SAGGISTICA 26

Re-Mapping Italian America

To our sons

Re-Mapping Italian America
Places, Cultures, Identities

Edited by

Sabrina Vellucci and Carla Francellini

BORDIGHERA PRESS

Library of Congress Control Number: 2017939528

St. George Terminal, Staten Island Ferry
from *SI3D*, film by Marylou & Jerome Bongiorno

Anaglyph 3D image courtesy of and © 2015
Bongiorno Productions Inc.

www.BongiornoProductions.com

Printed in the United States.

Published by
BORDIGHERA PRESS
John D. Calandra Italian American Institute
25 West 43rd Street, 17th Floor
New York, NY 10036

SAGGISTICA 26
ISBN 978-1-59954-116-5

TABLE OF CONTENTS

THE SILVER SCREEN

PERSPECTIVES & PROPOSALS

ACKNOWLEDGMENTS

This volume is the outcome of the conference *Re-Mapping Italian America. Places, Cultures, Identities*, held on May 12-13, 2016 at Roma Tre University, Dipartimento di Lingue, Letterature e Culture Straniere. On that occasion, we had the privilege of hosting as keynote speakers Mary Jo Bona, Fred L. Gardaphé, and Anthony Julian Tamburri, whose inspiring lectures and conversations fired up a lively exchange of views on a field of study still under-explored in many ways, especially in Italy. To our great delight, Maria Mazziotti Gillan and Tony Ardizzone generously accepted our invitation as guest writers and engaged in substantial readings from their works, while delivering captivating interviews that involved the audience and our students in a still ongoing dialogue. Filmmakers Marylou and Jerome Bongiorno were also part of this event via video-conference, sharing clips of their works—screened for the first time in Italy—and granting us a thought-provoking interview. We thank them also for providing the cover image to this book.

The idea of the conference was first conceived in the spring of 2010, in the aftermath of lectures held by Fred L. Gardaphé on Italian/American literature and culture that we both attended at the Centro Studi Americani in Rome, where we met. The entire project and the present volume were made possible by the continuous involvement and support provided by Anthony Julian Tamburri and the John D. Calandra Italian American Institute (Queens College, CUNY). A special "thank you" goes to Bordighera Press and to Nicholas Grosso for his editorial assistance.

Among our colleagues at Roma Tre University we wish to thank Veronica Pravadelli for granting us crucial support from the Centro di Ricerca Interdipartimentale di Studi Americani (CRISA). Our gratitude also goes to Richard Ambrosini, Cristina Giorcelli, and Luca Ratti (Roma Tre University), as well as to Donatella Izzo (University of Naples "L'Orientale") and Giorgio Mariani (Sa-

"Acknowledgments"

pienza University of Rome) for chairing panels and generating intense, lively discussions with the audience. We owe a heartfelt thanks to Giuseppe Nori for his presence on behalf of the Associazione Italiana di Studi Nord-Americani (AISNA). Marina Camboni and Valerio Massimo De Angelis, in turn, kindly accepted our invitation to present the Centro Interdipartimentale di Studi ItaloAmericani (CISIA) of the University of Macerata.

Invaluable technical support was provided by Claudio Mosticone and Davide Bevilacqua, while ongoing assistance was offered by the administrative staff of the Dipartimento di Lingue, Letterature e Culture Straniere at Roma Tre University. We wish to thank them all.

S.V., C.F.

INTRODUCTIONS

"Re-Mapping the Field"

Sabrina Vellucci
ROMA TRE UNIVERSITY

It is widely acknowledged that, especially in the last three decades, a growing number of American authors of Italian descent have gained both popular and critical attention in the United States. Successful TV programs, films, and documentaries consistently feature Italian/American writers, directors and actors, and portray Italian/American characters and settings. Accordingly, more and more scholars, on both sides of the Atlantic, have applied themselves to the study of a culture that has experienced, at last, a veritable renaissance, and has begun to be interrogated from diasporic, transnational, trans-lingual, and global perspectives.

As it is also well known, this was not accomplished quickly or without difficulty. For decades an embattled group of scholars and intellectuals, in the United States, Canada, and Italy, have engaged in the recovery and mapping of the predominantly Anglophone Italian/American culture—a linguistic, symbolic, and material world that has suffered a long period (almost a century) of neglect and has been subject to various forms of silencing or invisibility both in North America and Italy. This specific culture is the focus of this volume.[1]

Thus, it is especially poignant that since the mid-1980s *italianità* has become an "asset" to rediscover, reinvent, and re-envision in a transnational context that presumes the mobility and multiplicity of identity positions and encourages critical and intermedial reinterpretations. Such a framework allows, among other relevant changes, for the overcoming of stereotypes related to food and fam-

---

[1] I am referring to the field of the humanities in particular. Studies in history and the social sciences date back to several decades earlier.

ily (to name two of the most trite clichés), while recognizing their role in shaping Italian/American culture and integrating them into a wider, more complex, critical outlook.

Yet, still in 1993, the much discussed article, published in *The New York Times Book Review* by Gay Talese, entitled "Where Are the Italian American Novelists?" sparked a heated debate, that ultimately gave visibility to the issue of the existence of a canon of Italian/American literature. For, indeed, a canon had already been charted, as Rose Basile Green's *The Italian-American Novel* (1974) testifies. Several scholars have explored the reasons behind such a delay in acknowledging the cultural validity of the Italian/American tradition and have identified a number of concurrent factors, the most important of which is that for Italian Americans *italianità* has long been a troubling difference, before becoming a heritage to preserve and pass on to future generations. The history of this culture is, therefore, characterized by silences, lacunae, and disconnections—Anthony J. Tamburri writes, in this regard, about a "denied culture" (or more recently of a "denied biculturalism")[2]— that are also, clearly, the reason for the lack of awareness regarding the existence of literary and critical texts on the part of Italian/American writers themselves.

If in the United States the establishment of Italian/American literature and culture as a field of research has been long delayed, especially when compared to other so-called ethnic traditions like African/American, Jewish/American, Asian/American, or Latina/o Studies, in Italy the fortune of this culture has an even shorter history. After the first translations and reviews of authors like John Fante and Pietro di Donato by Elio Vittorini in the 1930s, it is since

---

[2] Anthony Julian Tamburri, "Beyond 'Pizza' and 'Nonna'! Or, What's Bad about Italian/American Criticism?: Further Directions for Italian/American Cultural Studies." *MELUS*, Vol. 28, No. 3 (Autumn, 2003) 152; Anthony Julian Tamburri, *Un biculturalismo negato: la letteratura "italiana" negli Stati Uniti* (Firenze: Franco Cesati Editore, forthcoming).

the end of the 1990s that translations and critical studies, in particular those of works by and about third- and fourth-generation Italian/American authors (those who, according to Fred Gardaphé, have generated an "Italian American Renaissance"), have begun to see the light. A fundamental step in this process is the inversion of the polarity that has transformed Italy from a point of origin to a destination for migrants. As Robert Viscusi has noted, "[f]or literary and cultural studies, this reversal amounts to a Copernican turn."[3]

Hence, Italian/American Studies seems to have finally found a home in Italy, too, as the contributions to this volume and other recent publications attest,[4] and as is also proved by the growing number of conferences organized on an international scale.[5] In-

---

[3] Robert Viscusi, "The History of Italian American Literary Studies."*Teaching Italian American Literature, Film, and Popular Culture*, ed. Edvige Giunta and Kathleen Zamboni McCormick (New York: The Modern Language Association of America, 2010) 43.

[4] A list of the works devoted to this subject, in a corpus that over the years has acquired increasing relevance, especially in disciplines such as history, literature, and cinema, exceeds the purpose of this brief introduction. Yet, as this volume goes to press, we wish to mention the publication of the special issue of the journal *Ácoma* dedicated to Italian/American literature, "Riflessi di un'America italiana. Studi sulla cultura italoamericana negli Stati Uniti," *Ácoma*, No. 13 (Fall-Winter 2017).

[5] Before the two-day conference, "Re-Mapping Italian America. Places, Cultures, Identities," from which this volume originates, in 1996 the Istituto Suor Orsola Benincasa held an international conference on Italian emigration to the United States and subsequently published a volume of essays (*Il sogno italoamericano: realtà e immaginario dell'emigrazione negli Stati Uniti*. Intro. Carmine Di Biase. Sebastiano Martelli, ed. [Napoli: CUEN, 1998]); the second conference of significant international regard was held in 1999 in Lecce at the University of Salento, "Emigrazione, esilio, sogno: il sogno americano," this too followed by the publication of a volume ("Esilio, migrazione, sogno Americano." Special issue Paolo A. Giordano and Anthony Julian Tamburri, eds. *Italiana* X [2001]); the third event to note here was the first conference of the Centro Interdipartimentale di Studi Italo-Americani of the University of Macerata, which took place in May 2017. The conference theme was "Democracies on the Move: Citizenships, Languages and

deed, in the past quarter century, Italian America has become a subject worthy of in-depth attention on the part of disciplines that have long neglected it, such as Italian Studies and American Studies. So much so that claims over the proper position that this field should occupy within the Italian academy, or what are the disciplines most entitled to deal with it, have recently been the subject of debate.

The notion of where Italian/American Studies should reside within the academy is addressed herein by Margherita Ganeri, who writes that Italian/American Studies might "more fruitfully" exist as "an integral part of Contemporary Italian Literature Studies" (315). Not wanting to exclude either of the two fields, Tamburri in turn sees Italian/American Studies co-existing both in American Studies and in Italian Studies. He articulates this concept through his rhetorical musing: "[O]ne may indeed wonder why Italian/American studies, on the other hand, does not enjoy the favorable positioning one might think it does—or should— within Italian studies (especially when conceived within the mindset of *italianistica*)—and I reference here both inside and outside of Italy—or, in similar geo-cultural fashion, within American studies" (53).[6]

Migrations across Italy, Europe, and the Americas." Other relevant events were: a ground-breaking four-day workshop of Italian and North American scholars, hosted by the Rockefeller Foundation in Bellagio, Italy, in March 2014, organized by the John D. Calandra Italian American Institute (Queens College, CUNY); the symposium of October 6, 2017, "'Effective Identities': Re-Envisioning Italian/Americanness through Everyday Lives and Actions," at the University of Naples "L'Orientale," organized by Donatella Izzo; and a follow-up to the 2014 Bellagio meeting, that will take place at the John D. Calandra Italian American Institute in New York on January 8-11, 2018.

[6] In *To Hyphenate or Not to Hyphenate*, Tamburri had already recognized the integral part Italian/American literature has in American literature: "Undoubtedly, Italian/American writers have slowly, but surely, built their niche in the body of American literature. Collectively, their work can be viewed as a written expression par excellence of Italian/American culture; individually, each writer has

I believe most scholars would agree that there exists an inherent cultural pluralism of Italian/American Studies as well as a predominant referencing of various forms of *italianità*. Thus, precisely because Italian/American Studies must "move beyond Little Italys and into the global arena of the many cultures of the Italian diaspora," as Gardaphé underscores (49), I believe that the more efficient and productive strategy is to broaden the playing field and thus not to compartmentalize or restrict scholarship on and/or of Italian/American Studies to either Italian Studies or American Studies, nor for that matter to Comparative Literature. Instead, the fruits of our collective, intellectual labors will profit exponentially from the concurrence and collaboration of these three disciplines, and others as well, which would allow for the deployment of different methodologies to analyze the various articulations that constitute the vast repertoire of *italianità* adopted by American writers and artists of Italian descent.

Such a strategy will also benefit from in-depth studies and analyses of Italian/American culture in conversation with other ethnic traditions as well as with the dominant cultures (both literary and artistic canons) of the places in which the Italian diaspora has set roots. For instance, Mary Jo Bona's book-length study, *Women Writing Cloth: Migratory Fictions in the American Imaginary* (2015), does as much in her interrogations of works by Nathaniel Hawthorne, Alice Walker, Sandra Cisneros, and Adria Bernardi. In similar fashion, books like John Gennari's *Flavor and Soul. Italian America at Its African American Edge* (2017) and Samuele F. S. Pardini's *In the Name of the Mother. Italian Americans, African Americans and Modernity from Booker T. Washington to Bruce Springsteen* (2017), both going beyond the literary while focusing on the relationship

---

enabled American literature to sound a slightly different tone, thus bringing to the fore another voice of the great kaleidoscopic, socio/cultural mosaic we may call Americana" (Anthony Julian Tamburri, *To Hyphenate or Not to Hyphenate. The Italian/American Writer: An Other American* [Montreal: Guernica, 1991] 48).

between Italian/American and African/American culture, have also helped pave the way for future research in this direction. Nonetheless, much more remains to be done.

Working from an interdisciplinary standpoint, and taking as basis the latest developments in the field, the essays in this book are meant as a contribution to this ongoing, collective effort at expanding and updating knowledge concerning Italian/American literature, cinema, and culture in its various articulations. Written and visual narratives by Italian/American authors are examined employing the diverse perspectives developed in such areas as cultural studies, gender and film studies—within a theoretical framework that problematizes the notion of "identity" as an unstable and porous category.[7] Particular attention is devoted to phenomena related to migration, language, and place as significant interpretative categories of the Italian/American experience, while also focusing on such broad, interrelated issues as mobility, identity/identification, and material cultures. The essays explore the effects that the texts' imaginary—often linked to the idea of space, mobility, and change—produces on our understanding of Italian/American culture, and how this knowledge can help construct a new narrative of Italian/American life, as well as provide a more complex understanding of American history and culture in a transnational context.

In the opening essay, "*Voci radicali*: Italian Americana as a Field and Its Experimental Voices," Mary Jo Bona stresses the importance of the Italian immigrants' "hybrid tongue," a "linguistic fact [that] made a literature of Italian America possible" (1), and highlights the key role of the culture of the southern regions forming the *Mezzogiorno* of Italy in shaping the "radical voices" that constitute the object of her study. Setting the Great Migration in the context

---

[7] For a critical reconfiguration of the unstable notion of "identity" in the context of Italian Americana, see the seminal study by Peter Carravetta, *After Identity. Migration, Critique, Italian American Culture* (New York: Bordighera Press, 2017).

of the hundreds of rebellions that followed Italy's Unification in 1861, Bona writes that "no rebellion was fiercer than the uprising of migration" (2). Indeed, paradoxically enough, it was precisely through the act of migration that the millions of people who went forth *en masse* came to recognize their country as a nation. In such a framework, mobility acquires a special significance, as it "enabled economically and linguistically disenfranchised Italians" to enact "a form of revolutionary resistance against being colonized by a homeland that starved them and a new world that exploited them" (2).

The experience of mobility and change also formed a relevant context for the transmission of narratives from one generation to the next. Looking at the ways in which Italian immigrants managed to resist cultural annihilation in their adopted country, Bona emphasizes the role played by their storytelling traditions and examines Tony Ardizzone's *In the Garden of Papa Santuzzu* and Adria Bernardi's *Openwork*. As children of immigrants whose tales revealed the "loss of both geographical and cultural sensibilities" (2), these experimental writers of the late twentieth century have been able to cope with the ensuing trans-generational trauma by paying creative tribute to their parents' cultural legacy and produce "cultural work with trans-geographic vistas and nontraditional representations of national cultures" (13).

Bona's essay also tackles epistemological issues related to Italian/American literature, a discipline that has still to contend with "a rigidified understanding of the canonical in academia" (6), and underscores both the allure and risk connected to its being subsumed under the aegis of transnationalism, which "threatened to dilute traditional understandings of ethnic cultures and paradigms within ethnic studies" (7). Thus, "[t]he unstable position of the field of Italian Americana both threatens and dilutes its cultural visibility and inspires broader conceptions of U.S. writings that are culturally resonant and invitingly comparative" (8). It is therefore necessary for scholars of Italian America in traditional disciplines "to offer an interdisciplinary approach to the study of Italian America, including its literature, employing comparative approaches that move us away from a consensus oriented sylla-bus [...] and toward an approach that offers counter-readings, which are fundamentally interventionist in purpose" (8).

In "Beyond Little Italys: The Future of Italian/American Stud-ies," Fred Gardaphé traces a genealogy of this discipline. In a his-tory marked by a lack of documentary evidence, he succeeds in collecting the foundational events that have been recorded. In so doing, he thus identifies its origins in the moment in which Ital-ians ceased to be the objects, and started to become the agents, of studies within the academy. Even admitting that the recognition of "when Italian/American studies began" is not as important as finding out "when it began to be taken seriously" (36), Gardaphé states that "[l]ocating those origins [...] enable[s] us to build upon them through revisionary criticism that sets a precedent for how to proceed with future histories" (35). In his defense of both "in-tra- and intercultural education" (45), of "an inter-ethnic/racial and class solidarity" (48) against recent anti-democratic acts in Ameri-can politics, such as the 2010 State of Arizona House Bill 2281, that abolished ethnic studies in state education, Gardaphé shows the pivotal role that Italian/American Studies can play within "the global arena of the many cultures of the Italian diaspora" (49).

Inviting scholars "to think differently," Anthony J. Tamburri stresses the need to bring "paradigm shifts" to discussions in the "notably vibrant field of intellectual interrogation" that is Italian/American studies (54). A consequence of this process of expand-ing our horizons and making the category of Italian/American lit-erature more inclusive is also, necessarily, the broadening of the concept of "Italian identity." Thus, Tamburri elaborates the notion of "effective identity," which, regardless of nationality or citizen-ship, recognizes the "Italian" quality of "everyday activity in which the individual lives out his/her daily life" (Tamburri 67). Beyond all traditional geo-cultural confines, the "Italian" world Tamburri envisions "surpasses every restrictive, reductive, and essentialist conceptual barrier" (69) and includes non-Italian writers such as Jhumpa Lahiri along with other writers of the Italian diaspora, in a process of "transcultural evolution" that allows for a more profound understanding of the "transnational discourse in which Italians engage but that, from a hegemonic point of view, they do not recognize" (75).

In her contribution entitled "Italian American Studies in the Italian University's System: Current and Future Perspective," Margherita Ganeri argues that introducing courses on Italian/American literature and culture in the Italian academic system would be a valuable and strategic move, especially in terms of curricula development. In order to substantiate her assertion, she illustrates the case of the successful pioneering program "Cultura e Letteratura Italiana Americana" (CLIA), established at the University of Calabria in 2014. Acknowledging the intrinsic transnational and interdisciplinary character of Italian/American Studies, Ganeri upholds the necessity of an ongoing exchange between Italy and the different countries and cultures of the Italian diaspora, not only to foster understanding of the "mobile and dynamic constructions of 'Italianità'" (Ganeri 308), but also as a way to further innovative research in Italian Studies and the humanities in general. Even more important, Ganeri asserts, "Diaspora studies have an ethical and social purpose [...] to promote civilization and social progress [...] on a national, but also on a transnational level" (Ganeri 317).

Stefano Luconi's essay, "Military Nationalism and the Re-Elaboration of Ethnicity: Italian Americans and World War I," examines how the patriotic discourse surrounding the Great War contributed to redefining the identity of both Italian newcomers and their progeny in the United States. If, at first, the dynamics of the Italian resettlement overseas strengthened the immigrants' localistic and insular allegiance to their village/community of origin, after the outbreak of World War I, and in the wake of Italy's entry into the conflict, many Italian immigrants developed "a sense of affiliation shaped by their mutual Italian ancestry" (Luconi 318). In outlining what he calls "wartime multifaceted patriotism," Luconi observes the tension deriving from the spread of Italian nationalism, on the one hand, and the "stimuli toward Americanization" coming from U.S. war propaganda on the other. He shows how the illusion of a possible reconciliation between "the newcomers' accommodation within the adoptive country and their identification with their ancestral roots" (332) was ultimately crushed in the 1920s, when "a resurgence of xenophobia and nativism ... again marginalized Italian immigrants, stamping them as undesirable and inassimilable aliens" (337).

In "I Am(s): Dantesque Strategies of Acceptance and Denial. And a Proposal," Martino Marazzi reaffirms his long, groundbreaking commitment to the study of early Italian/American literature. Stressing the intellectual creativity that is often testified by works in this tradition, as well as the moral engagement that is required of the scholar approaching them, Marazzi has made his own the advice Leslie Fiedler gave him years ago and has continued in his effort at opening up the canon of Italian literature with a view "to reap new riches, and explore new dimensions of a country notoriously keen on the dialogue between power and the arts" (Marazzi 341). An endeavor that inevitably leads to confront the larger question of "the role of power structures in shaping cultural blueprints, and the hypostasis of the criterion of aesthetic excellence, whatever we mean by that" (342). Marazzi also underscores the necessity for scholars in this field—regardless of their various positionings and identifications—to engage with "the privilege and responsibility of activating a critical reflection on a huge phenomenon that has affected ... well over twenty million Italians, and that, conversely, after the Fall of the Berlin Wall and the arrival in Bari of the Albanian cargo ship Vlora (August 1991) ... has changed the peninsula into a destination for migrants" (Marazzi 345).

Indeed, the transformation of Italy from a country of departure to a country of arrival, which Marazzi so cogently discusses, reminds us of Viscusi's "Copernican turn," which calls for a re-mapping of the field of Italian Diaspora Studies. From this perspective more recent scholarship has developed, giving us momentum for the conference whose outcome is the present volume.

The essays I have discussed herein provide the framing for the middle part of this collection, in which we find other contributions that shed light on the many facets of the cultural phenomenon we know as Italian America. Each, in its own way, offers further validation for yet another step toward the substantiation of the field of Italian/American Studies.

"Towards a New Visibility"

Carla Francellini
UNIVERSITY OF SIENA

The International Conference "Re-Mapping Italian America. Places, Cultures, Identities" moved from a deeply felt need to *reformulate* the notions of *place, culture* and *identity,* reaching a new, more dynamic definition of these concepts, flexible enough to make sense of the most significant changes in the field of contemporary Italian/American studies. The critical debate *about* and *around* this now full-fledged field of studies needs to focus on what comes next, hinting at different future perspectives in Italian/American criticism which may concentrate on the exploration of a great deal of material—literary, documentary, cinematic and so on—still in need of sufficient, critical consideration. And yet, great attention should be paid to the role played by *places* and *cultures* in the long process through which an Italian/American identity was forged through the decades, moving from the 1970s when some groundbreaking critical studies in the field were published. As Peter Carravetta maintains in his volume *After Identity* (2017), in fact, "[w]hich idea of identity one accepts and parleys in a heterological social reality betrays from the start a political stance, and the assumptions it rests upon."[8] Identity, in fact, turns out to be "a construct of multiple elements, all critically slippery, all historically contingent and multipronged, and perhaps constituting, deploying a post-modern moniker, a plurality of discourses in constant conflict and exchange. Identity has no contours, it is fluid, amoebic, viscous"(xii).

---

[8]Peter Carravetta, *After Identity: Migration, Critique, Italian American Culture* (New York: Bordighera Press, 2017) xii.

Though it becomes clear that we could better grasp the notion of Italian/American identity drawing up *maps of identity,* as Carravetta suggests, it seems we should never stop chasing it, at the same time, in the texts we interrogate—not only literary, of course—as the many contributors to this volume have done in their essays. At the same time, we need to go beyond the monolithic presence of the notion of identity in recent scholarship, to focus on *ethnic identity* as something "to be constituted by a cluster of different and not always coherent (sub)identities, some of which have little to do with nations and languages and much with politics and power" (xii). The exploration of those (sub)identities is a common denominator among all the essays collected in this volume, each one adopting a different perspective in order to examine diverse and engaging aspects of Italian America in different times and places through the decades. Through the various, indepth contributions to this volume, criticism, in fact, achieves its main function, that is to make "moderately readable" what, in its essence, "remains unreadable," as Paolo Valesio states in his essay, "The Writer Between Two Worlds."[9] If Italian/Ameri-can studies have long been in the shadow or, even worse, under the heavy cap of invisibility, this is partly because most of its fundamental theoretical, critical and literary texts have long been "unread" by the critics, the academics, and the general public as well. It is therefore of crucial importance to continue the long-lasting effort to make those texts "readable" through critical and literary analysis, moving from the theoretical assumptions on which Italian/ American studies rely. Going back to the ancient etymon of the word "theory," in fact, we find it alludes to a *procession* or *succession* of concrete images as opposed to a series of abstract statements. We need to focus on those concrete images and tableaux that make up Italian/American literature, cinema, and history, as

---

[9]Paolo Valesio, "The Writer between Two Worlds. Italian Writing in the United States Today." *Differentia: Review of Italian Thought* 3.3/4 (1989).

our contributors did in their challenging readings of different aspects of the ever-changing Italian/American idea of identity, places, and cultures. Only by focusing on concrete images and by proposing clear readings of those many subjects and matters gathering under the label of Italian/American studies,[10] we can make "readable" an entire tradition and a culturally relevant production.

In his *Buried Caesars* (2006), Robert Viscusi properly remarked that literature is usually born out of the most felt basic needs of society and Italian/American literature is no exception, it being the spontaneous outcome of the trauma of the Great Migration (1880-1924), a major cataclysm involving a consistent number of Italians mainly from the southern regions of Italy, but also from the Northern mountains of the Alps and the Apennines.[11] We should pay great attention, in fact, not to separate a work of art from its social usefulness, which quite often turns out to be an irredeemable mistake. If Italy's harsh condition of living provided the background for the massive emigration of Italians from different regions of the country, the extraordinarily racist moment in the constitutional development of the United States could give a clear idea of how distant the realities of the two countries were. When the first waves of immigrants arrived in the US, different "places" and distant "cultures" were forced to interact, as David J. Richards highlights in his *Italian American: The Racializing of an Ethnic Identity*:[12]

Both Italy and America were in this period in the midst of revolutionary struggles over the meaning of nationalism. One alter-

---

[10] This does not exclude the need to continue to explore new methodological strategies in order to approach the notion itself of literary, historical, cinematic representation.

[11] Robert Viscusi, *Buried Caesars and Other Secrets of Italian American Writing* (New York: SUNY Press, 2006).

[12] David A. J. Richards, *Italian American: The Racializing of an Ethnic Identity* (New York: New York UP, 1999).

native interpretation was liberal nationalism, a normative con-
ception of national identity defined in terms of protection of the
universal human rights of all people on fair terms. In both nations, the liberal interpretation was marked by appeals to universalistic principles of justice and by traditions of moral slavery
that corrupted public understanding of such ideals; in both cases, the people of Southern Italy were [...] among the victims of
such injustice. (5)

The Italians and the Americans, espousing the liberal interpretation of nationalism, conceived it as a struggle for universalistic
political values of justice according to which all peoples are, as
equals, participants. According to Richards, in fact, both the Italian massive emigration and the processes of Italian/American identity formation expressed aspects of that struggle.

And yet, Italian Americans—similarly to other immigrant groups
—have long been a target of the durable and continuous power of
American racism that "regarded [them] as non-visible black and
suppressed or tried to suppress multicultural traditions that might
protest such racism" (Richards 2). This question leads us to the
debate on the *invisibility* of the Italians in the U.S., an invisibility
that is connected to the marginal position of Italians in the social
and cultural fabric of their host country. While trying to make
sense of the forging of Italian/American identity, we have to take
into account its "privatization," that is the consequence of the "silencing of protest against the injustice inflicted on Italian Americans [as] a response to the group's finding itself the non-visibly
black target of American racism." Italian/American identity is,
therefore, the result of the durable and continuous effort to break
free from the boundaries, stereotypes, and prejudices cast upon
the Italian migrants by the dominant ruling classes in the United
States. The most evident sign of such a long-lasting attempt to
emancipate from this shocking frame of mind is, therefore, given

by the search for the voice common to most Italian/American women writers.

In "The Crow and the Cave," a long interview granted by Maria Mazziotti Gillan to Timothy Green, the poet explains that the metaphorical figure of "the crow"—recurrent in her poems—is "this creature who has in it the voice of every person who has ever been negative to you in your life—and that's a lot of people for most of us. Teachers who put us in the bluebird row instead of the redbird row in math, a friend who says you're not cool, or a man or a woman who treats you poorly, or your parents saying, 'How could you be so dumb as to get in a car with that person?' All those voices are caught in the beak of the crow."[13] As for the allegory of the "cave," she explains, "I think poems are in a very deep place inside yourself, the place I call the cave. It's really here [in the stomach]. So you have to be willing to knock the crow off your shoulder and move down into yourself, and tell the truth. And if you can't do that, then you aren't communicating anything. I really hate the kind of poetry that is all language and no gut. No feeling, no willingness to take a risk. Go to the edge, for God's sake. Take a little risk!"[14]

The variety of essays that makes up this volume provides the reader with this risk and as well as with an opportunity to listen to different critical voices, coming from diverse fields of study, embodying different—and not rarely distant and opposite—critical approaches to the very notion of identity in its multifaceted expressions. Each of the scholars involved in the Rome Conference of May 2016 adopts, in fact, a different perspective on a subject still far from having been fully explored and still far from having carried out its potentials.

---

[13]Timothy Green, "'The Crow and the Cave,' Conversation with Maria Mazziotti Gillan." *Rattle* No. 46 (Winter 2015): http://www.rattle.com/print/40s/i46/.
[14]See, http://www.rattle.com/print/40s/i46/.

In "Playing the American Tune: Ethnic and Cultural Identity in Horatio Alger Jr.'s *Phil the Fiddler*," Leonardo Buonomo proposes a close critical reading of Alger's stories of street boys. Buonomo demonstrates that the ultimate reward—very much in line with the Protestant ethic and the "Victorian myth of self-improvement" —was not wealth but, more soberly, a comfortable dwelling, an education, and steady employment. According to Buonomo's critical reading, Horatio Alger's works influenced twentieth-century writers of the caliber of Theodore Dreiser, Francis Scott Fitzgerald, and Nathaniel West.

Back to the issue of the visibility of the ethnic sign in Italian/American writers and poets, Maria Giuseppina Cesari's essay investigates the crucial importance of the Bronx in the process of building—as well as to that of recovering—an ethnic identity in Don DeLillo. She underscores in fine detail what significant role a *place* can play in the construction of a unique and peculiar point of view on life and literature.

Carla Francellini's essay, "'Nobody has to tell the whole truth, only pieces of the truth.' Chasing an Identity in Tony Ardizzone's Fiction," deals with the role ethnicity plays in Ardizzone's short stories and novels in shaping an ethnic identity for his characters, most often *hyphenated Americans*, disoriented and lost in a big dark world.

Giulia Iannuzzi's "An 'Eye-talian' in the New World: Cognitive Estrangement and Diglossia in Antonio Gallenga's Early Italian American Narrative" investigates Gallenga's work from the perspective of Darko Suvin's concept of cognitive estrangement. Iannuzzi proposes that any estrangement device may have a common matrix to place between the uneasiness, experienced by the subject during the migration process, and the projective and extrapolative mechanisms typically exploited in speculative fiction narratives to imagine future or alternate worlds. She maintains that the key to cognitive estrangement is the presence, in a story, of an element (*novum*), which, because of its absolute newness, stimulates a different way of conceiving our subjectivity and our world.

Gillan's poetry is at the core of Elisabetta Marino's essay "*Writing Poetry to Save Your Life*: Maria Mazziotti Gillan the Poet, the Healer," where she goes through some of Gillan's most significant poems to present some relevant aspects of her poetics. Through a close analysis of Gillan's *Writing Poetry to Save your Life* and *The Silence in an Empty House*, Marino sheds light on her artistic journey through universal, shared experiences of love, loss, mourning, and rebirth.

Sandra Paoli's essay, "Rita Ciresi. Spaces of Intimacy. Places of Diversity," presents Ciresi's short stories, focusing on the role of women in the traditional Italian/American family as well as on the complicated processes of emancipation and freedom.

Regarding the sensitive issue of Italy-US relations, Daniela Rossini presents the unusual figure of the Florentine-born Amy A. Bernardy, whose travel writings offer a new perspective on Italian immigration and on the two countries' mutual perception.

Maria Anita Stefanelli establishes a connection between Emily Dickinson's poems and some highly representative figures in Italian/American literature such as Sandra Gilbert, Helen Barolini, Daniela Gioseffi, Maria Mazziotti Gillan, Paul Di Filippo. Moving, in fact, from the legal concept of *patria potestas*, she proposes a critical appraisal of Italian/American writers and poets who embraced the intellectual challenge posed by Dickinson's writings, highlighting the invigorating connections existing between Dickinson's and Italian/American poetry.

In the section dedicated to the *Silver Screen*, Giuliana Muscio's essay, "Guido Trento: From the 'Neapolitan Synecdoche' to Italian American-ness," illustrates the various phases of Trento's artistic evolution and production, engaging the reader into a careful reconsideration of the issues of cultural identity in relation to language and culture, paying great attention to the passage from Neapolitan culture to Italian Americanness.

At the crossroad between cinema and history, Matteo Pretelli's study provides an analysis of some World War II movies produced by Hollywood from the time of the war onwards, paying attention to the presence of Italian/American servicemen and to the different roles ethnicity plays in Hollywood war movies.

Sabrina Vellucci's essay examines the depiction of domesticity and domestic labor in Italian-Argentinian-American director Nancy Savoca's *Household Saints* (1993) and *Dirt* (2003) through the lens of Homi Bhabha's notion of the *unhomely*. In both movies, the question of gendered domestic labor is compounded with issues of ethnicity, class, and citizenship, revealing the ambivalent outcomes of the irruption of the world in the home.

Francis Ford Coppola's penultimate film, *Tetro* (2009), released in Italy as *Segreti di famiglia,* is at the core of Vito Zagarrio's reflection on the Italian/American director eventually coming to terms with his roots. A hybrid of family drama, melodrama, and coming-of-age story, the movie turns out to be both a "formalist," as well as an "expressionist film," with its contrasting B/W and color scenes as well as its claustrophobic scenic designs aiming at showing, from different perspectives, the "secrets of the family," that is those hidden, irreconcilable conflicts among the members of the nuclear family, regarded by Coppola as a fundamental unit of society.

Groundbreaking studies such as *Are Italians White? How Race Is Made in America* (2003), edited by Jennifer Guglielmo and Salvatore Salerno, "We Weren't Always White: Race and Ethnicity in Italian/American Literature" (2012) by Fred Gardaphé, as well as works by Rudolph J. Vecoli, "Are Italian Americans White Folks?" (1996), or Werner Sollors's *Neither Black Nor White Yet Both: Thematic Exploration of Interracial Literature* (1997) have shown how in the last two decades the "conquest" of invisibility by the Italians in America, obtained by renouncing their ethnic color, had a long-lasting influence on the history of the complex relationship of this ethnic group with the other groups as well as with the dominant ruling classes.[15] Coming out of the shadow and re-gaining the status of a *visible* ethnic group, Italian Americans had to expend great effort in establishing the value, and before that, the existence of an Italian/American tradition, which is also something they recently achieved through the analysis of the historical, documentary and fictional works produced by Italians and Italian Americans in the U.S., from the moment of their arrival in *La Merica*. There is still a great deal to be done, but starting a discussion about the future perspectives of Italian/American studies here in Italy, where everything began, seems to be the necessary move to undertake. This international conference held in Rome, in the heart of a country that suffered—and still suffers—from the effects of a constant migration towards the United States, has offered us the opportunity to contribute to the bolstering of the foundation for a new positioning in which Italian/American studies can take permanent residence and hopefully thrive.

---

[15] Jennifer Guglielmo, Salvatore Salerno, *Are Italians White? How Race Is Made in America*, New York: Routledge, (2003); Fred Gardaphé, "We Weren't Always White: Race and Ethnicity in Italian/American Literature." *Lit: Literature Interpretation Theory* 13:3 (2012): 185-199; Werner Sollors, *Neither Black Nor White Yet Both: Thematic Exploration of Interracial Literature* (New York: Oxford UP, 1997); Rudoph J. Vecoli, "Are Italian Americans Just White Folks?" Mary Jo Bona, Anthony Julian Tamburri, eds., *Italian and Italian/American Images in the Media* (Staten Island: AIHA 1996) 3-17. See also, James Baldwin, "On Being 'White' ... and Other Lies" in David R. Roediger, ed., *Black on White. Black Writers on What It Means to Be White* (New York: Schocken Books, 1998) 177-80; David A. J. Richards, *Italian American. The Racializing of an Ethnic Identity* (New York: NYU Press, 1999); Thomas J. Ferraro, *Feeling Italian: The Art of Ethnicity in America* (New York: NYU Press, 2005).

KEYNOTE ADDRESSES

Voci radicali:
Italian Americana as a Field and its Experimental Voices

Mary Jo Bona
SUNY STONY BROOK

ITALIAN AMERICAN "STORIA": A MINI-HISTORY

My bilingual title deliberately exploits a linguistic phenomenon of migration history for many Italian immigrants post *Risorgimento* who left villages with oft-deemed incomprehensible and inferior dialects, but who did not speak the language of the *prominenti*, i.e., the standardized Italian of Toscana formalized by Dante's *Commedia* and considered the canonical standard-bearer for all educated Italians. The linguistic constraints created by the new, infuriating language of English, produced a hybrid tongue for Italian immigrants and their children: *that* linguistic fact made a literature of Italian America possible. I argue that the *voci radicali* of many Italian American writers has a deep history in the *Mezzogiorno*, those regions south and east of Rome. The revolutionary movement known as *il Risorgimento*, establishing northern Italian governmental control of all regions caused many Southern Italians to feel the sting of being "conquered" by their own country—the Piedmontese government—which was as foreign to those rural laborers south of Rome as the idea of nationalism itself as "many had never encountered the term *Italia* before" migration (Duggan, 135, 130).[1]

---

[1] Of the Italian populace, Duggan explains, "Italy remained an overwhelmingly rural society: according to the 1911 census, almost 59 per cent of the workforce depended on agriculture, and many others were employed on the land part-time. ... Despite the enormous exodus of peasants overseas in these years [1901-1911],

Of the hundreds of rebellions that erupted after Italian unification, no rebellion was fiercer than the uprising of migration, as so
many emigrants left villages bereft of all but the very old and ill.
In the peak years of their great migration—1880-1910—Italians left
a country that did not exist for them as a nation *until* they went
forth en masse. While Italian migration was part of a changing
global economy that enabled poor people to leave villages, migration also enabled economically and linguistically disenfranchised
Italians to use mobility as a form of revolutionary resistance
against being colonized by a homeland that starved them and a
new world that exploited them. Many Italian emigrants deflected
cultural annihilation by voicing their storytelling traditions, implicitly waging a "minority revolt against" the regulating effects
of assimilation.[2] As I examine later in this essay, Tony Ardizzone's
In the Garden of Papa Santuzzu deploys the folktale genre to assist
Sicilian immigrants, who experienced effects of cultural annihilation in America. Despite evidence to the contrary, children of immigrants listened well enough to pay creative tribute to their parents' loss of both geographical and cultural sensibilities, a trauma
that is reproduced generationally, as Adria Bernardi demonstrates

---

the Italian countryside remained hugely overpopulated." *A Concise History of
Italy*, 175. According to Donna Gabaccia, "After 1890, southern states of migration caught up with and then surpassed [migrations from northern and central
Italy]. Scholars have generally argued that areas of fragmented land ownership,
where peasant subsistence production was slowly giving way to a cash economy
and commercial agriculture, produced the highest emigration rates." *Italy's Many
Diasporas*, 68.

[2] Examining American nativism imposed on immigrant groups during the years
1860-1925, John Higham writes: "The minority revolt against Americanization, a
revolt accentuated by all the other manifestations of 100 per cent Americanism,
hurled large blocs of immigrants into compensatory chauvinisms of their own."
Strangers in the Land, 254. I add here that writers of Italian America created compensatory narratives as measures of protection and artistry, barricading themselves from a chaos that inherently negates the possibility of remedy, progress, or
contentment—perhaps storytelling itself.

in her novel, *Openwork*, also discussed in the second half of this essay.

This brief history of Italian migration was offered in the opening paragraphs to encapsulate my experience of working in the field of Italian American Studies since the 1980s. I herewith offer three anecdotes from different time periods and institutional settings that attempt to explain my reasoning for feeling the necessity of beginning a presentation on Italian America with a historical narrative that rehearses a specific immigration story of Italians who left their homeland during a period of time in migration history—after the *Risorgimento* and before U.S. immigration restriction laws halted the flow of movement for eastern and southern Europeans to America.

FOREGROUNDING THE FIELD OF ITALIAN AMERICA:
THREE ACADEMIC STORIES

My preliminary remarks regarding Italian migration history to the United States illuminate the issue of foregrounding for those of us working in area studies in American universities. The question, "How much introduction is enough?" persistently arises in a plethora of academic settings. Let me begin by way of an anecdote from the spring of 1988, when I delivered a paper at my graduate school's colloquium on Tina De Rosa's experimental novel, *Paper Fish*, to an audience largely comprised of English professors and graduate students who knew nothing of Italian diasporas into the Americas, and even less about the presence of a heritage group that produced writing during the first decades of the twentieth century. During the Q/A discussion, I was asked this: What makes Italian American writers unique, original, and worthy to be studied any more than, say, other ethnic groups? How is their history unique? My attempt to answer this question in 1988 was retrospectively instructive to me. Not only did I struggle with the essentialism implicit in the question but also I recognized that any

3

biographical response would make me susceptible to being perceived as filiopietistic in choosing my own heritage group to study, though I knew that Perry Miller, Henry Nash Smith, and my own professor in graduate school, Sargent Bush Jr., did not have to apologize for or justify their choice to examine the cultural lives and works of Anglo descended immigrants and writers.[3]

In 1988, I resisted providing a response to the questioner because I felt that the underlying presumption of the question was a covert attempt to diminish the topic of Italian American literature as worthy of being studied at the outset. Perhaps my defensive posture was abetted by the confusion and/or disinterest in my area study that I observed largely from academics in the department of English. Nonetheless, in my response, I chose to foreground as best as I could the post-*Risorgimento* migrations of Italians to the U.S., offering historical information without proffering either a defense of my choice or a direct response to a question I could not answer. At that time, I did not have the full benefit yet of the words of immigration historians like Rudolph Vecoli, who made the following pronouncement at a keynote address presented at the 1994 American Italian Historical Association: "I argue for the intrinsic significance of this [Italian-American] experience. It is an epic story of a diaspora, the story of the tragedies and triumphs of millions, the story of generations struggling to reconcile the old and the new. It is neither grander nor meaner than the story of other migrant peoples, *but it is our story.*"[4]

---

[3] Perry Miller's two-volume, monumental *The New England Mind*, Henry Nash Smith's *The Virgin Land: The American West as Symbol and Myth*, and Sargent Bush Jr.'s *The Writings of Thomas Hooker: Spiritual Adventure in Two Worlds*, represent a mere sampling of the myriad of critical studies on the subject of Anglo-descended cultural work, with a focus on Puritan heritage (Miller), New England divines (Bush), and empire-building, westward moving pioneers (Smith).

[4] "Are Italian Americans Just White Folks?" *Italian and Italian American Images in the Media*. Ed. Mary Jo Bona and Anthony Tamburri. Proc. of the 27th Annual Conference of the American Italian Historical Association. Staten Island, NY:

Having quoted Vecoli, let me add that taking Italian American cultural identity as an object of inquiry in fact dismantled my own claims of subjectivity as a descendant of Italian forebears. My own genealogical identification equipped me to examine this body of literature no more than an academic of Dutch or African descent. Nonetheless, it would be disingenuous of me not to stake a claim: as a scholar of literature, I recognize my stake, as Joan Scott explains, "in the production of knowledge" (96).[5] As Scott argues, subjects have agency, but they are not "unified, autonomous individuals exercising free will, but rather subjects whose agency is created through situations and statuses conferred on them" (93). In reading the literature of Italian America, I sought support from multiple disciplines and sources, however inflected they were at times by biased discourses on southern Italian peasants, Italian regional and class status, color and racial attitudes on both sides of the Atlantic. Despite their poverty and land hunger, I came to learn that Italian immigrants, like other marginalized groups, possessed narratives pre- and post-migration, and their stories were communicated in the context of their experience of mobility and in a social and historical context of change.

Allow me to scroll ahead nearly twenty years to December, 2007, to a second anecdote that instantiates the Italian American Discussion Group at our premier national convention of the Mod-

---

American Italian Historical Association, 1996. 3-17. This essay was reprinted in *Italian Americana* 13 (Summer 1995): 149-161 and *Beyond The Godfather: Italian Americans Writers on the Real Italian American Experience*, ed. A. Kenneth Ciongoli and Jay Parini Hanover: UP of New England (1997): 311-321.

[5] See Joan Scott's "The Evidence of Experience," 797, 793. Due to the concerted efforts of several leading scholars in the field of Italian American Studies, the Italian American Discussion Group (now Forum) was formally accepted into the premier organization of languages and literatures, the Modern Language Association (MLA) in 1998. Josephine Gattuso Hendin chaired the first formal Discussion Session devoted to Italian American literature with the panel title "Staking Claims: Defining Italian American Cultural Studies."

ern Language Association. The discussion group on Italian American literature was celebrating its 10th anniversary. By 2007, several full-length critical studies on Italian America had been published by university and academic trade presses.[6] The panel was organized as a roundtable that assembled well-known scholars in the field of Italian American literature. During the Q&A session, an attendee asked the kind of question that echoed my 1988 experience: why study Italian American literature? Does it really even exist? In his prejudgment, this questioner had already decided the terms of the answer, asking the question as a provocation rather than as an earnest inquiry. What remained evident to me was a mindset that exposed a rigidified understanding of the canonical in academia as this questioner employed that catch-all word, "excellence," thereby reinforcing an implicit universalism in his understanding of great works of literary art, i.e., "master"-texts, none of which he could conceive to be Italian American.[7] My first response was mild irritation as I thought to myself, "Do I have to say this again?" After *sotto voce* answering an uncontestable, "yes,"

---

[6] A brief list of full-length critical studies (monographs in North America by U.S. and Italian scholars) include the following: Fred Gardaphé's *Italian Signs, American Streets: The Evolution of Italian American Narrative*, Anthony Tamburri's *A Semiotic of Ethnicity: In (Re)cognition of the Italian/American Writer*, Mary Jo Bona's *Claiming a Tradition: Italian American Women Writers*, Mary Francis Pipino's *'I Have Found My Voice': The Italian American Woman Writer*, Edvige Giunta's *Writing with an Accent: Contemporary Italian American Women Authors*, Kenneth Scambray's *The North American Italian Renaissance: Italian Writing in America and Canada*, Leonardo Buonomo's *From Pioneer to Nomad: Essays on Italian North American Writing*, Martino Marazzi's *Voices of Italian America: A History of Early Italian American Literature with a Critical Anthology*, and Robert Viscusi's *Buried Caesars and Other Secrets of Italian American Writing*.

[7] In her recuperation of Harriet Beecher Stowe's *Uncle Tom's Cabin*, Jane Tompkins explains that "the issue of literary value cannot be settled by invoking apparently unquestionable examples of literary excellence as a basis of comparison, because [such] texts already represent one position in the debate they are being called upon to decide" *Sensational Designs: The Cultural Work of American Fiction, 1790-1860*. 187.

I recalled the same tenor of question asked in the 1980s about the study of feminism when developing the curricular field of Women's Studies in academia.

My own looming questions remain: How do I represent a cultural group who has not been embraced by traditional departments of English, at least not as a unitary field of study or as part of what we call in the United States, multiethnic American literature? When Italian American literature is examined at my university (Stony Brook University), it is sequestered in a department of European Languages and given minor status. Italian American literature has been confused and sometimes (understandably) merged with "Italian" literature in European Languages, or taught as an add-on or a supplement in American and Comparative Literature courses, only benignly reaping benefits of secondary critiques or anthology inclusion. Arriving late to the conversation about ethnicity, the scholarly study of Italian America occurred just as the shift into the age of transnationalism with its whiff of transcendence was taking hold. Just as processes of postmodernism threatened to disempower feminist scholars by insisting on the erasure of their own subjectivity or, at best, stipulating a necessary shift to multiple, fragmented selves, the processes of transnationalism threatened to dilute traditional understandings of ethnic cultures and paradigms within ethnic studies. Expressions of cultural identities certainly surpass national borders, thereby opening up discursive spaces for feminist, queer, and racial investigations, though doing such work "outside a United States framework," as Juana Maria Rodriguez argues, reveals the shift toward the transnational (811). As a result the study of ethnicity has been susceptible to being measured as a "mode of existence in need of correction or proper assimilation whereas transnationalism, situated beyond the regime of nationalism, is able to 'ex-nominate' itself and pass itself off as simultaneously ontological and epistemological, experiential and theoretical."[8]

The unstable position of the field of Italian Americana both threatens and dilutes its cultural visibility *and* inspires broader conceptions of U.S. writings that are culturally resonant and invitingly comparative. For ethnic studies in fact first problematized the idea of nationhood itself, as Agnes Lugo-Ortiz contends, and "subtly undermined traditional understandings of national culture.... [T]raditions, histories, and cultures ... may intersect with the national but which, in the last instance, are irreducible to it" (806). Thus the obligation for scholars of Italian America in traditional disciplines such as English, Italian, and Comparative Literature, would be to offer an interdisciplinary approach to the study of Italian America, including its literature, employing comparative approaches that move us away from a consensus oriented syllabus (in which textual themes are shared across a culture) and toward an approach that offers counter-readings, which are fundamentally interventionist in purpose.

Also, we must find ways to incorporate works on syllabi without performing minoritizing gestures such as placing works under the rubric of "recommended," without ever teaching them. Working simultaneously in the discipline of Women's, Gender, & Sexuality Studies has allowed me to refuse the header of "recommended," as I recognize the necessity of establishing broader intellectual alliances with other disciplines not only in a recuperative effort but also in recognition of the necessity of assuming a "troubled, self-conscious relationship with sources and traditions" in order to challenge my own cultural authority as I go about the task of

---

[8] R. Radhakrishnan, "Ethnic Studies in the Age of Transnationalism," 808. See also Juana Maria Rodriguez's "Ethnic Scholarship, Transnational Studies, Institutional Locations," 811. Both essays comprise syntheses of longer papers presented at the 2006 MLA conference panel on "Ethnic Studies in the Age of Transnationalism."

critical analysis (Rinehart 73). For example, my analysis of the topic of motherhood in the context of migration invites a cross-cultural discussion of how women negotiated the demands of reproduction through different kinds of mobility, whether it required an escape from plantation slavery in the antebellum American south or a forced migration from Lombardy to the United States with children in tow.[9]

My final story from the halls of academe returns me to the university classroom. In 2004, I was invited to give a lecture to graduate students taking a seminar on "Problematics in Italian/American Culture."[10] As Gregory Jay argues, replacing the term "theme" with its universalizing tendencies with the term "problematics" in our classrooms puts texts from "different cultures within the U.S. into dialogue with one another" (22). In my lecture to the graduate students, I attempted to problematize the conflicted and paradoxical relationship women writers of Italian America continue to have about the Catholic Church.

Quite in contrast to the code of *omertà*, women in Italian America have confessed much beyond the dark, enclosed stall of the traditional confessional. Women writers of Italian Catholic heritage often resisted the institution of Catholicism because it perpetuated the subordination of women. Moreover, the disciplinary structure of the official Catholic Church in America was largely

---

[9] Consider for example three texts emerging from very different social locations, therefore influencing the genre employed: Harriett Beecher Stowe's sentimental novel, *Uncle Tom's Cabin*; Harriet Jacobs's slave narrative, *Incidents in the Life of a Slave Girl*; and Marie Hall Ets's as-told-to autobiography of Rosa Cassettari, *Rosa: The Life of an Italian Immigrant*.

[10] In 2004, Anthony J. Tamburri created a Ph.D. seminar at Florida Atlantic University called "Problematics in Italian/American Culture" that prioritized secondary source materials from a variety of disciplines in an effort to examine current issues that surround Italian American culture, including definitional categories of race, ethnicity, gender, and sexuality alongside such topics as the myth of origins, linguistic strategies, and organized crime.

controlled by the Irish Catholic hierarchy, whose more doctrinal form of Catholicism felt at odds with the emotionalism derived from popular Italian Catholic practices. Add the common practice of immigrant parents sending their children to parochial schools and one may find that an intellectual girl could quickly become a bad girl. Helen Barolini was one such girl, harboring her father's anticlerical tendencies and using high school as her stomping ground for protest and dismissal.[11] What many an Italian American girl learned in Catholic school was not to ask questions, but, as Mary Gordon explains in *Good Boys and Dead Girls*, girls were taught thoughtlessly to accept a "tradition that provided them with answers before they thought of the questions" (190). Implicitly they were told: "don't ask, just tell."

The American Catholic Church's dual function was to maintain the faith and produce good American citizens—Italian American girls who asked questions were neither "good" citizens of their religious heritage nor apparently able to assimilate like their classmate citizens of Irish extraction. The next generation's daughters of these intellectual mothers also revealed tales about nontraditional sexuality; some writers explicitly chose queer sexuality as a fundamental determinant of their identity. From this situation, a rich brew of verboten information is blended into examinations of sexual practices, including a probing of the Catholic Church's inadvertent sanctioning of desire. Mary Cappello is one such probative writer who, in her memoir, *Night Bloom*, and a biographical essay that preceded it, "Nothing to Confess," forcefully denounced the official Catholic Church as an institution increasingly "devoid of language capable of expressing a new idea" ("Nothing to Confess" 101).

Aware that her marginalization as a lesbian compelled her into a secular (anti-)confession, Mary Cappello discloses the inter-

---

[11] See Helen Barolini's "Another Convent Story," in *Chiaroscuro: Essays of Identity* (114-128).

twining relationship between the traditionally separate categories of ethnicity and sexuality. Articulating an Italian Catholicity in which sacred and profane uneasily coexist in *American* culture, Cappello sensed "some unmet desire" that she observed on both sides of her Sicilian and Neapolitan Italian family, and that was "maybe even violently forced into religious or materialist forms" ("Nothing to Confess" 96). In an effort to explore a more "appropriate medium" to understand her family's love of opera and girl children's incredulous movement into religious cloisters, Cappello names "queerness in its broader sense," as the form of expression denied her family by Anglo-American standards, middle-class aspirations, and the official Catholic Church ("Nothing to Confess" 96). In a dramatic gesture, Cappello literally "outs" her Italian American family, asking the provocative question, "Is the lesbian in an Italian American family the *embodiment* of the family secret?" ("Nothing to Confess" 93). Cappello insists on the fluidity of the terms "lesbian" and "Italian American," dismantling the binary between ethnicity and sexuality that would render this coupling mutually exclusive: "In 'becoming queer,' I was becoming what my Italian forbears denied about themselves even as they provided the example" (*Night Bloom* 181). Instead of confessing a sin needing absolution, Cappello embraces a family that gave her the keys to a gay kingdom. Buttressed by several disciplinary fields, including feminist theorists of Foucauldian literature, I was better equipped to examine female empowerment within the context of the parochial school and the family home within literary Italian America.[12]

After my lecture, I fielded a question that paralyzed my tongue. After lauding the works of Chicana writers, one of the graduate students asked why Italian American women writers have not

---

[12] A longer version of this analysis appears in Chapter 2, "Faith/Fede: Plenty to Confess: Women and (Italian) American Catholicism." *By the Breath of Their Mouths: Narratives of Resistance in Italian America* (39-72).

been more inventive and revisionary like those she saw in Gloria Anzaldúa's conversation changing *Borderlands: La Frontera: The New Mestiza*? I was flummoxed by the tone and the content of this question: I did not want to enter into a conversation that required me to apologize for some supposed paucity of inventiveness on the part of Italian American writers, nor did I want to disclaim the groundbreaking work of Chicana lesbians like Anzaldúa, whose work highly influenced my own. I refused to play the game of competitive ethnicity or fall into defensive ethnic chauvinism, and responded in kind.

Later, however, I pulled off the bookshelf my dog-eared copy of *Borderlands* and re-read Anzaldúa's "How to Tame a Wild Tongue." In her section on "Overcoming the Tradition of Silence," Anzaldúa begins with the proverb "Flies don't enter a closed mouth," "en boca cerrada no entran moscas" (Anzaldúa 76), a saying also common throughout Italy: "nella bocca chiusa non entrano mosche." Both proverbs amount to the same bad advice: "well-bred girls don't answer back," but back talk as bell hooks reminds us is fundamental to feminist action—to resist the oppressions of silence with voices of protest, voices of poetry.[13] As poet Rose Romano has written in a poem called "The Fly," "Sicilians tell their children--/ 'A fly doesn't enter a closed mouth.' / I'm standing now and I'm / telling the Sicilians, / the Italians, / and the Lesbians— / You can't spit a fly / out of a closed mouth" (40).

Without submitting to a universalism that would claim essential greatness to literary Italian America, I examine in the second part of this essay those *voci radicali* of the late twentieth century who have been influenced by postmodern experiments in narra-

---

[13] In *Talking Back, Thinking Feminist, Thinking Black*, hooks writes, "In the world of the southern black community I grew up in, 'back talk' and 'taking back' meant speaking as an equal to an authority figure. It meant daring to disagree and sometimes it just meant having an opinion" (5).

12

tive, producing cultural work with trans-geographic vistas and nontraditional representations of national cultures.

THE ITALIAN AMERICAN IMAGINARY AND POST-MODERN NARRATIVES

The narrative voices emerging from what I call "the Italian American imaginary" embrace "a way to talk about shared mental life," as anthropologist Claudia Strauss explains, inclusive of a "person-centered approach [that] recognizes the importance of learned cultural understandings [but that] does not take 'culture' to be a fixed entity assumed to be held in common by a geographically bounded or [necessarily] self-identified group" (322, 323). As Donna Gabaccia explains, for migrants from Italy ... the concept of home meant a "place—the *patria* or *paese*—not a people, nation, or descent group," and migration "rarely created a national or united Italian diaspora" (7, 6). Rather, migrants experienced many "temporary and changing [diasporas of peoples] with identities and loyalties poorly summed up by the national term, Italian" (Gabaccia 7).

Contemporary Italian American authors, Tony Ardizzone and Adria Bernardi, tell post-*Risorgimento* stories of migration that are nontraditional in theme and structure. Publishing experimental novels in the millennium, Tony Ardizzone's 1999 *In the Garden of Papa Santuzzu* and Adria Bernardi's 2007 *Openwork* engage fundamental principles of feminism in works that might be called historiographic metafictions: as such these narratives problematize the relationship between supposedly objective recordings of the past (like the mini-history chronicled at this essay's beginning), and the "unstable nature of textuality and subjectivity" (Hutcheon 48). Both authors overlay their narratives with feminist revaluations of oral histories, storytelling voices, and other lacunae discovered in the ethnic archives of Italians whose migrations were vast.

Ardizzone and Bernardi read against the grain of canonical works of literature—Italian and Anglo—and also against traditional approaches to the social sciences. Both authors critique the relationship between capitalism and patriarchy, regarding issues such as family wages, modes of control of female sexuality, childrearing, and unpaid women's labor. While Ardizzone often uses parody, Bernardi tends toward covert critique, but both adroitly employ these strategies as forms of feminist subversion, specifically in Ardizzone's lavish use of allusions and Bernardi's representation of the wet-nursing industry. Both writers give emphatic value to the notion of lived experience in keeping with their ethnic and feminist commitments. As Josephine Gattuso Hendin explains, "Ethnic heritage is history in action; it subjects the fact of immigration to a scrutiny of its ongoing effects; ... it constitutes a revolt against the devaluation of the past, of heritage, of history, and the individual in postmodern critical discourse" (13). These writers re-think the value of personal-experience stories, the value of what Ilaria Serra calls "worthless lives" in her work on immigrant autobiographies.

While both writers focus on antipodal geographical locations, Sicily and Tuscany, respectively, they nonetheless deploy the trope of weaving in an effort to value the traditional way storytelling was done in village economies of scarce resources. As Roger D. Abrahams explains, stables were often the warmest places of domesticity where the dual activities of weaving and storytelling took place: "and it was here, too, that stories were spun and woven: the trope is not a conceit, for it is the traditional way in which storytelling is described in most of the world in which weaving is done" (xi). Both authors employ the trope of weaving through the voice of storytelling women, who literally and figuratively spin stories that encircle future generations as a web that is more of an embrace in the hopes of reconnecting to a transformed homeland.

The intersection between private and public history is revised in *In the Garden of Papa Santuzzu* and *Openwork* as each author problematizes the nature of representation in historiography, fusing storytelling traditions, family lore, and archival research to uncover the stories behind migration. As Linda Hutcheon argues, "If the personal is political, then the traditional separation between private and public history must be rethought" (160). While post-modern imperatives transform both narratives, the writers are simultaneously informed by a feminist re-evaluation of life-writing, thus collapsing standard borders between the narrator/author. While Ardizzone frames *In the Garden* with the voice of Rosa Dolci, "the emotional guide of the novel," as JoAnne Ruvoli describes it (224), narrative time is also informed by storytelling time, "in which the story is ... told and retold" (Timpanelli 140). Twelve migrating voices tell intersecting stories. All are relatives of Papa Santuzzu, the Sicilian patriarch, who initiates the migrations of his seven children out of paternal compassion for their impoverishment and land hunger. The stories that are told (and retold from the perspective of another character, whose version of the story is equally true) consider the topic of justice and the ancient conflict between disenfranchised peasants and powerful landowners. Also disclosing larger historical narratives that have shaped the destinies of powerless people, Bernardi's *Openwork* recovers and reimagines the memories of silenced voices, establishing a communal bond between a twentieth-century interlocutor and the central figure of sewing, a wounded storyteller, who navigates space and time differently.

As such, both Tony Ardizzone and Adria Bernardi destabilize the given history of what has been called the second great migration of southern and eastern Europeans to the Americas during the forty-year period of 1880-1920 before the 1924 Immigration Restriction Act in the U.S. For Italy's proletarian migrants "the most powerful magnets remained the home village, not the work sites of Europe or la Merica" (Gabaccia 72). Not uncommon, chain migration enabled immigrants to experience some connection with their home villages through the sharing of dialectal language and culinary traditions, though such connections were often severed due to subsequent migration and heterogeneity of the neighborhoods where they first settled. Nonetheless, after the golden doors were closed, migrating Italian women experienced a new reality once reproduction took place in the diaspora, laying a foundation for "incorporation into countries where migrants lived and worked" (67). Let me add here that most accounts of migration continue to focus on narratives of mobility, change, and agency, but such narratives then undervalue what Irene Gedalof calls the "embodied work of mothering, such as childcare and childbirth, and the work of reproducing cultures and structures of belonging, such as transmitting culturally specific histories and traditions regarding food, dress, family and other inter-personal relationships" (82). Both Ardizzone and Bernardi shape migration narratives to focus on women's embodied work within settings both domestic and communal.

TONY ARDIZZONE'S REVOLUTIONARY MADONNA

Tony Ardizzone's *In the Garden of Papa Santuzzu*, pays homage to multiple literary legacies, offering a textual repertory that both overwhelms and delights as it initiates readers into a persistently allusive and magical world. One of the back-cover blurbs on a paperback edition reads: "Not since *Christ in Concrete* have we had a novel so rich in language, so strong in story, so vivid in its telling, and so filled with history that it can be read over and over again. *In the Garden of Papa Santuzzu* should be required reading for everyone who is or knows an American of Italian descent" (Gardaphé *Fra Noi*). Ardizzone's textual repertory pays equal attention to Italian American writers as to European canonical authors such as Boccaccio and Chaucer. In an effort to place the diasporic experience of Sicilians on the map, Ardizzone plays the role of historian, folklorist, and contemporary magical realist, refusing to dictate a master protocol of reading through an all-knowing narrator. Rather, the author structures his novel around multiple voices, all of whom agree with Papa Santuzzu's anguished reasoning in initiating their migratory departures: "'I sent them away! I did! All seven! God sent only one! ... Seven against one! ... [T]here are some things on earth ... in the lives that we live, that are more sacred!'" (134). According to JoAnne Ruvoli, Ardizzone "uses traditional Sicilian stories and rewrites them in an American context, to construct Italian American urban folktales that help characters move forward in contemporary American life with an understanding of the past."[14]

Aware of the importance of intertextuality to decrease the hegemony of an individual narrative voice, Ardizzone employs rhetorical allusions with documentary value, prefacing his novel with epigraphs from Booker T. Washington, Karl Marx, Luigi Pirandello, and proverbial Sicilian culture. Such a paratextual convention "roots the fiction firmly in historical ... actuality" (Hutcheon 83), shaping the narrative that follows, merging stories of the visible and invisible, winners and losers, literate and illiterate: "In all human history," Marx wrote, "no country and no people have suffered such terrible slavery, conquest and foreign oppression, and no country and no people have struggled so strenuously for their emancipation as Sicily and the Sicilians" (*In The Garden*, front matter, n.p.)

Ardizzone's Sicilian characters are as different as their multicolored region. Yet, they share a tradition based on "the fact that the characters don't read, that they *tell* the stories they have heard and will tell again" ("Interview with Tony Ardizzone" 209), echo-

---

[14] 208. See Ruvoli's "Mythologizing Raconteurs: Performing the Folktale in Tony Ardizzone's *In the Garden of Papa Santuzzu* and Don DeLillo's *Underworld*" (207-267).

ing professional storyteller Gioia Timpanelli's comment that narrative time informed by storytelling means that the story is 'cunta e s'arricunta,' told and re-told. (140). Ardizzone extends his focus on justice, equality, and the rights of the poor in the voices of second-generational children born in America but bred on Sicilian folklore. The longest and arguably most radical chapter in the novel, "The Black Madonna," dramatizes a feminist contestation between the patriarchal Madonna of institutionalized Catholicism and the people's Madonna.

Anna Girgenti is sent by her father to a New York orphanage (which functions more as a work camp for poor girls either left by parents or bereft of them) after her mother's death in childbirth in early twentieth century America. Nearly killing her father in self-defense (after his crazed reaction to what in actuality is menstrual blood not the residuum of first sex), Anna shifts from violent defense to peaceful love through a belief in equality, prayerfulness, and nonviolence. As such, she inhabits a folk world in which the Madonna and saints resemble "peasant men and women" (Birnbaum 65). As Lucia Birnbaum explains, "In the vernacular world of Madonna ... closeness to the church signifies distance from goddess/god: *Vicino alla chiesa, lontano da Dio*" (65).

As in many areas of the world, in southern Italy "there are ... places where a major object of worship is the Black Madonna—Mary, mother of Jesus, in her aboriginal, mother-goddess aspect" (Di Stasi 90-91). Unsurprisingly, then, the Black Madonna appears to Anna in seven visitations in the chapel of the orphanage, enabling the young girl—despite *violent* protest by the white church fathers—to become *the* revolutionary spirit informing Ardizzone's novel. The ongoing conflict between the religion espoused by Church doctrine and the spiritual experiences of subaltern people is encapsulated by the apparition of the shift-changing Madonna, who denies hierarchy and insists on her equal position as the Holy Ghost of the Trinity: "J[G]esù and I are twin souls, and one with

God the Father'" (*In the Garden* 256). Constitutionally unable to tolerate equality, the priests respond to Anna's recounting of the Madonna's appearances to her by parroting received wisdom, spouting racist, sexist, and xenophobic comments, while Anna's advocate, a priest of color, refutes their groundless claims, as the following dialogue attests:

> "'[W]e should consider how Mary failed to lead a public life and as a result left behind no teachings.'
> 'What is the life of example,' said the advocate, 'but teaching in its highest form?'
> 'Yet none of it is recorded,' said the second priest.
> 'At least not officially,' said the advocate....
> 'Mary can hardly be thought of as an equal to Jesus since she was born a mere woman.'
> 'But in God's eyes both women and men are equal,' said the advocate.
>
> ...
> 'She'd [Anna] have us believe the Blessed Virgin was colored?' 'A Negro?'
> 'Forgive me,' my advocate said, 'but there is more than ample research to suggest that both Christ and Mary were of dark complexion. Further, there's a well-documented history of black Madonnas in Italy's Mezzogiorno region.'"
>
> (*In The Garden* 256-259)

The priests are refuted at every turn by a singular priest whom Anna describes as the "dark young priest," who, "for the sake of argument", challenges each insupportable assumption they make, reminding the men that Anna's experiences of seeing a dark-skinned apparition is perfectly in line with her native Sicily, "closer to Africa than it is to Rome" (*In the Garden* 259). Despite the Vatican's later refusal to acknowledge the miraculous powers executed by what the neighborhood folks call *la Madonna Nera*, her shrine continues to hold sway over scores of pregnant women and sick and invalid children.

Anna Girgenti spends her adulthood in east Africa doing missionary work, and re-witnessing the miraculous apparition of the black Madonna in the faces of "the beautiful Eritrean people for whom it was my blessing to care" (*In the Garden* 269). Surely Ardizzone strategically relocates his Sicilian character, fully aware that in 1890 Italy established a colony of the Kingdom of Italy, Italian Eritrea, through the fascist period. As Birnbaum further explains, "the indigenous goddess of Old Europe merged with African, Middle Eastern, and Asian dark goddesses and persisted in the Christian era in vernacular beliefs and rituals associated with black madonnas. The term vernacular connotes submerged beliefs visible in the everyday activities of [subaltern] people[s]" (*Black Madonnas* 4).

Dismantling hierarchical institutions, Ardizzone insists on the fundamental vernacular belief in equality with difference, shifting from veneration of the crucified male to love of the living female, marking the beginning of "God's third order, two thousand years of rule by the black Madonna, the Holy Ghost, and the third face of God" (270). ("*Son madre di Gesù, sposa di Dio*: I am mother of Jesus, wife of God") (Birnbaum 49). As justice is the "central value [that] emerges from studying the earth mother" (Birnbaum 23), the appearance of the black Madonna to Anna symbolizes the not-so-concealed figure of Giustizia, or the goddess of Justice. Anna's private experience, her lived life, becomes the official public record of historical injustice perpetuated by the Church. In his multivocal novel, Tony Ardizzone challenges many aspects of formalized history and the limitations of its archive: "the reliability of its recording", embracing the "unofficial personal record" (Hutcheon 163).

Migrants from Italy—north and south—despite their limited resources and land hunger, voluntarily left their homes, but their suffering has been equated by writers of Italian America with a trauma that damages beyond repair. Adria Bernardi's novel, *Openwork*, simulates the diasporic experiences of Italians, connecting them to a transnational identity that crosses borders, enabling more permeable boundaries and thereby keeping open the connections between families, generations, and places. Seven intersecting voices speak in *Openwork* as Bernardi sews the threads that connect them. Examining the unofficial personal record through multiple representations of the female body as a locus of power but also as a locus of pain, Bernardi describes the female body as vulnerable and injured (Hutcheon 154).[15]

Italian American writers often have represented the activity of sewing as a radical act and Bernardi's *Openwork* revitalizes and innovates on this tradition. Used to subvert and defend, the act of sewing offers women a means to protect their honor, reveal their inner desires, and also demonstrate their prowess. As such the needle is a metaphorical pen, expressing and concealing simultaneously.[16] The term "openwork" refers to ornamental or structural work as of embroidery or metal, combining numerous openings, usually set in patterns. The sewer represented in Bernardi's novel

---

[15] In her chapter "Postmodernism and Feminisms," Linda Hutcheon argues that master-works and mass culture both inscribe conventional feminine representations, but in "so-called high art ... gender is obviously a division of power here too, and the female body is a locus of power politics." Hutcheon references women writers such as Margaret Atwood, Maxine Hong Kingston, and Audrey Thomas as representing women's bodies as "vulnerable, diseased, injured, or as experiencing their own pleasure—from the inside—... implicitly protest[ing] the male erotic gazing at their external form." In *The Politics of Postmodernism*, 154-155.

[16] I take this idea of the needle as a metaphorical pen from Sandra M. Gilbert's and Susan Gubar's groundbreaking *Madwoman in the Attic: The Woman Writer and the Nineteenth-Century Literary Imagination*. They write, "Like Ariadne, Penelope, and Philomela, women have used their looms, thread, and needles both to defend themselves and silently to speak of themselves." For women, then, the literal and figural activity of stitching "both conceals and reveals a vision of the world in which such defensive sewing would not be necessary" (641-642).

reveals a vision of the world that is fundamentally unjust; she struggles to free herself from powerlessness; and she, and the author as her interlocutor, link the dual activities of sewing and storytelling, melding two forms of expression used by the poor around the world. The connection made between sewing and storytelling radicalizes Italian American narratives, serving liberating purposes for the woman who sews and with whom she shares her skills.[17]

ADRIA BERNARDI'S *OPENWORK* AND ITALY'S DIASPORAS[18]

Similar to *In the Garden of Papa Santuzzu*, Adria Bernardi's *Openwork* relocates migratory tales about ancestry within a regional context. Thus the author both refines and destabilizes given histories of Italian migrations and, in particular, myths about northern Italy. Italian openwork functions as a fabric text with transnational implications, connecting women, work, and "consciousness in more than one national territory," as Donna Gabaccia has argued (11). Bernardi's governing metaphor of sewing equally serves as a bulwark against the destabilization that occurs with migration and a counter-narrative to institutional forms of oppression by Church and state in post-Risorgimento Italy.

Disclosing larger historical narratives that have shaped the destinies of powerless women, Bernardi offers alternative documentation by reimagining memories of silenced voices. One such voice is Imola Bartolai, whose handwork liberates lives defined by poverty and maternity. The Roman equivalent of Clothos, *Nana* ("ninth") was originally a goddess called upon in the ninth month

---

[17] For an analysis of literary representations of a wide range of women sewers see Mary Jo Bona's "'A Needle Better Fits?': The Role of Defensive Sewing in Italian American literature." *Embroidered Stories: Interpreting Women's Domestic Needlework from the Italian Diaspora.* Ed. Edvige Giunta and Joseph Sciorra (144-164).

[18] See Mary Jo Bona's *Women Writing Cloth: Migratory Fictions in the American Imaginary* for a full-length chapter on Bernardi's *Openwork* (91-114).

of pregnancy; Imola's labor as a wet nurse aligns her with village women forced to abandon illegitimate infants. Bernardi unearths the linked activities associated with traditional women's work in nineteenth-century Italy: wet nursing and sewing, critiquing the highly organized system of infant abandonment in Italy by representing Imola's handiwork as a semiotic response to a form of institutional control that, if it did not condone, then, increased infanticide. In addition, Bernardi explores multiple ramifications inhering in a fictional migrating object, specifically the traveling tablecloth, eliciting a critique of institutionalized classism on both sides of the Atlantic.

Bernardi opens up a view of women's migration shaped by the cloth-worker's art, in this case, Imola's method of openwork. I argue here that by writing an "ethnographic counter-narrative," Bernardi discloses and links the gendered work common in nineteenth-century Catholic Europe: wet nursing and sewing (McCracken 10). I further contend that Bernardi's representation of Imola's hand work increasingly serves as a response to the oppressive system of infant abandonment in Italy, forcing women to leave their babies at the foundling wheel. This is Catholic Italy's response to controlling female sexuality by stigmatizing illegitimacy. For Imola and her cloth-working sisters, literary and historical, artistic production ultimately functions as an analog to storytelling, which allows for both imaginary and actual voyaging.

As *Openwork* demonstrates, Imola's work as wet nurse and cloth worker is not subsidiary to the family's economy. Sewing bridal linens by trade, Imola teaches sewing to her daughters and neighborhood girls, who then transfer those portable skills to another country. Imola's remunerated work more than shores up the family during lean times; it sustains them six months out of the year as they cannot rely on her seasonally migrating husband's money to arrive.[19] To evoke ideas of connectedness across space and time, Bernardi not only frames the beginning and ending of *Openwork* with the voice of *la sarta*, but also implements what Marie-Laure Ryan calls the "stack," a narrative technique that models "the mechanisms of the crossing of boundaries" (371). Three separate but interconnected paragraphs appear outside the pages of *Openwork*, which might also be called a prologue, from the Greek, *prologos*, literally meaning "before speech." Applying this paratextual convention of a three-paragraph prologue permits the author to incorporate, as Linda Hutcheon explains, "historical documentary value" into her fiction (82). Displaying both didactic and semiotic purposes, I suggest that this three-paragraph prologue functions as an extra-diegetic before-story, but simultaneously, it is "inevitably touched by the fictive, the shaped, the invented" (Hutcheon 82).

The spatial representation of the three block paragraphs in *Openwork* serves two interweaving purposes: to give the appearance of squares of cloth in deference to Imola's trade as a seamstress; and to express mobility of Italian migrants through a simulation of the picture postcard, an equally provocative traveling object invented during the period of the second great migration. Bernardi assures this connection spatially within the prologue and thematically through Imola's fascination with the postcards she collects from Africa, France, and the United States, the migratory destinations of her three brothers. To summon her brothers, Imola repeatedly views their postcards as a reminder of her longing for them, as a "commemoration of the Absent," to quote Derrida, but also, as Galit Hasan-Rokem explains, to recognize "the irreversibility of the migratory move [which is] thus metonymically allevi-

---

[19] As David Kertzer explains, in Apennine peasant culture, migration was a "major feature of mountain life for centuries.... The frequency with which men were away due to seasonal and other forms of migration gave considerable authority to the women left behind" ("History of the 'Truly Obscure'" [266, 267]).

ated by the countermovement of the postcard in the opposite direction" (Derrida, as qtd. in Hasan-Rokem, 507; 511). As emigration decreases face-to-face contact, postal communication becomes a compensatory mode of storytelling.

Imola's own regional migrations reiterate a family tradition of wet nursing as both her grandmother and mother engaged as *balie* (wet nurses). Thus Imola is deeply aware of the prevalence of foundling hospitals in northern Italy, and of the symbol of their institutional control, the wheel, *la ruota*, "'wooden cylindrical concave boxes ... which were in a windowlike aperture in the wall of the hospice and served as cradle turnstiles'" (Fuchs, qtd. in Kertzer, *Sacrificed for Honor* 101). Sensitive to the high rate of infant mortality, Imola knows that leaving one's children at the foundling hospital was a "form of socially condoned infanticide" (Jacobus 211). An entrenched social institution and a highly regulated industry, wet nursing in Italy was undergirded by a "thick network of informers: landlords, neighbors, employers, and various officials" (Kertzer, *Sacrificed* 53).

From her unofficial perspective as a maternal breast feeder, Imola is parent to the children she has suckled, despite the stigmatization of illegitimate children made by Church and state. Her compensated work never prevents her mourning the loss of children whom she nursed for a fee, for they were treated with the same devoted attention as her own. Imola's *seni dolorosi*—painful breasts—lament those children who are all but guaranteed to perish "within a few months" inside a "formal governmental system" (Kertzer, *Sacrificed* 10). In a final rendering of her thoughts, Imola recalls the faces of babies from her mountain village, her own, and others; whether she nursed them or not, their infant faces appear "like faint photographs. Intaglio. But translucent. Like figures stamped on tiny holy medals" (*Openwork* 296). Imola's intaglio is threaded into her body, a design incised or engraved in a material. An Italian Penelope, Imola believes that if she just keeps sewing, the babies will not be lost. For as dowry seamstress for her community, Imola knows that working the cloth affects a material satisfaction that signifies what has been lost to infant abandonment and migration: the children of Italy.

Openwork ultimately submits that milk is thicker than blood. Bernardi's portrayal of Imola as wet nurse and needle worker enables the author to draw attention to the peasant woman's historical role in nurturing generations of Italian children. A communal undertaking, cloth work transcends norms of reciprocity as women become the creators and "controllers of highly valued possessions—a currency of sorts made from 'cloth'" (Weiner, *Inalienable Possessions* 2-3). Imola's silent rebellion is revealed through the work of her hands. The specific needlework technique of openwork can be read as Imola's textual response to the closed system of the foundling wheel and its institutions, intricate networks of social control that regulated the lives of child-bearing women. Custodian of an Italian future in America, Bernardi honors the potential of cloth work to mend what seems are irreparable fissures. Beyond its utilitarian value as a source of economic support, cloth work's aesthetic value as represented through openwork embroidery illuminates the enduring nature of social ties.

While *Openwork* portrays traditional links between embroidery and femininity, it also examines the subversive potential of cloth work represented by Imola's tablecloth, serving as a testimonial to survival and resilience in the face of gender and class oppression. Refusing to exchange through commerce what she discerns is a coveted item, Imola instead sends the tablecloth to her brother's widow in the New Mexico desert. As Jane Schneider clarifies, embroidered trousseaux were deemed "wealth objects with significant liquidity in wide spheres of exchange" ("Trousseau as Treasure" 324). So desired an item of exchange is Imola's openwork that "a lady with pearl buttons on her boots," travels up the mountain to persuade Imola to sell her *magnum opus*, the creature-embroidered tablecloth (*Openwork* 303). Refusing her request, Imola will not be compelled to utilize her body to turn a profit. Like her wet-nursing capability, her artist's hands become an "alternative form of nourishment" in place of an absence (Costello 179). Like the biological mothers for whom she has substituted, Imola replaces scarcity with sustenance, embodying in her artist's hands the etymological meaning of the word "foster," which means "to feed or nourish" (Costello 179-80).

Imola intuitively recognizes that her tablecloth is a sacred cloth, and, by sending it to her widowed sister-in-law in New Mexico, she both reproduces kinship relations and honors sibling intimacy. The reproduction of kinship is legitimated in each generation through the transmission of inalienable possessions, "be they land rights, material objects, or mythic knowledge" (Weiner *Inalienable Possessions* 11). To defeat loss, Imola sends her enormous tablecloth to a weeping widow, keeping her brother's memory alive through this cloth rendition of Noah's Arc, a transnational symbol of migration. *Openwork* reproduces kinship connections across continents with the embroidered tablecloth signifying the quintessential Italian woman's communal art.

Authors like Tony Ardizzone and Adria Bernardi represent the innovative possibilities in narrative production that diasporic migrations of Italians have inspired them to create. The field of Italian American studies and its intersections with the study of migration and diaspora flesh out a cultural imaginary that varies by region, generation, gender, and sexuality, to name only a few categories of difference that require attention and guard us against nostalgic sentimentalism that is often borne of loss. As we move more fully into the millennium, my hope continues unabated: to read new and brilliant cultural productions by writers concerned by intersections between Italy and North America, with an increasing awareness that the very fact of globalization compels not only a transcending of borders, but also a bridging of gaps.[20]

REFERENCES

Abrahams, Roger D. Foreword. *Italian Folktales in America: The Verbal Art of an Immigrant Woman.* By Elizabeth Mathias and Richard Raspa. Detroit: Wayne State UP, 1988. ix-xv.

Anzaldúa, Gloria. *Borderlands: La Frontera, The New Mestiza.* 1987. Second Edition. San Francisco: Aunt Lute P, 1999.

Ardizzone, Tony. *In the Garden of Papa Santuzzu.* New York: Picador, 1999.

_____. "Interview with Tony Ardizzone." By Cristina Bevilacqua. *Italian Americana* 19.2 (Summer 2001): 207-213.

Barolini, Helen. *Chiaroscuro: Essays of Identity.* Madison: U of Wisconsin P, 1999.

Bernardi, Adria. *Houses with Names: The Italian Immigrants of Highwood, Illinois.* Urbana and Chicago: U of Illinois P, 1990.

_____. *Openwork: A Novel.* Dallas: Southern Methodist UP, 2007.

Birnbaum, Lucia Chiavola. *Black Madonnas: Feminism, Religion and Politics in Italy.* Boston: Northeastern UP, 1993.

Bona, Mary Jo. "'A Needle Better Fits?': The Role of Defensive Sewing in Italian American literature." *Embroidered Stories: Interpreting Women's Domestic Needlework from the Italian Diaspora.* Ed. Edvige Giunta and Joseph Sciorra. Jackson: UP of Mississippi, 2014. 144-164.

_____. *By the Breath of Their Mouths: Narratives of Resistance in Italian America.* Albany: SUNY P, 2010.

_____. *Women Writing Cloth: Migratory Fictions in the American Imaginary.* Lanham, MD: Lexington Books/Rowman & Littlefield), 2016.

Buonomo, Leonardo. *From Pioneer to Nomad: Essays on Italian North American Writing.* Toronto: Guernica, 2003.

[20] Here I refer specifically to a consortium established in 2014 at the Rockefeller Foundation Center in Bellagio, Italy. This conference brought together eighteen scholars from Italy and the United States in diverse disciplines to discuss the future of Italian American studies. The collection of essays emerging from this conference is called *Transcending Borders, Bridging Gaps: Italian Americana, Diasporic Studies, and the University Curriculum.*

Bush, Jr., Sargent. *The Writings of Thomas Hooker: Spiritual Adventure in Two Worlds*. Madison: U of Wisconsin P, 1980.

Cappello, Mary. *Night Bloom*. Boston: Beacon, 1998.

_____. "Nothing to Confess: A Lesbian in Italian America." *Fuori: Essays by Italian American Lesbians and Gays*. Anthony Julian Tamburri, ed. West Lafayette: Bordighera, 1996. 89-108.

Costello, Bonnie. "Maria Edgeworth and the Politics of Consumption: Eating, Breastfeeding, and the Irish Wet Nurse in *Ennui*." *Inventing Maternity: Politics, Science, and Literature, 1650-1865*. Susan C. Greenfield and Carol Barash, eds. Lexington: UP of Kentucky, 1999.173-192.

Di Stasi, Lawrence. *Mal Occhio: The Underside of Vision*. San Francisco: Northpoint P, 1981.

Duggan, Christopher. *A Concise History of Italy*. Cambridge: Cambridge UP, 1994.

Gabaccia, Donna R. *Italy's Many Diasporas*. Seattle: U of Washington P, 2000.

Gardaphé, Fred. *Italian Signs, American Streets: The Evolution of Italian American Narrative*. Durham: Duke UP, 1996.

Gedalof, Irene. "Birth, Belonging and Migrant Mothers: Narratives of Reproduction in Feminist Migration Studies." *Feminist Review* 93 (2009): 81-100.

Gilbert Sandra M. and Susan Gubar. *Madwoman in the Attic: The Woman Writer and the Nineteenth-Century Literary Imagination*. New Haven: Yale UP, 1979.

Giunta, Edvige. *Writing with an Accent: Contemporary Italian American Women Authors*. New York: Palgrave, 2002.

Gordon, Mary. *Good Boys and Dead Girls: And Other Essays*. New York: Viking, 1991.

Hasan-Rokem, Galit. "Jews as Postcards, or Postcards as Jews: Mobility in a Modern Genre." *The Jewish Quarterly Review* 99.4 (Fall 2009): 505-546.

Hendin, Josephine Gattuso. "Social Constructions and Aesthetic Achievements: Italian American Writing as Ethnic Art." *MELUS* 28.3 (Fall 2003): 13-39.

Higham, John. *Strangers in the Land: Patterns of American Nativism, 1860-1925*. 1955. New Brunswick: Rutgers UP, 2004.

hooks, bell. *Talking Back: Thinking Feminist, Thinking Black.* Boston, MA: South End P, 1989.

Hutcheon, Linda. *The Politics of Postmodernism.* London: Routledge, 1989.

Jacobus, Mary. *First Things: The Maternal Imaginary in Literature, Art, and Psychoanalysis.* New York: Routledge, 1995.

Jay, Gregory. "The End of 'American' Literature: Toward a Multicultural Practice." *The Canon in the Classroom: The Pedagogical Implications of Canon Revision in American Literature.* Ed. John Alberti. New York: Garland, 1995. 3-28.

Kertzer, David. "History of the 'Truly Obscure': Peasants of the Apennines." *Peasant Studies* 13.4 (Summer 1986): 265-69.

_____. *Sacrificed for Honor: Infant Abandonment and the Politics of Reproductive Control.* Boston: Beacon, 1993.

Lugo-Ortiz, Agnes. "Ethnic Studies in the Age of Transnationalism: Framing a Forum." *PMLA* 122.3 (May 2007): 805-807.

Marazzi, Martino. *Voices of Italian America: A History of Early Italian American Literature with a Critical Anthology.* Trans. Ann Goldstein. Madison: Fairleigh Dickinson UP, 2004.

McCracken, Ellen. *New Latina Narrative: The Feminine Space of Postmodern Ethnicity.* Tucson: The U of Arizona P, 1999.

Miller, Perry. *The New England Mind: From Colony to Province.* Cambridge: Harvard UP, 1953.

_____. *The New England Mind: The Seventeenth Century.* Cambridge: Harvard UP, 1939.

Pipino, Mary Frances. *"I Have Found My Voice:" The Italian-American Woman Writer.* New York: Peter Lang, 2000.

Radhakrishnan. R. "Ethnic Studies in the Age of Transnationalism." *PMLA* 122.3 (May 2007): 808-810.

Rinehart, Jane. "Feminist Theorizing as a Conversation: The Connections between Thinking, Teaching and Political Action." *Women and Politics* 19.1 (1998): 59-89.

Rodriguez, Juana Maria. "Ethnic Scholarship, Transnational Studies, Institutional Locations." *PMLA* 122.3 (May 2007): 810-812.

Romano, Rose. *Vendetta.* San Francisco: malafemmina press, 1990.

Ruvoli, JoAnne. "Framing Ethnicity: Storytelling in Italian American Novels." Diss. University of Illinois at Chicago, 2011. Print.

Ryan, Marie-Laure. "Stacks, Frames, and Boundaries." *Narrative Dynamics: Essays on Time, Plot, Closure, and Frames*. Ed. Brian Richardson. Columbus: Ohio State UP. 2002. 366-386.

Scambray, Kenneth. *The North American Italian Renaissance: Italian Writing in America and Canada*. Toronto: Guernica, 2000.

Scarry, Elaine. *The Body in Pain: The Making and Unmaking of the World*. New York: Oxford UP, 1985.

Schneider, Jane. "Trousseau as Treasure: Some Contributions of Late Nineteenth-Century Change in Sicily." In *Beyond the Myths of Culture: Essays in Cultural Materialism*. Eric B. Ross, ed. New York: Academic P, 1980. 323-356.

Scott, Joan. "The Evidence of Experience." *Critical Inquiry* 178:3 (1991): 773-97.

Serra Ilaria. *The Value of Worthless Lives: Writing Italian American Immigrant Autobiographies*. New York: Fordham UP, 2007.

Smith, Henry Nash. *Virgin Land: The American West as Symbol and Myth*. Cambridge: Harvard UP, 1950.

Strauss, Claudia. "The Imaginary." *Anthropological Theory* 6.3 (Sept 2006): 322-344.

Tamburri, Anthony Julian. *A Semiotic of Ethnicity: In (Re)cognition of the Italian/American Writer*. Albany: SUNY P, 1998.

Tamburri, Anthony Julian, and Fred L. Gardaphé, eds. *Transcending Borders: Bridging Gaps: Italian Americana, Diasporic Studies, and the University Curriculum*. New York: John D. Calandra Italian American Institute, 2015.

Timpanelli, Gioia. "Stories and Storytelling. Italian and Italian American: A Storyteller's View." *Italian American Heritage: A Companion to Literature and Arts*. Pellegrino D'Acierno, ed. New York: Garland P, 1999. 131-148.

Tompkins, Jane. *Sensational Designs: The Cultural Work of American Fiction, 1790-1860*. New York: Oxford UP, 1985.

Vecoli, Rudolph. "Are Italian Americans Just White Folks?" *Italian and Italian American Images in the Media*. Ed. Mary Jo Bona and Anthony Tamburri. Proc. of the 27th Annual Conference of the American Italian Historical Association. Staten Island, NY: American Italian Historical Association, 1996. 3-17.

Viscusi, Robert. *Buried Caesars and Other Secrets of Italian American Writing.* Albany: SUNY P, 2007.

Weiner, Annette B. *Inalienable Possessions: The Paradox of Keeping-While-Giving.* Berkeley: U of California P, 1992.

Weiner, Annette B. and Jane Schneider, eds. "Introduction." *Cloth and Human Experience.* Washington: Smithsonian Institution P, 1989. 1-29.

Beyond Little Italys:
The Future of Italian/American Studies

Fred L. Gardaphé
QUEENS COLLEGE, CUNY

Italian/American studies probably began the moment the first Italian immigrant wondered to him or her self "What the hell am I doing here?" Until recently, knowing the date and time of that precise moment never mattered. Since Italian/American studies were not taken seriously enough—even by some of its practitioners—to warrant historicisation, the moment of its birth has never been a concern. Its parents, both American and Italian Studies in the U.S. and Italy had abandoned the child at birth, so it doesn't even know its own birthday. And this would remain true as long as Italians were the objects of, and not the agents of, studies in the academy.

The study of Italians in the United States has long been a function of social scientists, primarily the anthropologists, historians, and sociologists. Robert Forester's *The Italian Emigration of Our Times*, published in 1919 by Harvard University, is one of the first major English language studies of why people left Italy in such large numbers between 1876 and 1909 and throughout this over 500 page study the words "Italian American" never appear. Turn-of-the-century magazines are filled with articles decrying the coming of the Italians or arguing for their acceptance as Americans. These accounts range from crime to work accidents; see such articles as "What Shall We Do with the Dago" (*Popular Science Monthly* December 1890, February 1891 in Moquin 259) and "Italians Can Be Americanized" (*The North American Review*, 1896 in Moquin 264). In many of these early studies, the authors used descriptions of their eating habits to demonstrate their strangeness, as in the April 1897 edition of *Arena* magazine, where Frederick O. Bushee, of South End House, a Boston settlement house in the manner of Jane Adams Hull House, writes:

> The dinner of the ordinary Italian is made up largely of macaroni, French or Italian bread, and usually some meat and potato. That form of flour preparation known as spaghetti is the most frequently used. This is boiled whole and served as a first course. The Italian experiences no difficulty in eating this slippery food, for he merely sucks it into his mouth from his fork in a very unconventional if not elegant manner. (Moquin 52)

If the tone of this seemingly innocuous article is not offensive enough out of context, then a brief look at the conclusion will show you that Bushee's purpose is to argue for the relocation of Italians from the city to rural areas into "agricultural colonies composed of Italian peasants" (58). The authors of these early studies and accounts saw the options as being Italian or becoming American, thus, the words Italian American could not be used.

I began a search for the first usage of the hyphenated "Italian-American" and found, what I will offer as the unofficial earliest usage in an article Viola Roseboro wrote for the January 1888 *Cosmopolitan.* Her "The Italians of New York," is based on "an unusually careful examination of the lower place in Little Italy, as Mulberry Street, particularly the part known as 'The Bend'" (Moquin 301). Roseboro can't ignore what she calls the Italian's "defects." "There is no doubt," she writes, "that they do a great deal of slashing and cutting of each other" (Moquin 301), but also posits the possible transformation of the Italian living in New York into the Italian-American: "The Italian-American," she writes toward the end of her article, "is to be a considered part of our population" (Moquin 302).

At what point then do the words Italian American begin to be used regularly to refer to Americans of Italian descent? At what point then can the shift from the study of Italians to Italian/American studies be identified, tagged, and used as a point-of-departure for those wishing to enter the field of Italian/American studies? While that precise moment may never be documented, this paper hopes to collect and present those foundational moments that have been recorded so that we may have a more extensive understanding of the development of Italian/American studies.

The predominant image of Italian Americans in today's media comes through the representation of the working class. The predominant voice of protest of those images comes from Italian Americans in the middle class. What we have here is classic class struggle. Those educated out of the working class no longer connect to those who have remained working class. Often, the result of this class mobility through education is the creation of Americans with Italian names who do not see anything wrong with writing, producing, directing, and acting in films that, while protected by the First Amendment, offend other Italian Americans, because there is nothing in their education that makes them aware of the reality of Italian American experiences outside the family and Italian American contributions to the creation of American culture.

It is important that scholars search for, if not find, the origins of Italian/American studies because we are now in the business of developing curricula, planning conferences, and creating a great deal of published information in the field. Locating those origins will enable us to build upon them through revisionary criticism that sets a precedent for how to proceed with future histories. Where do you begin, for example, a survey course in Italian/American studies? Start with Columbus? With the Italian contribution to the Revolutionary War? With the mass immigration of the 1800s?

There should be many stories on the origins of Italian/American studies, for only through a multiplicity of perspectives will we ever be able to achieve a sense of inclusion that defies the exclusion of anything but lies and false scholarship, though even those have their place in the field when they incite mindful challenges. And so, what is important is not when Italian/American studies began, but when it began to be taken seriously.

Italian/American studies begin in earnest in this country when the scholar, trained in America begins applying a disciplinary focus to the phenomenon of Americans of Italian descent living in the United States. However, Italian/American studies becomes realized as a (serious) field of study only when the very subjects of earlier studies turn the interpretative gaze back on the scientists, sociologists, scholars, and artists and begin studying them and when these encounters become the material for writing about their own experiences. Italian/American studies becomes legitimized as a serious field of study when institutions begin developing programs of study.

Without scholarly societies or formal programs inside institutions dedicated to the study of Italian/American Culture, American intellectuals of Italian descent who were intent on defining and developing Italian/American studies had to do so independently, and more often than not their work was considered adjunct to their "real work." There are at least two generations of Italian/American scholars who could hardly teach a course dedicated to the study of Italian Americans, let alone vie for a professorship in Italian/American studies.

While there were many Italian/American newspapers in which appeared creative and critical work by Italian/American writers, so much of it was in Italian and mattered only to its readers and certainly not to those who were studying Italian in the universities at the time. Popular culture and journalism was simply not something seriously studied at the time in institutions of higher education. It would not be until the children of Italian immigrants came of age in the 1930s that an articulate voice of Italian Americana would begin to be heard in the mainstream media.

One of the earliest acts of indigenous Italian/American study in the field of literary criticism was the late Jerre Mangione's 1935 *New Republic* review of Garibaldi Lapolla's *The Grand Gennaro*. Mangione introduces the rarity of meeting Italian Americans in American literature and credits Lapolla for "creating Italo-Americans who are vivid and alive and probably a novelty to the average person who, not knowing them intimately, is likely to draw his conclusions about them from the gangster movies" (313). A few years later, Mangione reviewed Pietro di Donato's *Christ in Concrete* in the *New Republic*, and while he praised the young writer's rendition of the Italian/American life, he did not succumb to what I call *Paesan Patting* or blind boosterism; he did not hesitate to point out the novel's roughness and its "minor deficiencies" (111).

During the same time period, Leonard Covello, the New York school teacher who helped shape the social consciousness of progressives such as Vito Marcantonio, completed the first study of the Italian/American school child. His work led to major school reforms in New York City and ushered in the concept of community education. He told his story, with the help of novelist Guido D'Agostino, in *The Heart is the Teacher*.

Giuseppe Prezzolini was a member of the executive council that directed the Institute of Italian Culture in the United States, founded in 1923, and became director of the Casa Italiana of Columbia University in 1930. While Casa Italiana was denounced as a proponent of Fascism, it often published commentaries on Italian/American writers and encouraged the production of a catalogue of Italian/American literary activities, resulting in Olga Pera-gallo's *Italian-American Authors and Their Contribution to American Literature*, which was edited by her mother and published posthumously in 1949. The survey was introduced by a preface from the author and can be considered one of the first attempts to historicize American authors of Italian descent. This primal text paved the way for the next major step in the development of Italian/American literary history by an indigenous intellectual.

The first thorough attempt to organize Italian/American literature was Rose Basile Green's 1962 dissertation at the University of Pennsylvania: "The Evolution of Italian-American Fiction as a Document of the Interaction of Two Cultures." Published in 1974 as *The Italian American Novel: A Document of the Interaction of Two Cultures*, Green's study was the first major attempt to identify and to critically examine the contributions of American writers of Italian descent to American culture. Her work reflects an early stage of cultural examination, one that invites readers and critics to consider the fiction of Italian/American writers through an essentially universal sociological paradigm related to understanding the process of Americanization through the experience of immigration. Green's scholarship enabled the formation of new dimensions of critical examination of the Italian/American contribution to American literature. Like Giovanni Schiavo's attempts to historicize Italian immigrant contributions to U.S. history, Green's work is more a catalogue than criticism, and while flawed in a variety of ways, it reflects the need of early scholars to simply get it down, to chart the presence of Italian Americans in the sea of American culture.

During the 1960s, Italian/American intellectuals began producing books based on studies of their own culture. Two, which best characterize Italian/American studies during this period, are Richard Gambino's *Blood of My Blood*, and Patrick Gallo's *Ethnic Alienation: The Italian Americans*. Only now are these books being read seriously and critiqued properly. For years Richard Gambino attempted to develop Italian/American studies through a minor at Queens College in New York. However, his efforts never were realized on a grand enough scale to claim anything more than start.

One key stage in the *risorgimento* of Italian/American studies occurred in 1967 with the founding of the American Italian Histor-

ical Association (later transformed into the Italian American Studies Association). Though not dedicated specifically to literary studies, with its founding members being primarily historians and sociologists, it did welcome and encourage literary analysis and dedicated its second conference to the Italian/American novel. It was
through that association that some of Italian Americana's best literary criticism has come to be known.

While early intellectuals like Basile Green were well acquainted with what was happening within Italian/American culture, few
knew enough about the literature, and American studies, to speculate as to what was to come. A number of contemporary critics of
the Italian/American narrative have produced exciting and vital
alternatives to Green's methodology by turning their gaze into the
direction of the future. Such critics as Helen Barolini, Robert Viscusi, founder of the Italian American Writers Association, Frank
Lentricchia, Mary Jo Bona, Anthony Tamburri, Louise Napolitano,
Justin Vitiello, Franco Mulas, Edvige Giunta, and Paolo Valesio
with Luigi Fontanella, who formed the Italian Poetry Society of
America, represent the development of an indigenous criticism and
are those whom Robert Viscusi refers to as interpreters "of the minority culture to which [they belong] to by birth" ("A Literature
Considering Itself" 278).

Robert Viscusi, whose work on Italian/American literature has
paved the way for subsequent critics through his prescient and
innovative articles, has contributed tremendously to the construction of a foundation upon which an Italian American discourse
can be built. In many of his articles he offers a culture-specific approach that educates the reader about Italian culture and the context it creates for interpreting the Italian/American narrative. Viscusi was the first critic bold enough to challenge the then nostalgia
that permeated Italian/American studies with the composition of
complex essays that were the result of rigorous thought and an
incredible sense of humor. However, even the power of Viscusi

was not enough to generate the force necessary to birth Italian/ American studies. It wasn't until the John D. Calandra Italian American Institute filed a lawsuit that an institution finally awarded permanent standing to a research institute dedicated to Italian/American studies, which has grown into the U.S.'s leading Italian/American public institution of research and community development,. As part of the City University of New York through Queens College, the lawsuit also resulted in a distinguished chair in Italian American studies. The late Dr. Philip Cannistraro, when he assumed that position after a national search, became the first Distinguished Professor in Italian American studies.

The critical writing and the editing of such scholars as Anthony Tamburri, Mary Jo Bona, and Edvige Giunta combined with their teaching, have probably done more to create a sense of development of Italian/American studies than the work of any other scholars and teachers. Tamburri's early study, *A Semiotic of Ethnicity*, and Bona's *Claiming a Tradition: Writings of Italian American Women* treat Italian/American literature as a colonized body of writing that gains its identity through its interaction between Italian and American culture. Both of these studies will no doubt serve literary scholars in the future.

Francesco Durante's anthologies and Martino Marazzi's work on the earliest of Italian American literature brought attention to writers nearly untouched by previous scholars who may have been daunted by the language. Giorgio Bertellini's fundamental study of early Italians in American cinema, and Stefania Taviano's groundbreaking work in theater, all represent important new directions that will enable us to rescue lost publications and recuperate a tradition. In folklore studies there are the works of Frances Malpezzi and William Clements, Joseph Sciorra, Luisa DelGiudice, Joan Saverino and many others.

In light of the exciting work being done today, more and more of the previously submerged American scholars, critics and writers of Italian descent are surfacing to contribute to the journals *Italian Americana, VIA*, the *Italian American Review*, and a few other ethnic specific publications dedicated to Italian Americana. These publications reveal the work being done to institutionalize the serious academic study of Italian/American culture.

In spite of these developments in the U.S., Italian/American studies still has never fared well in Italy and only recently has it been given some attention. In spite of this lack of attention I do believe that the future of Italian/American studies depends very much on its development in Italian institutions of higher education. In his recent keynote address at the "Re-Mapping Italian America" conference held at Roma Tre University, Anthony Tamburri, Distinguished Professor of Italian and Dean of the John D. Calandra Italian American Institute, crystalized his observations into questions that advance my notion that the future of Italian/American studies lies in Italy. Why does Italian diaspora studies have problems entering the academy, both in the United States and in Italy? and, What is its position within ethnic studies across the U.S.? As Tamburri said in his keynote address, "Alternatively, one might ask, 'Why, then, haven't programs of Italian studies out-side Italy picked up the mantle, given the vast number of Italians who left Italy during the great wave of emigration?'"

Now could this be due to anti-Italian Americanism in Italy? Or could it be simply that the ripple effect of Anti-Italianism in the U.S. that keeps Italian Americans out of mainstream courses of study, those most likely to be taken by Italians who return to Italy to teach American Studies? I would say that while it might not be outright discrimination of Italian Americans in Italy, though many of us Italian Americans know that Italy has always been very receptive to our presence in its field of academic studies, it does represent the Italian academy's lack of interest in the growing field, and its inability to incorporate relevant scholarship into its programs. And while things are obviously getting better—we all have a lot of work left to do, work that I would argue provides benefits to both of our countries socio-cultural well-being.

There are new areas, being worked in by scholars who have new ideas, such as seeing Italian/American studies as part of the development of Italian Diaspora studies, and new tools, such as electronic databases and digital humanities resources, to work with that will take us beyond the twentieth century focus on identities built on immigration experiences and into new previously unexplored areas of Italian Diaspora and Italophone studies. And this, I assure you, will benefit Italy as it learns to expand traditional definitions of what it means to be Italian today and tomorrow in light of its shift from a country of emigration to one of immigration.

One thing about the work that I have reviewed is that most of what has been developed thus far in the field of Italian/American studies, has been accomplished by individuals. And while the efforts have been valiant, there is little hope that this field will thrive unless individual intellectuals come together to identify tasks, share existing resources and co-develop new resources. The future of Italian/American studies needs a new sense of cooperation among scholars of Italian and American cultures. For years, we wanderers in the field have been wondering when what we do would be taken seriously, and it is beginning. There have been professorships in Italian American studies at CUNY (1996), SUNY-Stony Brook (2008), California State University at Long Beach (1997), John Carroll University, (1999), Hofstra University (2008), Montclair State University (2010), and a new position is opening at Loyola University in Chicago (2016). So the homelessness of scholars of Italian/American studies is beginning to be addressed. However the greater needs include archival centers so that the papers of our writers, our intellectuals, can be of use to a new generation of scholars. Right now, most of those papers are in basements of surviving relatives' homes, gathering dust and mildew, when they should be garnering attention in proper research facilities. From these archives scholars need to create critical editions of works that have too long been out of print. We need to take advantage of new developments in technology to create electronic databases, to create multi-media programs that introduce and document the careers of our writers. And in order for all of this to be developed and put to use, we need presence in academic programs that can provide encouragement and direction for graduate students.

Another way of institutionalizing the field is to present relevant materials to the general public. Trends in material culture point to more public exhibits such as those pioneered by the Calandra Institute, working with the New York Historical Society to produce 500 Years of Italians in New York, "Tutti a Tavola: Italian Food in America" and B. Amore's art installation, "Lifeline: filo della vita" both at the Ellis Island Immigration museum.

In terms of publications, the current situation is that we have a number of interesting islands, which is better than earlier when intellectuals were floating in the mainstream or in ponds; but the future needs to see a greater sense of interaction between and among publications through consultation on issue planning and resource development and sharing. We need a good, on-going bibliography project that would identify, locate, and annotate relevant primary and secondary publications. We need book-length studies on all of our major writers—the two studies of Pietro di Donato represent the greatest critical depth we've achieved, but we are standing deep in the shallow end; we need studies of our finest writers; we need to reprint deserving books that are out-of-print. While we have activists and politicians, too few have turned attention to their own culture. While we have a few journals, none are quarterly; we also lack a publishing center; there is Bordighera Press, and Farleigh Dickinson University Press, Fordham University Press, and SUNY Press have vibrant series in Italian/American studies, but something that we could benefit from would be a publishing/editorial network that could be used as a clearing house to recommend books to publishers, and if possible, provide them with a subvention. Yes, this all takes money, but before we can achieve the necessary financial support we need to connect the streets to the academe by uniting the efforts of such organizations as the National Italian American Foundation, the Sons of Italy, and UNICO to the needs of the intellectual community. We, the intellectuals, must create products that they need, and they need to be able to see that we are creating products that can further their agenda. In conjunction with a greater development of intra-cultural studies, we need to establish a strong Italian/American presence in the field of inter-cultural studies. This requires a greater awareness of the history and evolution of the cultural studies of other groups that make up America.

Conclusion
"In the new age, Little Italy can be anywhere."
Robert Viscusi, "Making Italy Little" 75

During the 1980s I spent much time studying the many cultures that make up the USA. I had studied African American, Jewish American, Irish American, Asian American, Hispanic American, and was wondering, as does Spike Lee's character Mookie in the film *Do the Right Thing*, where were the pictures of my people on the walls of the local institutions. That's when I decided to focus my time and energy on Italian/American studies. Through my articles, books, curriculum and program development I did not follow the traditional American studies path, and in doing so defied status quo expectations of what a good American Studies student would produce.

Throughout all my studies I learned much, but nothing more important than what I learned about two different nations and what happened when a person migrated from one to the other. These were some of the most important lessons I ever learned in or out of school, and it prepared me to devote my life to developing Italian and American studies in the context of American studies.

I did this outside of school with the hopes that if I worked hard enough future generations would be able to do this within their own education. What I object to most about the 2010 State of Arizona House Bill 2281 that abolished ethnic studies in state education, is not what it says, but what it implies. One of the first implications is that ethnic solidarity is a bad thing and runs counter to individualism. That's something I don't understand. We are constantly working the tension between individualism and community identities and this bill assumes that it's either one or the other. The principle of ethnic (and class) solidarity is worth fighting for. Good education requires both intra- and intercultural education that would alleviate the fears brought out by the unknown, and the thinking behind this bill is the fuel that ignited the current reaction to the Syrian (among others) refugee crisis.

Good education is always about revolution that makes the old new, that turns the unknown into the known, and it will continue to be. Students need to learn about all the cultures that are part of their country; whether it is through textbooks or other resources we need to be reminded that the USA was founded on the principle of resistance to economic, social and political tyranny, and this bill suggests a tyranny of culture. Thomas Jefferson reminds us that we need to keep the spirits alive that helped to found this government. "The spirit of resistance to government is so valuable on certain occasions, that I wish it to be always kept alive. It will often be exercised when wrong, but better so than not to be exercised at all. I like a little rebellion now and then. It is like a storm in the atmosphere," from a letter by Thomas Jefferson to Abigail Adams, 1787.

The storm in Arizona is something that we all need to understand as the seeds of a worse storm are brewing on the global horizon. Developing transnational studies is a good and, I might argue, the only way to grasp an understanding of the complex cultural weather of today's world.

One of the first signs that the U.S. Government was not going to tolerate difference (besides the efforts to eradicate the presence of the Native Americans) came in the 1780s through what has been called Shays' Rebellion. This insurrection of farmers against the merchant classes and their attempts to achieve economic equity has been rarely emphasized in established American studies, but it is worth a re-examination of this event to understand the precedents that have created the basis for recent actions taken by the state and federal government to quell the attempts of working-class people to assert their rights and protect their livelihoods.

Shays was a soldier in the Revolutionary War who organized Massachusetts farmers to rebel against the U.S. Government in order to stop the foreclosures of property that were taking place as the economy struggled with post-war inflation and the deflation of American currency. Farmers began to borrow money in order to survive the subsequent economic crisis that hit the country after the war. Unable to meet the demands of their loans, many lost their land and found themselves in debtor prisons. Today we may no longer have physical debtor prisons, but we have retained the prison of debt that has affected working-class Americans in ways similar to this post-Revolutionary War period. Shays' rebellion targeted the judicial system that supported the merchants and brought about retaliation by the state's militia. It was the beginnings of a first civil war.

This was a lot like what we see happening today as the government uses an economic crisis to enact legislation that drains the power of the people to react to what Naomi Klein has labeled as "shock doctrine," in her 2007 book on "disaster capitalism." Klein surveyed the last 30 years of U.S. history and observed that local and national democratic governments perpetrated anti-democratic acts as a guise to push through unfavorable reforms that benefit the upper classes formed by free market capitalism. I would argue that a similar type of shock therapy has been applied to American studies over the same years—the result of reactionary political acts that affected both social and cultural activities and studies resulting in such acts as the Arizona bill.

A simple transnational approach comparing the formations of the U.S. and Italy nation formation can inform our thinking about problems we face today. This can be seen through the case of Shays' Rebellion, which resulted in the creation of the U.S. Constitution in which reference to labor or work appears only once. Meanwhile the Italian working class has a more established and solid base through the power of strong unions recognized by the government from which to counter threats from those wishing to diminish their power. While it might be easy to laugh at some of Italy's corrupt leaders, no one is laughing at Italian labor. Workers have respect, if not power, granted to them by the Italian Constitution. A big difference between Italy and the U.S. is that Italy was constructed on a fundamental belief in the importance of labor. Italy is founded on work. In fact, labor is in the very first sentence of the constitution: "Italy is a Democratic Republic founded on labor." In comparison, the word "labor" appears three times in the entire U.S. Constitution, all in same paragraph three of the fourth Article, and here in reference to the responsibility of the worker to fulfill a contract of labor even if he flees the state, and the right of the employer to have that worker retuned to fulfill the contract:

> 3: No Person held to Service or Labour in one State, under the Laws thereof, escaping into another, shall, in Consequence of any Law or Regulation therein, be discharged from such Service or Labour, but shall be delivered up on Claim of the Party to whom such Service or Labour may be due.

Interesting is the difference, and it is one not identified by pundits and journalists reporting on recent congressional actions such as the oral reading of the Constitution that occurred in the Congress in 2011. While I am not an expert in Constitutional interpretation, I do think that this simple comparison between Italy and the United States raises an important issue that we the people of work and the people who study work in the U.S. need to address. Failure to do so would be fatal for the working classes of the U.S and the world.

We need to rethink the meanings of multiculturalism in American studies so that the result is the creation of an inter-ethnic/racial and class solidarity rather than fragmentation and that we recognize the continued centrality of racism in American culture in our efforts to realize a truly transnational American Studies. And so, in light of recent anti-democratic acts in American politics, disguised as attempts to save the economy, I suggest we take a good look at just at how transnational approaches to single disciplinary studies, such as comparing the way work is presented in two different national documents, can lead us into new thinking, to better ways of understanding how perceived differences are formed, acted and reacted to in today's world, and in the Internet age, global consciousness has gone from being a luxury to a need, especially as the U.S. moves ever closer to becoming the very fascist nation it once fought against.

I leave you with an observation and a challenge. Italian/American Studies courses in college curricula can be seen as alternative entry into the study of Italian language and culture, as we found it to be when I was directing the Italian/American studies program at Stony Brook University. I suggest that through socio-cultural components added to courses in the Italian language can make students aware of the rich contributions Italy has made to U.S. culture. This can be accomplished when scholars of Italian language and culture work with scholars of Italian/American studies. Together we can move the future of Italian/American Studies beyond Little Italys and into the global arena of the many cultures of the Italian diaspora.

Works Cited and Selected Bibliography

Barolini, Helen. "Introduction." *The Dream Book*. Ed. Helen Barolini. New York: Schoken, 1985. 3-56.

_____. "Preface." *The Dream Book*. New York: Schocken Books, 1985;

Bertellini, Giorgio. *Italy in Early American Cinema: Race, Landscape, and the Picturesque*. Bloomington: Indiana UP, 2009.

Bona, Mary Jo. *By the Breath of Their Mouths: Narratives of Resistance in Italian America*. Albany, NY: SUNY P, 2009.

_____. *Claiming A Tradition Italian/American Women Writers*. Carbondale, IL: Southern Illinois UP, 1999.

Bona, Mary Jo. Ed. *The Voices We Carry*. Montreal: Guernica Editions, 1994.

Covello, Leonard, with Guido D'Agostino. *The Heart is the Teacher*. New York: McGraw Hill, 1958.

Diomede, Matthew. *Pietro di Donato, The Masterbuilder*. Cranbury, NJ: Fairleigh Dickinson UP, 1995.

Durante, Francesco. Ed. *Italoamericana. Vol. 1: Storia e letteratura degli italiani negli Stati Uniti 1776-1880*. Milano: Mondadori, 2001.

_____. *Italoamericana: Vol. 2, The Literature of the Great Migration, 1880-1943*. Bronx, NY: Fordham UP, 2014.

Gambino, Richard. *Blood of My Blood*. 1973. New York: Anchor, 1975;

Gardaphe, Fred. *Italian Signs, American Streets*. Durham, NC: Duke UP, 1996.

Giordano, Paul, and Anthony Tamburri, eds. *Beyond the Margin*. Cranbury, NJ: Farleigh Dickinson UP, 1998.

Giunta, Edvige. "Afterword. 'A Song from the Ghetto.'" *Paper Fish*. Tina DeRosa. New York: The Feminist Press, 1996. 123-149.

_____. *Writing With an Accent*. New York: St. Martin's Press, 2002;

Green, Rose Basile. *The Italian-American Novel*. Cranbury, NJ: Associated UP, 1974.

Harney, Robert F. and Vincenza Scarpaci, eds. *Little Italies in North America*. Toronto: The Multicultural History Society of Ontario, 1981.

Krase, Jerome. "New Approaches to the Study of Italian Americans in Metropolitan New York." *Italian Americans on Long Island: Presence and Impact.* Kenneth P. LaValle, ed. Stony Brook, NY: Filibrary, 1996. 32-51.

Maffi, Mario. *Gateway to the Promised Land: Ethnic Cultures in New York's Lower East Side.* New York: New York UP, 1995.

Lentricchia, Frank. "The American Writer as Bad Citizen." *Introducing Don DeLillo.* Frank Lentricchia, ed. Durham: Duke UP, 1991. 1-6.

_____. *The Edge of Night.* New York: Random House, 1994.

_____. "Luigi Ventura and the Origins of Italian-American Fiction." *Italian Americana.* 1.2 (1974): 189-95.

_____. "My Kinsman, T.S. Eliot." *Raritan.* 11.4 (Spring 1992): 1-22.

_____. (Rev.) of *Delano in American & Other Early Poems. Italian Americana.* 1.1 (1974): 124-5.

Klein, Naomi. *The Shock Doctrine.* New York: Picador, 2007.

Mangione, Jerre. *America is Also Italian.* New York: G.P. Putnam's Sons, 1969.

_____. "A Double Life: The Fate of the Urban Ethnic." *Literature and the Urban Experience.* Michael C. Jaye and Ann Chalmers Watts, eds. New Brunswick, NJ: Rutgers UP, 1981. 169-8.

_____. "Little Italy." Rev. *Christ in Concrete. The New Republic.* 100.1291 (August 30, 1939): 111-12.

_____. Rev. *The Grand Gennaro. The New Republic.* 84.1090 (October 23, 1935): 313.

Mangione, Jerre. and Ben Morreale, eds. *La Storia.* New York: Harper-Collins, 1992.

Marazzi, Martino. *Voices of Italian America: A History of Early Italian American Literature with a Critical Anthology Reprint Edition.* Bronx, NY: Fordham UP, 2012.

Moquin, Wayne, ed. *A Documentary History of the Italian Americans.* New York: Praeger, 1974.

Mulas, Francesco. *Studies on Italian-American Literature.* Staten Island, NY: Center for Migration Studies, 1995.

Napolitano, Louise. *Christ in Concrete: An American Story.* New York: Peter Lang, 1995.

Peragallo, Olga. *Italian-American Authors and Their Contribution to American Literature.* New York: S.F. Vanni, 1949.

Schiavo, Giovanni. *Italian American History.* Volume 1. New York: Arno P, 1975.

State of Arizona House of Representatives Forty-ninth Legislature Second Regular Session 2010 HOUSE BILL 2281, http://www.azleg.gov/legtext/49leg/2r/bills/hb2281s.pdf.

Steinhauer, Jennifer. "Constitution Has Its Day (More or Less) in House." *New York Times*. January 6, 2011: A15.

Tamburri, Anthony Julian. "The Coincidence of Italian Cultural Hegemonic Privilege and the Historical Amnesia of Italian Diaspora Articulations." Keynote address, "Re-Mapping Italian America" conference. Roma Tre University. May 13, 2016.

_____. "In (Re)cognition of the Italian/American Writer: Definitions and Categories." *Differentia*. 6-7 (Spring/Autumn 1994): 9-32.

_____. *To Hyphenate or Not to Hyphenate*. Montreal: Guernica Editions, 1991.

_____. "Re-Thinking Italian(/American) Studies in the Third Millennium: Where Have We Been? Where Can We Go?" The Frank J. De Santis Lecture at the University of California, Long Beach, 2011.

_____. *A Semiotic of Ethnicity: In [Re]cognition of the Italian/American Writer*. Albany, NY: SUNY P, 1998.

_____. *Re-reading Italian Americana: Specificities and Generalities on Literature and Criticism*. Madison, NJ: Fairleigh Dickinson UP, 2014.

Tamburri, Anthony Julian, Paolo A. Giordano and Fred L. Gardaphe, eds. *From the Margin: Writings in Italian Americana*. West Lafayette, IN: Purdue UP, 1991.

Tamburri, Anthony Julian and Ron Scapp, eds. *Differentia*. Special Double Issue on Italian American Culture. 6-7 (Spring/Autumn 1994).

Viscusi, Robert. "Breaking the Silence: Strategic Imperatives for Italian American Culture." *VIA*. 1.1 (1990) 1-14.

_____. "A Literature Considering Itself: The Allegory of Italian America." *From the Margin: Writings in Italian Americana*. Anthony Julian Tamburri, Paolo Giordano and Fred L. Gardaphe, eds. West Lafayette, IN: Purdue UP, 1991. 265-81.

_____. "Making Italy Little." *Social Pluralism and Literary History: The Literature of Italian Emigration*. Francesco Loriggio, ed. Toronto, Guernica Editions, 1996. 61-90.

Viscusi, Robert. *Buried Caesars, and Other Secrets of Italian American Writing*. Albany, NY: SUNY P, 2006.

Vitiello, Justin. *Poetics and Literature of the Sicilian Diaspora: Studies in Oral History and Story-Telling*. Lewiston, NY: The Edwin Mellen P, 1993.

The Coincidence of Italian Cultural Hegemonic Privilege and the Historical Amnesia of Italian Diaspora Articulations

Anthony Julian Tamburri

JOHN D. CALANDRA ITALIAN AMERICAN INSTITUTE

My intellectual profile is that of someone who migrates regularly between both Italian—a.k.a., *Italianistica*, as we know it in Italy—and Italian diaspora studies. Now, before going on, let me explain what I mean by my terminology here. For "Italian studies," and for this context only with the Italian sign */italianistica/* as my referent, I refer to the study of literature predominantly, an interrogation that has as its base a philologico-historical foundation. In turn, my use of the term "Italian diaspora" (I use a small "d" here) is used not in opposition to the more popular binomial "Italian/American"; indeed, I use it here to underscore the concept of necessity of the historical migratory act. After all, diaspora, in its many definitions, has at least two that relate to any notion of what we can consider an "Italian diaspora." As such, then, it can refer to, (1) "any group migration or flight from a country or region," and, surely more pertinent, (2) "any group that has been dispersed outside its traditional homeland, especially involuntarily."[1]

Clearly, the approximately four million Italians fleeing from Italy to the U.S. during the historical period of immigration (1880-1924) constitute a "group migration." I would further submit that, in similar fashion, these same four million immigrants constitute a

---

[1] *Dictionary.com*, s.v. For more on the complexities of the use of "diaspora" with regard to Italians, see, Donna Gabaccia, *Italy's Many Diasporas* (Seattle: U Washington P, 2000) 5-6, passim. For a counter argument, see, Stefano Luconi, "The Pitfalls of 'Italian Diaspora'," *Italian American Review* 1.2 (Summer 2001): 147-76.

"group ... dispersed" beyond "its traditional homeland." The fact, then, that having remained in their "homeland" might have readily led to starvation for many, the phrase "especially involuntarily" is equally relevant here.

This is my semiotic point of departure; it constitutes, to some degree, my hermeneutical "pre-judices" in this context. That said, I do not propose to furnish you with the magic wand that, to quote Montale, "mondi possa aprirti" (can open up worlds for you), something that will resolve the issues presented herein. Rather, I shall offer some musings and observations as both food for thought and, as well, an invitation for us all to think differently; and as we do, to bring such paradigm shifts to our intellectual discussions, be those conversations within the classroom or at the base of our writings on such matters.

As we know, Italian/American studies constitute, on the one hand, a notably vibrant field of intellectual interrogation; in both the social sciences and the humanities, a plethora of studies and critiques have appeared over the past century, for sure, especially within the social sciences. One need only think back to the many sociologists and anthropologists who began publishing their studies soon after the first decades of the twentieth century.[2] Save history, within the humanities—and, more specifically, the literary and cinematic fields—studies are more recent, dating back to the 1970s for the written, and to the 1980s for the visual. Considering both major fields together, we have indeed an impressive number

---

[2] In addition to Herbert J. Gans, *The Urban Villagers: Group and Class in the Life of Italian-Americans* (New York: The Free Press of Glencoe, 1962), I would add Edward C. Banfield, *The Moral Basis of a Backward Society* (New York: The Free Press of Glencoe, 1958); Irvin L. Child, *Italian or American? The Second Generation in Conflict* (New Haven: Yale UP, 1943); Leonard Covello, "The Social Back-ground of the Italo-American School Child," unpublished Ph.D. dissertation, New York University, 1944; William F. Whyte, Jr., *Street Corner Society* (Chicago: U Chicago P, 1943); Robert Foerster, *The Italian Emigration of Our Times* (Cambridge, MA: Harvard UP, 1919).

of books and articles that number in the hundreds.[3]

That said, one may indeed wonder why Italian/American studies, on the other hand, does not enjoy the favorable positioning
one might think it does—or should—within Italian studies (especially when conceived within the mind-set of *italianistica*)—and I
reference here both inside and outside of Italy—or, in similar geo-
cultural fashion, within American studies. Indeed, with regard to
the situation in Italy, I have already discussed it elsewhere.[4]

The paradox of omissions, in Italy or in the United States, clam-
ors ever more loudly when one looks to the aesthetic positioning
of someone like John Fante in Italy, or the cultural/literary history
of the United States with the likes of (Yes, it is a long list of many,
indeed not all, whom we should surely know): Tony Ardizzone,
Helen Barolini, Mary Jo Bona, Grace Cavalieri, Mark Ciabattari,
John Ciardi, Peter Covino, Don DeLillo, Pietro di Donato, Rachel
Guido deVries, Louise DeSalvo, Emanuel di Pasquale, W. S.
DiPiero, Louisa Ermelino, Gil Fagiani, Maria Famà, Lawrence Ferlinghetti, Mario Fratti, Fred Gardaphe, Dana Gioia, Daniela Gi-

---

[3] In addition to what we might find in the early proceedings of the then American Italian Historical Association, the pioneering works that I have in mind are
the following: (1) for literature, Rose Basile Green, *The Italian-American Novel: A
Document of the Interaction of Two Cultures* (Madison, NJ: Fairleigh Dickinson UP,
1974); for visuality, in turn, Joseph L. Monte, "Correcting The Image of the Italian
in American Film and Television," *Ethnic Images in American Film and Television*.
Randall M. Miller, ed. (Philadelphia: Balch Institute) 109-110; Joseph Papaleo,
"Ethnic Pictures and Ethnic Fate: the Media Image of Italian-Americans," *Ethnic
Images in American Film and Television*, 93-97; Michael Parenti, "The Italian-
American and the Mass Media," *Ethnic Images in American Film and Television*, 105-
107; Allen L. Woll and Randell M. Miller, "The Italians." *Ethnic Images in American
Film and Television*, 275-307; and Andrew Brizzolara, "The Image of Italian Ameri-
cans on U. S. Television." *Italian Americana* 6.2 (Spring/Summer 1980): 160-8.

[4] I refer the reader to my "Note sulla cultura diasporica degli Italiani d'America:
ovvero, suggerimenti per un discorso di studi culturali," *Campi immaginabili* 34–
35 (2007): 247–64, now in my *Una semiotica dell'etnicità: nuove segnalature per la
scrittura italiano/americana* (Florence, Italy: Franco Cesati Editore, 2010).

oseffi, Maria Mazziotti Gillan, George Guida, Gerry La Femina, Philip La Mantia, Annie Rachel Lanzillotto, Frank Lentricchia, Maria Lisella, Paul Mariani, Donna Masini, Stephen Massimilla, Fred Misurella, Joey Nicoletti, Jay Parini, Mario Puzo, Joseph Ricapito, Nicole Santalucia, Felix Stefanile, Maria Terrone, Lewis Turco, Joseph Tusiani, Anthony Valerio, Pasquale Verdicchio, Richard Vetere, Robert Viscusi, Arturo Vivante, Frances Winwar, and so on. These are writers who have, and continue, to be published by presses that range from the boutique, specialized publisher (e.g., Bordighera Press; Guernica Editions; Legas) to the larger more popular publisher (e.g., Farrar, Straus, Giroux; Harper Collins; Knopf; Random House).

Or, better yet, in a desire to complicate the issue further still, there are those who have and continue to write poetry and/or fiction in Italian and live in the U.S.: Luigi Ballerini, Emanuel Carnevali, Peter Carravetta, Alessandro Carrera, Tiziana Rinaldi Castro, Giovanni Cecchetti, Ned Condini, Alfredo de Palchi, Rita Dinale, Franco Ferrucci, Luigi Fontanella, Arturo Giovannetti, Ernesto Livorni, Irene Marchegiani, Mario Moroni, Pier Maria Pasinetti, Emanuele Pettener, Mario Pietralunga, Giose Rimanelli, Joseph Tusiani, Annalisa Saccà, Victoria Surliuga, and Paolo Valesio are some of the names that come to mind in this regard.

Some might wish to argue against any critique of said omissions, underscoring a plethora of references to Italian/American history and culture in some Italian venues and fora. Perhaps, but I am not too sanguine about the benefit of the doubt in this regard. For, in addition to the various writings of Mario Soldati, Giuseppe Prezzolini, and the like, when Italian Americans are discussed or merely referenced, it seems it is most often critical.[5] In the visual sphere it can sometimes be even more frustrating. Alongside the

---

[5] One need only consult Soldati's *America primo amore* (Florence: Bemporad, 1935) and Prezzolini's *I trapiantati* (Milan: Longanesi, 1963) to see how some Italians looked to Italian Americans with a most critical eye.

early representations at the turn of the twentieth century,[6] I would point to two contemporary examples. In cinema, one need only think back to Paolo Virzì's *My Name is Tanino* (2002). Tanino is a young Sicilian in search of his American love interest, Sally, and along the course of the film meets up with his immigrant relatives in Rhode Island. As one might expect, they are boorish, to a notable degree, and local *Mafiosi* to boot; and in so doing, Virzì readily underscores the most popular of U.S. stereotypes vis-à-vis Italian Americans. Yet, a more offensive image—paradoxical, to be sure—might be that which accompanied a positive review essay of the anthology *From the Margins: Writings in Italian Americana*,[7] which appeared in a 1992 issue of the Italian monthly, *L'indice dei libri del mese*, in the rubric "Secondo me."[8]

Needless to say, the editors of the anthology were most perplexed by such an illustration, especially given both the positive review

---

[6] For examples in the United States, see my "Reflections on Italian Americans and *Otherness*" in *The Status of Interpretation in Italian American Studies. Proceedings of the First Forum on Italian American Criticism*. Jerome Krase, ed. Stony Brook: FILibrary, 2011. 45-60.

[7] Anthony Julian Tamburri, Paolo A. Giordano, and Fred L. Gardaphé, eds. *From The Margin: Writings in Italian Americana* (West Lafayette, IN: Purdue UP, 1991).

[8] Cosma Siano, "Cosa leggere sulla letteratura italoamericana negli Stati Uniti," *L'indice dei libri del mese* No. 5 (1992): 27.

there, as well as elsewhere, and the historical positioning of the volume, second only to Helen Barolini's ground-breaking *The Dream Book: An Anthology of Writings by Italian American Women*.[9]

Notwithstanding such offensive imagery that has recurred throughout our history, all is not lost. Fortunately, the Italian studies journal, *Studi italiani*, housed at the Università degli Studi di Firenze and edited by Gino Tellini, launched in 2014 the section "Oltreconfine," which is dedicated to the Italian diasporic voice, especially that voice articulated in Italian. Then, at the AISNA (Associazione Italiana di Studi Nord-Americani) biannual conference at the Università degli Studi di Napoli L'Orientale in September 2015, the Association dedicated a plenary session to the volume, *Transcending Borders, Bridging Gaps: Italian Americana, Diasporic Studies, and the University Curriculum*, a collection of essays that originated from a four-day workshop at the Rockefeller Foundation Center in Bellagio, Italy. So, surely, *Spes ultima dea*! Things are looking up!

Given as much, then, a few simple questions arise, "Why does Italian diaspora studies linger in the academy, both in the United States and in Italy?" and, "What is its position within ethnic studies across the U.S.?" Alternatively, one might ask, "Why, then, haven't programs of Italian studies outside Italy picked up the mantle, given the vast number of Italians who left Italy during the great wave of emigration?" In this regard, let us not forget that the current numbers of Italian residents abroad is not insignificant. The Registry of Italian Residents Abroad (AIRE), for instance, counts more than 85,000 Italian citizens living in the greater New York area for more than twelve months, which is the period recognized by AIRE. Yet, there is another intriguing aspect to this phenomenon of Italians living abroad and those who are involved in departments of Italian studies at many universities in the United States. Thus, the question becomes more specific: namely, "How

---

[9] Helen Barolini, ed., *The Dream Book: An Anthology of Writings by Italian American Women* (New York: Schocken, 1985).

is it that departments and programs of Italian studies, in which there is a notable number of more recent Italian immigrants — those, that is, who left Italy after earning their "laurea" and came to the United States to complete a PhD in Italian—do not include course-work, if not concentrations as well, in Italian/American culture and history?" Of course, the question is further complicated by those departments and programs that allow students to study migration literature in Italy, a phenomenon that is less than thirty years old, give or take a few.

One might assume, for instance, that many of Italian descent have, perhaps, engaged in an act of identity descension (pun intended) for which any reference to their Italian ancestry is null and void, and, consequently, their identity politics is solely articulated within a U.S. profile.[10] In yet another sense, one might readily assume that there indeed exists a sort of hegemonic privilege among scholars of "Italian" (Read, peninsula. Yes, the privilege of hegemony, I would submit, is restricted to those on the peninsula; the islanders are not always invited into the club.) cultural history and practice (Read, literature and cinema especially.) for which any notion of an extra-Italy articulation of something that resembles "Italian" in some manner or form, simply does not exist. Ultimately, then, one might speak in terms of the historical omission of any sort of cultural manifestation of an Italian diaspora.

It is, indeed, a doubled-edged sword. On the one hand, Italian Americans who write in English seem to garner very little if any attention at all from those in the positions of cultural power in the United States. In a similar fashion, those who write in Italian and live beyond the geo-cultural borders of Italy extract even less attention from their confreres in both Italy and elsewhere among those in Italian studies, a.k.a., *Italianistica*. Then, of course, there are the

---

[10] The one thing we must recognize here is that self-identity in one manner or another is optional; if someone of Italian heritage decides not to identify as "Italian," "Italian American," or the like, that is entirely acceptable.

new Italian writers, the so-called "migrants," the veterans among whom we find the likes of Pap Khouma, Amara Lakhous, and Igiaba Scego. They constitute, in turn, a third wheel in this greater categorization of migration writing, or, to use a term not yet in vogue but has its qualities for sure, *Italici*, as Piero Bassetti might consider all three groups mentioned at this point.[11] Namely, that ever encompassing term that collects under its large umbrella these groups for sure: (a) Italians, (b) those of Italian origin living outside of Italy, and (c) those who love things Italian though not of Italian descent. Of course, in this regard, we can surely complicate the issue even further by adding the likes of Jhumpa Lahiri, someone who is not of Italian origin, is not an Italianist, does not permanently live in Italy, but yet did spend three years in Italy and, eventually, wrote and published a book that she composed in Italian.[12]

অ

So what are our options to remedy some of what we've seen above and elsewhere, and what might be some of the reasons that have occasioned such issues? These are the two questions we need to confront before we can truly move on in a more productive direction with regard to the above-mentioned marginalized, Italian diasporic aesthetic production. The very first step is a change in the dominant cultural thought paradigms that reign both in Italy and in the United States with regard to not only Italian/American studies but, more important, Italian diaspora studies. I would

---

[11] I realize that I might be problematizing Bassetti's notion to some degree, my slightly particularized version with the addition of Jhumpa Lahiri is still in full concert with what Bassetti has been articulating since 1998. See his latest publication in this regard: *Svegliamoci italici: manifesto per un futuro glocal* (Venice: Marsilio, 2015), available in English, *Wake Up, Italics! Manifesto for A Glocal Future* (New York: Calandra Institute, 2017).

[12] I refer to her most recent literary deed, her *In altre parole* (Parma: Guanda, 2015), which also appeared subsequently in a bilingual edition, *In Other Words*, trans. Ann Goldstein (New York: Knopf, 2016).

submit to you that they go hand in hand notwithstanding a possible initial resistance to such coupling; for I could hear the purists telling us how the [im]migrants are not of "our culture" and cannot understand what it means to be Italian.[13]

I have already mentioned some of the examples with regard to obstacles for American writers of Italian descent that we have seen in Italy. There are analogues, to be sure, in the United States. For example, in spite of names like John Ciardi, Paul Gallico, Mario Puzo, Henry Rago, Frances Winwar, and Don DeLillo, Italian/American studies has no standing whatsoever within the most powerful organization dedicated to American Studies in the United States, namely, the American Studies Association. Yes, it is true that some *infiltration* into mainstream United States culture has already been successful; as mentioned earlier, for the past twenty-plus years a handful of university presses and American studies journals have published or republished significant work.[14] In this sense, then,

---

[13] Among the many items on Italian and/or Italian/American identity I refer the reader to Anthony Julian Tamburri, ed. *Meditations on Identity • Meditazioni su identità* (New York: Bordighera P, 2014).

[14] Some examples include: SUNY Press series in Italian/American Studies, directed by Fred Gardaphè; Josephine Gattuso Hendin's "The New World of Italian American Studies," *American Literary History* 13.1 (2001): 141-57, or Thomas Ferraro's less conspicuously titled essay, "'My Way' in 'Our America': Art, Ethnicity, Profession," *American Literary History* 12.4 (2000): 499-522; other mainstream press books include: Mary Jo Bona. *Claiming a Tradition: Italian American Women Writers* (Carbondale: Southern Illinois UP, 1999); Edvige Giunta's *Writing with An Accent: Contemporary Italian American Women Authors* (New York: Palgrave, 2002); as well as Gardaphè's earlier pioneering *Italian Signs, American Streets: The Evolution of Italian American Narrative* (Durham: Duke UP, 1996). Most recently, Thomas Ferraro published *Feeling Italian* (New York: NYU P, 2005), Robert Viscusi published *Buried Caesars* (New York: SUNY P, 2006), Fred Gardaphè published his *From Wiseguys to Wise Men* (New York: Routledge, 2006), and Mary Jo Bona published *By the Breath of Their Mouths: Narratives of Resistance in Italian America* (New York: SUNY P, 2010). Let us not forget that the first study to be published in this area was Rose Basile Green's *The Italian-American Novel* (Madison, NJ: Fairleigh Dickinson UP, 1974).

a good part of a foundation has been laid. But much more has yet to be done. In perusing the last seventeen annual addresses of the American Studies Association, for example, it is a curious fact that, among all the topics mentioned dealing with issues immediate also to Italian Americana, there is no mention at all of Italian/American studies, not even an occasional, oblique reference to the ethnic origin of an American writer of Italian descent.[15]

Such absences of attention raise a number of issues, and, to some degree, add yet another challenge. For while there are a number of excellent books in English on Italian Americana,[16] what is still missing, for example, is a rigorous study that, first, examines those whom we might consider the major writers of Italian Americana and, second, then contextualizes them within the greater United States literary panorama in which we normally situate the corresponding great "American" writers.[17] Yet, more significant is the fact that an organization of the scale and stature that is the American Studies Association engages in a type of hegemony that *de facto* discounts any validity to Italian Americana as an accepted field of study. Indeed, while it is truly troubling to see such dismissal in Italy, as I have discussed elsewhere with regard to the Italian jour-

---

[15] All presidential addresses are included in the following year's first issue of the *American Quarterly*.

[16] For a review of what was available until and through the first half of 2003, see my "Beyond 'Pizza' And 'Nonna'! Or, What's Bad about Italian/American Criticism? Further Directions for Italian/American Cultural Studies." *MELUS*. 28.3 (2003): 149-74. To this list, one would add at this juncture Robert Viscusi's *Buried Caesars*, and Fred Gardaphè's *From Wiseguys to Wise Men*. I would also reference an expanded version of my *MELUS* essay as the last chapter of my *Re-reading Italian Americana*.

[17] Other questions are begged at this point. What should be, if at all, the relationship between Italian Studies and Italian/American studies in the United States? Should intellectual outlets—journals and book series—dedicated to Italian Studies open their doors, so to speak, to Italian/American essays and creative works? To date, if memory does not fail me, three Italian journals in United States have already done so: *Forum Italicum*, *Italian Culture*, and *Italica*.

nal *Ácoma*,[18] it is more perplexing to see this take place in the United States, especially within the realm of American studies, a field that has at its base both history and literature, in addition to other subject matter relevant to the discipline.

Fred Gardaphé has maintained in various venues and conversations that the future of Italian/American studies is in Italy, referring specifically to members of the younger generation who, among other things, are both methodologically and linguistically equipped to investigate such subject matter. I am not going to rehearse all that he has said; he would do a much better job at unpacking his new geo-cultural cartography. But what I would like to do, in recognizing his geo-cartographic lens, is make my point of departure for a call for paradigm shifts from an Italian point of origin. That said, there are at least three individuals who come to mind.

One of the most poignant observations in this regard—and one, I would contend, that has gone unnoticed, as I have not seen it mentioned before by any of the expounders of "[im]migrant" literature—is something Armando Gnisci stated almost fifteen years ago. In his *Creolizzare l'Europa: Letteratura e migrazione*, he stated the following with regard to Italian migration literature, that which is written in Italian by the "new" [im]migrants to Italy:

> [N]oialtri italiani dobbiamo imparare a imparare dal nostro passato migratorio, oltre che dalla breve ad esagerata (in tutti i sensi) esperienza di potenza coloniale, ad avere a che fare con il presente interculturale, in casa e dovunque nel mondo. Quest'ultima considerazione ci aiuta, infine, a formulare in maniera più compiuta la rivendicazione di una letteratura italiana della migrazione. Essa deve essere pensata innanzitutto come un fenomeno della modernità avanzata, senza precedenti. Inizia con le migrazioni di intere popolazioni di italiani verso tutto il mon-

---

[18] See my "Appunti e notarelle sulla cultura diasporica degli Italiani d'America: ovvero, suggerimenti per un discorso di studi culturali," *Campi immaginabili* 34/35 (2007): 247-64, especially 250-52.

do alla ricerca di lavoro a partire dall'immediato periodo post-unitario e trova il suo completamento nella letteratura scritta dagli immigrati, venuti in Italia da tutto il mondo in cerca di lavoro, a partire dall'ultimo decennio del XX secolo.

[We Italians have to learn to learn from our migratory past, beyond the brief to exaggerated (in every sense) experience of colonial power, to deal with the intercultural present, at home and wherever in the world. This last consideration helps us in the end to formulate in a more complete manner the claim of an Italian literature of migration. It needs to be considered first and foremost as a phenomenon of advanced modernity, without precedent. It begins with the migrations of entire populations of Italians throughout the world in search of work, beginning with the immediate post-unification period, and it finds its completion in the literature written by immigrants, having arrived in Italy from all over the world in search of work, beginning with the last decade of the twentieth century.][19]

To invoke the emigrants of the past, as we read Gnisci's words above, was at the time a solitary act. There were a few other voices, but they, too, found themselves working in an environment that, for reasons beyond their means, did not include a community of scholars who envisioned the one-hundred-fifty-plus-year diaspora as a resource in a variety of ways. Instead, they found obstacles if not barriers in their respective paths. In this regard, I have in mind a scholar who has written books and anthologized Italian diaspora writers in both Italian and English; yet, to keep his current position and hope for promotion, he should publish, first and foremost, on *Italianistica*. Then, of course, there are the two anthologies that truly made history—*Italoamericana* I (2001) and *Italoamericana* II (2005)—which, first, were never issued in paperback, and, second, are now out of print.

---

[19] Armando Gnisci, *Creolizzare l'Europa: Letteratura e migrazione* (Rome: Meltemi, 2003) 83.

These voices are not alone. Others, as well, are beginning to abound in Italy and/or in Italian with regard to the "migrant" writer in Italy today: Franca Sinopoli and Daniele Combierati are two names of later generations engaged in profound interrogations of this and other pertinent issues.[20] I would, at this juncture, further contend that we can readily see the "migrant" writer in Italy as a parallel experience to the writer in the United States who is (a) of Italian origin, or (b) born and socialized in Italy but later moved to the United States and has lived there for a significant amount of his/her life. What I am stating here has not only been expressed by Gnisci, in fairly general terms as we saw above, but even earlier, Graziella Parati stated the following with specific regard to the aesthetic literary act:[21]

> It is not enough to displace our attention to Italian American literature to discover that the fact that a first generation did not have the language to express their experience has by far not suffocated the later creation of a large Italian American literature. It is a literature that is generationally marked, which might also be the case in Italy. In Italian cultural history there are a number of repressed historical narratives, among them the history of Italian migration and of Italian colonialism.

More pertinent to the discussion at hand is, obviously, the comparison of Italian migration literature to Italian/American literature. Equally important—and one might say it is something many have stated *ad nauseam* and yet always falls by the wayside—is Parati's mention of "repressed historical narratives," especially the "history of Italian migration." Such repression of "historical narra-

---

[20] See, especially, Daniele Combierati, *Scrivere nella lingua dell'altro: la letteratura degli immigrati in Italia (1989-2007)* (Bruxelles: Peter Lang, 2010) and Franca Sinopoli, *Interculturalità e transnazionalità della letteratura: questioni critiche e studi di casi* (Rome: Bulzoni, 2014).

[21] Graziella Parati, "Introduction" in Graziella Parati, ed., *Mediterranean Crossroads: Migration Literature in Italy* (Madison, NJ: Fairleigh Dickinson UP, 1999): 21.

tives" is, surely, what we have seen in the example of *Ácoma* in Italy.[22] In this same introduction, Parati goes on to underscore the necessity of such a comparison: "I would argue that the link between the two Italys—the Italy of both immigration and migration— must not be broken because it offers a way to read recent migration issues in Italy" (21). In so doing, she brings to the fore yet another issue equally important: the recognition of the emigrants and their progeny as belonging to "Italy," be it another "Italy," when she states ever so naturally, "the link between the two Italys."[23]

Yet a third voice I would invoke here is Michele Cometa and, specifically, his work on cultural studies, and I am referring here to his book *Studi culturali*.[24] His notion that migration literature should not remain enclosed within either a "marginality" or an "exceptionality" of "such experiences" (97) in literature, resonates to a significant degree with what I had brought up elsewhere in my *A Semiotic of Ethnicity* with regard to a different geo-cultural arena and different manifestations of ethnic literature. I was specifically interested in a couple of types of writers, those in both English and Italian, and thus suggested that "we expand our own reading strategy of Italian/American art forms in order to accommodate other possible, successful reading strategies"; and "[w]ith regard to Italian/American literature we should thus consider it a series

---

[22] As an update, I am delighted to note the forthcoming issue of *Ácoma* dedicated entirely to Italian/American Studies. For more information, see Sabrina Vellucci's introduction to this volume.

[23] Parati continued her bi-focal interrogation of migrant literature to Italy in her follow-up book to her 1999 anthology. She later stated that her theoretical framework was not only grounded in the work of those such as Homi Bhabha, Julia Kristeva, Rosi Braidotti, and Alex Hargreaves, but that "the work of Fred Gardaphé, Anthony Tamburri, and other scholars of Italian American culture have created the fundamental work without which my discourse on Italian multiculturalism throughout the centuries could not be discussed" (see her, *Migration Italy: The Art of Talking Back in a Destination Culture* [Toronto: U Toronto P, 2005] 12).

[24] *Studi culturali* (Napoli: Guida, 2010).

of on-going written enterprises which establish a repertoire of signs, at times *sui generis*, and therefore create verbal variations (visual in the case of film, painting, sculpture, and drama) that represent different versions that are dependent, of course, on one's generation, gender, and socio-economic condition. Turning now to the Italian-language writer, having established such a working paradigm, I would now also add language to this working definition — that is, Italian, English, or some conscious maccheronic combination thereof — of what can be perceived as the Italian/ American interpretant" (110-111).[25] The fundamental idea then, as it is now with Cometa, is that we expand our horizons and thus broaden once and for all the category.

We must, for sure, as Cometa states, "compel Italianists to [engage in] a reformulation of the canon and of canons partially put forward in recent decades" (97), broadening as a consequence, and necessarily, I would underscore here, the concept of "Italian identity," which currently is changing into something that goes beyond the traditional confines of that concept. An "effective identity," therefore, in as much as it recognizes the quality of everyday activity in which the individual lives out his/her daily life; an "effective identity" also insofar as it recognizes that what an individual does within a largely Italian milieu — and not necessarily only in Italy — unfolds in that way specifically because s/he feels "Italian-ly" — *italianamente*, let us say — as part of his/her ordinary existence, and not in any honorary or affected sense, but actually "effective," such that whatever s/he does — and that s/he knows, as an Italian — is part of the every-day life of that person. And so, that "Italian effect" of his/her daily life is precisely that blending of Italian characteristics and/or Italianistic-ness of his/her identity.

What I am suggesting here echoes what Rebecca West wrote

---

[25] See my *A Semiotic of Ethnicity. In (Re-)cognition of the Italian/American Writer* (Albany, NY: SUNY P, 1998), chapter 7 *passim*, and the essay by Aijaz Ahmad, "Jameson's Rhetoric of Otherness and the 'National Allegory.'"

more than twenty-five years ago about a concept of Italian and/or Italian/American identity, of someone who is not of Italian origin but who lives out his/her daily activities—be they professional or personal—if not specifically within, then at least for the most part close to what is coming to be called *Italianità*, or s/he lives her daily life *italianamente*:

> By bringing non-Italian or Italian/American perspectives to Italian literature and culture [...], we implicitly (and at times explicitly) question essentialist views of ethnicity. I could go so far as to say that I am, by dint of twenty-five years of study, scholarship, and professional engagement in Italian culture and literature, a kind of "Italian/American" (or "American/Italian"). This identity is not to be found in my genes, my blood, or in any part of my material body, but rather in my orientation, my knowledge, and my commitment. [...] Similarly, adopted cultures may be seen in the same light as adopted children. If those children are more truly the children of their adoptive parents who nurture and cherish them than of their biological parents, then perhaps an adopted culture is eventually as much (or in some cases even more) "mine" as it is that of someone born into it. I recognize that I may never "feel" Italian or Italian/American in the same way that natural sons and daughters of Italian culture may feel, but I would at the very least like to believe that my investment in that culture has marked me more than superficially as someone who is part of *italianità*" (337).[26]

If we accept just the very basics of what West is saying, that she in some way—and maybe on the strength of "twenty-five years of study, research, and responsibilities having to do with Italian culture and literature," belongs within the rather vast confines of *italianità*, we must then include in this world of *italianità* also those

---

[26] "Scorsese's *Who's That Knocking At My Door?*: Night Thoughts on Italian Studies in the United States." *Romance Languages Annual*. Ben Lawton and Anthony Julian Tamburri, eds. (1991): 331-338.

who, while born and raised in Italy, live elsewhere, and in our case, in the United States.[27] And we can do it fairly easily from the scientific point of view if we are willing to break free from those limiting, and dare I say, arbitrary confines. In so doing, we thus recognize that kaleidoscopic mosaic that is North America, as I classified it more than twenty-five years ago,[28] and what now resonates in what Cometa states in his *Studi culturali* with regard to the "migrant" writer: "The mosaic of identities that migrant writers carry around with them is much more complex and variegated" (107), as is true, as we have seen above, even in the case of someone like West. Following, then, such an intellectual trajectory with regard to migrant writers, ethnic writers, and/or writers of other "limitations," we can only end up colliding—and happily so —with the Bassettian discourse of "italici" and, in the broader sense of the concept of "Italian" identity. We thus find ourselves in an "Italian" world that surpasses every restrictive, reductive, and essentialist conceptual barrier. This, ultimately, I would submit, should be our end goal in our continued endeavors to change paradigms.

ঽ

I mentioned above the triangulation of Italian/American writers, Italian-language writers who live outside of Italy, and the so-called "migrants" within Italy who now write in Italian. I have complicated it further with the non-Italian who does not live in Italy and yet—analogous to who writes in Italian yet lives outside

---

[27] If we must enlarge further this concept of West's, we find ourselves in the end converging with the concept of "Italicity," which Piero Bassetti has been promulgating since 2002. He spoke about it first in his essay "Italicity: Global and Local", in *The Essence of Italian Culture and the Challenge of a Global Age*, edited by Paulo Ianni and George F. McLean (Washington, DC: The Council for Research in Values and Philosophy, 2002) 13-24, and he further elaborated it in *Italici. Il possibile futuro di una community globale* (Milano: Casagrande, 2008).

[28] I addressed it for the first time in my *To Hyphenate or Not to Hyphenate* (1991) 48-51, and later in my *Una semiotica dell'etnicità* (2010) 62-64.

of Italy — "lives Italy," as I have mentioned elsewhere (Tamburri, *Semiotica*, chap. 1); and thus in addition to Rebecca West, I have in mind someone like the above-mentioned Jhumpa Lahiri.[29]

Now, setting aside for the moment this fourth category — which I shall momentarily keep in reserve for argument's sake in our current forum — this seemingly odd triad of writers does not consist of what some may call distinct and disparate categories. Who, then, is this writer, who — regardless of his/her language — may very well be discussed within a context greater than the geo-cultural territory that we know as the United States with Italy as the so-called backdrop? S/he is undoubtedly, for one, a writer of Italian social and cultural upbringing, who writes in Italian but lives in the United States. S/he is even, in a rather obvious way, a writer who has much in common with other writers who work in Italian and live in Italy; which is, as Gnisci wrote, "a reciprocal transcultural co-evolution." In turn, this writer may also be someone of Italian origin who, because s/he lives in a different linguistic context, writes in the language of that country, in our case, English. In this case as well, there is a cultural relationship however indirect it might appear. Thirdly, there is the so-called "migrant" writer who, having inserted his/herself into an Italian cultural context through his/her move to Italy, adopts his/her host country's language, Italian. All of these writers share commonalities within the greater scheme of a "transcultural co-evolution."

Yet it is also true that even if they have such a transcultural evolution in common, they remain different writers insofar as their relations depend on a series of characteristics that are simultaneously similar and different. And identity depends on this rapport

---

[29] I would hasten to underscore at this juncture that in these two instances I am talking about people who do not reside on a quotidian basis in Italy, notwithstanding an occasional lengthy stay, as is the case with both Rebecca West and Jhumpa Lahiri.

between institutional/traditional and not,[30] similar in fact to what Charles Sanders Peirce says when he speaks of identity not as something founded on dissimilarity but, on the contrary, a state of being that distinguishes itself from another state that will certainly be similar to the first one but that possesses something unique; and so it has to do ultimately with a concept of identity that is perforce based on the haecceites of the individual.[31] And to underline the distinction between two things that are fairly similar but not the same, Peirce offers the following clarification:

> Two drops of water retain each its identity and opposition to the other no matter in what or in how many respects they are alike. Even could they interpenetrate one another like optical images (which are also individual), they would nevertheless react, though perhaps not at that moment, and by virtue of that reaction would retain their identities. (Peirce, 1.458)

Two writers as well, therefore, who are not identical as writers but who nonetheless live either for the culture that has in some manner formed them, or for the language via which their work develops, as a result belong *sensu amplu* to a larger cultural and/or linguistic community that is, in general terms, Italian. Linked, in a Benoistian sense, even while different in a Peircean sense, the geographically Italian writers along with those who are culturally Italian can be placed in a larger category that we can readily label Italian. And so in this sense they are writers who are similar in many ways, but who also, owing especially to the fact that they inhabit two different geo-political areas, are distinct from one an-

---

[30] I direct the reader to Alain de Benoist, *Identità e comunità* (Napoli: Guida, 2005).

[31] He says on this topic: "Otherness belongs to haecceities. It is the inseparable spouse of identity: wherever there is identity there is necessarily otherness; and in whatever field there is true otherness there is necessarily identity. Since identity belongs exclusively to that which is *hic et nunc,* so likewise must otherness." See his, *The Collected Papers of Charles Sanders Peirce.* Vols. I-VI ed. Charles Hartshorne and Paul Weiss (Cambridge, MA: Harvard UP, 1931-1935) 1.566.

other like the drops of water that Peirce used as examples.

More specifically, it becomes clearer still that these writers share a closer relationship than some might imagine. First, they are all dia-loguing to some degree or another with the sign we know as /Italy/. Second, at least two of the groups are "de-riva-tive" of Italy where-as the third, in its own right, is "ar-riva-tive";[32] the first two leav-ing, the third arriving, yet the common denominator is still Italy; it remains the central point of commonality, as the graph shows:

Italian "[im]migrant" writers

↓

"ar-riva-tive"

/Italy/

"de-riva-tive"

↙   ↘

Writers of the Italian diaspora   Writers of the Italian diaspora
in local language (e.g., English)   in Italian

↑

[Non-Italian diaspora writer = *italici* (e.g., West, Lahiri)]

---

[32] My coining of such a term in this instance is my reaction, in linguistic terms, to an "accidental gap," for which a non-existing word which is expected to exist given the hypothesized morphological rules of a particular language; this is usu-ally thought of as a hole in a paradigm. And since in English it is possible to de-rive nouns from verbs by adding the suffixes *-al* and *-(a)tion* to the verbal stem, I have taken even greater liberty here by adding the suffix *–(a)tive*. Indeed, even though some derivations as just mentioned do not exist, there are no grammati-cal reasons for their nonexistence. Hence, my seemingly arbitrary lexical anoma-ly. For more on the notion of "accidental gaps," see M. Halle, "Prolegomena to Theory of Word Formation," *Linguistic Inquiry* 4 (1973): 3-16.

I would also add at this juncture that my use of "ar-riva-tive" should not be confused with the term "arriviste," both of which signal someone newly arrived. The difference is that the latter term has negative connotations, as it refers to an upstart/newcomer who generally behaves in a brash or arrogant manner and is not yet integrated into the host society.

Further still, and returning to Peirce's drops of water, Italy is the metaphorical centrifuge, of which the three groups make up its content. Namely, like the literal machine that is the centrifuge, these three groups are analogues to the various fluids of different densities that the centrifugal force of the machine typically separates. As such, they remain separated not only from each other but, indeed, from the original center-point of the dialogue—Italy—and as a consequence, are kept adrift from the so-called mainland of Italian cultural discourse. Yet, they are like the above-mentioned liquids, all of the same ilk, just as those who arrive and those who depart are "migrants" all involved in the act of aesthetic production that, to one degree or another, dialogues with what can only be seen in this context as the ur-sign that is /Italy/, as the following graph depicts:

Italian "[im]migrant" writers

⬇

/Italy/

[↗]   [↖]

Writers of the Italian diaspora   Writers of the Italian diaspora
in local language (e.g., English)   in Italian

[Non-Italian diaspora writer = *italici* (e.g., West, Lahiri)]

The difference is one of perspective—going or coming—but the commonality is the sign /Italy/ and all that it pertains. Perspective, then, is the operative word; and changing it, which is tantamount to changing one's conceptual paradigm, go hand in hand.

The above-proposed paradigm recognizes, first and foremost, the changing dynamics of the ever-increasing phenomenon of migration and thus responds in an aesthetic-critical manner. This, I would contend, is the initial stage of what I consider the necessary, conceptual paradigm shift if Italian studies is to broaden its horizons and catch up to other socio-aesthetic fields of intellectual interrogation. In as much as it does, this new schemata also calls attention to the two types of writers that, to date, have been considered significantly different either for linguistic reasons (the hyphenated Italian writer in English), if not then for geography (the emigrant who writes in Italian in another country); yet, at the same time, they each dialogue in their own way with the ur-sign.[33]

That said, we might re-consider, ever more profoundly, the linguistic element and, precisely because of these writers' analogous coterminous dialogue with the ur-sign /Italy/, assign it less of an essentialist value. In so doing, these two seemingly different writers—the "arrivative" (immigrant) and the "derivative" (emigrant / diasporic)—now become more similar in a classificatory manner and thus form a group unto themselves; they are similar to each other, like Peirce's two drops of water ("could they interpenetrate one another like optical images"), yet "by virtue of [their individual-based] reaction[, they] would retain their identities." The result in all of this is the constitution of a greater group of writers we could readily classify as "Italian" even though these writers (a) do not live in Italy (the emigrant who writes in Italian), (b) adopt a different linguistic medium (e.g., Italian, English, or any other language of a host country that is different from Italian), and (c) are not of Italian origin (the [im]migrant to Italy who writes in Italian). These are three characteristics that, while highly significant, do not necessarily trump the dialogue in which these three types of writers engage with /Italy/ and all that pertains.

If, in the end, we decide that this is a logically aesthetic modification in paradigms that we should make, as I have demonstrat-

---

[33] Of course, in a more sustained discussion of paradigm shifts within Italian studies, we would need to include another types of writer, s/he who writes in dialect.

74

ed above with the two graphs, then it proves equally logical to include in this greater category of the new "Italian" writer even those who are not somatically Italian yet, as mentioned earlier, "live Italy." In as much, to continue, as what we have seen above, then, it is not farfetched to add our two non-Italians (genetically speaking), Rebecca West and Jhumpa Lahiri. Having now arrived as far as we have with our new paradigm shift, the inclusion of West and Lahiri helps create an even broader group of "Italian" writers, as we now know them at this juncture in time.

In our post-structuralist world of all sorts of borders having been readily traversed, diminished, if not completely eliminated, the expansion of this new "Italian" group of writers allows for a more profound understanding of the current situation at hand, as well as for a more fertile field of study of the trans-national discourse in which Italians engage but that, from a hegemonic point of view, do not recognize. The insistence on a limited and, dare I say, limiting group of writers restricted to Italy-born and bred can only stifle the critical voice that wishes to make the evident connections that indeed exist under a more broad umbrella that we can still readily call "Italian."[34]

---

[34] My *caloroso grazie* goes to Sabrina Vellucci and Carla Francellini for having invited me as one of the keynote speakers for the conference from which this volume emanates. I also wish to thank friends and colleagues of the Italian Diaspora Studies Summer Seminar, Mary Jo Bona, Fred Gardaphé, and Joseph Sciorra, for their keen comments on earlier drafts of this essay.

THE WRITTEN WORD

Playing the American Tune:
Ethnic and Cultural Identity in Horatio Alger Jr's *Phil the Fiddler*

Leonardo Buonomo

UNIVERSITY OF TRIESTE

Contrary to popular belief, the phrase "from rags to riches," to which Horatio Alger Jr owes his chief claim to fame, bears only scant relation to the actual contents of his books. To read Alger's stories of street boys—*Ragged Dick, Mark, the Match-Boy, Paul the Peddler*, etc.—is to discover that a more accurate—though admittedly less catchy—description of his typical plot formula would be "from rags to respectability."[1] In line with the Protestant ethic and the "Victorian myth of self-improvement," the ultimate reward for most of his young heroes is not wealth but, more soberly, a comfortable dwelling, an education, and steady employment.[2] This is an *actual* Horatio Alger story, as distinct from the label "Horatio Alger story" which, since about the late 1920s, has been synonymous with the rise from humble beginnings to spectacular economic success. That label seems to have taken on a life of its own, becoming much better known than the author it is named after.

Born in 1832, Alger died in 1899 in near obscurity. While the status of literary artist, to which he aspired so keenly, always

---

[1] Michael Moon, "'The Gentle Boy from the Dangerous Classes': Pederasty, Domesticity, and Capitalism in Horatio Alger," *Representations* 19 (Summer 1987): 89; Ann Scott MacLeod, "From Rational to Romantic: The Children of Children's Literature in the Nineteenth Century," *Poetics Today* 13.1 (Spring 1992): 149.

[2] Carl W. Brucker, "Virtue Rewarded: The Contemporary Student and Horatio Alger," *The Journal of General Education* 35.4 (1984): 273.

eluded him, his books influenced twentieth-century writers of the caliber of Theodore Dreiser, Francis Scott Fitzgerald, and Nathaniel West. The author of biographies of U.S. presidents James Garfield and Abraham Lincoln, Alger was the subject, in 1928, of an entirely fabricated biography by Herbert R. Mayes. Titled *Alger: A Biography Without a Hero*, it was regarded as the standard text on him for forty years and continued to be quoted even after its author, in the early 1970s, finally admitted it was a hoax. Among other things, Mayes's book included quotes from letters and diaries Alger had never written.[3]

To be sure, in the 1920s very little information about Alger's life seemed to be available, which is hardly surprising since Alger had scrupulously covered his tracks. Before becoming the literary champion and benefactor of New York street boys, Alger had been a Unitarian minister in Brewster, Massachusetts, a chapter of his life he did his best to keep out of public record. He feared his reputation would be severely damaged should the public ever learn the truth, namely that Alger had been forced to resign from his post and flee to New York, having been found guilty of "gross immorality" and "unnatural familiarity" with at least two boys of his congregation.[4]

Widely regarded as the prophet of the American myth of success, during his lifetime Alger published only one indisputable bestseller, *Ragged Dick* (1868), the first and best-known of his street-boy stories. Not one of the many sequels, spinoffs, and variations on that formula that Alger churned out in the following years ever came close to the original in terms of sales. It was only when they were reprinted in cheap (and often abridged) editions, at the turn of the twentieth century, that Alger's books finally enjoyed an

---

[3] Herbert R. Mayes, *Alger: A Biography Without a Hero* (New York: Macy Masius, 1928).

[4] Qtd. in Gary Scharnhorst and Jack Bales, *The Lost Life of Horatio Alger, Jr.* (Bloomington, IN: Indiana UP, 1985) 67.

enormous popularity which lasted for a couple of decades (though too late for him to enjoy the fruits of his labors).

As he declares in his preface to the book edition of *Ragged Dick* (which had been previously serialized), Alger saw himself as combining the roles of storyteller, social advocate, and philanthropist. He hoped his books would have "the effect of enlisting the sympathies of his readers in behalf of the unfortunate children whose life [they] described, and of leading them to co-operate" with the Children's Aid Society and other charitable organizations.[5] Alger had observed and befriended the young boot blacks, newsboys, and peddlers who trod the streets of New York, often until late at night, regardless of weather conditions, trying to sell their services or wares to frequently indifferent passers-by. These children numbered in the thousands and were a troubling visual and — with their cries — auditory reminder of the growing social inequality that plagued the American metropolis.

In 1872 Alger turned his attention to a particularly conspicuous and vulnerable sub-group of the New York street-boy population, the Italian child performers whose numbers had increased since 1860 and whose predicament had become a matter of concern for socially-minded citizens and the press. Before Alger, other American writers had taken notice of that presence, even when it was still a small-scale phenomenon. As early as 1843, Lydia Maria Child had mentioned the young Italians in her *Letters from New-York*. Both Herman Melville and Nathaniel Hawthorne had followed suit, introducing an Italian boy performer respectively in *Redburn* (1849) and *The House of the Seven Gables* (1851).[6] Before

---

[5] Horatio Alger Jr, *Ragged Dick: or, Street Life in New York with the Boot-Blacks* (Boston: A. K. Loring, 1868) viii.

[6] Lydia Maria Child, *Letters from New York* (Athens, GA: U Georgia P, 1998); Herman Melville, *Redburn, White Jacket, Moby-Dick* (New York: Library of America, 1983); Nathaniel Hawthorne, *The House of the Seven Gables* (New York: Penguin, 1967).

1860, the young street performers had come primarily from the North of Italy, specifically from Emilia Romagna and Liguria. However, from 1860 on, the vast majority of them hailed from the South.[7] Having researched his subject matter, Alger chose Calabria as the native region of the young protagonist and his best friend in the novel *Phil the Fiddler: The Story of a Young Street-Musician*. In his preface, Alger acknowledges the "unusual difficulty" he had encountered in the preparation of *Phil*, due to his inadequate information.[8] Contrary to his custom, he had been unable to communicate directly with the children he wished to portray because of their diffidence towards strangers and, most importantly, the formidable language barrier that stood in his way. The vast majority of the Italian children spoke only the dialect of their villages or towns, and the Italian that Alger had learned as a student at Harvard proved of little use. But the door to the Italian children's otherwise nearly impenetrable world had been opened for him by two very prominent members of the New York Italian community with whom he had become acquainted: A. E. Cerqua, superintendent and teacher at the Italian school in the notorious Five Points neighborhood; and Francesco Secchi de Casali, editor of the Italian-Language newspaper *L'eco d'Italia*. Through this newspaper, de Casali had been one of the first to sound the alarm on the Italian children's terrible living conditions and their cruel exploitation by the unscrupulous adults—the *padroni*—for whom they toiled. In his preface to *Phil*, Alger pays significant homage to de Casali, stating that without the aid of his articles he would "have been unable to write the present volume" (Alger, *Phil the Fiddler*, vi).

---

[7] John E. Zucchi, *The Little Slaves of the Harp: Italian Child Street Musicians in Nineteenth-Century Paris, London, and New York* (Montreal: McGill-Queens UP, 1992) 37-41.

[8] Horatio Alger Jr, *Phil the Fiddler: The Story of a Young Street-Musician* (New York, n.d.) v.

It is possible that, like many other New Yorkers, Alger had first become aware of the plight of Italian child performers after reading a letter to the editors of the *New York Evening Post* on 23 March, 1868. Titled "Midnight Doings in New York: Abuse of Boys," the letter had been written by a concerned citizen who had noticed the presence of small boys, "Italians or gypsies with their fiddles and harps," on the ferry returning to Manhattan from New Jersey around midnight. From a fellow passenger he had learned that "an active trade is carried on in these helpless mortals, that they are really bought in the streets of Rome and London of their parents, who are glad to sell them. The wretches who bring them here are the worst of slave masters." The letter ended with an urgent appeal to the Police Commissioner to put a stop to this "outrage on human nature" and to the *New York Evening Post* to dispatch its reporters to investigate and expose "these midnight doings" and help "bring their authors to justice."[9] But it was not until the beginning of 1872, a few months after the publication of *Phil the Fiddler*, when not the *New York Evening Post* but *The New York Times* began to explore that underworld in a series of sensational articles with titles like "The Italian Slave-Trade: How Boy Musicians are Entrapped and Imported" (7 July, 1872) and "The Italian Slaves" (19 June, 1873).[10] These articles insistently aligned the Italian children's removal from their homes and their cruel treatment in New York with American slavery, whose horrors were still very fresh in the memory of the American public.[11] This "traffic of children," claimed the 7 July 1872 piece, was "as absolute a slave-trade as ever existed down South," but "infinitely more repul-

---

[9] "Midnight Doings in New York: Abuse of Boys," *The New York Evening Post*, March 23, 1868.

[10] "The Italian Slave-Trade: How Boy Musicians are Entrapped and Imported," *The New York Times*, July 7, 1872; "The Italian Slaves," *The New York Times*, June 19, 1873.

[11] Zucchi, *The Little Slaves of the Harp*, 131-132.

sive." What made it worse than its precedent was that *after* the Civil War "Americans should know of these things and should suffer them... for all must confess that he who allows cruelty shares in the crime," and that this slave-trade should be conducted in the very heart of the North.[12]

In *Phil the Fiddler*, Alger, who came from an abolitionist family, evokes the specter of slavery from the very beginning. In the preface he mentions the "inhuman treatment" which the Italian children "receive from the speculators who *buy* them from their parents in Italy" (italics mine). "It is not without reason," he goes on to say, "that Mr. De Casale [sic] speaks of them as the 'White Slaves' of New York" (Alger, *Phil the Fiddler*, vi). In many ways, the comparison with slavery was a gross exaggeration. In particular, since the parents signed a contract of limited duration (usually four years), the children's plight, however harsh, was closer to that of the indentured servants of old. Significantly enough, Charles Loring Brace, social worker, author and founder of the Children's Aid Society, in his 1872 book *The Dangerous Classes of New York and Twenty Years' Work Among Them* described the Italian children as "indentured by their parents."[13] But clearly, in post-Civil War America slavery was a far more powerful term of reference and one which resonated strongly in the North.[14] Alger was keenly aware of this. Even though in *Phil the Fiddler* he relied on character types and situations he had already used in *Ragged Dick* and other boy stories, he also tried to emulate Harriet Beecher Stowe. His most ambitious project to date, *Phil the Fiddler* was to be an Italian American *Uncle Tom's Cabin*; like that novel, it was intended to denounce the horrors, and contribute to the demise, of

---

[12] "The Italian Slave-Trade."

[13] Charles Loring Brace, *The Dangerous Classes of New York and Twenty Years' Work Among Them* (New York: Wynkoop and Hallenbeck, 1872) 195.

[14] Charles J. Scalise, *"Phil, The Fiddler*: How Horatio Alger's Harvard Unitarianism Played Among Italian Americans," *Italian Americana* 27.2 (Summer 2009): 163n.

a shameful system. However, contrary to the boastful claims Alger would make in later years, evidence suggests that the impact of *Phil the Fiddler* on public opinion and, more importantly, on legislation, was minimal. The novel was practically ignored by the New York press and its sales were unremarkable.[15]

Phil the Fiddler departs from previous Alger books in its graphic depiction of brutal, sadistic violence. Clearly Alger was aiming for the emotional and sensational power of Harriet Beecher Stowe's anti-slavery bestseller *Uncle Tom's Cabin* (1852), which had exposed the cruelty of the Southern slave system to an enormous readership and had thus contributed to mobilizing public opinion in support of abolition.[16] At the same time, as Gary Scharnhorst and Jack Bales have suggested, Alger was probably trying to compete with the increasingly popular violence-ridden dime westerns.[17] If his previous books had featured the occasional fist fight, *Phil* showed the *padrone* inflicting horrific beatings on the young boys who had failed to bring him enough money or had dared to spend some of their earnings on food. The *padrone's* brutality, and the pleasure he obviously takes in punishing those in his power, reveal his close kinship to Beecher Stowe's slave owner Simon Legree ("he had one of those hard, cruel natures that delighted in inflicting pain and anguish upon others" [Alger, *Phil the Fiddler*, 70]). As is well known, in *Uncle Tom's Cabin* Legree is the epitome of sadism and the tormentor of martyr-like Tom, whose very mildness and Christian faith seem to goad Legree to paroxysms of ruthlessness. Determined to "break" Tom and assert his complete authority over him, Legree subjects him to repeated and savage punishments, ultimately causing his death. Like Tom, one of the *padrone's* victims dies in *Phil*. While the immediate cause of death in the Italian boy's case is a cold-induced fever, Alger makes it

---

[15] Scharnhorst and Bales, *The Lost Life of Horatio Alger, Jr.*, 96-97.

[16] Harriet Beecher Stowe, *Uncle Tom's Cabin* (New York: Norton, 2010).

[17] Scharnhorst and Bales, *The Lost Life of Horatio Alger, Jr.*, 97.

very clear that the *padrone* hastened him to his grave by viciously beating him and denying him proper food and care. Taking inspiration from an actual case, Alger took the opportunity to stage a lachrymose death scene clearly modeled upon the much celebrated (and parodied) death of little Eva, the angelic white girl who befriends Tom in *Uncle Tom's Cabin*. Like Eva, who expires with a vision of heaven in her eyes, the boy who dies in *Phil the Fiddler*, named Giacomo, is too good for this world. Squeezing every little drop of sentiment from the scene, Alger has a delirious Giacomo make his final wishes to his torturer, whom he mistakes for his beloved friend Filippo (the "Phil" of the title). Unaware that Filippo, having escaped from the Padrone's clutches, is not there with him, Giacomo addresses his final words to the very man who is responsible for his suffering and impending death:

> "When you go back to Italy, dear Filippo, go and tell my mother how I died. Tell her not to let my father sell my little brother to a padrone, or he may die far away, as I am dying… kiss me, Filippo," said the dying boy. One of the boys who stood nearby, with tears in his eyes, bent over and kissed him. Giacomo smiled. He thought it was Filippo. With that smile on his face, he gave one quick gasp and died—a victim of the *padrone's* tyranny and his father's cupidity. (Alger, *Phil the Fiddler*, 273)

As if to compensate for this sentimental flourish, Alger provides his readers with factual information, and identifies his sources, in a footnote: "It is the testimony of an eminent Neapolitan physician (I quote from Signor Casale [sic], editor of *L'Eco d'Italia*) that of one hundred Italian children who are sold by their parents into this white slavery, but twenty ever return home; thirty grow up and adopt various occupations abroad, and fifty succumb to maladies produced by privation and exposure" (Alger, *Phil the Fiddler*, 273n).

Like Secchi de Casali and others who wrote about the *"padrone* system," Alger used the expression white slavery (or white slaves), with an implicit emphasis on *white*, to arouse the indignation of the public. And yet that expression is somewhat belied by the uncertain racial status of his Italian characters. With few exceptions (in particular, see his 1894 novel *Only an Irish Boy*),[18] Alger made his young heroes impeccably Anglo-Saxon, and endowed them with moral and physical qualities that reflected the prevailing ideas about racial and ethnic ranking of his day. In many respects the protagonist of *Phil the Fiddler* is an identical twin to those American heroes by virtue of his inherent goodness, his honesty, his determination, his bravery, his readiness to protect the weak, his good looks, and his physical vigor. What distinguishes Phil from the typical Alger hero is the color of his eyes (he has "the dark eyes peculiar to his race") and, most importantly, the color of his skin (Alger, *Phil the Fiddler*, 1). Except in the first chapter, in which his complexion is said to be "a brilliant olive," Phil's skin tone is categorized as brown. Thus the Italian boy is placed in a kind of racial in-between-ness: he is not black, but he is not quite white either. Indeed, early on in the story, when Phil is invited into an elegant house to play his fiddle for a sick child, Alger makes the most of the chromatic contrast between the rich child's paleness and the fiddler's "brilliant brown face" (Alger, *Phil the Fiddler*, 6). Similarly, when Phil plays for the Hoffmans, a German American family, we are told that the younger boy Jimmy "had taken a fancy to the dark-eyed Italian boy, whose brilliant brown complexion contrasted strongly with his own pale face and blue eyes" (Alger, *Phil the Fiddler*, 48). To some extent, Phil is like a junior version of the enticing exotic males who, as Leslie Fiedler famously argued, are the real romantic attraction in a number of nineteenth-century

---

[18] Horatio Alger Jr, *Only an Irish Boy: The Story of Andy Burke's Fortunes* (New York: A. L. Burt, n.d.).

American classics.[19] Phil is dark enough, exotic enough, to function as an aesthetically (and perhaps even erotically) pleasing or-
nament to the scene, without being too unsettlingly Other. His
complexion literally brings a touch of color, it evokes warm and
sunny southern climes in the midst of the cold, busy, modern landscape of New York City.

But if, on the one hand, Alger calls attention to Phil's dark eyes
and brown face as tell-tale signs of his non-Anglo-Saxon-ness
(practically synonymous, in Alger's world, with "non-American-
ness"), on the other he makes it clear that he is morally *and* physically different from the novel's Italian villains, namely the *padrone*
and his nephew Pietro. Tellingly, the word brown, which identifies
Phil's complexion is never used to describe the appearance of his
Italian antagonists. Both the *padrone* and Pietro are said to be *dark*,
a term which applies as much to their inner as their outer traits.
The *padrone*, we are told, "was a short man, very dark, with fierce
black eyes and a sinister countenance" (Alger, *Phil the Fiddler*, 27).
In a later scene, Pietro, having been reprimanded by his uncle in
the presence of the younger boys, "glowed beneath his dark skin
with anger and shame" (Alger, *Phil the Fiddler*, 258). A *padrone* in
the making, Pietro is every bit as ruthless and sadistic as his uncle,
whom he will indeed succeed at the end of the story. Significantly,
when he tries to pass himself off as Phil's brother, those who
know what Phil looks like immediately realize that Pietro is lying
because his dark skin and harsh features betray him. Equating
aesthetics with ethics, Phil's friend Paul Hoffman dismisses
Pietro's claims in no uncertain terms: "Phil is a handsome little
chap. He wouldn't have such a villanous-looking brother as you"
(Alger, *Phil the Fiddler*, 204). Though brown rather than white,
Phil's attractive countenance matches that of the other Alger heroes inasmuch as it bespeaks his good character, thus inducing

---

[19] Leslie Fiedler, "Come Back to the Raft Ag'in, Huck Honey!" *The Partisan Review*
15 (1948): 664-71.

fair-minded, compassionate people to trust him and befriend him. As Roy Schwartzman has noted, for Alger "appearance signifies an individual's true nature." Alger's firm belief in physiognomy is a measure of the persistence and continuing appeal of this pseudoscience in the American popular imagination long after its heyday (throughout the first half of the nineteenth century). In America's increasingly multiethnic metropolises, physiognomy, although scientifically discredited, could offer reassuring indications on how to tell friend from foe: "In the midst of urban perils such as swindlers, unemployment, gambling houses, drunks, and derelicts, Alger offered his readers some assurance that there were reliable guides for behaving and interacting with others."[20]

Alger also calls attention to the difference in body and character between Phil and his friend Giacomo, a difference which ultimately accounts for Phil's successful admission into the middle class of American society and Giacomo's premature demise. Like his attractive features, Phil's bodily strength announces his moral fitness to become a good American citizen. His "naturally vigorous frame" (Alger, *Phil the Fiddler*, 78). and his irrepressibly lighthearted outlook, stand in sharp contrast to Giacomo's feebleness, despondency, and hopeless longing for sunny Italy. Phil too is deeply attached to Italy, but he is also resourceful, adaptable and forward-looking, and these distinctive traits qualify him as an ideal candidate for Americanization. In the novel's first scene he sings the patriotic "Hymn of Garibaldi," and a little later he is characterized as possessing, "like most of his nation, ... a love of whatever was beautiful, whether in nature or art" (Alger, *Phil the Fiddler*, 1, 5). Asked by Jimmy Hoffman if Italy is like America, Phil replies, "with natural love of country," that Italy is much nicer (Alger, *Phil the Fiddler*, 44). And yet, unlike Giacomo and most of the other Italian children, Phil has made an effort to enter into

---

[20] Roy Schwartzman, "Recasting the American Dream Through Horatio Alger's Success Stories," *Studies in Popular Culture* 23.2 (October 2000): 83.

meaningful communication with his new country: he has learned to speak some English. Moreover, the translation of his name (from Filippo to Phil), which Alger adopts, as he puts it, "for the benefit of [his] readers," suggests a transformation, or a passage into a new dimension (Alger, *Phil the Fiddler*, 2). By contrast, Giacomo stays Giacomo. By not anglicizing his name, Alger seems to suggest that Giacomo cannot change. He cannot be assimilated into American culture because he lacks Phil's resourcefulness and adaptability: Giacomo "was not self-reliant, like our hero, but always liked to have someone to lean upon" (Alger, *Phil the Fiddler*, 90). To Phil, the possibility of escaping the *padrone*'s tyranny, however fraught with danger, becomes in time something he believes to be within his reach. To Giacomo, on the other hand, words such as freedom and independence are literally incomprehensible. When Phil decides to defy the *padrone*'s rules and spend some of the money he and Giacomo have earned to buy a proper meal, Alger invites us to take notice of the difference between the boys' mindsets: "Phil had begun to think, and the essential injustice of laboring without proper compensation had impressed his youthful mind. Giacomo was more timid. He had not advanced as far as Phil, nor was he as daring" (Alger, *Phil the Fiddler*, 92). Interestingly enough, it is after talking to Mr. Pomeroy, a kind American gentleman he met in a grocery store, that Phil begins to harbor his daring thoughts. It takes an educated, benevolent American (a typical Alger mentor-figure) to bring Phil to the full realization of his exploitation and bondage-condition. Phil does not seem to possess that innate love of liberty, which in Alger's time was believed to be the most distinctive heritage of the Anglo-Saxons. But Phil, unlike Giacomo, with time acquires that feeling because he is imaginative and brave enough to aspire to a better life. Tellingly, when Mr. Pomeroy asks him if he and Giacomo would like to go back to Italy, Phil replies: "[Giacomo] would ... I would like to stay here, if I had a good home" (Alger, *Phil the Fiddler*, 86). Phil's quest for that good home appears to begin after a particularly cruel beating by the *padrone*. It is almost as if, in Phil's mind, the figures of the brutish Italian tyrant and the sympathetic American adviser stood before him, pointing in opposite directions: "There seemed no prospect except of continued oppression and long days of hardship, unless—and here the suggestion of Mr. Pomeroy occurred to him—unless he ran away" (Alger, *Phil the Fiddler*, 120). For Phil, the journey to freedom and a new life as an American is both a physical and a mental undertaking. Indeed, freeing his mind is the harder task, as he realizes when Paul Hoffman, a second-generation American (and as such more "advanced" than Phil) shows no fear at the prospect of confronting the *padrone* should the latter come in search of Phil: "Phil looked admiringly at [Paul] … Though he had determined to run away, his soul was not free from the tyranny of his late taskmaster" (Alger, *Phil the Fiddler*, 186).

In addition to the Hoffmans, another "ethnic" family helps Phil after he runs away: the Maguires, from Ireland, who not only give him shelter when he moves to Newark but put Pietro and his uncle to flight when they attempt to recapture the young fiddler. Both families offer him a permanent home but Phil, though grateful, decides to move further on. It is plausible and understandable that he should wish to put as much distance as possible between himself and his pursuers. And yet, given the novel's ending, in which an all-American couple, a country doctor and his wife, take Phil into their home and adopt him, a different explanation comes to mind. One suspects that Phil turns down the Hoffmans and the Maguires because, within Alger's system of societal hierarchy, he can do better and indeed he does. He becomes part of an "authentic," comfortable American household. Rather shamelessly, Alger stages the doctor's rescue of a half-frozen Phil on Christmas Eve. Phil wakes up the next day in his new role as the soon-to-be adopted child of an American family: "So our little hero had drifted into a snug harbor. His toils and privations were over. And for the doctor and his wife it was a glad day also. On Christmas day, four years before they had lost a child. On this Christmas, God had sent them another to fill the void in their hearts" (Alger, *Phil the Fiddler*, 294). Like many other Alger boys before and after him, Phil gets a new wardrobe, because good clothes are the badge of respectability. By the time he starts to go to school, he has come as close as possible, for someone of his ethnicity, to the typical Alger hero. Now fluent in English, "he might have been mistaken for an American boy," were it not for the color of his eyes and his complexion (Alger, *Phil the Fiddler*, 296). It is a sign of Phil's new identity, however, that his brown complexion, previously qualified as brilliant or radiant, is now "clear," as if Americanization had brought him a shade closer to whiteness.

Don DeLillo as The Kid From The Bronx: "Time, finally, to go home"[1]

Maria Giuseppina Cesari

UNIVERSITY OF MACERATA

1. AN INTRODUCTION

Don DeLillo is widely acknowledged as a major figure of American literature and has been analyzed and scrutinized under various and multiple aspects: as the theorist of America's secrets and conspiracies (*Running Dog, Underworld, Libra, Point Omega*); the narrator of American history throughout the last fifty-odd years in its most strategic moments, like Kennedy's assassination (*Libra*), the Cold War (*Underworld*) or the twin-towers attack and its post-traumatic consequences (*Falling Man*); the critic of mass media influence (*Americana*); the keen analyst of eco-criticism (*White Noise*), and lately the pioneer of the studies on how to bypass death by preserving life through cryonic freezing (*Zero K*). The list could go on and on with the abundance proffered in his insightful narration of the major events and critical issues in 20th and 21st century America.

But, throughout his long eclectic career, one of the thorniest matters is his and/or our own questioning his Italian American descent. Several Italian American scholars have long been persuaded that he is a writer of Italian descent or an American Italian writer, if not an Italian American writer in the strictest sense.[2] A

---

[1] Don DeLillo, *Underworld*, 676.
[2] For the problem of definition and ethnic positioning, see Anthony Julian Tamburri, *A Semiotic of Ethnicity*; Fred Gardaphé, *Italian Signs, American Streets*; Robert Viscusi, *Buried Caesars and Other Secrets of Italian American Writing*.

traditional definition for an Italian American writer was usually given accordingly to what Frank Lentricchia suggested, "Italian American writing is a report and meditation of first-generation experience usually from the perspective of a second-generation representative."[3] Second-generation writers have treated Italian American subjects and narrated their own experiences and difficulties in adapting and assimilating to American society. In the novel *Christ in Concrete* (1939) Pietro di Donato recounts the story and tragic death of his immigrant father as a bricklayer in New York City on Good Friday. In John Fante's *Wait Until Spring Bandini* (1938), the author recounts the harshness of the new American life for an immigrant Italian family, the Bandinis. According to Francesco Durante, the 1930s second-generation Italian American writers, such as Pietro di Donato and John Fante, are "figli di due mondi" because they represent the bridge between the two cultures. This bridge can turn into a clash, as Lentricchia argues: "... Italian American experiences and values are delineated as they appear in dramatic interaction with the mainstream culture" (Lentricchia, 124).

Although DeLillo unquestionably belongs to the "second-generation," being the son of Italian immigrants, his narrative choices and ethnic positioning are very different from earlier second-generation Italian American writers. In fact, according to Daniel Aaron's analysis of the hyphenate writer,[4] DeLillo is to be regarded as a "third stage" writer,[5] the so-called "American." A "third stage writer" does not replicate the historical experience of Italian Americans, neither does he narrate the immigrant journey of his

---

[3] Frank Lentricchia, "Delano in America and Other early poems," 124-125.

[4] Daniel Aaron, "The Hyphenate Writer and American letters," 214.

[5] For a better explanation of the classification (first, second, and third stage writer) see Aaron, "The Hyphenate Writer and American letters." See also Tamburri, "In (Re)cognition of the Italian American writer: Definitions and Categories." In *A Semiotic of Ethnicity*, 3-20.

parents or grandparents with a descriptive or critical approach, as first stage or second stage writers do (Aaron defines them as "local colorist" and "militant protester"). But he contributes to "our understanding of the process by which Italians have assimilated into American culture" (Gardaphé, *Italian Signs*, 192).[6] While his *italianità* is visible in his early works, he relegates his ethnicity to some invisible signs in his later works, traveling from the margin to the mainstream "viewing it no less critically, perhaps, but more knowingly" (Aaron, "The Hyphenate Writer," 214).

Aaron's third stage is comparable to Fred Gardaphé's third stage of his tripartite Vichian framework whereby DeLillo epitomizes "the philosophic mode"[7] (*Italian Signs*, 16-17) reflecting on his Italian roots and depicting post-modern American characters with implicit or hidden signs of *italianità*. Anthony J. Tamburri also agrees that DeLillo is a "third stage writer" because he went all the way from the margins to mainstream American literature (9).

A "third-stage" writer is comparable to being "third-generation," although they do not always perfectly coincide, as Aaron's difference between a second and a third stage writer can sometimes be blurred. According to generation-based "Hansen law," "What the son wanted to forget, the grandson wished to remember."[8] Therefore, first-generation immigrants, as foreign born, inevitably maintained the language and customs of their Old World identity, whereas their children sought to assimilate and deliberately distanced themselves from the customs and language of the Old World. Finally, the grandchildren or third-generation Italian American writers sought to recover the original ethnic identity.

All these definitions and classifications are not enough to clarify DeLillo's ethnic starting point, his positioning in mainstream America (assimilation) and subsequent return to his Italian roots

---

[6] Gardaphé, *Italian Signs*, 192.
[7] The three stages are the poetic, the mythic and the philosophic mode.
[8] Marcus Lee Hansen, "The Third Generation in America."

(recovery) in *Underworld,* if his journey is not contextualized within the emergence of a large group of third-generation Italian American writers and critics. "Thus the 1980s and the 1990s saw a bountiful harvest of third-generation creative and critical writers, aware of and writing about the complexities and variable meanings of the binomial nomenclature 'Italian American.'"[9] Ethnic and social refusal of Italian American identity was overcome by this generation: they did not have to worry about assimilation, since they had already assimilated, but they could look back on their past and think over their Italian American roots and their relation with Italy. It goes without saying that profound changes had intervened in the meanwhile, such as Italian Americans' higher social and economic conditions, a profound change in inter-ethnic relations culminating with the 1980s ethnic revival and the new vision of America as a kaleidoscope of different races and not as the American melting pot (where Italian Americans had to assimilate for fear of being excluded).

Don DeLillo was born in 1936, in the Italian American Bronx, near Arthur Avenue, where from he took inspiration for his early short stories, and which he later moved away from to write about a variety of American topics. He has become a post-modern mainstream American writer who has *also* looked back to Italian American subjects through the lens of parody and myth. And he has come to terms with his Italian American heritage by keeping a certain distance and reflecting on it. While Tamburri and Gardaphé see a clear line in DeLillo's writing, Daniel Aaron argues instead that there are no grounds for supporting the existence of Italian signs in DeLillo's works: "... nothing in his novels suggests a suppressed 'Italian foundation': hardly a vibration betrays an ethnic consciousness. His name could just as well be Don Smith or Don Brown" (Aaron, 67-68). The critic is suggesting that not even his

---

[9] Mary Jo Bona, "*Italianità* in 2003: The State of Italian American Literature," 4.

Italian name can be regarded as an ethnic sign. In Aaron's opinion, DeLillo is a mainstream American writer with no ethnic foundation. Additionally, DeLillo's own declared skepticism about his being an Italian American writer has made academic debate even more lively.

However, in recent years, things appear to have changed. First of all, DeLillo's Italian origins seem to be coming out like a slip of the tongue in a single Italian word like *"frittata"* (*Point Omega*, 48) or like the "buried"[10] memory of an Italian cultural reference like "Morandi paintings" (*Falling Man*, 48). This happens even in the novels that are not concerned with Italian stories or characters and it does happen when he refers to his old neighborhood. Secondly, from his own admission, for the first time he publicly recognized that, in an interview with Ian Brooks in May of 2016, "... in fact, more and more I think of myself as the kid from the Bronx" (DeLillo, 2016).

My purpose here is to highlight how the Bronx has been crucial to his identity as an American writer of Italian descent and also a point of departure and arrival of his "circular journey"[11] into the vast American society and back home.

2. DON DELILLO AND THE OLD NEIGHBORHOOD

The Bronx is not only Don DeLillo's old neighborhood, but also the place where he has lived quite secluded for many years.[12] I personally tried to find out where he lived in New York while engaging in research for my PhD thesis in 2010, but I did not succeed. Vague rumors circulated about his real address in the Bronx,

---

[10] For an in-depth analysis of the "buried" Italian heritage see Robert Viscusi, *Buried Caesars*.

[11] I am referring to the well-known book by Helen Barolini where she describes her own circular journey as an Italian American woman and writer: Home-Abroad-Return. Helen Barolini, *A Circular Journey*.

[12] For insights into DeLillo's life see Anthony Remnick, "Exile on Main Street: Don DeLillo's Undisclosed Underworld," 131-144.

but it was widely acknowledged that he wished to keep his personal life private. When asked about this secrecy, he answered Tom LeClair: "Silence, exile and cunning, and so on. It's my nature to keep quiet about most things" (*Anything Can Happen*, 80). Despite his reluctance to speak about his Italian name and origins, it is clear from his works that DeLillo has often engaged the city of New York and particularly the Bronx as his special place of choice, analyzing its changes throughout the second half of the twentieth century from an historical, spatial, and temporal perspective.

If we look at DeLillo's early production, two of his short stories, *Take the 'A' Train* and *Spaghetti and Meatballs*, are totally,set in the Bronx. They show *explicit*[13] references to the life of the "Little Italy" and the main characters are Italian Americans. The settings, characters, and words spoken are ethnic-centric and denote his knowledge of the life of the Italian American neighborhood of his youth. In the short story *Take the 'A' Train* (1962),[14] DeLillo depicts the life and fall of the young Italian American Angelo Cavallo. He has to leave "his apartment in a garlic-and-oil Bronx tenement" (9) because of the money he borrowed "from loan sharks" (89). The apartment is the only thing he has left after his wife abandoned him and he lost contact with his Italian American family (struggling with a difficult relationship with his father, anticipating Nick Shay's father-son trauma in *Underworld*). He is forced to abandon the ghetto to live in New York's metro anonymity and is on the way to becoming a bum as his father had predicted. "A bum for a son… I got a bum for a son"(15).

The writer has to abandon his old home (the Italian American Bronx) to become part of the modern American society, as DeLillo has acknowledged in a recent Italian interview of 2016: "I used to write about my personal experiences with friends and rela-

---

[13] On this matter, see Tamburri, 7.
[14] Don DeLillo, "Take the 'A' Train," 9-25.

tives in the Italian Bronx. Short stories. And then I made a clean break. That is why my first novel is called *Americana*" (my translation).[15] In the logic of Sollors's notion of "descent/consent," DeLillo has to leave his past and assimilate in order to build a new future for himself as an American writer. If we apply the idea of natural "growth" of ethnic literature to Italian American literature, as proposed by Sollors (241), whereby there is a natural "growth" of ethnic writers from non-fiction to fiction and from local forms to universal significance, DeLillo's "growth" from ethnic to mainstream literature seems to be a natural consequence. It is also obvious that a born-ethnic writer fears the fact that by writing mostly on his ethnic past he can be pigeonholed to his ethnic upbringing and then rejected by the big American literary world. Since the publication of *Americana* in 1971 and his abandonment of ethnic "centrality," DeLillo has been widely acknowledged as a one of the most highly regarded mainstream American writers.

However, his invisible signs[16] of *italianità*—his direct or indirect references to the Bronx among them—have continued to be recurrent through his works published from the seventies into the nineties. As Anthony J. Tamburri says: "What do we do about those works of art—written and visual—that do not *explicitly* treat Italian/American subject matter and yet seem to exude a certain ethnic Italian/American quality, even if we cannot readily define it?" The answer is that the "absentia" is actually a sign of them "*in potentia*" (7). We can see invisible signs of ethnicity through implicit references or even denials, or through different perspectives on American society and values. As Tamburri well pointed out (7), we should stretch our readings of Italian American works by

---

[15] "Scrivevo delle mie esperienze personali con amici e parenti nel Bronx italiano. Racconti brevi. E poi ho dato un taglio. Ed è per questo che il mio primo romanzo si chiama *Americana*." It is an excerpt from a very recent interview with Francesco Pacifico on October 21, 2016. "DeLillo ci parla di cinema."

[16] For visible and invisible signs of *italianità* see Fred Gardaphé (1996).

analyzing them in a wider perspective, looking at their content, form and (I would like to add) contextualizing them within their settings, bearing in mind that ethnicity is a fluid concept that changes over time.

As a matter of fact, in most interviews in the '70s and '80s (until early '90s before *Underworld*, published in 1997), DeLillo offered very little information about his early days in the Bronx. As Vince Passaro revealed in a 1991 interview, Don DeLillo had no interest in delving into biographical matters, "his work is without even a trace of the usual autobiographical resonances" (*Dangerous Don DeLillo*, 1991). And in that interview there is an illuminating statement by Gerald Howard, DeLillo's editor: "The way I've explained Don's psychology to myself is that here is an absolutely normal guy of the sort that's very familiar to me, attached to a literary genius. And I don't think the two parts necessarily communicate all that much." This hint at DeLillo's inner conflict (private life/public sphere) can explain the long-term denial of his ethnic roots: he needed to separate from his family background in order to assimilate and expand his literary potential and develop a career. That there would be a regret within him can be seen through the detachment full of regret of *Underworld*'s main character, Nick Shay, that is defined as "distance or remoteness" (116) or *lontananza* (275).

When Terry Gross interviewed him after the publication of *Underworld*, DeLillo extensively recalled the Bronx Italian American jargon of the '50s and being exposed to the Bronx games and street life, and he admitted that he regretted not having learnt Italian in those days, that he had to erase his ethnic origins: "The last thing kids my age wanted to do in those years was to appear European"(DeLillo, *Fresh Air*, 1997). In some recent interviews, things have changed. He has clearly referred to his *italianità* and reflected upon his ethnic roots in the Bronx. In a 2010 interview with *The Guardian's* reporter Robert McCrum, he admitted: "I suppose I have the Italian element of enjoying a certain amount of leisure".

He also compared his leaving the old neighborhood to his parents' journey: "In a strange kind of way, [...] what I did was to repeat the journey of my parents. That's to say, they left the old country to find a better life." [17]

His journey into American life started with *Americana* (1971), as he explained in the aforementioned interview with McCrum: "But then it came time for me to make my journey—into America." [...] "It was no coincidence that my first novel is called *Americana*. That became my subject, the subject that shaped my work" (DeLillo, 2010). In fact, in the novel *Americana* the main character, David Bell, is a 28-year-old successful TV executive working for the WASP establishment in a 1970's Manhattan. When his TV project is cancelled and many other executives are fired, he decides to leave New York and starts on a journey westward to work on a Navajo-themed documentary for the network. The second part of the book becomes David's road movie in search of meaning in American society.

In *Americana* the autobiographical aspect is clear: not so much for the fact that in his early days as a writer DeLillo worked at a Manhattan advertising agency as for a young, conflicted narrator standing in for a young, conflicted writer. DeLillo searched for an identity outside the physical and conceptual boundaries of the Bronx's Little Italy. But his allusion here is also to the system of America that forces immigrants into this place of otherness and isolation, unless they assimilate (his Italian foundation still peeping out from a short sentence at the beginning when he references to such as "Italian women with hairy legs" [*Americana*, 5]). Critics have different points of view about the years following the publication of *Americana*, when he was building a career in mainstream America. If Daniel Aaron is persuaded that his sympathy for marginalized people or his grotesque parody have nothing to do with

---

[17] https://www.theguardian.com/books/2010/aug/08/don-delillo-mccrum-interview.

his Italian roots (Aaron, 1991), Fred Gardaphé instead speaks of an "American Masquerade: *Italianità* in a Minor key" (Gardaphé, 1996). He argues instead that Italian signs can be found in many of DeLillo's works, even in those novels where American subjects or contents are predominant.

In the light of his "circular journey," home-abroad-return, (Barolini, 1996), I would like to find a way through by saying that *implicit* Italian signs do exist in some of his "abroad" novels (I mean those novels written after the two short stories and before *Underworld* when he left his old neighborhood subjects), but they probably were unconsciously or at least unintentionally included by the writer at the time. His focus then was the unveiling of American plots and great traumas, American history, the analysis of the large world he had plunged in and to "make interesting, clear, beautiful language" (*Anything Can Happen*, 82). That he was induced to assimilate to be able to build a literary career in the American mainstream, I do believe that he also intended to broaden his horizons at the time. In many ways one view fuels the other.

Some *implicit* or unconscious Italian American signs can be found in other "abroad" novels through a reading focused on the Bronx's presence, even in those with the strongest American characterization, when DeLillo had then become an acclaimed author of American mainstream literature. An example for all is *Libra* (1988), the well-known novel about the Kennedy assassination. If we open the first pages of *Libra*, we can see that the first chapter (Part One) is entitled "In the Bronx." There DeLillo depicts a young Lee Oswald living with his mother: "They were not wanted anymore and they moved to the basement room in the Bronx"(4), "near the Bronx zoo" (5), and some of the girls around there were "Italian girls in tight skirts" (12).

3. DON DELILLO AND THE BRONX IN *UNDERWORLD*

Although DeLillo has tried to explore this neighborhood before *Underworld*, all of previous explorations culminate in a fuller understanding of his identity and background with the publication of *Underworld* in 1997. Entire parts of the novel are devoted to the Bronx and it is the first time in one of DeLillo's novel that an Italian American character, Nick Shay, plays the role of the protagonist. Additionally, the novel's settings and characters of the Bronx's Little Italy epitomize DeLillo's homecoming to his Italian American origins and *Italianità* through language and myth. Both the language used by DeLillo and the mythical reconstruction of his old neighborhood reveal the complexity of his Italian American identity, moving from the denial of the second generation to the recovery of the third generation, as explained by sociologist Lee Hansen.

The language DeLillo spoke as a boy was English and not Italian. For many Italian Americans of his generation speaking Italian was not a privilege but a secure way to exclusion. Assimilation demanded total immersion into American culture and language, hence the "Americanization" of some Italian American names. In *Underworld*, DeLillo exemplifies this aspect through Nick Shay, the main character of Italian descent, who changes his name from Nicholas Costanza into Nick Shay. Italian Americans who stayed on in the Little Italys preserved some of the language they had learnt from their parents, as Albert Bronzini did in the novel: "Albert talked to his mother in his boyhood Italian" (683).

"The intrinsic connectedness of temporal and spatial relationships" (Bachtin, 15) shows that the language of the Italian American characters depicted in the novel is particularly evocative of the language learnt and spoken by DeLillo's Italian American community in the Bronx. Speaking of this uniqueness in an interview to Terry Gross on Fresh Air in 1997, he refers to "the pleasure of rediscovering a language of the 1940s and 1950s" in writing *Un-*

derworld. He continues, "when I tried *to reconstruct* the street jargon of my own background in the Bronx, one of the curious
pleasures of this endeavor was figuring out spellings for such
strange words, words that in many cases I don't think ever found a
life out of this narrow neighborhoods" (DeLillo, *Fresh Air*, 1997).
When asked to give an example, he cited the word "brouch," explaining its meaning as "to welsh on a deck." He uses the word
twice in the novel, in "It's a brouch" (778) and "I'm pulling a
brouch" (meaning that there is no way he is going to return the
five dollars he owes to his friend, Juju). DeLillo adds that "this
word comes from an Italian word that means to burn, so I am
burning you for this money, but I have never heard it since I was
seventeen years old" (DeLillo, *Fresh Air*, 1997).

Most of the Italian words in the Bronx chapter "Arrangement
in Gray and Black" are typical oral expressions ("*Mannaggia
l'America*" [766], or "*baci a tutti*" [709], "*che succese?*" [710]), swear
words ("u'gazz'" [778]) or food–related terms ("biscotto" [672],
"capozella" [667]), all terms that Italian Americans normally included in their English without interrupting its cadence.

Therefore, by reconstructing the spoken words of the Bronx in
the 1950s, the writer is exerting a typical function of third-
generation writers who were born in the US, i.e. the preservation
of the spoken language and oral storytelling of Italian Americans
in the New World by the means of their narratives. According to
sociologist Richard Alba,[18] the third generation of Italian Americans is the last generation with a living memory of their grandparents' storytelling and Italian past. The (present) fourth and fifth
generations of Italian Americans have lost their historical memory
and have been completely assimilated by American culture. There-

---

[18] My words summarize what Richard Alba said during the conference *Re-thinking
Italian American Studies* at the John D. Calandra Italian American Institute, New
York (10-11 September 2010).

fore, the third generation is a "bridge" generation worthy of careful examination.

All of this brings to light an important issue concerning the building of mythical "sites of memory" on American soil. The immigrant circular journey has changed its course: immigrants do not go from Italy to the US and (eventually) back to Italy as they used to do in the past centuries (the so-called birds of passage) when their residence in America was only temporary. As underlined by Fred Gardaphé in *Leaving Little Italy* (2004),[19] they have moved from Little Italys to Big America. Gardaphé argues that urban renewal programs in the 70's caused the destruction of Italian ghettoes, hence the residents' flight to the suburbs or somewhere else "outside their traditionally ethnocentric Little Italys" (38). This journey is mapped by DeLillo in Nick Shay's own journey from the Bronx to Arizona. When/if Italian Americans decide to return to their old neighborhoods, the journey back can be interpreted as a mythical and/or cognitive journey.

4. NICK SHAY AND THE BRONX IN *UNDERWORLD*

Don DeLillo devotes one hundred and twenty pages to the description of the Bronx in the fifties at the end of *Underworld* (661-781), but surprisingly enough, the first time he mentions and recalls the Bronx we are not in New York, but in the desert of Arizona at the beginning of the novel (Part I "Long Tall Sally" Spring-Summer 1992). In fact, *Underwold* is built on an inverted chronological order whereby the novel goes back in time from the 1990s (Part 1) to the 1950s (*Arrangement in Gray and Black*), briefly from the desert of Arizona to the Bronx. The only chapters that are not built accordingly are the Prologue (*The Triumph of Death*) and the Epilogue (*Das Kapital*), respectively set in the 1950s and in the 1990s.

---

[19] Gardaphé, *Leaving Little Italy*, especially Chapter 3, "Mythologies of Italian America. From Little Italys to Suburbs" (37-50).

When we first encounter Nick Shay, we are in the desert of Arizona in the 1990s. Nick is fifty-seven years old and he is heading west towards the desert, looking for the long-lost lover from his Bronx youth, Klara Sax (DeLillo, *Underworld*, 63). Klara is now a conceptual artist, trying to create a work of art by recycling the relics of the U-bombers and the Vietnam War helicopters. It is the first time that an Italian American character takes center stage in a DeLillo's novel. It is what Fred Gardaphé defines as a "postmodern prerogative" (*Italian Signs*, 22), meaning the possibility for Italian American authors to identify themselves with the Italian American heritage through a main character of Italian American descent. In such a way they can reconstruct their heritage and question themselves about it by creating a certain distance from their Italian American immigrant past. The time is ripe for Italian Americans to take a step forward and look back with no fear of exclusion or marginalization. They can do it through their narratives, so the written word will replace the spoken word of their ancestors' storytelling.

Nick Shay is a typical self-made man who has made his fortune by leaving the Italian Bronx, moving to the suburbs and setting up a new life in Phoenix, Arizona, as many other Italian Americans of the post-war years. By "discarding" his past and "recycling" his Italian American identity through the American melting pot, Nick resurfaces as a successful waste manager at which point is finally able to return to his Italian American roots. An external reason, the accidental killing of Joe Manza, triggers his departure from the Bronx. The subsequent period spent in "a juvenile correction center" and in "the small Jesuit outpost in Northern Minnesota" (299) deeply changes him. When he abandons the Italian American life of the Bronx, he also leaves behind a fatherless childhood with very little money and opportunities and an early life of petty crimes that turned into serious crime. Nick wants to shed his identity above all things and become a completely assimilated American. But, when in Phoenix, he lives as if he were someone else: "Like someone in the Witness Protection Program" (66). He doesn't hide now out of fear, he has paid for his crime, but lives in Arizona as a form of rejection of his old life in the Italian American Bronx, "to escape the hard-luck past with its gray streets and crowded flats and cabbage smells in the hall-way" (90), towards "the westward dreams" (89), towards a dreamy place that immigrants like his ancestors could have moved to in search of a better life

His journey is the quintessential quest of the hero's circular journey, as depicted in Joseph Campbell's mono-myth (30): the hero starts on an (identity) quest after a major event in his life (homicide), he overcomes a boundary (the Little Italy's borders) and moves into the New World (Big America) where his initiation (assimilation) takes place. At the end of a series of trials (career, marriage, adaptation to mainstream America), when the hero's quest has been accomplished (building of a new American identi-ty), the hero returns to his point of departure by crossing a return threshold (the desert). The hero (Nick) must complete his identity quest by returning to his first source of knowledge (the Bronx).

The loss of his Italian American identity through his assimila-tion into American society brings the loss of his selfhood, hence his attempts at recovering it in two ways. Nick Shay wishes to re-capture the past by looking for Klara Sax in the desert and by try-ing to buy Thomson's ball from a baseball memorabilia collector. This is the ball launched by Bobby Thomson during the baseball match of the Giants against the Dodgers at the New York stadium, on October 3, 1951. It is defined as the "shot heard around the world," a home-run that gave the Giants the pennant, an event eternalized by DeLillo in the Prologue of *Underworld*.

Nick's identity is clearly split between resorting to the healing power of memory to overcome the traumatic experiences of his life in the Bronx (the killing of George the Waiter and his father's abandonment) and the defensive stance of keeping some "distance" (64) between his new identity of "made man" (275) with no cracks or weaknesses like a "sturdy Roman wall" (275) and his past. The word *distance* is referred to the chronotopic dimension, as well as to Nick's alienation and split personality. As scholar and critic John N. Duvall, underlines: "an awareness of one's alienation is the last best hope to construct an opposition to the forces of consumer culture" (Introduction, from Valparaiso to Jerusalem, 561).[20] Nick is aware of his alienation, since this distance between the "American self" and "the Italian American self" allows him to defend himself from assimilation, but at the same time it creates alienation and nostalgia. When he is found out to be half Italian by his colleagues, they say "they hear it in that voice he does" (165), a gangster voice, "Expert stereotyped, pretty funny" (165). As Nick makes a parody of his origins, distancing himself from them.

If we compare Don DeLillo's life with Nick Shay's, we can easily perceive the similarities between the writer and the fictional character. They were born in the Italian American Bronx, as DeLillo recalls: "I was brought up in the Fordham section of the Bronx, a neighborhood of mostly Italian-Americans" (Passaro, 1991). They share a Catholic upbringing. DeLillo studied in Cardinal Hayes High School, a Catholic Boys School in the Bronx, and then at Fordham University, also in the Bronx, where he majored in communication arts in 1958.[21] Nick Shay moves west and changes his name and becomes a success in waste management before reconnecting with his roots, while DeLillo stops writing about spe-

---

[20] John Duvall is one of the major critics and scholars of Don DeLillo. He is the author, among other texts, of the *Cambridge Companion to Don DeLillo* (Cambridge: Cambridge UP, 2008).

[21] Information about DeLillo's life can be culled from Vince Passaro's Interview cited herein and from other interviews, for example, Robert R. Harris's Interview, "A Talk with Don Delillo."

cific Italian and Italian American characters, as described earlier in his approach to *Americana* in 1971, and becomes a prominent novelist before returning to an Italian American protagonist in 1997's *Underworld*. In the light of the hero's quest, Nick Shay is Don DeLillo's alter ego when he completes his circular journey back to his Italian American roots and the old neighborhood.

When Nick Shay explains this distance he uses an Italian term *"lontananza"* (276)[22] and he translates it to his wife Marian as "Distance or remoteness" (276). *"Lontananza"* to me sounds like *"ricordanza,"* a term used by Giacomo Leopardi to indicate the remembrance of an ancient image (*immagine antica*). Instead, *lontananza* would probably recall for DeLillo the song "La Lontananza" by Domenico Modugno, since DeLillo spent his youth in the Bronx. As Modugno beautifully sings, "distance, you know is like the wind, puts out the little fire, but makes bigger the big ones...." A perfect metaphor for the distance DeLillo puts between himself and his Italian American neighborhood. And, in Modugno's words, *"Ritornerò, te lo giuro, amore, ritornerò"* (I'll be back, I swear it my love, I'll be back).[23]

,

4. Conclusion

In *Underworld* the Bronx becomes a spatial and time-consuming metaphor of the past and presently disappeared life of one of the old Italian American neighborhoods in New York City. It is also a metaphor of Nick Shay's circular journey from denial to homecoming through the mythical return to his old neighborhood. This homecoming goes hand in hand with DeLillo's own circular jour-

---

[22] "I tell her there is an Italian word, or a Latin word, that explains everything. Then I tell her the word. She says, what does this explain? And she answers. Nothing. The word that explains nothing in this case is 'lontananza'" (*Underworld*, 275).

[23] "I was born on Nov. 20, 1936." [...] "Except for a short stint in Pennsylvania when I was quite young, I was brought up in the Fordham section of the Bronx, a neighborhood of mostly Italian-Americans" (Don DeLillo, interview with Vincent Passaro, "Dangerous Don DeLillo").,

ney and mythical and cognitive return to the old neighborhood. From the first Italian American short stories and after the clean break with Italian American topics, De Lillo travels into Big America and becomes an American literary giant. In 1997, with the publication of *Underworld*, for the first time in his novels an Italian American character plays a central role, and so does the old Italian American neighborhood. The great American novelist is back home, as "the kid from the Bronx."

DeLillo said to Ian Brooks in 2016: "But I circle back literally, in that I go back to the same neighborhood. I have a regular meal with the guys I grew up with, who now all live elsewhere. We all meet in a restaurant on Arthur Avenue, which is in the heart of the Italian Bronx. All these guys—I didn't see them for years, but I never forgot. And when we meet, we talk about growing up. And all of us remember absolutely everything the same way" (DeLillo, 2016). Even for Don DeLillo it is "time, finally, to go home" (67).

WORKS CITED

Aaron, Daniel. "The Hyphenate Writer and American Letters." *Smith Alumni Quarterly* (July 1964): 213-17.

_____. "How to Read Don DeLillo." In *Introducing Don DeLillo*. Frank Lentricchia, ed. Durham, NC: Duke UP, 1991.

Bachtin, Michail. "Forms of Time and the Chronotope in the Novel: Notes towards an Historical Poetics." In *Narrative Dynamics: Essays on Time, Plot, Closure, and Frame*, Brian Richardson, James Phalen, Peter Rabinowitz, eds. Columbus, OH: Ohio State UP, 2002.

Barolini, Helen. *A Circular Journey*. New York: Fordham UP, 2006.

Campbell, Joseph. *The Hero with a Thousand Faces*. Princeton, NJ: Princeton UP, 1973(1949); Italian translation, *L'eroe dai mille volti*. Parma: Guanda, 2000.

DeLillo, Don. *Underworld*. New York: Scribner, 1997. London: Picador, 1998; Italian translation by Delfina Vezzoli. Turin: Einaudi, 1999.

_____. "Take the 'A' Train." *Epoch* 12.1 (Spring 1962).

_____. "Spaghetti and Meatballs." *Epoch* 14.3 (Spring 1965).

_____. *Americana*. New York: Houghton Mifflin (1971; rev. Penguin, 1989).

_____. *Running Dog*. New York: Knopf, 1982.

_____. *White Noise*. New York: Viking Press 1985.

_____. *Libra*. New York: Viking Press, 1988.

_____. *Mao II*. New York: Viking Press, 1991.

_____. *Point Omega*. New York: Scribner, 2010.

_____. *Zero K*. New York: Scribner, 2016.

_____. "The Power of History." *New York Times Magazines*, September 7, 1997. Retrieved April 22, 2016 from http://www.nytimes.com/ library/books/090797articles3.html.

DeLillo, Don. Interview with Vincent Passaro, "Dangerous Don DeLillo." *The New York Times*, May 19, 1991, Retrieved September 5, 2010 from http://www.nytimes.com/books/97/03/16/lifetimes/del-v-dangerous.htm.

_____. Interview with Robert R. Harris, "A Talk with Don DeLillo." *New York Times Book Review*, October 10, 1982.

_____. Interview with Thomas. LeClair, "An Interview with Don DeLillo." *Contemporary Literature* 23.1 (1982): 19-31. Rpt. in *Anything Can Happen: Interviews with Contemporary American Novelists*. Thomas LeClair and Larry McCaffery, eds. Urbana: U. of Illinois P, 1983. 79-90. (Interview conducted in Athens, in 1979.)

_____. Interview with Herbert Mitgang, "Reanimating Oswald, Ruby et al. in a Novel On the Assassination." *The New York Times*, July 19, 1988 retrieved on October 2016 from http://www.nytimes.com/ books/97/03/16/lifetimes/del-v-oswald.html

_____. Interview with Ian Brooks, "Don DeLillo, I think of myself of the kid from the Bronx." *The Guardian*, May 6, 2016. Retrieved on September 10, 2016 from https://www.theguardian.com/books/2016/ may/06/don-delillo-kid-from-the-bronx-interview-xan-brooks.

_____. Interview with Francesco Pacifico "DeLillo ci parla di cinema." *Il Sole 24 ore Magazine* 85 (November 2016). Retrieved on November 2nd, 2016 from http://24ilmagazine.ilsole24ore.com/2016/10/che-cose-la-poetry-fiction-leggete-zero-k/?refresh_ce=1#massimoscroll.

_____. Interview with Terry Gross on *Fresh Air*. "Don DeLillo & Terry Gross & Underworld/part 3. October 2, 1997. Retrieved November 3rd, 2016 from https://www.youtube.com/watch?v=FSyRbFWoqUo.

Dizionario di Storia Moderna e Contemporanea. Retrieved on October 22, 2010, http://www.pbmstoria.it/dizionari/storia_mod/m/m133.htm.

Durante, Francesco, ed. *Figli di due Mondi. Fante, di Donato, & C. Narratori italoamericani degli anni '30 e '40*. Rome: Avagliano Editore, 2002.

Duvall, John N. "Introduction: From Valparaiso to Jerusalem: DeLillo and the Moment of Canonization." *Modern Fiction Studies* 45.3 (Fall 1999).

Fabietti, Ugo, Vincenzo Matera. "Luoghi di memoria." In *Memoria e identità. Simboli e strategie del ricordo*. Rome: Meltemi, 1999.

Gardaphé, Fred L. *Italian Signs, American Streets. The Evolution of Italian American Narrative*. Durham, NC: Duke UP, 1996.

_____. Mythologies of Italian America. From Little Italys to the Suburbs." In *Leaving Little Italy*. Albany, NY: SUNY P, 2004.

Kerouac, Jack. *On the Road*. New York: Penguin Books, 1976 (1957).

Hutcheon, Linda. *The Politics of Postmodernism*. New York: Routledge, 1989.

Hansen, Marcus Lee. "The Third Generation in America." *Commentary* 14 (1952).

Lentricchia Frank. "The American Writer as Bad Citizen." In Frank Lentricchia, ed. *Introducing Don DeLillo* (Durham, NC: Duke UP, 1991.

Leopardi, Giacomo. "Le ricordanze." In *Canti*. Milan: BUR Rizzoli, 1998 [1835].

Luconi, Stefano. "Little Italy." In *The Sage Encyclopedia of Economics and Society*. Los Angeles: SAGE Publications, 2015.

Modugno, Domenico. "La Lontananza." Retrived on September24, 2016 from http://www.timmusic.it/www/artist/537006774.

Premo Steele, Cassie. *We Heal from Memory. Sexton, Lorde, Anzaldúa and the Poetry of Witness*. New York: Palgrave, 2000.

Puzo, Mari, *The Godfather*. New York: G.P. Putnam's Sons, USA, 1969.

Remnick, Anthony, "Exile on Main Street: Don DeLillo's Undisclosed Underworld." In Thomas De Pietro, ed., *Conversations with Don DeLillo*. Jackson, MS: UP Mississipi, 2005.

Russo, John Paul. "Technology and the Mediterranean in DeLillo's *Underworld*." In *America and the Mediterranean*. Massimo Bacigalupo and Pierangelo Castagneto, eds. Turin: Otto Editore, 2003.

Sollors, Werner. *Beyond Ethnicity: Consent and Descent in American Culture*. New York: New York UP, 1986.

Tamburri, Anthony Julian. *A Semiotic of Ethnicity. In (Re)cognition of the Italian/American Writer*. Albany, NY: SUNY P, 1998.

Viscusi, Robert. *Buried Caesars and Other Secrets of Italian American Writing*. Albany, NY: SUNY P, 2006.

"Nobody has to tell the whole truth, only pieces of the truth."[1] Chasing an Identity in Tony Ardizzone's Fiction

Carla Francellini
UNIVERSITY OF SIENA

Tony Ardizzone's stories seem to originally inflect the inextinguishable search for identity in a contradictory world — "a big dark world" — where nobody can ever elude nonsense, absurdity, and uncertainty.[2] Most of the characters in his collections — *The Evening News. Stories* (1986, Flannery O'Connor Award), *Larabi's Ox: Stories of Morocco* (1992), and *Taking It Home: Stories from the Neighborhood* (1996) — are people who live the condition of hyphenation:

> Ardizzone's characters are the so-called hyphenated Americans who occupy a world seemingly different from what one might expect. They are very much ensconced in a world of memory and recollection that keeps them ineluctably tied to their past, either in search of some form of understanding their present situation or, in certain cases, in an attempt to escape from their present situation.
>
> (Tamburri 23)

In most cases — except for a few stories about college — Ardizzone's characters are working-class and middle-class men and women of all ages, ordinary people who end up facing the fact that nobody in this world has to tell the whole truth, but only pieces of the truth. Using everyday language, setting his narratives in an ordi-

---

[1] Ardizzone, Interview with Bevilacqua, 210.
[2] Ardizzone, "The Eyes of the Children," *passim.*

nary—even though, almost always, ethnic—context, Ardizzone succeeds in fixing a set of referents, symbols, metaphors, and images,
to create a layered photograph of his protagonists. Identity, in his
works, is described as something made up by an infinity of different layers of existential meanings, obscure perceptions of signifi-
cances well beyond the surface of things and the limitations of
language.

As Peter Carravetta points out, "ethnic identity is found to be
constituted by a cluster of different and not always coherent (sub)-
identities, some of which have little to do with nations and languages and much with politics and power" (Carravetta xii). In
what follows I shall highlight those instances in some of Ardizzone's more popular works—novels and short stories—in which
Italian/American identity is forefront.

Ardizzone's Italian origins—his paternal grandfather was from
Menfi near Agrigento—are deeply intertwined with his ideas of
Italianità and *Americanness*.[3] Precious insights to understand better
how it feels to be an artist writing on the hyphen between different cultures are provided in his many short stories focusing on
ethnicity, where Ardizzone goes deep into the analysis of how being—and even more feeling to be—ethnic can influence our point
of view on life and society. Ardizzone's characters—confused and
somehow lost in a world whose meaning gets through only in-
termittently—share a disquieting feeling of uneasiness and fear
and they dramatically experience a devastating loss of inner balance when forced to face their origins and the widespread nonsense around them. Carravetta, in his volume *After Identity* (2017),
maintains the need to pay attention to the complicated dynamics
within the Italian American (self)narrative arising from the relationship with la Madre Patria:

---

[3] For a definition of *italianità*, see Tamburri, Giordano, Gardaphé; see also, Gardaphé, *Italian Signs*. For biographical information about Ardizzone's grandfather,
see Bevilacqua, 207-213.

[W]e should begin to assess the dynamics, within the Italian American (self)narrative, of the degree and type of associations that actual agents and fictional characters alike make with la Madre Patria [...] Although this will turn out to be highly symptomatic of how multilayered and differentiated the Italian American psyche is and has been, what will prove most shocking is the incredible (and, to me, absurd) chasm that has existed and tenaciously persists between the sense of *italianità* of the Italian Americans (or, better yet, the Americans of Italian descent), and the sense of *italianità* of the Italians from Italy...the whys and wherefores of this paradoxical situation would require long interdisciplinary analyses, and must be taken up somewhere else, but I think it represents a field for future research. (23)

Tony Ardizzone—whose works highlight not only a great vitality of the Italian/American ethnic element but also evident signs of *Italian Americanness*—is among those Italian/American writers that Fred L. Gardaphé defines as "visible" since they deal mostly "with the Italian/American experience through Italian/American subjects."[4] In marked contrast with Richard Alba's theory, according to which evident and stable signs of Italian/American ethnicity were bound to diminish over time and gradually disappear, in Ardizzone's stories a new idea of ethnicity as something dynamic and changing in a most active and twinkling society comes to light, fresh and alive.[5] According to Michael Fischer, ethnicity is not simply passed on from generation to generation, but it is, in

---

[4] For the distinction between "visible" and "invisible" Italian American writers, cfr. Gardaphé, *Italian Signs*: "I propose dividing contemporary Italian American writers into two categories: the 'visible' and 'invisible.' Those Italian American writers who choose to deal with the Italian American experience through Italian American subjects I will call the visible. Italian American writers who choose to avoid representation of the Italian American as a major subject in their works can be referred to as the invisible" (123).
[5] See Richard Alba and Michael Fischer.

fact, reinvented and reinterpreted again and again in different ways and with variable degrees of intensity. Tony Ardizzone's stories seem to prove that identity is the final result of a long, complicated process which consists in reinventing and reinterpreting one's ethnic roots in view of a possible coexistence of a double identity, American and Italian, an aspect on which not enough reflection has been focused, as Carravetta remarks:

> Not enough reflection has been focused on the question of how someone—especially if an artist, or a writer, or a public persona— can identify as being both, an American and an Italian, without confronting the thus revealed possibility that identity is a construct of multiple elements, all critically slippery, all historically contingent and multipronged, and perhaps constituting, deploying a post-modern moniker, a plurality of discourses in constant conflict and exchange. Identity has no contours, it is fluid, amoebic, viscous. (xii)

Tamburri, on this same topic of *italianità*, maintains:

> ethnicity—and more specifically [...] *Italianità* is redefined and reinterpreted on the basis of each individual's time and place, and therefore is always new and different with respect to his/her own historical specificities vis-à-vis the dominant culture. (14)

ॐ

From his very first novel, *In the Name of the Father* (1978), to his last one, *The Whale Chaser* (2010), passing through his many short stories and that marvelous maze of tales which is the novel, *In the Garden of Papa Santuzzu* (1999), Ardizzone creates a wonderful labyrinth of distracting meanings and ambiguous signs. Here, most readers would easily get lost were it not for the precious Arianna's thread offered them by the writer's Joycean style leading them through the maze to learn once more that none of the protagonists in his works has the whole truth, but only pieces of it.

In his first novel, *In the Name of the Father* (1978), Ardizzone deals with ethnic identity as he would do with a magmatic jumble having the power to throw his characters off center. Tonto Schwartz, a young American boy with Jewish origins—and an embarrassing name which is the only thing his mysterious father, Abraham, left him—is the protagonist of a novel, whose title highlights the two central elements of the story, the *father* and the *name*, elements not so uncommon in Ardizzone's narratives.[6] Here the story is structured around a powerful reference to the Jewish "Father and Son" sacred relationship with the figure of Abraham—the Father—profoundly intertwined with that of the Son engaged in an almost mystical research of deeper meanings beyond the surface of his unusual name. As a result of the premature loss of his father, who died before the boy was named, Tonto's life is devoted to the tireless search for his mysterious father's identity, while his mother is torn by a strong desire to change her son's name immediately followed by a feeling of uneasiness at the idea of going against Abraham's last will. Still, even the last name "Schwartz"—so openly ethnic if not distinctly Jewish—would be muffled by a strongly American first name. *Naming things*, though, is obviously a very important act hinting at the task assigned to Adam by God himself in the Garden of Heaven: that's why the young Tonto persuades himself he needs to know why his father wanted to give him such an unusual name in the belief that answering this question will help him understand who he is. Tonto's mother, on the contrary, soon realizes that his son's name can make life much harder for him and the day before the young boy has to start

---

[6] In "My Mother's Stories," the first-person narrator's name is Tony and he tells his mother's story reporting many autobiographical details. In Gardaphé's *Dagoes Read*, we read: "[this story] is about as autobiographical a piece as I've ever written. [...] I even used my own name in that story. I tried to tell all truth, though my mother now tells me I got many details wrong" (22-23).

school, she takes into consideration the hypothesis of changing it in an engaging dialogue with her emancipated sister Jenny:

> "He starts school tomorrow," [Mary] said. [...]
> "He's a good boy. But I'm afraid of what the other children might do to him because of his name."
> Jenny stirred her coffee. Mary sat at the plain wood table.[...]
> "Well, you remember we talked about this," Jenny said. "There still is time to do something, you know. We can call the school, we can tell Tonto that when a boy begins school he gets a new name. We can name him after Abe. That's what I would do, Mary." She sipped her coffee.
> "But you know that I can't," Mary said. (3-4)

Mary is so resistant to changing her son's name because she doesn't want to go against Abraham's last will, no matter how much her sister insists on the opportunity to give the boy a new name:

> Jenny shook her head. "Abe was sick, kid. He was goddamn crazy sick when he told you to name the boy Tonto. It was because of the radio program and him coming back that way from the war. You've done it for what, five or six years now. You can change it." [...]
> She pushed her cup away and looked around the kitchen.[...]
> "Call the school and tell him his name is Abraham," Jenny said. "Or give him another name, like John or like Richard. Richard Schwartz, John Schwartz, Thomas Schwartz. And besides those names don't even sound that Jewish." (3-4)

ॐ

Something very similar takes place in one of Ardizzone's most compelling pieces, "My Mother's Stories," probably the most autobiographical of the collection *The Evening News*. The everlasting search for the mother plays a fundamental role in the wider search for identity, which is at the core of many Italian/American writers and, of course, of Ardizzone's short stories. Mothers, grandmothers, and other powerful figures of matriarchs populate some of his most interesting short stories, even though each of these women can be very different from the others.

Indeed, in "My Mother's Story," there's a woman extremely talented in the art of storytelling. She's on her deathbed while her son—the first person narrator—terribly scared at the idea of losing her, goes through the numerous stories she told him.[7] Her life as a daughter first, and then as a wife and as a mother—eventually a dying mother on the verge of disappearing forever from her son's horizon—is at the core of all her stories. What stands out in this narrative is the fact that Ardizzone presents the reader with a great piece of meta-literature discussing the importance of telling stories.[8] Narrating stories from and of the past—no matter how distant this past is—has something to do with giving it a new chance to be born again: it is clear from the incipit of the story, in which the woman's birth is described as a terrific moment, since the baby was too tiny and too frail to live:[9]

> They were going to throw her away when she was a baby. The doctors said she was too tiny, too frail, that she wouldn't live. They performed the baptism right there in sink between their pots of boiling water and their rows of shining instruments, chose who would be her godparents, used water straight from the tap. Her father, however, wouldn't hear one word of it. He didn't listen to their *she'll die anyway* and *please give her to us* and *maybe we can experiment*. No, the child's father stood silently in the corner of the room, the back of one hand wiping his mouth and thick mustache, his blue eyes fixed on the black mud which caked his pants and boots.

---

[7] Ardizzone, "My Mother's Stories," 1-13.
[8] For a narratological reading of this story, see Tamburri (24-28).
[9] See also Magrini.

> *Nein*, he said, finally. *Nein*, die anyway.
>
> With this, my mother smiles. She enjoys imitating the man's thick accent. She enjoys the sounds, the images, the memory. Her brown eyes look past me into the past. She draws a quick breath, then continues.
>
> ("My Mother's Stories," 1)

It is the contrast between the father's sharp words pronounced with a definite German accent and the mother's mocking version of the fact to set the theme of the short story that is ethnicity and what it means to be an American of ethnic descent. Not by chance, the narrating voice in this short story belongs to the son who has inherited from her the art of storytelling.

> ...the child lived. If she hadn't, I wouldn't be here now in the corner of this room, my eyes fixed on her, my mother and her stories. For now, the sounds and pictures are *my* sounds and pictures. Her memory, my memory. (1)

Narrating ethnicity, though, seems the only way to find a passage in the thick jumble of meanings that characterize an ethnic identity. The power of the narrating voice is, therefore, underlined and established once more at the end of the short story when the woman is said to be dying, losing her body but reinforcing her presence on earth through her compelling stories. Like in the sad myth of the nymph Echo, who ended up wasting away—her beauty faded, her skin shriveled, and her bones turned to stone—while only her voice survived though condemned to repeat the last word of another person, the woman—whose body is about to become as cold and hard as a rock—will leave behind only her voice which will resonate in her son's words telling over and over again her stories (Ovid, 395-397). Once she's gone, her children will be left with the numerous stories she told them and the vivid memory of her voice:

> She knows how to tell a pretty good story. I think. She's a natu-
> ral. She knows how to use her voice, when to pause, how to
> pace, what expressions to mask her face with. Her hand slices
> out the high fence. She's not in the same room with you when
> she really gets at it; her stories take her elsewhere, somewhere
> back. She's there again, back on a 1937 North Side street. My fa-
> ther and I are only witnesses. (3)

The unbridgeable distance between the different ethnic groups
of the narrator's parents triggers many of the stories his mother
told her children. Her parents were, in fact, from Alsace Lorraine
and had a hard time accepting the idea of her daughter marrying
an Italian/American man, the son of Italian immigrants from Sicily. The description of the first encounter between the narrator's
parents begins with a little detail, apparently even baneful—"She
was sweeping"—and ends with a strong sentence "She never tells
the rest of the details":

> She was sweeping. This story always begins with that detail.
> With broom in hand. Nineteen years old and employed as a mil-
> liner and home one Saturday and she was sweeping. By now
> both her parents were old. Her mother had grown round, ripe
> like a fruit, like she would. Her father now fashioned wood. A
> mound of fluff and sawdust grows in the center of the room and
> she is humming, perhaps something from Glenn Miller, or she
> might have sung, as I've heard her do while ironing on the back
> porch, when from behind the locked back screen door there was
> suddenly a knock and it was my father, smiling. But this was the
> afternoon he proposed. Why he chose that afternoon, or even af-
> ternoon at all, are secrets not known to me. I ask her and she
> evades me. *Ask your father.* (3-4)

"My Mother's Stories," though, is so much more than a simple
short story. The beginning and ending insist on the same theme
that is the impending death of the woman so much that, at the end

of the story, we see the Ohio doctors' prophecy—*"Please, give her to us. Maybe we can experiment"*—eventually come true. Telling his mother's life in a story of his own gives the narrator a chance to dwell on the art of telling stories and, more precisely, on the relation between autobiography and fiction—quite a central aspect in Ardizzone's writing. His mother's stories will teach her son—the first-person narrator—to reveal, communicate, and tell his own experience in this life without ceding to the temptation of changing any little detail or modifying the ending:

> I stand here, not used to speaking about things that are so close to me. I am used to veiling things in my stories, to making things wear masks, to telling my stories through masks. But my mother tells her stories openly, as she has done so all her life—since she lived on her father's farm in Ohio, as she walked along the crowded 1930 Chicago streets, to my father overseas in her letters, to the five of us children, as we sat on her lap, as we played in the next room while she tended to our supper in the kitchen. She tells them to everyone, to anyone who will listen. She taught Linda to read her lips. I learn now to read her lips. (12)

Not by chance, the mother in the story taught her deaf daughter Linda to read her lips so that she could participate with her brothers in the storytelling moments of the family. Linda is presented as the one who had the great gift to understand the deep meaning beyond the words. The deepest meaning of the art of storytelling is eventually a direct communication of feelings and moods, entrusted to the written or spoken word.

At the end of the text, there is a last story our narrator wants to share with the readers, that of the encounter with death:

> And I imagine one last story.
> Diana and I are children. Our mother is still young. Diana and I are outside on the sidewalk playing and it's summer. And we are young and full of play and happy, and we see a dog, and

it comes toward us on the street. My sister takes my hand. She senses something, I think. The dog weaves side to side. It's sick, I think. Some kind of lather is on his mouth. The dog growls. I feel Diana's hand shake.

Now we are inside the house, safe, telling our mother. Linda, Bob, and Jim are there. We are all the same age, all children. Our mother looks outside, then walks to the telephone. She returns to the front windows. We try to look out the windows too, but she pushes the five of us away.

No, she says. I don't want any of you to see this.

We watch her watching. Then we hear the siren of a police car. We watch our mother make the sign of the Cross. Then we hear a shot. Another, I look at my sisters and brothers. They are crying. Worried, frightened, I begin to cry too.

Did it come near you? Our mother asks us. Did it touch you? Any of you? Linda reads her lips. She means the funny dog. Or does she mean the speeding automobile with its lights off? The Ohio doctors? The boy behind the alley gate? The shards of broken glass? The wolf surrounded by butterflies? The ten-and-a-half-pound baby?

Diana, the oldest, speaks for us. She says that it did not.

Our mother smiles. She sits with us. Then our father is with us. Bob cracks a smile, and everybody laughs. Alfie gives a bark. The seven of us sit closely on the sofa. Safe. (12-13)

Ardizzone's ideas about the role of the narrator and the importance of the point of view in a short story are openly expressed in this piece. The woman, the mother, stands between her children and the tragic scene taking place outside the house. She wants to protect them from seeing the final scene where someone finds a violent death—a wolf, a rabid man, a mafioso. We readers are not told. "I pray none of us looks at that animal's face" ("My Mother's Stories," 13).

১

Lost in the midst of confusion, haunted by the ghosts of his past as a soldier in the Vietnam war, the protagonist of another short story, "The Man in the Movie," is one of the most revealing and fascinating characters in Ardizzone's collection *The Evening News*. Deeply convinced that details are "what makes up this world" and that details can make the difference between life and death, this unusual character reminds the reader of some disquieting characters of a Joycean memory. The veteran in his agitated and obsessive wandering in Chicago, in fact, reminds the reader of the character of *Ulysses*, almost lost in the streets of Dublin, in the homonymous novel by Joyce. The soldier's "piece of truth" relies completely on the devastating experience of the war where he learnt to pay attention to any detail, even the least significant one in order to save his life as he repeats obsessively to himself as he wanders through Chicago's streets and alleys after a robbery and, most importantly, after having shot the owner who had tried to start the alarm.

> The trick to survival is to notice everything. It's the least significant details that are the most important, like suddenly not hearing birds or seeing something unusual move or not move in the bush, I must notice the details.
>
> ("The Man in the Movie," 82)

In addition to the reference to details and their significance in understanding the world around him, this passage especially reminds the reader that s/he must be vigilant in her/his own reading of Ardizzone's text(s). Here, for example, we find a nicely ironic situation in which, to use Ardizzone's own words, "the least significant details ... are [in fact] the most important." This implied self-reflexivity is further signaled in the very title of the short story, "The Man in the Movie," since while watching a movie we may easily lose track of those images that populate the margins of the screen and not the center. Such marginality, we know, often plays an important role in our viewing of a film.

ॐ

Disillusionment, fear, anxiety are, instead, the dominant feelings in Paul and Mary, the protagonists of "The Evening News." The arrival of their first baby causes them to fall in a negative and depressed mood that becomes more and more severe as they try to distillate some truth from every bit of the evening news relating about traumatic events taking place all over the world. As they wonder about the consequences of bringing a new life in this sad, confused world, they foresee dreadful sceneries about the end of the world, but nothing can bring peace and joy to their tormented lives. Ethnicity plays a significant part in this story since both of them are ethnic: Paul has Italian origins for which he feels nostalgia, while Mary, who is Hispanic, seems not to care so much about recovering her past, at least at the beginning of the story. The colors on the television screen are an open metaphor and a clear allusion to the ethnic theme and, in fact, it is Paul playing with the control knob of the colors. Paul is a professor of sociology, quite an interesting field of research, whose meaning turns out to be very relevant, as Tamburri states:

> [Sociology] is pertinent both to Paul's idealistic period of adolescent protests as a university student and metanarratively to the overall thematics of Ardizzone's fictional world of the ethnic. In both cases sociology proves significant: 1) it is the intellectual world in which he believes he can make a difference; 2) it is also the epistemological world that will allow him to understand better, perhaps, his own world experience as an Italian American. (Tamburri 30)

In a different narrative situation, only pieces of an intermittent dialogue between Maureen and Suor Bagnola, trigger the imagination of Gino, the young, fervent Catholic boy, protagonist of "The Eyes of the Children," a beautiful story set on Chicago's mixed-ethnic North Side. He's induced to believe that a miracle happened in the church of his school on a windy afternoon when two girls reach the courtyard of his school running and screaming, claiming to have met a bleeding man in the choir loft. Gino wants to believe that the bleeding man in the choir was Jesus, opening his arms to the two lucky girls. Ardizzone's narrative talent wraps the narration into a suspended and sacred atmosphere so that we readers learn the truth only in the epiphany, when the priest explains to the young boy at the end of the story that it was only vandalism. Gino's world—suddenly deprived of the great truth he had believed in for several hours—becomes "dark and big."

ৎ

The exceptional figure of the "father" in Ardizzone's novel, *In the Garden of Papa Santuzzu*, who seems to have genuinely internalized the lesson according to which nobody has the whole truth deserves considerable attention. This novel consists of different tales, whose detailed descriptions have the power to evoke a world distant in time—the story takes place during the Risorgimento—and in space—the story's protagonists live in Sicily:

> Once there was a poor, but honest man, *un'omu d'onuri*, a man of honor, who worked the whole day—day after day—in the unrelenting heat of the blazing sun, scratching the pitiful dirt at his feet with a wooden hoe, coaxing the useless dust first this way and then that way, like a mother combing her feverish child's thin, dulled hair, urging the earth to release something he and his children and wife might eat, so that they might live to work beneath the scorching sun another day, and not starve. (1)

In this highly symbolic novel, Ardizzone's talent as a storyteller, as well as his deep interest in oral history appears to be connected to both Italian and English literary tradition. He makes use of Boccaccio's artifice of the frame and caesurae and Chaucer's frescoes of a distant past. The novel's incipit reminds the readers of the style of the folktales and Calvino's *Italian Folktales* turned out to be highly influential on Ardizzone's style:

> I was working on a scene in which a mother is telling a story. About that time Calvino's book, *Italian Folktales*, came out and I realized that other people tell stories, too. I was after the sense of the oral story and the way that aunts and uncles don't tell you literally what happens; they relate it metaphorically and leave it to you to read between the lines.
>
> (Gardaphé, *Dagoes Read*, 29)

Soon after having announced the name of the man ("The man's name was Papa Santuzzu" [1]), and after having established the relation existing between the man and the addressee of the whole novel ("He was your nonnu, father of your father" [1]), the narrator declares the content of the text and the final aim of her narration openly:

> This is his story and the story of his children. It's also the story of people like me, whose destiny was to marry into the Girgenti family. God willing, one day you'll pick up the thread and tell these stories to children of your own. May you be blessed, figghiu miu, with a fair wife and many children! May you have a clear gaze and a strong back! (1)

In *The Garden of Papa Santuzzu*, the resistant voice of Rosa Dolci—the storyteller who binds together the different pieces—is an extraordinary example of "the continuous importance of voice—libratory, healing, resistant—within the mouth of ordinary folk whose thoughts and beliefs were neither heard or respected much in the old or the new worlds" as Mary Jo Bona stated in her *By the Breath of Their Mouths* (5). Ardizzone's characters seem to share an oral tradition, based on "the fact that the characters don't read, that they *tell* the stories they have heard before and will tell again" ("Interview with Tony Ardizzone," 209). The physical description of Papa Santuzzu is the portrait of *italianità*:

> Well, his skin was as dark as an olive soaked in brine. His nose was long and sharp, like the beak of a great bird. He had a big black moustache that drooped next to his chin. He wore a gray cap to protect his head from the sun. You could see at once in his brown eyes that he was gentle. When he laughed, your mouth had no choice but to laugh, too. (2)

The physical references in this passage recall both the stereotyped descriptions of Italians at the beginning of the twentieth century especially in the various media as well as some descriptions that Ardizzone himself adopted in some of his short stories.

Papa Santuzzu's unforgettable laughter is due to bring him good luck since luck is like a person's shadow that chases those who flee from it (*In the Garden*, 3). Magic realism—a critical category often applied to the works of Ardizzone—is often used to represent unusual events or illogical outcome of situations, as it happens in this novel with the sudden apparition of the tiny spirit in the melon Papa Santuzzu finds "trapped in the tangle of thorns [...] a small and modest melon, hardly worth eating" (*In the Garden*, 6):

> Papa Santuzzu [...] tore the melon from its vine, then managed with his knife to slit the fruit open. Inside the slit crouched a tiny spirit. The spirit tried to escape, but Papa Santuzzu caught it and held it fast in his hand.
> "Let me go!" the spirit cried. "Let me go!"
> "Not until you've helped me," Papa Santuzzu said.
> So the spirit stopped squirming and told Papa Santuzzu he could have three wishes. (6-7)

In the very moment, Papa Santuzzu realizes he can wish for something, he tries to solve his problems—he wanted Gabriella, the donkey, to be free from the thorns of the bushes and the field to be cleared—and then he becomes more ambitious.

> With his last wish, Papa Santuzzu was tempted to ask that the field be filled with grain. But instead, maybe for the first time in his life, your father's father stopped thinking like a wretched labourer whose sole purpose was to put coins into another man's pocket. Papa Santuzzu took a gulp and wished for a house as big as the baron's. At that point the spirit made fun of him and scampered away, after having replied: "Hey [...] do you think that if I had a house as big as the *baruni*'s I'd be living in this scrawny melon?" (8-9)

The first metamorphosis of the novel has already been acted out: Papa Santuzzu was turned from a "wretched labourer" into "a man" with ambition and desires to be fulfilled. A few lines after, Papa Santuzzu is said to have dreams:

> He stared at the bits of light dotting the deep and endless sky, and just then a shooting star arched westward across the heavens. (8)

And what he is dreaming about are endless possibilities, "even more fantastic than the perfect run of cards that had brought him Gabriella or the spirit that had nearly granted him the baruni's house." (*In the Garden*, 8) He dreams "about a wonderful, faraway land [...] a marvellous new land." He dreams about "La Merica," a land he depicts through a series of hyperboles in climax, moving beyond what Papa Santuzzu knows best, the fields:

> This place was said to have such vast, fertile fields that all you had to do was to push a seed into the ground and it would grow!

You had to step back fast [...] or the plant's stalk would knock you right down!" (8)

Then Papa Santuzzu starts thinking about the rivers and the seas —"leaping with fish"—and the mountains filled with gold, "so much gold that roads were actually paved with it!" (8). In this abundance, "[n]o one went to sleep hungry!" (8). In any of the three "villages" that made up America—New York, Brazil and Argentina—"a working man could earn a real bundle" (8).

Once he realized that the right and only thing to do was leave the sad conditions of living in Sicily to reach "La Merica," Papa Santuzzu sees the departure of his seven sons who will settle in the New World waiting for their father to reach them. But in the little piece of truth Santuzzu has learned in his life, there's the strong belief that he can't leave his homeland. This truth is revealed when Salvatore, while working in the fields with Santuzzu and Gabriella, the donkey, "again saw the flying tuna" bringing in his mouth a message from Gaetanu and Luigi, who asked him to join them bringing the rest of the family with him.[10]

In this enchanting and tragic moment of the narrative Santuzzu is forced to explain why he will never leave Sicily and his wife Adriana, who is buried there. Through the metaphor of the rock and its pieces, Santuzzu gives voice to his inner feelings of belonging to his island.

"Do you remember that rock we found five springs ago," Papa Santuzzu said as he pointed toward a distant field, "or was

---

[10] In the magic style of the novel, a flying fish delivers messages from those who have already left Sicily for "La Merica" and this one recites as if follows: "'Brother,' the letter said, 'it's time that you joined us. Here are coins for five, the rope and a basket of food. Don't let go of the rope, no matter what. Bring Papa and the twins, Rosaria and Livicedda, as well as the infant Assunta. Tell everyone we miss and love them. Say a prayer on behalf of each of us on the ground beside our dearest mother's grave.'" (*In the Garden*, 14)

it seven, eight, nine, ten? [...] We worked on it for weeks. [...] You remember that in the end, [...] we decided that it wasn't a rock at all. It was a hard edge of the world."

"You said it was an edge of the bedrock, Papa. It was a part of the island of Sicilia herself," [Salvatore said.]

"A living edge of the world itself," Papa Santuzzu said. "I climbed down into the hole around it and could hear the earth breathe. [...] I didn't want to leave there [...]. The rock's breathing seemed to match my own." (16)

Santuzzu is one thing with his island: he cannot be removed from it since he *is* the island. In such a perfect identification with his land, Santuzzu finds his own identity, his "breathing," and this keeps him alive. His children, being "pieces of rock" can be carried away from the land and are, therefore, free to leave Sicily:

"[P]ieces of rock that have broken off," Papa Santuzzu said, "even very big pieces, in time you can drag them or break them apart and carry them from the fields. But you can't move the earth itself.

For several moments he patted Gabriella's side. "You know, when I started all this years ago, I think at first I meant to move only one rock. Or maybe three. I should have remembered that once you begin clearing a field of stone, you're tempted to clear it all." He gave us a hard stare. "Don't leave anyone behind, you two, you understand? Not Livicedda and Rosaria, or even Assunta. Do I have your promise on that?" Salvatore nodded. "But don't be fools and try to move the world itself." (17)

It is probably the most tragic moment of the novel, the acme of a narrative that is only at its very beginning, as properly remarked by Rosa's narrative voice:

Papa Santuzzu opened his arms, and his third and youngest son embraced him. Then I embraced him and covered his face with my kisses and tears. By then I was one of his children, too. I didn't know how to tell him good-bye. There were no words to say. (17)

A series of changes describes the difficult process of assimilation of Papa Santuzzu's sons in America, the most powerful of which is portrayed in "The Wolf of Girgenti." Here, Luigi Girgenti undergoes a process of transformation into a wolf, after having decided to reach the wolves "up in the hill, deep in the forest, calling to one another" (*In the Garden,* 72). Once he reached the *banditi's* camp, he eats their food until his stomach is full and, eventually, surrenders to the temptation of stealing some coins from a big sack of gold:

> In the blink of an eye, one coin hopped its way into my empty pocket. Then a second coin joined the first, then a third. That did it! A streak of lighting shot up from a fissure in the ground, right through the crack of my *culu.* You should have heard me holler! Then thick tufts of hair sprouted from every pore of my body. My back constricted and bucked and twisted me so fiercely that I fell down on all fours. My hands and feet shrivelled into paws. A bushy tail sprang out just above the spot where the lightning had got me. My skull collapsed and warped in shape. My ears stretched up and out, gravitating to the top of my skull. My nose grew so keen and pointed that I could smell the colors in the air. My eyes shrunk to the size of *ceci* beans. Teeth long as nails protruded wildly from my muzzle. I gave mother moon a howl. I'd transformed into a wolf! (76)

Suddenly hit by lightning, Luigi Girgenti is transformed into a wolf, this wild animal being, in fact, an allegory for the *banditi*:

> [w]olves are often used to symbolize characteristics associated with the gangster: success, perseverance, intuition, independence, thought, intelligence. Ardizzone utilizes these in creating his *banditi* (bandits). There are local men who fight for the honor of their existence. Ardizzone flips the historical association of the

> Mafia with the barons by having his Mafiosi or *banditi* become the wolves who fight those in power.
>
> (Gardaphé, *From Wiseguys to Wise Men*, 165)

Not by chance, "[t]he typical weapon of the Sicilian Mafioso is the lupara, a short-barreled shotgun good for spraying the shot out to drive away packs of wolves" (Gardaphé, *From Wiseguys to Wise Men*, 165).

After having said goodbye to his sons leaving for "La Merica," a world of wonders and richness he will never see, Papa Santuzzu comes to terms with his decision to stay, while his descendants on the other side of the ocean will have to face the fact that "[e]very immigrant has a double identity and a double vision, suspended between an old and a new home, an old and a new self" (Grunwald 43). Papa Santuzzu, therefore, avoids the whole issue at the heart of migration and border-crossing, finding *a new home*. A *home*, in fact, cannot be found again elsewhere if not in the old place we are used to calling *home*, as Henry Grunwald wrote in his autobiography, *One Man's America*:

> The very notion of a new home is absurd, as impossible as the notion of new parents. One's parents are who they are: one's home is what it is. It is one's birthplace, ratified by memory. It is the nursery wallpaper, the family dining room, the stories and songs that surround one's growing up.
>
> Yet home, like parentage, must be legitimized through love; otherwise it is only an accident of geography or biology. Most immigrants to America received little love in their homelands or saw it betrayed; whether they starved in Ireland, or were persecuted in czarist Russia and Nazi Germany, or, later, were driven into the sea in Vietnam, they did not abandon their countries— their countries abandoned them. In America they sought not only a new life, but a new love. (43)

২

In 2010, Ardizzone went back to the crucial issue of identity in his novel, *The Whale Chaser*, where the search for identity meets another theme, that of the border-crossing, in the ethnic character of Vincent Sansone, a young American boy with Italian origins who leaves Chicago—the "*stinking onion creek* in the tongue of its First Nation people. City of big shoulders [...] tool maker, stacker of wheat, hog butcher for the world" (*The Whale Chaser*, 11)—to move to Tofino in search of his identity and of a new life.

Ardizzone's novel dwells insistently on the meaning of crossing a border connected with the idea of putting distance between the protagonist and the place that is home to him, Chicago. Eventually, this distance will be—more than everything else—distance between the past and the present. If crossing the border, in fact, means traversing a frontier, a barrier, going beyond some limit of sort, it is the fundamental action connected with migration which itself implies movement, crossings, journeying between origins and destination (Carravetta 12).

Mobility is, in fact, a primary feature of Vince who walks in his Italian predecessors' steps when moving from Chicago to Tofino: the two places are so different from each other that it is possible to see them as dialectical opposites in the protagonist's journey from his origins—genetic, ethnic, familial origins—to his destination—the future outcome of his personality. What Vince gains, though, in his crossing the border, is a *sguardo mobile*, that is a different, not fixed way of looking at things and people around him. He becomes generous, open-minded, forgiving: he learns how painful making mistakes can be. His experiences in Chicago first, and in Tofino later, soon become metaphors in his life, cognitive symbols enabling the character to read through the loomings of his past. His journey to Tofino can also be interpreted as a redemptive path toward the truth, as a lesson on the difficulties of crossing obstacles in life to reach a closer contact with one's own identity. In the novel, Vincent comes to terms with his past and its ghosts and this is the first step towards his claim for an identity which will only be reached—though partially and temporarily—at the end of the novel:

> [T]he past echoes in my ears. I listen to the voices. Like something out of Shakespeare, ghosts from the past rise and swell and splash angrily against one another, then dissolve like a surfacing gray whale's blow into spray and foam and the least bits of light.
>
> (The Whale Chaser, 12)

Identity for Vincent is a work in progress and the unpredictable result of a dialectical opposition between past and present, without any possibility to change the past and without any chance to come to terms with pain, nostalgia, disillusionment, loss. All these emotions, in fact, are the result of his feeling guilty for the wrong turns he took, for the blind choices he made and for the abrupt, often nonsensical, decisions he made. All these feelings are obviously part of his own identity: experiencing them, in fact, gives the protagonist a unique possibility to get in touch with the kind of boy he used to be in the past and, as a consequence, gives him the opportunity to understand why he has become the man he is now.

> Sometimes I talk to the ghosts over the noise of the boat's engine. I invite them to join me, take a seat, go over how things might have turned out differently. Sometimes in winter I walk through town in the persistent rain, reasonably dry inside my gumboots and Smelly Hansen, and past hovers along the sidewalk beside me, then reaches inside my shirt past my scar and squeezes my heart so firmly that I have to stop and bend at the waist, barely able to breathe. I sip bits of breath as the episode passes and I calm myself. Together, the ghosts and I go over everything that happened, and I think of all the things I might have done, or not done, all the words I should have said and all I should have never given voice to. (12)

Sensing the impossibility to move the pawns back and forth in his past—scared of not being able to move the pawns in his future either—Vince reaches the harsh conclusion that we are nothing more than spectators in a life whose grander designs are already completed for us. Here lies all the beauty and significance of this novel. Here is the little piece of truth Vincent conquered throughout his many painful geographical and emotional border-crossings:

> [A]s my heart slows I wonder if it's naïve to believe that people can control the directions their lives take. Oh, sure, I think, we can change the scenery and select a few of the cosmetic details, opt for a soup over the salad, the blue shirt over the brown, the rutted roads of Tofino over the streets and alleys of Chicago, but as for the grander designs our lives inscribe, aren't we ultimately little more than spectators? Tourists in orange deck suits, out on the blue water, chasing whales? (13)

As "tourists ... out on the blue water, chasing whales," Ardizzone's characters prove that truth and identity are tightly connected. In their attempt to grasp the truth about their past, in their tenacious effort to get in touch with their ethnicity, nobody has ever to tell the whole truth, since nobody can ever find a way to grasp an indisputable truth about their magmatic feelings.

Identity, therefore, is nothing more than the enigmatic result of numerous tiles not perfectly matching one with the other.

WORKS CITED

Alba, Richard. *Italian Americans: Into the Twilight of Ethnicity*, Englewood Cliffs, NJ: Prentice Hall, 1985.

Ardizzone, Tony. *In the Name of the Father*. Garden City, NY: Doubleday, 1978.

————. *Heart of the Order*. New York: Henry Holt and Company, 1986.

————. *The Evening News. Stories*. Athens and London: U Georgia P, 1986.

————. *In The Garden of Papa Santuzzu*. New York: Picador USA / St. Martin's P, 1999.

_____. *Larabi's Ox: Stories of Morocco*. Minneapolis: Milkweed Editions, 1992; republished as *The Arab's Ox. Stories of Morocco*. New York: Bordighera P, 2018.

_____. "Interview with Tony Ardizzone." By Cristina Bevilacqua. *Italian Americana* 19.2 (Summer 2001): 207-213.

_____. *The Whale Chaser*. Chicago: Academy Chicago Publishers, 2010.

Bona, Mary Jo. *By the Breath of Their Mouths, Narrative of Resistance in Italian America*. Albany, NY: SUNY P, 2010.

Carravetta, Peter. *After Identity. Migration, Critique, Italian American Culture*. New York: Bordighera P, 2017.

Fischer, Michael J. "Ethnicity and the Post-Modern Arts of Memory." In *Writing Culture: The Poetics and Politics of Ethnography*. James Clifford and George E. Marcus, eds. Berkeley: U California P, 1986.

Gardaphé, Fred L., *Dagoes Read: Tradition and the Italian/American Writer*. Toronto: Guernica Editions, 1996.

_____. *Italian Signs, American Streets: The Evolution of Italian American Narrative*. Durham, NC: Duke UP, 1996.

Gardaphé, Fred and Tano Gullo. "Palermo, Brooklyn. I siciliani d'America che raccontano l'isola senza stereotipi." *La Repubblica* (16 June 2013).

Grunwald, Henry. *One Man's America*. New York: Anchor Books, 1997.

Magrini, Giacomo. "Il racconto (di) gravidanza." In *Conversazione su Tolstoj*. C. Graziadei and D. Colombo, eds. Roma: Artemide, 2011.

Ovid. *Metamorphoses*. Translated by David Raeburn. New York: Penguin, 2004. 3. 395-397.

Tamburri, Anthony Julian, Paul A. Giordano, and Fred L. Gardaphé, eds. *From the Margin: Writings in Italian Americana*, West Lafayette, IN: Purdue UP, 1991.

Tamburri, Anthony Julian. *A Semiotic of Ethnicity: In (Re)cognition of the Italian/American Writer*. Albany, NY: SUNY P, 1998.

An "Eye-talian" in the New World: Cognitive Estrangement and Diglossia in Antonio Gallenga's Early Italian American Narrative*

Giulia Iannuzzi
UNIVERSITY OF TRIESTE

There is a promising territory of theoretical dialogue between Italian American and speculative fiction studies, which may be developed starting from *estrangement mechanisms* as a common matrix between the *disadjustment* experienced by the subject during the migration process, and the projective and extrapolative mechanisms typically exploited in speculative fiction narratives to imagine future or alternate worlds. In some ways, the migrant has encountered in actuality that radical *otherness* that speculative fiction puts on page, be it in a New World in which the utopian imagination that governed expectations is put to the test or in a new idea and narration of the self, emerging after deep processes of identity negotiations, when in contact with new social groups, forms of collective organization, physical places, languages and mindsets.

Darko Suvin, pre-eminent scholar in the foundation and affirmation of science fiction studies in the English-speaking academic world (and beyond), derived his concept of *cognitive estrangement*, on the one hand, from the Formalist notion of *ostranenie* theorized by Viktor Shklovsky as the elective instrument of art to disrupt our automatic mechanisms of perception and conceptualization,[1]

---

* I wish to express my deepest gratitude to Leonardo Buonomo and Nicholas Grosso for all their valuable suggestions and notes on the first draft of this essay.
[1] See, for example, "The purpose of art is to impart the sensation of things as they are perceived and not as they are known. The technique of art is to make objects

and on the other, from Bertoldt Brecht's closely related but Marx-inflected development (*alienation*), arguing that it was fundamental to distinguish the concept for the genre of science fiction writing. The key to *cognitive estrangement* is the presence, in a story, of what Suvin called a *novum*, namely an element which, because of its absolute newness, impedes our automatic conceptualization, inviting us to imagine a different way of conceiving our subjectivity and our world.[2] I think that the *displacement* experienced in the course of migration[3] provides significant moments of *disadjustment*, having a similar effect to a *novum*, and foster more complex processes of identity problematization and critical reflections on society, which we may now read in Italian American narratives, including early narratives—written and/or published and/or referring to experiences occurring before the 1880s.[4]

'unfamiliar,' to make forms difficult, to increase the difficulty and length of perception because the process of perception is an aesthetic end in itself and must be prolonged. Art is a way of experiencing the artfulness of an object; the object is not important." Viktor Shklovsky, "Art as Technique" (1917), in Julie Rivkin and Michael Ryan, eds., *Literary Theory: An Anthology* (New York: Blackwell, 1998) 15-21, qt. 16. Cfr. Carlo Ginzburg, "Making Things Strange: The Prehistory of a Literary Device" (1996), in *Wooden Eyes: Nine Reflections on Distance*, tr. by Martin Ryle and Kate Soper (New York: Columbia UP, 2001) 1-24.

[2] Suvin went further, proposing a rather exclusive definition of science fiction based on the idea of cognitive estrangement, which emphasizes the rational scientific dimension of the genre and rigorously excludes fantasy fiction. Subsequent generations of scholars have pointed out the limitations of Suvin's approach and were able to refine it (for example, by replacing the idea of *reality*) with a more epistemologically negotiable concept of *paradigm of reality*. See Patrick Parrinder, ed., *Learning from Other Worlds: Estrangement, Cognition and the Politics of Science Fiction and Utopia* (Liverpool: Liverpool UP, 2000) esp. 36-50.

[3] Teresa Fiore, "Lunghi viaggi verso 'Lamerica' a casa: straniamento e identità nelle storie di migrazione italiana," *Annali d'Italianistica*, 24, *Negotiating Italian Identities* (2006), 87-106; Ginzburg, "Making Things Strange."

[4] Francesco Durante, *Italoamericana: Storia e letteratura degli italiani negli Stati Uniti, 1776-1880* (Milan: Mondadori, 2001).

NARRATING A NEW SELF

Antonio Gallenga's autobiography, *Episodes of My Second Life (American and English Experiences)*, is a case in point. Published in London in 1884-85 (in two volumes) and again in Philadelphia in 1885,[5] the *Episodes* narrate Gallenga's life starting with his decision to move to America to where he embarked in 1836, at the age of 26.

Antonio Gallenga (alias Luigi Mariotti), 1810-1895, was born in Parma; and was a medical student before taking part in the 1831 insurrection in Parma. He became member of *La giovine Italia*, and in 1833 planned the assassination of Carlo Alberto, King of Sardinia, but in Turin he changed his mind and did not carry out the plan. In 1834, working as private tutor for a Neapolitan diplomat, he was in Malta, and then in Tangiers, from where he set sail for New York in 1836. From New York he went to Boston, where he did not manage to obtain the teaching position he wanted at Harvard University, but worked in David Mack's School for Young Ladies. In 1839 he moved to London, where he collaborated with cultural reviews, and in 1840 he was in Florence. After a new attempt at teaching in Nova Scotia he went back to London, where he continued his writing activities and had contacts with Mazzini. In 1848, back in Italy, the Alfieri government gave him a diplomatic post in Frankfurt.[6]

Between 1849 and 1859 he taught at University College in London before being hired by *The Times*, for which he wrote reportages and analysis on Italy (1859-60) as well as the United States during

---

[5] Antonio Gallenga, *Episodes of My Second Life (American and English Experiences) (1884-85)* (Philadelphia: J. B. Lippincott & co., 1885). Subsequent quotes are taken from this edition.

[6] The diplomatic appointment was short-lived after he attempted to promote an alliance between Sardinia and Austria, which would have left Lombardy and the duchies abandoned to their own fates instead of defending the cause of Italian independence, as he was supposed to do. Other political parentheses will come between 1854 and 1856, when he was elected to the Piedmont parliament, and in 1861, with the election in the national parliament.

the Civil War (1863), Denmark during the conflict with Prussia in 1864, revolutionary Spain (1865-66, 1868-69), Prussia (1866, 1870-71), Cuba (1873), Istanbul (1875). He was fired in 1884 after the English first edition of the *Episodes*, in which he made an open depiction of *The Times'* internal affairs. He retired with his second wife to the countryside in Llandogo, where he died in 1895.[7]

The first half of the *Episodes* is dedicated to his years in the United States (1836-38), the second to the years 1839-80, emphasizing the important role the American experience played in the author's life. In the *Episodes*, it might be argued that Gallenga is testifying on the migration experience as "the ultimate form of cognitive estrangement." "On the 15th of August, 1936, I was born again:" no formulation could be more effective than the one forecasting the trip to America at the beginning of the first chapter of the *Episodes*, to describe how deep the turning point constituted by the migration movement affected the author's identity, its construction and narration. Antonio Gallenga's autobiography *Episodes of My Second Life: (American and English Experiences)*, offers us an incredible testimony of an early Italian American experience,

---

[7] Scholarship on Gallenga includes mostly historical reconstructions of his life, but the most exhaustive is still Aldo Garosci, *Antonio Gallenga: Avventura, politica e storia nell'Ottocento italiano* (Turin: Einaudi, 1964); Garosci's biography was preceded by Hugh Chisholm, ed. "Gallenga, Antonio Carlo Napoleone," in *Encyclopædia Britannica*, 11th ed. (New York: Cambridge UP, 1911); and followed by briefer entries in biographical dictionaries and encyclopedias: Luca Codignola, "Gallenga, Antonio Carlo Napoleone," in Chiara Evangelista, ed., *I primi italiani in America del Nord. Dizionario biografico dei liguri, piemontesi e altri. Storie e presenze italiane tra Settecento e Ottocento* (Reggio Emilia: Diabasis per la Fondazione Casa America, 2009) 103-106; Giuseppe Monsagrati, "Gallenga, Antonio Carlo Napoleone," in *Dizionario Biografico degli Italiani* 51 (1998), http://www.treccani.it/biografico/, *ad vocem*. Especially on the Boston years: Renzo Dionigi, *An Italian Exile in Brahmin Boston 1836-1839: Antonio Gallenga* (Como: Insubria UP, 2006); on the English years: Toni Cerutti, *Antonio Gallenga: An Italian Writer in Victorian England* (Oxford: Oxford UP for the University of Hull, 1974); of some interest on the experience at the Harvard School for Young Ladies: Claudia Biraghi, "Following in the Footsteps of Antonio Gallenga," *New England Ancestors* 7.1 (Winter 2006): 29-31.

marked by a high degree of literary and linguistic self-awareness and by a relevant distance between narrating and narrated "I"s. It might be worth emphasizing that, as we shall see in subsequent paragraphs, Gallenga's migration was professionally driven: a comparable cognitive estrangement would be all the more striking for people following his steps with a far less secure professional and personal situation.

The narration of the self epitomizes the migration experience as a source of estrangement, underlined by the presence of mark-edly discrete narrating and narrated "I"s, of which the linguistic self-consciousness (of the narrator *and* the character) is a conspicuous correlative objective. The relationship between different selves, belonging to different moments in time, is made more complex by the relatively long period elapsed between the narrated events and the actual writing—almost 50 years—and by the literary self-awareness of the author. Gallenga is a learned man; during his political exile he was first in Corsica, and then in Tangiers, earning a living as a teacher of Italian—or as he puts it ironically "a dealer in participles"[8] just as many of his compatriots in the United States during the same years.[9]

The text is interspersed with comments and judgments offered by Gallenga the narrator, on the actions and thoughts of the nar-rated Gallenga, with a retrospective gaze that reveals the extent to which the experience changed him and how he perceived himself, often in an amusing way, occasionally patronizing his younger self. For example, the captain of the ship *Independence* taking him to New York (so much for "talking names!") "came up to the ideal I

---

[8] Gallenga, *Episodes of My Second Life*, 8, cf. Durante, *Italoamericana*, 203.

[9] Emilio Goggio, "Italian Educators in Early American Days," *Italica* 8.1 (1931): 5-8; Howard R. Marraro, "Pioneer Italian Teachers of Italian in the United States," *The Modern Language Journal* 28.7 (1944): 555-82; Joseph J. Fucilla, *The Teaching of Italian in the United States: A Documentary History* (New York: American Association of Teachers of Italian, 1967).

had, *in my silly imagination,* conceived of the typical Yankee" (Gallenga, *Episodes,* 17; emphasis added). Gallenga would soon move to Boston, but his first stop was in New York, that

> might at that time be described as a town with one street. Broadway was its only real thoroughfare ... I had seen nothing like it, unless it might be Toledo at Naples, — a street which might boast ten times the noise but not half the actual movement of this transatlantic Babylon. ... The impression of novelty, however, was not very deep, and soon wore off. ... *What struck me as the wonder of wonders in the place was "to see myself there."*
>
> "What!" I said to myself, "was I really in America, — alone in a world to which I came unbidden, unexpected, utterly unknown, with barely the most rudimental acquaintance with its language, and no knowledge of its ways, its laws and customs, — without one friend, with credentials the value of which was yet to be tested, and with only forty poor dollars on my pocket?" (Gallenga, *Episodes,* 29-30; emphasis added)

That "[t]he impression ... soon wore off" is not exactly true: the text is scattered with depictions of people, their customs, places, the narrating self always commenting, explaining and putting into perspective what his young eyes registered, with an informative attitude, in its depiction of Boston Brahim society, religion, politics, customs, and culture derived from the prolific activity of *reportage* writing which Gallenga did for the London *Times* between 1849 and 1859.

Many other descriptions follow of the American streets and crowds — in Boston for example, "the Athens of the United States, and the 'Hub of the Universe'," where the young Gallenga wandered around in great need and difficulty (being out of a job and with no friends to help him, in a situation that seemed briefly to be hopeless), while the older Gallenga comments "All this seemed very hard to me at the time. But I have learned what the world is since...." (Gallenga, *Episodes,* especially 71, 58-60, 61-62).

An *Eye-talian* in Boston Brahmim Society

Focusing attention on the language and specifically on peculiar expressions of literary self-awareness,[10] in Gallenga's case we find a particular, linguistic self-consciousness, which is possible thanks to Gallenga being a learned person[11] and partly a consequence of the intellectual distance that separates the narrating and the narrated "I"s.

Teacher of Italian and then Modern Languages, amateur writer, the young Gallenga in Tangiers also composed, in Italian, "*Romanze*, or ballads on chivalrous subjects ... attuning my verses to some of Bellini's airs, popular at that epoch. They belonged to what was called the 'romantic school', based on the study of German and English literature, of which Manzoni, Grossi, Berchet, and other Lombards had taken the lead" (Gallenga, *Episodes*, 132), poems the reading of which will be friendly and affably demanded by Henry Wadsworth Longfellow, at the time Professor of European Languages at Harvard, whom Gallenga met during his months of teaching at the Harvard Young Ladies' Academy of Cambridge, Massachusetts.[12]

---

[10] In devoting specific attention to the language and to the peculiar expression of linguistic self-awareness, we are following Martino Marazzi, *A occhi aperti: Letteratura dell'emigrazione e mito americano* (Milan: FrancoAngeli, 2011).

[11] Among the literary references that punctuate the text, Dante appears as a milestone of the Italian canon (Gallenga, *Episodes of My Second Life* 4, 41, 63, 64, 83, 87, 103, 140, 148, 221, 226, 319, 331, 372, 374, 451). Dante is quoted by the narrator to comment on what happens to his young self (e.g. "the salt that savors other people's bread," 4), on various subjects, often as a life mentor or historical point of reference (41, 140, 319, 374, 451) and as a father of the Italian identity and national cause (along with Machiavelli, 372); it is a topic of conversation and learned discussions with Pietro Bachi and Pietro D'Alessandro (63-64), of teaching (83, 87, 221, 226, 331), of translation (by Longfellow, 103). Other "literary founding fathers" of Italian identity appear, including Pellico, Alfieri, Manzoni, Foscolo. Cf. Gallenga's essays and companions of Italian literature, such as his article on "Romantic Poetry in Italy," *The North American Review* XLVII (1838); *Italy: Past and Present*, 2 vols. (J. Chapman, 1848-49).

[12] The Academy has been more recently identified with the School for Young

While reporting on his American experience, the narrator often describes the struggle of his young self with spoken English (Gallenga, *Episodes*, 17, 52). During a conversation with Edward Everett, the Governor of Massachusetts,[13] the narrator notes: "Though he was a great linguist, it was only in cases of extreme necessity that he spoke in any other language than his own, — his principle being that if one of the talkers was to be embarrassed and at a disadvantage it should be rather his interlocutor than himself; whilst for my own part I was glad that such was his choice, as when any language has to be murdered I always prefer that it should be any other than mine" (Gallenga, *Episodes*, 36).

While trying to improve his English, he received precious help from a woman, a widow, at the first boarding-house he stayed at in Boston. The young Gallenga took a fancy to her (the narrator commenting "What defence [sic] I had against her?" [Gallenga, *Episodes*, 55]) and she gave him some English lessons: "There was an ecstasy of the senses, but there was also improvement to the mind, as I watched the movements of her lips and the expression of her eyes, to catch the peculiar lisp of the 'th,' the hissing of the 'sh,' the stronger or softer aspiration of the 'h'" (Gallenga, *Episodes*, 56).

Along with his own personal difficulties and struggles, Gallenga's being a foreigner was often exposed — deliberately or not — by others, singling him out, calling him "*eye-talian*" or "*signiò*" or "*signor*" (Gallenga, *Episodes*, 50 and ff., 57 and ff), as much as for his own communication shortcomings in everyday life, let alone the limitations posed by a poor mastery of the language in the image of the self presented in social and professional relationships (e.g. lacking ease, self confidence and naturalness in verbal interaction, which was felt all the more important by a professional lan-

---

Ladies directed in Cambridge by David Mack (imprecisely mentioned as "Marx" in the *Episodes*): Dionigi, *An Italian Exile in Brahmin Boston 1836-1839*, 99 and ff.; Biraghi, "Following in the Footsteps of Antonio Gallenga," 29.

[13] Dionigi, *An Italian Exile* 47-53, esp. note 115 for further references.

guage teacher and writer, projecting himself as a well educated person):

> The reader must not imagine that I had been very ready with my English even in my intercourse with Mr. Everett, Mr. Quincy, or young Mills, educated men though they were, who spoke slowly and deliberately, shaping their sentences in that manner and giving them those turns which they thought could best convey their meaning to one who knew only as much of English as book-learning could impart. With illiterate persons, as those only conversant with one language may in our days be called, as with mere children, the beginning is much harder; but when you perceive that they have only one word for an idea, when they insist on screaming out that word till they think they have overcome your deafness, somehow you get on better, – in this as in any other study necessity being after all the best mistress. (Gallenga, *Episodes*, 52-53)

Given the efforts Gallenga made during his first twelve months in the US to became fluent enough to work as a teacher, it came as the highest mark of praise to be asked by Henry Ware Jr.— professor of pulpit eloquence and pastoral care at the Harvard Divinity School, and co-editor of the *North American Review*—to lecture at Harvard, where he had not been able to fulfill his ambition of obtaining a professorship in Italian (a position filled by Pietro Bachi).[14] While the invitation came after the circulation of a manuscript in which Gallenga mocked and parodied the style of previ-

---

[14] "'I maintain, that you have acquired a mastery over our language that seems to me surprising, and that I find in your manner something quaint and outlandish, maybe, but not un-English,—some happy turn of your Latin phrase into our Saxon idiom, by which you almost seem to teach us our English, and to find in it what we would vainly seek in it ourselves.' It may be easily believed that such words from such a man called up a flush of color on my cheeks. But I gulped down the emotion of gratified vanity that was rising in my breast, and answered, without affected humility" (Gallenga, *Episodes*, 129).

ous lecturers, the author still ironically lamented lacking confidence in speaking:

> how could I muster an accent that would make me intelligible? I can tell you that I hardly ever address a street-porter, a housemaid, or even the postman, to ask my way, without being met by a blank stare, and a *'Me no parle vous'*. ... Consciousness of unconquerable shyness disquieted me; and there were peculiar combinations of English consonants, such as the *w* and *wh* and still more the *s* after the *th* in *months*, *truths*, etc., to which my Italian teeth and lips positively refused to give utterance. (Gallenga, *Episodes*, 129, 132)

Proficiency and command of pronunciation were in fact perceived as markers of social position and/or integration, and the emerging of an Italian inflection was feared as comparable to the ones typical of low social statuses, or, when counterbalanced by the awareness of the richness and beauties of the native tongue, anyway as a limitation in the second language mastery, cause of unwelcome distinction: "We have also no aspirations in Italian, and, do what I might, I never felt sure that I would not, in an unguarded moment, drop my *h*'s like a cockney. The natural melody and smoothness of our Italian language, besides, rendered it extremely difficult to keep my intonation from falling into a monotonous *cantilena*, or sing-song" (Gallenga, *Episodes*, 52-53).

The contention that English is a language better learned by use than by the systematic study of the grammar (Gallenga, *Episodes*, 134, 152) had to come to terms with the necessity of becoming competent beyond mere correctness, to be able to give voice to one's literary aspirations,[15] in the persuasion that "[t]hought must come

---

[15] "[A] language like the English is best learned and written by use. Grammar, however, is as indispensable for a writer as drawing for an artist, and we must master it, no matter whether by precept or practice; there were a thousand pit-

forth soul and body from the brain that conceives it: it only lives through the words. Hence is translation so difficult" (Gallenga, *Episodes*, 155). Gallenga's Italian mindset inevitably appeared in his construction of sentences and speeches, but it may be forgiven, and even appreciated by his audience as "quaint and outlandish" (Gallenga, *Episodes*, 170), part of the speaker's personal style and competence in a foreign language which enjoys the association with the community of Italian exiles in Boston, a small group of well educated, literate people including Pietro Bachi and Pietro D'Alessandro (Durante, *Italoamericana*, 201-237, 292-311).

The relationship, therefore, between the narrated and narrator and English is an effective synecdoche of Gallenga's relationship with the migration experience both in the present of the story and of the discourse. In the present of the story language is an "objective correlative" of the cognitive estrangement experienced through the migration process, symptom of the young Gallenga's relative extraneousness in the new context; in the present of the discourse, the narrator's reflections on his past struggles with language effectively mark the distance between the narrated and narrating "I"'s (also, implicitly, being described in a text written in English). On the English backdrop, Italian language became part of a peculiar diglossia. Dante's speech, associated with the Risorgimento's exiles in the United States, acted, for Gallenga, as primary indicator of the self: a symptom of his otherness in the new country, but also a source of income, thanks to teaching positions, at the same time an element that prevented a full assimilation as part of the local elites, as well as a positive element in the building of a presentable social image of the self.

---

falls and snares about some parts of speech, and especially about the prepositions *in* and *on*, *at* and *to*, *by* and *with*, etc. But I aspired to something more than mere correctness. I wished my English to be as much as possible like that of the authors I most admired, Bulwer, Disraeli, Carlyle, Washington Irving, and the like" (Gallenga, *Episodes*, 152).

DISTANTIATING UTOPIA

Utopian projections[16] interact with identity-building processes in Italian American experience, an *American otherness* was repeatedly imagined and conceptualized at different levels and in different moments of the migration process. I am assuming as a working hypothesis that mechanisms of utopian (in the broader sense) extrapolation offered critical tools that authors were able to exploit while conceptualizing their experience of the North American *otherness*—which became an ideal mirror, and a vantage point from which to reflect on the present state of the country of origin and personal trajectory (a critical perspective that in recent years is being fruitfully applied to other cultural and/or linguistic areas, within the framework of postcolonial studies as it intersects with speculative fiction studies).[17]

In *Episodes of My Second Life*, we can notice a utopian drive at work in the building of certain expectations. Before arriving in the United States, the narrator came into contact with other people, who tended to present a positive image of the country. For example, when Gallenga decided to leave Tangiers, the English consul advised against England ("London, he said, was, for a friendless stranger, a terrible place. Competition in every branch of business was appalling, overwhelming, crushing," 10), and directed him to his American colleague, who, in turn, depicted an opposite image of the United States:

---

[16] Tom Moylan, *Demand the Impossible: Science Fiction and the Utopian Imagination* (1986) (New York: Lang, 2014); Tom Moylan and Raffaella Baccolini, eds., *Utopia Method Vision: The Use Value of Social Dreaming* (New York: Lang, 2007).

[17] E.g. Lyman Tower Sargent, "Utopianism and National Identity," *Critical Review of International Social and Political Philosophy* 3 (2000): 87-106; Ralph Pordzik, *The Quest for Postcolonial Utopia: A Comparative Introduction to the Utopian Novel in the New English Literatures* (New York: Lang, 2001); Pordzik, "A Postcolonial View of Ireland and the Irish Conflict in Anglo-Irish Utopian Literature since the Nineteenth Century," *Irish Studies Review* 9.3 (2001): 331-46.

"A big country that! Room for everybody there! You will find your place ready for you as if you had bespoken beforehand. It is of men like you that want is particularly felt in our trading community. We have plenty of storekeepers, land-agents, and politicians. Give us scholars and gentlemen, men of taste and refinement. I shall be more than happy—I shall be proud—to introduce you to the best of my acquaintance " (Gallenga, *Episodes*, 12-13)

The narrator was here reporting the American consul's words, while he himself appeared from the beginning to be more skeptical and aware of the uncertainties that lay ahead. In a chapter significantly entitled "The Pillars Of Hercules"—underlining that an invisible, yet intensely perceived line had been crossed—, the trip to America is described as an unsettling "leap in the dark:" "I had torn myself from my moorings, and was like a waif adrift in the ocean, with no other prospects on landing than to be launched into another unknown sea of trouble and dangers" (Gallenga, *Episodes*, 16). The decision was made, the young Gallenga had resolved to carry out his project, but there would appear to be no promises: "If I was to go, the sooner and the farther I went, the better. I would follow in the wake of Columbus and Cortes. Like the latter, I would burn my ships. Like the former, I would find a new world—a new life—or be drowned" (Gallenga, *Episodes*, 12). A sensation that the young Gallenga would not lose, even after arriving in New York and then Boston, when his new life had to be faced with all its (mostly financial and professional) difficulties: "I felt now, as I had expected, that it would not be without a struggle that I could obtain a footing on this slippery and stubborn though on the whole friendly and hospitable Yankee-land" (Gallenga, *Episodes*, 35).

When he spoke to the captain of the *Independence*, with his little English, "the dialogue soon sinking to a pattering monologue, in which all I could make out was that, what with the bigness of his country, the Boston gals, mint-juleps and sherry cobblers, and dollars, and again dollars, and many dollars, I had only to wait till I came in sight of Sandy Hook, and would soon see what a Paradise 'Merikey' would be for me" (Gallenga, *Episodes*, 18). While it is clear that the young Gallenga moved to the United States in search of a better professional position for himself, we can sense how the perspective of the narrator is weighing up the words of others critically even while he is reporting them, using the knowledge of his experience. Gallenga is reporting on an early American dream, quite conscious of its volatile substance.

The ship's captain's exaggeration is made rhetorically clear, the black cook on the *Independence* is a runaway slave from Georgia, the whole trip to New York is described as an excruciating experience (sea sickness and lethargy, equinoctial tempests, the "horrid monkey" [Gallenga, *Episodes*, 20] that the captain keeps as a pet, the shortage of food...). America is a land of trades, of dollars, of self-promotion,[18] but also of women's independence,[19] of the religious tolerance that characterizes New England after an early season of prosecution and bigotry (Gallenga, *Episodes*, 72),[20] and so on.

---

[18] When the young Gallenga is looking for a job as a private tutor and has to write an advertisement to be published in a newspaper in Boston, he is advised by Pietro Bachi: "'That I call blowing my own trumpet,' said I. 'Who do you expect will blow it for you?' Bachi answered. 'How do you like America?' And he went on without awaiting my answer: 'You will like it, I am sure. A great country, sir! Room for everybody here! ...' They were apparently the stereotyped phrases with which a stranger in want of employment was usually encouraged in the United States" (Gallenga, *Episodes*, 40, 48).

[19] For example: "I knew absolutely nothing of the nature and fashion of American women. Women in the States were then, and are still more now, absolute mistresses of their own world and of themselves" (Gallenga, *Episodes*, 54).

[20] Here the narrator comments with curiosity on Congregationalist communities and religious discussions which are "daily bread to the Anglo-Saxon race ... I had lived in countries where tyranny forced me to agree; I had come to countries where liberty allows them only to agree upon disagreeing" (Gallenga, *Episodes*, 75).

FINAL REMARKS

Sampling those *loci* in which Gallenga's narrating "I" throws a retrospective gaze on how his younger self, we focused how the migration experience, working as a source of estrangement, changed the author and his self-perception. The linguistic self-consciousness of the narrator—his working as a teacher of Italian and Modern Languages and his being part of Boston literary society, the relationship that the young Gallenga had with his first and second languages are important parts—and at the same time effective synecdoches—of his relationship with the migration experience, both in the present of the story, when the young Gallenga is struggling to find a socially and professionally well integrated and successful position, and in the present of the discourse, when an older Gallenga is looking back on his American experience.

Language contributed to how an *American otherness* was imagined and conceptualized by Gallenga. Here pragmatism and disenchantment—for example in the skeptical and/or ironic reception of ideal images of the US proposed by other characters, and in the lucid pondering of small and big difficulties encountered while trying to settle in the country of adoption—influenced identity-building processes, affecting the articulation of expectations, the metabolization of new encounters and circumstances, the creation of narratable images of America, and, in them, the (cultural, social, professional) placement/locating of the self.

The *Episodes* case shows how critical categories refined in speculative fiction studies such as cognitive estrangement and utopian projections can be put to use to better study and understand early Italian American narratives, bringing into focus the *disadjustment* experienced through migration and how it is at work in the complex identity negotiations of which these narratives are testimony.

Writing Poetry to Save Your Life:
Maria Mazziotti Gillan the Poet, the Healer

Elisabetta Marino
UNIVERSITY OF ROME "TOR VERGATA"

From her first collections of poetry, Maria Mazziotti Gillan has acted as a powerful healer, dressing her own deep wounds while curing the traumas of an entire generation of Italian Americans. Her urge to blend in, her aspiration not to be stigmatized, the shame she felt for displaying the wrong shade of white led her down a path of "a deeply internalized and complicated self-deprecation," in the words of Edvige Giunta (25), a grievous and tell-tale silence,[1] that only writing "as a source of personal and social healing" (134) could break. And suddenly, we begin to find in her lines both the charming storytelling of her parents, the long ancestral line of formidable women nested within her, and the cherished memories of food and rituals from a distant land juxtaposed against the compromises, the anxieties, and insecurities of being a second generation Italian American.

As I have elsewhere argued, in her more recent poems the focus has widened, stretching to include subjects every reader may

---

[1] One of the most remarkable examples of Maria Mazziotti Gillan's induced self-denigration is featured in her poem entitled "Public School No. 18. Paterson, New Jersey." Humiliated by her teacher's rebukes, at school she was "silent, grop[ed] for the right English/ Words, fear[ed] the Italian word/ [would] sprout from [her] mouth like a rose" (Mazziotti Gillan, *Where I Come from*, 12). As Anthony Julian Tamburri has pointed out, the difficulty to blend in and to fully conform to WASP standards led to the creation of a set of stereotypes of the Italian Americans that were "rampant at the end of the nineteenth century and through the first half of the twentieth century for sure" (*Re-reading Italian Americana*, 112).

relate to; her notion of *family* has expanded to embrace the whole of humankind.[3] Her concept of *home* now transcends cultural, ethnic, and geographical boundaries, being identified with the network of cherished interpersonal relationships each of us builds throughout our lives. Being such a committed, socially responsible writer, Maria Mazziotti Gillan decided to *carry her old* and new *delicious burdens, men and women* (to quote Walt Whitman),[4] teaching them how to work their way out of tragedy, leading them towards long-lasting healing. At times, in fact, we all undergo the ordeals suffered by immigrants: we all have to face and defeat our *individual crow*, "the critic in [our] head, that voice that tells [us] what is wrong with everything [we] do, that voice that makes [us] doubt [ourselves]," as Maria defines it in her handbook, *Writing Poetry to Save Your Life* (16). Using a symbol already established in her 1995 poem "The Crow," the reader is taken into her own disparaging inner dialogue: "you aren't really very much/ you guinea, you wop" (Mazziotti Gillan, *Where I Come From*, 68). Following the poet on her personal journey of healing leading to the 2013 volumes *Writing Poetry to Save your Life* and *The Silence in an Empty House*, the poet also reveals her artistic journey; initially writing from the margins of society, she reaches a place with these collections that is universal, poignantly delving into the shared experiences of love, loss, mourning, and rebirth.

---

[3] Focusing on *The Place I Call Home* (2012) by Maria Mazziotti Gillan and *Mystics in the Family* (2013) by Maria Famà, I have elucidated that their poems "no longer aim at overcoming the traumas of displacement, shame, and discrimination but rather deal with issues every reader can relate to, regardless of his/her background; they build bridges across the wider community; they encourage sympathy and understanding among people; they expose social problems, and provide successful tools to heal collective wounds and empower oneself" (Marino, *The Italian American Family*, 80).

[4] In his "Song of the Open Road," Whitman wrote: "Still here I carry my old delicious burdens;/ I carry them, men and women—I carry them with me/ wherever I go" (Whitman, *Leaves of Grass*, 177).

Writing Poetry to Save your Life is a book about the writing process, about enabling people to melt their sorrow into song, composing poems "that reach across the barriers of age, ethnicity, gender, social class to connect with all that is human inside us" (Mazziotti Gillan, *Writing Poetry*, 7). Mazziotti Gillan believes everybody has a story to tell, everybody can offer valuable contributions, even if at times we may remain silent, either for fear of being judged or simply because we cannot find the courage to *write aloud*. Language is inextricably linked with a tremendous power and in her poetry Mazziotti Gillan invites readers to seize upon this power, replacing the insidious, undermining whisper of her ominous crow with the warm message of encouragement: "I want you to hear my voice in your head, when you begin to doubt what you're doing, when you're writing your life and your stories into your work: *believe in yourself*" (Mazziotti Gillan, *Writing Poetry*, 22-23). In order to further empower readers, she explains the cathartic possibilities of writing; telling her own story, she contrasts her grief with the transformative experience of putting the most harrowing, insufferable memories into words, a method of almost *physically* expelling these traumas from her system thereby depriving them of their destructive, undermining potential.

But writing is not only a place in which to struggle against personal and societal demons, it can also be a refuge, a therapy, as we discover in Mazziotti Gillan's *The Silence in an Empty House*. This collection is dedicated to Dennis, the man she shared 46 years of married life with before he passed away after a 25-year battle with Parkinson's disease. The volume is divided into four sections that chronicle Maria's long journey towards serene acceptance (which is never a synonym for resignation). Unlike Dante Alighieri who, in his *Divina Commedia*, carved his path through the horrors of Hell, ascended Purgatory and finally reached Heaven, Maria begins her poetic narrative in the earthly paradise of her premarital and newlywed life. In the opening section called *All about*

Love, Dennis is a handsome, reassuring figure, with his gray-blue eyes and a fair complexion, as the author recalls in the poem entitled "In the Photograph, 1978." He is her "ticket to America" (Mazziotti Gillan, *The Silence*, 21), offering her the delightful opportunity to broaden the horizons of her stifling world in Little Italy, which she would at last leave behind.

In another poem, Maria recalls the "bright/ orange universe"[5] (22) of their new apartment, with its orange shag-pile rug, deep orange chairs, orange "cheese platter with a sunflower painted/ in the middle" (22), where she would serve orange cheddar: everything glows and shines, mirroring the prospect of a happy life ahead, far away from "the drab tenement where [she] grew up, the colorless/ world of [her] mother's house" (22). Like all dreams, however, her expectant vision of a blissful future will prove to be both ephemeral and fragile: as readers will gather in the following parts of *The Silence in an Empty House*, pain, fear, and loss will be the poet's lot before her final rebirth. It is not surprising, therefore, that even at this early stage of her journey (and of her married life) a feeling of uneasiness seems to lurk behind apparent serenity. The portrayal of the couple holding hands, anxiously looking for mutual support, is thus recurrent,[6] as it is Maria's craving for security and protection, identified with Dennis's "arm around [her]"[7] (20) and the "big stone house" (18) they had decided to buy, a house that had withstood tornadoes for countless years, protecting their family and guarding their beloved nest.[8] The image of the tornado, with its destructive power, is just one of the many signifiers of an impending tragedy scattered in the poems of

---

[5] "What Were We Thinking?," *The Silence*, 2013.

[6] See, for example, "I'll remember this moment/ forever, you holding my hand" (14) in the poem entitled "Going to the World's Fair, 1964", or "you and I holding buttery hands" (20) in the poem called "Going to the Movies in Kansas City."

[7] "Going to the Movies in Kansas City," *The Silence*, 2013.

[8] "My First Tornadoes," *The Silence*, 2013.

this first section: the threatening manager of the motel they stayed in when they first arrived in Kansas City[9] (the poet describes her fear that "the manager would come into the room/ and murder [them] all" [16]), the "huge thunderstorm, lightning cracking/ the sky in half"[10] (21), and the reference to the Vietnam War, with its "dead bodies/ of young men unloaded in bags from planes"[11] (20), deserve to be added to the list. What happens in the outer world (which is unsafe and laden with dangers and sorrow) may be interpreted as an ominous anticipation of the catastrophe that is soon going to strike the couple.

In "Watching the Bridge Collapse," the opening poem of the second section, *What We Carry* (corresponding to Maria's descent into her own version of the Dantesque Hell), the poet develops a parallel between an unexpected disaster and the startling change that has just affected her family: the deep terror and utter disbelief experienced by the people driving over a bridge in Minnesota the very moment it collapsed are compared with what she felt when her husband was diagnosed his condition. This correspondence allows the poet the opportunity for a wider reflection on what every person feels when an unforeseen event shatters his/her life, when the metaphoric ground beneath his/her feet crumbles to dust:

> Sometimes I think all our lives
> are like that. We really believe we are safe,
> the roads we travel built to last, and are shocked
> no matter how many times it happens,
> when the ground falls away [...].
>   (*The Silence*, 27).

Over many long years, Dennis's ailment increasingly destroys his body and annihilates his mind; day-by-day it cruelly cancels

---

[9] "Driving to Kansas City," *The Silence*, 2013.
[10] "In the Photograph, 1978," *The Silence*, 2013.
[11] "Going to the Movies in Kansas City," *The Silence*, 2013.

even his most elementary skills; it impairs his language compre-
hension and expression so that he seems to regress to an infantile
state. In "How My Husband Escapes," Loretta (his caretaker) harsh-
ly rebukes Dennis when he tries to run away: "'Dennis, Dennis,
where are you going?' She brings/ you back inside, scolding as
though you were a child" (Mazziotti Gillan, *The Silence*, 37); after a
few lines, he strives to defend himself, to preserve his own dignity, by proudly stating, "I am not a child" (37). In "How Do We
Ask for Forgiveness," Maria sadly observes that "for him time is
moving backwards/ and he is becoming a child again" (49). Once
more, in "Watching the Pelican Die," the poet describes her husband's body, "so thin [he] look[s] like a boy" (50); elsewhere in the
same poem she focuses on his lunch, on the way he even needs to
be fed, having lost his autonomy: "Althea feeds you a jar of baby
applesauce. You open/ your mouth and accept the food" (51-52).
Impotent before what, in real life, is out of her control, Mazziotti
Gillan tries to combat her husband's cruel disease by turning her
poetry into a weapon: in her lines, she contrasts his painful shrinking and his piercing agony with vivid memories of the man Dennis used to be. She tries to restore him back to health, at least in
her words, like in "How My Husband Escapes," where she describes her strategy to imagine him free from his illness:

> How did it come to this? I want to superimpose the picture
> of you young and fit, your mind full of Aristotle and John
> Dewey, over what I see now, you sliding down in your chair,
> your skinny behind hanging over the edge, your head resting
> sideways on your neck, your face like the crucified Christ
> in Spanish paintings [...]. (37-38)

In "Last Night at the Hampton Inn," she forcefully conjures up the
lost image of her spouse, a brilliant intellectual with his "Ph.D. in
philosophy" (30) and the books he "always loved to read" (30),
not simple novels "but books on the nature/ of time and astrono-

my and history" (30). Moreover, in "Winter Landscape in Sunlight," Maria's storytelling succeeds in recreating and nurturing the same atmosphere of love and protection that had enveloped the couple in the first years of their union:

> [I] help you to believe that nothing has changed
> and that we can still be the people we were
> so many years ago, our arms around each other,
> your hand in my hair. (32)

However, the solace she derives from writing as well as the magic spell of her words are only transitory. Just like Dante, when he met the Leopard, the Lion and the Wolf, barring his way to salvation and causing him to plunge into Hell, even Mazziotti Gillan has to face her own monsters: she has to push away the urge to hide away from the enormous pain she encounters, the wish to "close that door in [her] mind" in the vain attempt "not to think of the way/ this disease is killing off brain cells, more cells each day [...]" (Mazziotti Gillan, *The Silence*, 30). And in this way she fortifies herself; exposing her fragility and offering it to readers, lingering on descriptions of herself, she confronts feelings of extreme guilt and shame for having deserted the man she loves (albeit only temporarily while driving away to a conference or to a poetry reading). In "Driving into the Dark Sky," she reveals:

> [...] I am ashamed that I drive faster
> and faster to escape the image of you with your lost
> frightened eyes, your hands that can no longer hold
> a piece of toast or a cookie, your head so bent
> it is like an iris with a broken stalk.
> I am ashamed at how hard I try
> to leave you behind. (35)

Maria has to learn how to ask for forgiveness,[12] but first of all, she has to discover how to forgive herself, for wishing her nightmare to be over, for surrendering Dennis's body to the peace only Heaven could actually grant him:

> [...] though I love you, I need this
> to be over. I want to put down the burden you have
> become, want to stop worrying about you and crying
>
> for you and myself, want to let you go, your body in heaven
> restored to what it used to be–healthy, strong, athletic. (33)

By voicing her innermost thoughts, the poet releases herself from their shackles and begins to heal. Eventually unleashed, her individual pain reverberates like an echo into the lives of others in both the human and animal families, and into a natural environment that is too often heedlessly violated and disregarded. The "California wildfires in Santa Barbara" (43),[13] the suicide of a man who could no longer afford to pay taxes,[14] the birds and fish killed by pollution[15] are just a few of the many instances of how, even as an optimist, as she describes herself three times in the volume,[16] the whole world (not just her life) may seem too full of grief. This section significantly ends with "Watching the Pelican Die," in which Maria alternates between the excruciating portrayal of her husband's agony and the depiction of the dying bird completely cov-

---

[12] Read "How do We Ask for Forgiveness" (Mazziotti Gillan, *The Silence*, 49).

[13] "There is No Way to Begin," Mazziotti Gillan, *The Silence*, 2013.

[14] "We're into It Now, This New Year," Mazziotti Gillan, *The Silence*, 2013.

[15] "Watching the Pelican Die," Mazziotti Gillan, *The Silence*, 2013.

[16] "I, optimist that I am, can't find a spot/ of joy anywhere" (Mazziotti Gillan, *The Silence*, 34) in "Driving into the Dark Sky." "Even an optimist, like me/ can no longer deny you are getting ready to die" (42) in "This Year Is Difficult." "Even I, the ever-ready optimist, cannot deny that/ the world is filled with grief" (73) in "The Workshop in Hingham."

ered in oil, "its mouth wide open,/ a picture of torment and despair" (51).

The third section, *The Loneliness that Lives*, corresponds to Maria's Purgatory. At this stage, she has to come to terms with what she failed to express when her husband was alive; as she confesses in the first poem of the section, "You Never Gave Up": "I am sorry I did not tell you enough how brave you were,/ wish I could tell you now, how much I miss you" (Mazziotti Gillan, *The Silence*, 56). The second stage of her healing process is a recognition of her grief and learning how to cry and then to let go of grief. And even in this emotionally fraught situation, the profound empathy she nurtures for all the living beings of the planet enables her to approach the unapproachable *sideways*. The dead deer at the side of the road moves her to tears: "when I see that dead deer, the way life is gone from it/ I cry for you and for the deer and for all the other creatures/ lost"[17] (57). In this phase of mourning there is a clash between the moments in which the poet feels devastated and disempowered—like in "The Silence in an Empty House," where she describes the silence of her home broken only by the sound of an alarm she does not know how to stop (because Dennis used to take care of that)[18]—, and moments of unexpected bliss, when her soul is awakened to the beauty and consolation of nature, when she feels thankful for what she still has and can still achieve. For example when Maria gazes at the warm colours of autumn leaves (reminiscent of the orange of her newlywed apartment) she is, "for the moment, cheered and hopeful" (91): "I want to believe I still hold/ the fire of those autumn trees inside me" (91).[19] "The flash of fire of trees flaring into autumn" (65) is evoked in another poem, meaningfully entitled "Sometimes I Am Blind-sided by Beauty," to-

---

[17] "The Dead Deer on the Side of the Road," Mazziotti Gillan, *The Silence*, 2013.

[18] As she emphasizes, "I am shaking. 'I don't know how I'll manage without you,' I tell you" (Mazziotti Gillan, *The Silence*, 76).

[19] "Leaving New Jersey and Autumn behind," *The Silence*, 2013.

gether with the purple of the African violets given to her by a student, and the smile of an unknown little child:[20] "How gratified I am for these moments, blessed and perfect/ as a new moon," (65) elucidates the poet.

Travelling through her personal Inferno and Purgatory, her version of Virgil (Dante's guide) is not a human figure but her job as a teacher, her powerful art that, at times, seems to act as an exoskeleton, capable of supporting and shielding her. We see this survival strategy in "There is No Way to Begin," where her temporary loss of hope gives way to the comforting memory of a poetry reading:

> After the first poem, the second, the cloud
> thick as a woollen muffler that covered me, lifted.
> I felt the power of the poems, the way they moved me,
> made everything else fall away.
>
> (*The Silence*, 44)

One would expect Mazziotti Gillan's journey to end like the *Divina Commedia*, with an ecstatic vision of heaven. Instead, she concludes it where she began, in an earthly paradise, which is eventually regained, appreciated in its fullness, never taken for granted. She has learnt not to be too hard on herself and a sense of gratitude fills almost every page of this last section, *Getting Ready to Stand*. The painful and so far unsolved questions—*How do we get to the other side of grief? How can we overcome such a heartbreaking loss?*—finally find their answer in one of the final poems: "when we allow/ momentary beauty, iridescent as dragonfly wings,/ to carry us through grief and terror to the other side"[21] (90). The poet's world, that had seemed to have lost its colours, can now *again*

---

[20] In "Sometimes I Am Blind-sided by Beauty," the poet mentions both the violets and "the child whom [she's]/ never seen before who turns to [her] and smiles" (Mazziotti Gillan, *The Silence*, 65).

[21] Compare the poem entitled "Travelling in Style."

display all of its most vibrant hues of oranges, reds, and yellows; contemplating the trees "that line the hills [...] on fire/ with autumn" (91): "Some days I am like these trees,/ my colours scarlet, bright orange, and I am,/ for the moment, cheered and hopeful"[22] (91).

And it is in the last poem of the collection, "When the Christmas Cactus Blooms," that we find Maria Mazziotti Gillan transcending her place from the margins, once with the help of Dennis, now independently, with the creation and acceptance of her role as the poet-healer, and delivering a potent message of hope, gratitude, endurance, and a metaphor for life. In these almost oxymoronic lines, a Christmas cactus (as thorny as life can be) touchingly blooms, in the dead of winter:

One November morning, when the Christmas cactus blooms,
When I walk into the dining room and find it there,
All red blossoms in a profusion of green,

The way sometimes we too come alive again after a gray season,
The world so full of grief and loss, and even you, whom I loved
So long, dead now two years already, though I am certain
You sent me the amazing blooms of the cactus as a reminder
Of all those sweet years we had together, even when you
Became so ill; such blessings, as spectacular as the cactus.

How difficult it is to learn to be grateful, to cherish
All the patterned hours that braided our lives together,
And only now, greeted by the flowering cactus,
Only now, am I ready
To let go of your hand.

(*The Silence*, 92)

---

[22] The lines come from the above-mentioned "Leaving New Jersey and Autumn behind."

WORKS CITED

Giunta, Edvige. *Writing with an Accent*. New York: Palgrave, 2002.

Marino, Elisabetta. "The Italian American Family between Past and Present: *The Place I Call Home* (2012) by Maria Mazziotti Gillan, and *Mystics in the Family* (2013) by Maria Famà." In Leonardo Buonomo and Elisabetta Vezzosi eds., *Discourses of Emancipation and Boundaries of Freedom*. Trieste: EUT, 2015. 79-85.

Mazziotti Gillan, Maria. *Where I Come From*. Toronto: Guernica, 1995.

_____. *The Silence in an Empty House* (New York: NYQ Books, 2013).

_____. *Writing Poetry to Save Your Life. How to Find the Courage to Tell Your Stories*. Toronto: Guernica, 2013.

Tamburri, Anthony Julian. *Re-reading Italian Americana. Specificities and Generalities on Literature and Criticism*. Madison, NJ: Fairleigh Dickinson UP, 2014.

Whitman, Walt. *Leaves of Grass*. Mineola, NY: Dover Thrift Editions, 2001.

Rita Ciresi. Spaces of Intimacy. Places of Diversity

Sandra Paoli
ROMA TRE UNIVERSITY

The Italian-American[1] writer Rita Ciresi[2] has the rare gift of portraying contemporary American society with an unconventional and profound approach. She describes the world she comes from with empathy and yet with detachment and open-mindedness. She focuses on the relationship between the individual and her community, with all the conflicts and dynamics it involves. Ciresi is a writer who maintains a balance between and amongst different worlds in a period in which cultural homologation crushes identities. At the same time, she pushes identities to claim their own existence in radical forms, and accomplishes this by using parodic narrative forms.

Involvement and abstraction are the distinctive features of Ciresi's narratives, whose irony sheds light on the stereotypes and the contradictions of our contemporary society in its continuous

---

[1] As Anthony Julian Tamburri and Caterina Romeo observe, the phrase "Italian American" represents in equal terms the culture of departure and that of arrival, unlike "Italo-American," in which the first word—Italian—is distorted (Caterina Romeo, *Narrative tra due sponde. Memoir di italiane d'America* [Rome: Carocci, 2005] 13; Anthony Julian Tamburri, *Una semiotica dell'etnicità. Nuove segnalature per la scrittura italiano/americana* [Florence: Franco Cesati Editore, 2010] 17-18).

[2] Rita Ciresi was born in 1960 in New Haven, Connecticut, to a mother of southern Italian origin born in the United States and to a Sicilian father who emigrated to America as a child in 1921. The neighborhood she lived in as a child was in the suburbs of New Haven, an ethnically mixed working-class community inhabited above all by Italian Americans, many of whom could not speak English. They spoke Italian, or more often an Italian dialect. They were practicing Catholics.

and unpredictable transformations. At first glance, her work may not seem as elaborate and rich as, in fact, it is. As Anthony Julian Tamburri remarks, for a long time she was unfairly ignored in academic circles, becoming an interesting subject of research only recently.[3] Mary Jo Bona compares her work to that of other Italian-American women writers such as Anne Calcagno and Renée Manfredi, whose stories are set in the popular context of a working-class Italian-American enclave. As Bona puts it, what these writers seem to have in common is the use of wordplay and the continuous reference to the culture of communities of origin.[4]

Making use of techniques of memoir writing, Rita Ciresi tries to tell her own story in an ironic style whose main goal consists of retrieving memories and rewriting history from non-official perspectives. Through the narrative dynamics of memoir, she, in fact, challenges official accounts, going beyond both the American mainstream and Italian-American patriarchal culture, in order to give emphasis to the life of a community traditionally considered marginal.[5] She, therefore, insists on the most private, complex, conflicting aspects of her personal experience in the strong belief they deserve further reflection and elaboration.

In one of her most interesting collection of short stories, *Sometimes I Dream in Italian*, Ciresi focuses on the experiences and pranks of the two Lupo sisters, Angel and Pasqualina/Lina, and their parents, Filomena and Carlino—who are first-generation immigrants. They all live in New Haven, Connecticut, during the 1970s and 1980s and, once adults, they choose to live very different lives. This is the case of the two sisters: Pasqualina is a housewife with

---

[3] Anthony Julian Tamburri, "Beyond 'Pizza' And 'Nonna'! Or, What's Bad About Italian/American Criticism? Further Directions for Italian/American Cultural Studies," *Melus*, 28.3 (Autumn 2003): 149-174; interview with Anthony Julian Tamburri, New York City, April 29, 2015.

[4] Mary Jo Bona, *Claiming a Tradition: Italian American Women Writers* (Carbondale: Southern Illinois UP, 1999) 163-165.

[5] *Ibid.*

two children, while Angel is a single and independent woman. In this short story, Angel deals with some important aspects of the Italian-American experience. Her memories also reveal her family's problems of integration and their daughters' desire to be all American, the girls' experience at school, encounters that at times became clashes with children from other ethnic communities: the profound and the conflictual bonds between the various members of the family and the misunderstandings between them as well as the contrast between appearances and reality.

The difficulties involved in the process of assimilation are shown through the experience of the Lupo family living in an Italian-American community in an ethnic context. Donna Gabaccia and Colin Wayne Leach help us to understand what Ciresi dramatizes when they write that the United States seems to "[function] symbolically as a cultural plural or multicultural nation of individuals with complex identities."[6]

Set in transcultural places and spaces, in a world that is continuously changing, Ciresi's short stories cannot be framed within a rigid identity logic. Being an Italian-American author, and some of her main characters being Italian-American, is for her neither a symbol of pride nor a stigma, it is her peculiar key to read the contemporary American reality in which the story takes place. Ciresi is a "transversal" writer as she is in between two worlds *in fieri*: the Italian community opens her boundaries to an American society accepting her growing diverse identity in historical phases, which follow each other with a transformational intensity and speed never experienced before.

The distressing lacerations of her characters are explored and described while taking into account the continuous exchange between the members of the different communities in the ethnic neigh-

---

[6] See their "Introduction" to *Immigrant Life in the U.S. Multicultural Perspectives.* Donna Gabaccia and Colin Wayne Leach, eds. (New York: Routledge, 2004) 3.

borhood where most of her short stories are set.[7] The stories reflect on a complex contemporary society, where the single communities and relative cultures are not sharply divided from each other but contaminate and influence one another, they are woven together.

The protagonists of Ciresi's work are mainly women who distance themselves from their original community, in the hope of becoming part of the mainstream. Their continuous comparison of realities different from their experiences forces them to question themselves unceasingly. As in the novels *Sometimes I Dream in Italian* and *Blue Italian*, ancestral origins seem to have left a mark on these women, changing their own self-perception. It is not simply a matter of ethnicity but ultimately of social class. Working class and Italian-ness overlap and mingle with each other. Aspiring to be part of the mainstream is the desire and quest for a higher rung on the social ladder, the prosperous middle class. Such relentless and yet legitimate aspirations for social promotion belong to the women—Italian-American women—in a conservative environment. Ciresi was one of them in her years in New Haven, so are her female characters in *Sometimes I Dream in Italian* and *Blue Italian*.

Ciresi's work can also be observed from the perspective of geography, topography, mapping, and literature.[8] This type of study

---

[7] There are several studies about places in the contemporary, global and transcultural society; see, among others, Homi Bhabha, *The Location of Culture* (New York: Routledge, 1994); Donna Gabaccia, *Foreign Relations. American Immigration in Global Perspective* (Princeton: Princeton UP, 2012); Christiane Harzig, Dirk Hoerder with Donna R. Gabaccia, *What is Migration History?* (Cambridge: Polity, 2009).

[8] See, among other important studies, the following publications: Francesco Fiorentino, ed., *Cultura tedesca. Topografie letterarie* XXXIII (2007); Francesco Fiorentino, Giovanni Sampaolo, eds., *Atlante della letteratura tedesca* (Macerata: Quodlibet, 2008) and the conference Francesco Fiorentino organized, *Letteratura e cartografia, Giornate di studio*, Rome May 8–9 2015. These recent studies confirm what Homi Bhabha asserts: that the concept of nation is anything but static, it proves to be an

goes beyond the traditional assumption of a one-dimensional national culture to a point of view that is particularly in tune with
the peculiar characters of America's kaleidoscopic society.[9]

In a kaleidoscope, as it is moved, colors keep mixing, overlapping, making new figures and forming unusual shapes. What is
called diversity today for a long time was actually a crystallized
reality in which the sum of America's different parts made it
something bigger and richer: because of a rich array of races, classes and religions, most notably in big cities. Only after the sixties,
with the full power of the Civil Rights movement, the melting pot
starts to really work as a positive, inclusive force for all communities. Italian Americans had an important role in this process,
which has to be fully acknowledged. Rita Ciresi belongs to one of

---

ambivalent and mobile space at a crossroads of cultures he defines as "transnational" (Homi Bhabha, "Introduction: Narrating the Nation," in *Nation and Narration*. Homi Bhabha, ed. [New York: Routledge, 1990] 1-7).

[9] The United States is constitutionally and historically a multi-ethnic, multicultural, and multi-religious nation. For the past thirty years the United States
has experienced a dramatic demographic transformation. A significant population growth has been accompanied by an astounding change in power relations
between its different components. The WASP majority seems destined to become
a minority. The United States of America is no longer the black and white country. This polarization remains, but is now inside a polyhedron of communities, of
different colors, origins, religions, and characterized by a significant crust of cultural homologation linked to the hegemony of consumerism. At the same time,
these are communities increasingly proud of their own roots that have in recent
times been rediscovered, exhibited, cultivated, and promoted. It is double layer-
ing in which even the "lower" level of origins, of roots, has an acknowledged
importance. In the mingling of the many ethnic identities, there is the pride of
every community for contributing to the continuously changing creation of a
shared identity. In this context of diversity, speckled with contradictions and periodical steps backwards, conflicts and impasses, increasing importance and visibility are assumed by artistic and cultural expressions that explicitly lay emphasis on the varied complexity of identity provided by belonging to a community,
or simply by the origins of a given community. Among these expressions, an
important role is played by those linked to the Italian-American community.

the generations in the middle of this very transformative process, which makes America the country it is today.

The Italian-American world in Ciresi's stories is set in a diverse context and her narratives focus on events of redemption set within the family context, a sphere dominated by women.[10] In her works, Ciresi describes different kind of women, from the traditionalist archetype of the Italian mother to the daughters following in their mothers' footsteps trying to achieve emancipation and freedom. All of them are frail in their rich and nuanced psychologies.

A virtual tour in the spaces of diversity and in places of intimacy in Rita Ciresi's work starts in New York's Central Park in her short story "Mother Rocket," that narrates the vicissitudes of Jude, a fragile young Jewish-American woman. Jude is a young ballerina from New York, married to a photographer. She is hypersensitive and carries lively and painful memories of the past, characterized by acute feelings of guilt sparked by a conflicted relationship with her adoptive parents. Unable to accept her past, she suffers from a neurosis that led her to threaten to commit suicide. Rob, the man she loves, persuades her not to, promising to marry her. It is precisely at that moment that the young girl experiences an uncontrollable desire for a hot and salty pretzel: "Only a pretzel delivered from the wrinkled hands of a vendor in Central Park would do" (58).

In "Mother Rocket" America is depicted as a land of immigration, an ethnic, cultural, and religious melting pot, even though

---

[10] Fred Gardaphé, "'What'ya Mean I'm Funny?': Ball-Busting Humor and Italian American Masculinities," in Delia Chiaro, Raffaella Baccolini, ed., *Gender and Humor: Interdisciplinary and International Perspectives* (New York: Routledge, 2014) 243. Fred Gardaphé quotes Ciresi, alongside a few other authors, all male, as an example of particularly successful irony (Fred Gardaphé, "Italian American Humor. From Sceccu to Chooch: the Signifying Donkey," in Fabio Finotti and Marina Johnston, ed., *L'Italia allo specchio. Linguaggi e identità italiane nel mondo* (Venezia: Marsilio, 2014) 353-362.

there is no direct hint at the Italian-American environment of her biography. And yet her very background as immigrant plays an important role as it gives her the gift of understanding the experience intimately and rendering the chemistry of an interethnic relation. The story takes place in New York, a city closely associated with social and cultural intertwinements in our modern times.

In the story "Miss Liberty," Filomena, who emigrated to the United States many years earlier, when she was a child, believes that the Statue of Liberty is on Staten Island, confusing the island's name with "statue island," an expression she herself has coined. It is Luigino, her brother-in-law, who knows the history and explains to her that when they emigrated to the New World, Americans already lived on Staten Island, and that the ships carrying Italians landed at Ellis Island, whereas the Statue of Liberty was on a nearby island. Readers feel tenderness for Filomena when they learn that she arrived on the new continent when she was five years old.

Visiting the monumental place as tourists, some remember the immigrants' hard work and the long hours spent waiting. Yet, for some immigrants, disenchantment dominates their memories. This disenchantment is the result of the broken dream of hope for the Promised Land that was believed to be America, when they discovered only a hard life of poverty and labor awaited them.

The confrontation between cultures is again present in *Blue Italian*, Rita Ciresi's first novel, even though in this case there is not a crystallized polarization inside the family and between two generations, rather, it is featured as a peculiar interethnic and social debate in progress—both in the form of clashes and encounters. It appears even in the characters' most intimate moments and in their interactions, as in the meeting, courting, and marriage of two young people, the Italian-American Rosa Salvatore and the Jewish-American Gary Fisher: a woman and a man from different backgrounds, not only from an ethnic and religious perspective, but also socially. Rosa's family is working-class, while Gary's is upper middle-class. The two young people meet at Yale Hospital in New Haven. Rosa is employed as a social worker, while Gary, who is a law student, is a voluntary apprentice in the hospital's legal department.

What Rosa and Gary share is the same generation, the same city, the same working place; it is a solid common ground upon which they build a mutual understanding, and yet, especially in Rosa's case, their respective roots may end up dominating the scene of their interaction, when the reader least expects it. This happens when her Italian-American roots are associated with the perception of her community of origin as irredeemably backward and even archaic (at least this is the view that she conveys to Gary). Rosa is obsessed with what Gary will think of Pizza Beach. But it is also her own judgment, which is even more critical, that torments her. She imagines seeing her old neighborhood through the eyes of her fiancé and then again through her own. The picture looks even worse. Her parents and their house become ridiculous in her eyes. Pizza Beach is distant in every possible way from the well-off suburb where Gary grew up. It is slightly run-down, but Rosa knows the reasons for its decline. People who get up early in the morning and come home late; people who work hard, make sacrifices, and have no time to devote to their homes and gardens, these are the people who live in Pizza Beach. They are people who deserve respect. There is a wealth of values in those homes and on those streets, the values of people who sweat to make it to the end of the month. Here Rita Ciresi plays a double game, making the reader understand how working-class values and principles are the backbone of Rosa's (and Rita's) world. At same time she is compassionate with a young woman who basically shares those same principles and values and yet she is not defending them as she is psychologically fragile during the development of a new relationship with a man who does not belong to the same world, to the same social class, and may be judgmental.

How then can the reader be judgmental with Rosa?

When Gary meets her parents for the first time, she is under constant stress of how Gary will react. Here, again, it is a matter of class conflict. Class conflict characterizes Rita Ciresi's writings; she too is a child of the working class in the city that acts as the backdrop for *Blue Italian*. These are the years in which the American working class, more than previously, was more inclined to assume the consumer patterns and social characteristics of the middle class; a process greatly encouraged and idealized in a society that mythicizes success, social mobility, and the possibility to overcome one's status, not with a collective struggle, but assuming the values of the dominant classes and individually working toward obtaining them.[11]

The class and cultural conflict is again revealed in Rosa's family garage where a portrait of Benito Mussolini hangs. Just as Aldo, Rosa's father, is about to meet his future son-in-law, Gary. Gary notices the dictator's photo and is, understandably, appalled:

> Aldo is sitting at a worktable he had improvised out of a sheet of plywood and two wine barrels. On the wall above him hung a faded felt Yankees pennant. And next to that—a small detail that Rosa had forgotten about—hung a black-and white portrait of Benito Mussolini which had been on display in their father's garage for as long as Rosa could remember. [...] Rosa had suggested that her father take down the picture. [...]
>
> [...] Gary's eyes lingered for a moment on the portrait. "Whoa," he said, beneath his breath, and Rosa felt herself turning hot and red. But there was no time to deal with Il Duce, because Rosa's father had looked up when they came in the garage. Aldo did not get up from his stool.[12]

---

[11] Arnaldo Testi, *Il secolo degli Stati Uniti* (Bologna: il Mulino, 2014).
[12] Ciresi, *Blue Italian*, 75.

The Duce's photograph has been there for a very long time. It belonged to Rosa's grandfather, and, after his death, Aldo had not wanted to take it down. Her grandfather said he admired Mussolini because when he was in power the trains ran on time. At the time, there were Italian Americans who had been victims of discrimination, who felt well-represented by a man who, at least in the early days of his history, seemed a strong, well-known leader respected all over the world. And yet the Salvatores prove to be insensitive in their lack of awareness of what memories the Italian dictator, an ally of Nazi Germany, would bring back for Gary, who is Jewish. Aldo welcomes Gary in his garage, a "male" place, the correct setting for a meeting as her father sees it, and it is as informal as a basement can be.[13]

What in a middle-class context would appear to be a lack of consideration for a guest and a future son-in-law is, in fact, the informal style of the head of a family who immediately treats him like a relative. His almost excessively relaxed attitude in reality hides bewilderment and embarrassment as the culture and established roles do not allow, traditional Italian-American men to reveal their weaknesses, especially in front of other men, as Gardaphé asserts.[14]

Gary is affected but keeps his composure. Rosa, who has meticulously anticipated and forestalled any possible reason for potential conflict between her fiancé and her family, had banished from her mind that photograph that would soon be the site of great embarrassment to her. The photograph of the very symbol of the dictatorship clearly portrays the political ideas of an Italian family who seems to be nostalgic of Mussolini's times and power.

---

[13] Lara Pascali, "The Italian Immigrant Basement Kitchen in North America," in Joseph Sciorra, ed., *Italian Folk: Vernacular Culture in Italian-American Lives* (New York: Fordham UP, 2011) 49-61; Joseph Sciorra, "Vernacular Culture," lessons held during the Italian Diaspora Studies Summer Seminar, Arcavacata (Rende) Calabria, June 15 - July 3, 2015.

[14] Fred Gardaphé, "What'ya Mean I'm Funny?" 243.

It is thus that Mussolini's portrait becomes an incongruous orna-
ment, both outrageous and yet inoffensive, in the garage where
Gary is welcomed by Aldo.

Ciresi then amusingly emphasizes the differences and misunderstandings in the communication codes between men and wom-
en. The dining room has been prepared by Rosa's mother with the
Venetian lace tablecloth and the pale pink hexagonal set of plates,
obsessed with the idea of making a good impression, a "bella figura."[15]

The Salvatores, in Gary's progressive if slightly patronizing
eyes, may be positive figures because they belong to the working
class, unlike his well-off middle-class parents. He is more interested in their surreal and grotesque features and behavior. He describes them as "a weenie bit on the Fellini side, but basically well-
intentioned."[16] Gary is ironic, while Rosa is anxious about her
parents' behavior.[17]

For Rosa even the meeting with Gary's parents is a source of
anxiety. Entering the Fischer home (Mimi and Artie's home), the
reader observes the extent to which a family living in a well-to-do
neighborhood can be distant from the frankness and simplicity of
the Salvatores. "She gazed out the windows at the neatly manicured
gardens and unnaturally green grass—courtesy of Chemlawn—and
the large houses set back from the quiet, wide streets."[18]

Mimi is very elegant, neat, and a little eccentric. Mimi's eccen-
tricity is contrived. Her outfit conforms to a certain dominant ste-

---

[15] The concept of making a *bella figura* in Italian culture is the object of study of
several essays. Quoted here: Gloria Nardini, "A Definition of *Bella Figura*." *Che
Bella Figura! The Power of Performance in an Italian Ladies' Club in Chicago* (Albany,
NY: SUNY P, 1999) 4-33. Furthermore, Italian-American studies have been the
object of debates, as expressed by Joseph Sciorra in his above-cited seminar
"Vernacular Culture."

[16] Ciresi, *Blue Italian*, 90.

[17] Cfr. Fernandez and Taylor Huber, *Irony in Action*, 3.

[18] Ciresi, *Blue Italian*, 97.

reotype of femininity, that femininity on which beauty and perfection are imposed.[19] Mimi's portrait is not only the result of her flaunted elegance and affected mannerisms, but also of her exhibited class difference. This is something Rosa compensates for with caustic irony by imagining her as the Fisher's cleaning lady. The way the house is furnished and Mimi's behavior seem dictated by deference to appearances and not by a sincere desire to welcome guests. The attitude and the feelings of the characters change over the course of the story. Rosa's and Gary's families are very different from each other. Their relationship did not begin at Pizza Beach, nor in Long Island, but in the pizzeria "Progressive Pizza." Food is nourishment, but, most of all, it is culture.[20] It is identity. At the same time, being able to appreciate dishes from traditions that are not one's own means leaving one's own community and approaching another.[21] This is what happens in "Progressive Pizza." It is this being equally both Italian and American further symbolizing the meeting between the two and the developments that will arise from this encounter. When Rosa and Gary leave the pizzeria, their lives will no longer be the same. This episode reveals the two young people's conflicting sentiments, and in particular Rosa's:

> Definitely not Rosa's kind of place.
> The hostess led them to a dark booth in the back. The plastic covering on the bench made a melancholy fart sound when Rosa

---

[19] Delia Chiaro and Raffaella Baccolini, "A Many Gendered Thing" in *Gender and Humor: Interdisciplinary and International Perspectives*. Delia Chiaro and Raffaella Baccolini, eds. (New York: Routledge, 2014) 1-9.

[20] As observed by Anthony Julian Tamburri, this was the object of the film co-directed by Stanley Tucci, *Big Night*, USA 1996 (Anthony Tamburri, seminar on "Italian-American Film," which was part of the *Italian Diaspora Studies Summer School*, Università della Calabria and John D. Calandra Italian American Institute, Arcavacata (Rende) Calabria 2015.

[21] Donna Gabaccia, private communications with Donna Gabaccia, Naples, September 26, 2015.

sat down. Considering this was their first date, Rosa thought it prudent to ignore it. [...] All her suspicions were immediately confirmed. Progressive offered pizza with pineapple, broccoli, and avocado on top, and calzone stuffed with peaches and mangoes. Rosa shook her head with sorrow. Anything beyond mushrooms, peppers, black olives, and sausage seemed complete sacrilege.[22]

The young woman could be portrayed simply as an emancipated person, critical of the backwardness of her family and community of origin. But Ciresi does not describe her as such and, instead, she insists on the subtle transformation of American society. She seizes the ambiguities and contradictions, as noted by Fernandez and Taylor, of the modern and post-modern worlds.[23]

Gary senses Rosa's shock, and is delighted that he likes a young woman with such different tastes. They work up the courage to share their life stories and over the course of the meal their respective cultural identities are stripped away and a connection is made.

Despite Rosa's inner conflict, the class differences and the clash of cultures, a very significant encounter of the two families becomes unexpectedly intimate. After Rosa and Gary's wedding, Gary's parents attend the party held in the Salvatores' garden with the bride's relatives, a simple, informal and intimate place. The encounter of two different families does not become a clash of cultures, and class difference does not spoil the harmony of the moment between the two sets of parents. In fact, Gary's parents, Mimi and Artie, comforted by the atmosphere, have no inhibitions about sharing with everyone the story of the night when Gary was conceived, information received with satisfaction by Rosa and her aunts, but with indignation by Gary:

---

[22] Ciresi, *Blue Italian*, 39.
[23] Fernandez and Taylor, *Irony in Action*, 2.

> Throughout all this, Gary looked down at his shoes, which had become dusty from the garage. He was preoccupied, disconcerted. For once, he had nothing to say for himself. Artie and Mimi were doing all the talking. They began to laugh and trade stories about Italy with Rosa's relative.[24]

There is an exchange of roles with Rosa who is instead amused, and now it is she who supports him. This is a downplaying of an inversion of roles, as often happens in Ciresi's books, with the way she avoids character, cultural, personal, or ideological fixations in the American world of her novels.

> [...] he said, "I'm gonna puke. I'm not kidding. I am dangerously close to barfing the big one all over this rug, right now, and I mean right now. Why did my mother tell that story?"
> "I thought it was cute, " Rosa said. "Romantic."[25]

Now almost thirty years old, Gary has never seen his mother speak so openly, revealing her intimate self. He has criticized but also idealized his parents. We see his naivety, like that of a child who cannot imagine how he can have been conceived on an occasion that was very romantic for his parents. A moment that was unique only for them.

In Rita Ciresi you can witness this delicate style of humor at work, miraculously swinging between sweet and sour, between compassion and friendly mockery. Her irony stops short of sarcasm. You can feel it, the sarcasm, looming, and yet magically, it never materializes. Her humor is never derisive. Her smile is never grimace. Because she is never judgmental. Irony is just the key to open gently the door of the intimacy of a couple—Gary and Rosa—not to spy them but to share their feelings. It's the key to get discreetly in the kitchen of a family—the Salvatores, the Lupos. To

---

[24] Ciresi, *Blue Italian*, 157.
[25] Ibid, 158.

enter a bourgeois house and watch, respectfully, a rich family—the Fishers—acting just like a proletarian family, with a bigger dose of hypocrisy.

Ciresi's sense of humor fills the irony deficiency she finds in Italian Americans, rediscovering a certain comicality in her Italian ancestors and elaborating it in her peculiar way, that of a contemporary Italian-American writer.

Amy A. Bernardy:
A Writer between Two Cultures

Daniela Rossini
ROMA TRE UNIVERSITY

A my Bernardy was an unusual figure in the field of Italian-American relations during the first decades of the twentieth century: one might even consider her "American-Italian" as a writer, rather than the other way around.

Born in Florence in 1879, she was the daughter of the U.S. consul and his Italian wife. She grew up and was educated in the same city where she would be one of the first women to obtain a university degree. Of course she was fluent in both English and Italian, indeed the "pure" Italian of the Florentine upper class. As Pasquale Villari, supervisor of her dissertation, put it, Bernardy was "a foreigner by origin, but an Italian by birth and education."[1]

What is of interest from our point of view is the fact that she felt passionately Italian, and more so as her sojourns grew longer in the States, and the fiercer the cultural and political antagonisms became between the two countries. Her writings thus offer an interesting perspective on the sensitive points in Italy-U.S. relations, including Italian immigration to the States and the two countries' mutual perceptions. Her witty observations regarding the differences between the two cultures and their customs made her one of the most successful writers in the rapidly growing field of travel

---

[1] Pasquale Villari, "Preface," in Amy A. Bernardy, *Venezia e il Turco nella seconda metà del secolo XVII* (Florence: G. Civelli, 1902) V.

literature: a vehicle for the promotion both of the American myth in Italy, and of Italy's image in the States.[2]

After graduation, Bernardy was faced with the difficult problem of finding a suitable occupation. She wanted to earn her living and at the same time to travel extensively. In Italy this seemed an impossible aspiration.[3] The path she chose to follow, undoubtedly a courageous one, was to accept a university teaching post in America. Thus it was that in 1902, at the age of only twenty-three, she moved to the United States, where Smith College, one of the first women's colleges, had offered her the position of teacher of Italian, first as an Instructor and then from 1905 to 1909 as an Associate Professor.[4]

From the very beginning, a donation of art books and engravings from the Foreign Ministry to the College of Italian demonstrated the high regard paid to her work promoting Italian culture in the USA. Though it must be said that part of the attention was due to her acquaintance with persons of influence such as the statesman Sidney Sonnino, the historian and politician Pasquale Villari and the art historian and archaeologist Giacomo Boni.[5]

However, life on the isolated women's campus was hardly congenial to her outgoing temperament: in her letters she characteriz-

---

[2] For her prominence as a writer in the first decades of the twentieth century to World War II, see Maria Bandini Buti ed., *Poetesse e Scrittrici*, Vol. II (Rome: Carlo Tosi, 1941) 88; *Enciclopedia Biografica e Bibliografica Italiana*, VI Series; and Mario Gastaldi, *Donne luce d'Italia: panorama della letteratura femminile contemporanea* (Milan: Quaderni di Poesia, 1936) 269.

[3] Amy A. Bernardy, *Paese che vai: il mondo come l'ho visto io* (Florence: Le Monnier, 1923) 6-18.

[4] *President's Annual Report* [hereafter *PAR*] 1901-1902, 3, *PAR* 1905-1906, 4, and *PAR* 1908-1909, 25, Office of the President, Opening and Early History, and the folder "Bernardy Amy A., Assoc. Prof. 1902-1909," box 676, Faculty Biographical Files, Smith College Archives.

[5] Bernardy to Villari, September 27, no year [probably 1904], Carteggio Villari, box 5, folder 245-6, Biblioteca Apostolica Vaticana [hereafter BAV], Vatican City; "In Italian Colors," *Boston Daily Globe* [hereafter *BG*], March 27, 1904.

es the small town of Northampton as a "necropolis,"[6] or exclaims that "one dies of boredom in the college!" Bernardy felt herself to be not just isolated, but an exile yearning to return to Italy, if only a chance of work there would present itself.[7]

University life however formed only one part of her American experience. Bernardy wrote prolifically, from articles to books, and was published both in Italy and in America, all the while making frequent trips, principally to Boston, but also to New York, Washington, and Chicago, as well as traversing the length and breadth of the enormous West in the final years of her sojourn. Through her traveling, writing, and lecturing, she expanded the range of her activities, appearing even to American eyes as a "woman of unusual energy and personality."[8] And at the same time that she became an expert on Italian immigration, aided by her frequent visits to the "Little Italies" around the country, she developed and maintained a rich and active social life as a sought-after representative of the Italian elite in America.

THE IMAGE OF THE UNITED STATES IN ITALY

In the early decades of the century, Bernardy wrote numerous articles, essays, and books on the United States: Pier Paolo D'Attorre, tracing the evolution of the American myth in Italy, mentions her works alongside those of Edmondo De Amicis as among the most widely read about America.[9] Her best-known travel books are notable for their verve and a talent for observation, as well as a mas-

---

[6] Giacomo Boni to Bernardy, March 7, 1903, Corrispondenza Boni-Bernardy, Epistolario B, XXXIX, Archivio Boni, Accademia di Scienze e Lettere, Istituto Lombardo, Milan.

[7] Bernardy to Villari, February 26, 1906, box 5, folder 237-8, Carteggio Villari, BAV.

[8] "Smith College Teacher helps Italian Immigrants," *BG*, May 26, 1907, see also "Italian in the South," *New York Tribune* [hereafter *NY Tribune*], March 31, 1907, and "War on Black Hand," *Washington Post* [hereafter *W. Post*], October 9, 1910.

[9] Pier Paolo D'Attorre, "Sogno americano e mito sovietico nell'Italia contemporanea," in P. P. D'Attorre ed. *Nemici per la pelle. Sogno americano e mito sovietico nell'Italia contemporanea* (Milan: FrancoAngeli, 1991) 16.

tery of language,[10] even if today they might seem "oversized" and "lacking in cohesion."[11]

The broadening of horizons characteristic of the *Belle Époque* had produced a public hungry for information about the legendary America. Bernardy was one of a host of writers—albeit the only female among them—describing this new transatlantic society which promoted itself as a model for the entire world to follow.[12] She poked fun at the many writers who regaled their readers with impressions gained from hurried visits:

> None of those who have written of America [...], or almost none, have left Europe, their own occupations, their own everyday lives, and gone to America with the single aim of living there, working there, being there as if it were home; of allowing themselves to be swept along by the American current, doing purely and simply as the Americans do. Their books' concerns betray the lot of them, journalists and lecturers, diplomats and *touristes*. They may give us a complete history of the Mormon sect, and fail to note, which is much more to be marveled at, the public honesty that permits you to leave a package of pamphlets unguarded in the open street beside the postbox with no fear that urchin delinquency will cause it to disappear *ex abrupto*. They

---

[10] Her main volumes on the United States are: *America vissuta* (Turin: Bocca, 1911), *Italia randagia attraverso gli Stati Uniti* (Turin, 1913), *Paese che vai:* (1923), *Passione italiana sotto cieli stranieri* (Florence: Le Monnier, 1931).

[11] Giuseppe Massara, *Viaggiatori italiani in America (1860-1970)* (Rome: Storia e letteratura, 1976) 103.

[12] Giuseppe Giacosa, *Impressioni d'America* (Milan: Cogliati, 1898); Ugo Ojetti, *L'America vittoriosa* (Milan: Treves, 1899) and *L'America e l'avvenire* (Milan: Treves, 1905); Alberto Pecorini, *Gli americani nella vita moderna osservati da un italiano* (Milan: Treves, 1909); Vico Mantegazza, *Agli Stati Uniti: il pericolo americano* (Milan: Treves, 1910); Ferdinando D'Amora, *Gente dell'altro mondo. Gli americani più interessanti d'oggi* (Milan: Milan: Trevis, 1918); Emilio Cecchi, *America amara* (Florence: Sansoni, 1939). For a bibliography of Italian volumes about the United States, see Michel Beynet, *L'image de l'Amerique dans la culture italienne de l'entre-deux-guerres* (Aix-en-Provence: U Provence, 1990) 1151-1218.

notice the skyscrapers, but do not tell you that this is the land *par excellence* of wooden houses, a land abundant in oysters, bananas and pineapples but content to do without wine and almost without bread. (Bernardy, *America vissuta*, 7-8)

New York, a *topos* in discussions of American civilization, was for her a "city of wonders ... a spectacle ... awe-inspiring" (Bernardy, *Paese che vai*, 222), "monstrous and formidable" (Bernardy, *America vissuta*,1). Her accounts concentrated above all however upon everyday life in the American metropolises. She emphasized the comfort of the houses, even if they were "too uniform," the ease of movement and travel, including railway restaurant-cars, the feminine mania for department stores and widespread consumption of canned food, the well-equipped kitchens, the presence of elevators in buildings and of cinemas and libraries even in the smallest towns, as well as the huge circulation of newspapers, consisting of dozens of illustrated pages, some in color. While her gaze was a critical one, stressing the country's "abundant mediocrity," in line with the view prevailing amongst European elites, her descriptions fed into the construction of the American myth in an Italy far removed from such standards of living.[13] However, there were moments at which she was compelled to recognize in herself a "dual" spirit, split between a "Latin" and an "American" soul:

And it happens that I surprise in myself, with a sense of both curiosity and dismay, the existence of what I would almost call a dual soul, which in the Latin world quivers with Latin pride and joy, and in America finds its gratification in the panting of trains and jingling of telephones, in a superimposition of ideas and habits which somewhat resembles the sudden turning on of the great electric light globes against the red sunset, here on Riverside Drive. (Bernardy, *America vissuta*, 1-2)[14]

---

[13] Ibid, 9, 26-27, 49-50, 120-23, 431-33, 460-64; Bernardy, *Paese che vai*, 129-30, 235.

[14] See also, *America vissuta*, 4 and 6.

She also singled out aspects of everyday life which were soon to disappear with the triumph of consumerism; for example, the "colossal" boredom of Sundays spent in that puritan land, where the day of rest was devoted to the family and to prayer, with shops, restaurants, cafés and theatres closed: "a full-scale funeral for the living." The weekly holiday had not yet become a day for shopping and leisure. What a contrast to the cheerful Sundays of Paris or Rome! (Bernardy, *America vissuta*, 442-443)

And yet, at times an exaltation of American opulence and modernity slipped almost inadvertently into Bernardy's writings. She lingered over descriptions of the splendours of society events she attended, including her own elegant costumes and those of her hosts. Her accounts of the exclusive ambiences inhabited by the metropolitan elites served to promote not just her own image, but the American lifestyle. The newspaper society columns traced her life, reporting her disembarkations as a first-class passenger from the steamers, her lectures, her participation in events in various cities, her work as a teacher at Smith College, and even her resignation therefrom.[15]

Appealing too were her sketches of women she encountered on social occasions, immersed in the futuristic urban landscape.[16] When she addressed directly the theme of the New American Woman, however, she displayed considerable impatience with this emancipated and socially influential type of female, who to her appeared tiresome and lacking in culture. Bernardy deplored this "formidable gynecocracy extending from fashion to religion, from literature to manners, from public opinion in certain matters to public action

---

[15] See the following: *BG*, June 9,1907; January16, 1903; November 3, 1903, April 10, 1905; October 2, 1905; April 5,1908; December 13,1913; January 30, 1914; *W. Post*, April 19, 1903; December 24, 1907; *New York Times*, April 19, 1903; *Los Angeles Times*, January 9, 1910 [hereafter *LA Times*].

[16] Bernardy, "Vita Americana. Un Natale a Chicago," *La Donna* (December 20, 1907): 26-7; and "Vita Americana. Un Capodanno a Chicago," *La Donna* (January 3, 1908): 9-12.

in others...," a gynecocracy "that is ignorant of the virtue of leaving one's neighbor in peace" (Bernardy, *America vissuta*, 15-16).

How did Bernardy manage to reconcile this opposition to new feminine roles with her own life as a prominent professional woman? As Ginevra De Nobili observed, there existed "an odd contrast" in this young lady, who whilst on the one hand competing with the most glittering male intelligences, on the other declared not only that she was not a feminist, but that feminism was indeed "her *bête noire.*"[17] Bernardy personified a type of woman closer to American than to Italian models: alone and independent, she was continually on the move and encountering a vast diversity of situations, armed with pen and paper and often with her camera to compile her successful features and reports. It would seem, however, that she regarded herself as an exception: a woman who thanks to her endowment of courage, culture, and intellect was able to take on the masculine world, whilst for other women, generally inferior to men, different standards applied. And Valeria Benetti hit the mark, exactly, accusing her of "masculinism"—that is, of having adopted "male" criteria in the evaluation of her own sex, as happened in the case of certain women who were themselves fortunate in the struggle for existence in competition with *the stronger sex.*[18]

The positions she took explained too her sense of solitude, the price paid for her "vagabond" and eccentric style of life, but also the consequence of a certain immaturity and incapacity to perceive herself as part of a wider reality, as other emerging figures in the new feminine world were able to do. In an article in which she described the terror she experienced during an Atlantic crossing, when a thick fog had entirely obscured the course of the ship, we catch a despondency at her own dearth of emotional bonds:

---

[17] Ginevra De Nobili, "Amy A. Bernardy," *La Donna* (May 5, 1911): 14-15.
[18] Valeria Benetti, "Polemica sul femminismo," *Giornale d'Italia* (September 4, 1907): 3.

> I am sailing, alone in the vast loneliness. [...] I will arrive one day
> in a port, so I was told upon departure. Yes, but I could equally
> be obliterated in an instant in the all-enveloping sadness, la-
> menting in vain a life in which the hours of joy, the only ones,
> the longed-for ones, were never lived or known.[19]

Though replete with contacts, interests and occupations, Bernardy would appear to have been a woman who was profoundly alone.

Her books of *reportage* gained the approval of certain literary critics. The influential Giuseppe Saverio Gargano, reviewing *Paese che vai*, expressed his appreciation for the way in which Bernardy diverted the attention of her young female readers from novels entirely concerned with matters of the heart and instead dragged them out into "the great wide world," where she herself seemed "always at home." He described her as "a woman of action and at the same time a meditative and poetic spirit," "a felicitous union of the Latin and Anglo-Saxon temperaments," deriving from the former "that sense of the fantastic that evolves out of the real" and from the latter "a love for clarity and solid pragmatism." She had a sure eye for the most telling details of a country, which she presented to us "in a style at once plain and colorful, precise and yet poetic, with a sound and subtle humor that stirs our sense of the pleasure in life." Hers might seem "hardly a feminine temperament"; but then at certain moments an "unexpected and delightful" femininity would disclose itself. His final verdict was that *Paese che vai* was a remarkable book, in which "literary quality gushes from fresh and unquenchable springs and exerts an allure that surpasses any greater beauty imagination may devise."[20]

---

[19] Bernardy, "Lettere dall'Atlantico. Nebbia in mare," clipping from unknown periodical, box 175, folder 3964, Fondo Ambasciata d'Italia a Washington 1901-1909, Archivio Storico Diplomatico, Ministero Affari Esteri, Roma.

[20] Giuseppe Saverio Gargano, "Rassegna letteraria," *Almanacco della Donna Italiana* V (1924): 308-9.

THE IMAGE OF ITALY IN THE USA

These literary facets of Bernardy's *oeuvre* are all but forgotten. She is remembered today not as a wide-ranging writer and cultural mediator but essentially as a student of the Italian emigration, with a talent for incisive description of the phenomenon in the initial phases. Her writings thus continue to be referred to, if only in studies on emigration.[21] On the contrary, what is most interesting are her descriptions of Italy and the United States and more generally her analysis of and influence on the images the two countries had of one another.

From the earliest years of the twentieth century, Bernardy was publishing articles in both Italy and the United States. In Italy she wrote for *Il Regno, Il Giornale d'Italia, La Donna, Il Corriere della Sera, La Nuova Antologia, Il Marzocco,* and *La Rassegna Nazionale.* In the U.S., apart from occasional collaborations with magazines like *Outlook* and *Good Housekeeping,*[22] she had a steady association with the *Boston Evening Transcript,* the historic Boston daily, which was published for over a century (1830-1941) before being supplanted by the *Boston Globe.* On account of this paper's circulation in the "Little Italy" districts and in Italophile cultural *milieu,* it maintained

---

[21] See Piero Bevilacqua, Andreina De Clementi, and Emilio Franzina, eds., *Storia dell'emigrazione italiana* (Rome: Donzelli, 2009). For Bernardy's studies on Italian immigration, see Anna Gasparini, "Amy Allemand Bernardy, studiosa dell'emigrazione italiana in Nord America," *Il Veltro* 34.1-2 (January-April 1990): 169-180; Nicoletta Serio, "Italiane in rotta per l'America: emigranti e studiose dell'emigrazione 1900-1914," *Il Veltro* 34.1-2 (January-April 1990): 181-204; and Maddalena Tirabassi, *Ripensare la patria grande. Gli scritti di Amy Allemand Bernardy sulle migrazioni italiane (1900-1930)* (Isernia: Cosmo Iannone Editore, 2005).

[22] "How to see Italy," *Outlook* (April 20, 1907): 890-93; "A New Influence in Music: the Pope," *Good Housekeeping* (October 4, 1904): 379-384; "The Italian Gift of Song: An Interview with Pope Pius the Tenth," *Good Housekeeping* (April 1907): 386-390; "Our Graceful Tyrants," *Good Housekeeping* (July 1908): 33-34.

a consistent interest in Italy: Bernardy called it one of Italy's "oldest and most faithful friends."[23]

She began writing for the paper in 1902, describing her first meeting with Giacomo Boni, the celebrated archeologist involved in the excavation of the Roman Forum, who had at that time come into the attention of the international press for having been entrusted with the reconstruction of the belfry of San Marco in Venice, which had suddenly collapsed the previous July. In what the newspaper's editorial board called "brilliant characteristics by a personal friend," Bernardy recalled her accidental introduction to Boni while visiting the Roman Forum with mutual friends. She described "the man of the day" as an unassuming, little man, who led a simple, even frugal life, centered on his studies and excavations that had drawn great attention from the scientific as well as the literary world. After that first meeting, she spent hours of pleasant conversation with him in his small abode in Clivus Antonini, close to the Forum.[24] Their correspondence created the foundation of a friendship that lasted throughout the rest of their lives.[25]

From then on her articles in the *Boston Evening Transcript* grew in frequency: a dozen appeared in 1903 alone, concerning Guglielmo Marconi, the Pope, life in Rome and in other cities and centers of art in Italy, including the Venice exhibition, in connection with which she discussed John Singer Sargent's portrait of the three Hunter sisters and the stereotypes with which Italy and America regarded each other.[26] Amongst these stereotypes was the wide-

---

[23] Amy A. Bernardy and Vittorio Falorsi, *La Questione Adriatica vista d'oltre Atlantico (1917-1919)* (Bologna: Zanichelli, 1923) 151.

[24] Bernardy, "Giacomo Boni, the architect who will rebuild the campanile," *Boston Evening Transcript* [hereafter *BT*] (November 15, 1902): 20.

[25] Corrispondenza Boni-Bernardy, Epistolario B, XXXIX, Archivio Boni, Accademia di Scienze e Lettere, Istituto Lombardo, Milan.

[26] Bernardy's articles in the BT during 1903: "With Marconi on Cape Cod," January 21, 1903; "Marconi, Civis Romanus," May 23, 1903; "Marconi in Europe," November 28, 1903; "A Successor to Leo," March 7, 1903; "The Man Who Smiles," August

spread notion that while Italy, by the richness and beauty of its historical and natural landscapes and relaxed lifestyle, fostered artistic expression, this could find no place in the States, the land of mechanical and commercial progress. Even some of her Italian acquaintances subscribed to the notion that: "to our own Latin mind, to the really Latin mind, the United States stands as the negation of art and of delicate artistic intuition and sensitiveness. To be sure, they have what we lack, the power to make money. Well, we do not have it, and we may safely boast of it." Bernardy believed, on the contrary, that art could flourish too on American soil: the very fact that at the Venice exhibit the principal piece was an American painting demonstrated that the United States were taking rank among the best art producers of the world. However, American art was still "somewhat too European," it did not show yet the "vigorous stamp of a personality unmistakably American." "Why—she observed—don't American artists turn awhile from Italy and Normandy and Brittany and give us some artistic portrayal of the characteristic features of their homeland?" There were surely elements of beauty also in "the land of iron and steam and electricity." American artists had potential sources of inspiration in the great cities of the East, in the shores of Maine, or in the magnificent scenery in the West and South at their disposal. And American wealth could have been used to enhance this artistic process. Bernardy concluded: "It appears to me that there is a broad and triumphal way open in this direction to American art."[27]

22, 1903; "Easter Pilgrims at Rome," April 11, 1903; "Three Emperors in Rome," April 29, 1903; "The Heart of Rome" November 25, 1903; "The New Campanile," May 13, 1903; "Uncovering the Forum," December 9, 1903; "Socialists in Italian Universities," February 18, 1903; "Monsignor Guidi," January 7, 1903; "American Art at the Venice Exposition," October 28, 1903.

[27] Bernardy, "American Art at the Venice Exposition," *BT*, October 28, 1903, 16.

For Bernardy, politics too derived from the way in which each of the two countries regarded its own history and culture. She noted an excess of pride in the one case, and of modesty in the other; that is to say, the widespread conviction in the USA that America was "the number one country in the world," and the "vague self-dissatisfaction" that prevailed in Italy,[28] the latter accompanied by an "acute americanitis" on the part of more or less superficial Italian observers (Bernardy, *America vissuta*, 35). She was critical of either excess—of US pride and Italian modesty— since she thought that the American culture lacked the "fine-grained emery," the "finesse of the ancient races" which only time can provide (Bernardy, "Refugium," 6). And therefore, as an inveterate nationalist, she set out to passionately defend *italianità* in the United States, whether it appeared clad in the rags of the immigrant masses, at that time subject to virulent social rejection, or took the form of Italian foreign policy, much denigrated in the difficult wartime years. Most of her activities in the States as a writer, as a conference speaker, or even as a socialite, had this defense of *italianità* as its primary target. She was conscious of the fact that the backdrop upon which misunderstandings between the two countries were projected was the result of a complex tangle of prejudices and stereotypes that sprang from recent intense interactions (amongst them being Italian immigration to the U.S. on a massive scale) following upon centuries of reciprocal ignorance.[29]

Her articles attracted public attention and in the United States circulated also locally. Bernardy recalled the frequency with which articles she published in Italy were taken up by numerous Italian-American newspapers, and the resulting invitations she received

---

[28] Bernardy, "Modestia sbagliata," *Il Regno* 1.35 (July 24, 1904): 8; Bernardy, "Refugium peccatorum," *Il Regno*, 1.8 (February 21, 1904): 6.

[29] See the first chapter of Daniela Rossini, *Woodrow Wilson and the American Myth in Italy. Culture, Diplomacy and War Propaganda* (Cambridge: Harvard UP, 2008) 4-32.

from the immigrant communities.[30] Her Italian articles about the United States echoed too in the most widely-read American dailies: for example, the *San Francisco Chronicle* summarized two of her pieces on American women and Italian emigration originally published in *La Nuova Antologia* and *La Minerva*, while the *Washington Post* referred to other articles on Italian-American criminality which had originally appeared in *Il Giornale d'Italia*.[31]

In Italy her voice was heard with ever-increasing frequency, as it passed from magazines to the daily papers, and from these into books she authored. Indeed, her freelance journalism and her book authorship were mutually sustaining, generating a readership pool large enough to support her creative work in its entirety.[32] However, the fact that she denounced the exploitation of the immigrants, supported the establishment of associations in their defense, and held lectures for them[33] should not blind us to the totality of her perspectives. As Martellone observes, her attitude was a paternalistic and elitist one, the direct offshoot of her nationalism.[34] Bernardy was concerned above all by the "damage" done to the image of Italy by this poor and ignorant immigrant horde.[35]

---

[30] "Smith College Teacher helps Italian Immigrants," *BG*, May 26, 1907, 46.

[31] "Affectations of American Women," *San Francisco Chronicle* (October 26, 1906); "American Books Popular in Italy," *San Francisco Chronicle* (January 2, 1910); "War on Black Hand," *W. Post* (October 9, 1910) and "Black Hand Exposed," *W. Post* (December 25, 1910). Bernardy writes about the Black Hand in *Italia randagia attraverso gli Stati Uniti*, 189-194.

[32] Silvia Franchini and Simonetta Soldani, eds., *Donne e giornalismo. Percorsi e presenze di una storia di genere* (Milan: FrancoAngeli, 2004) 24.

[33] "War on Black Hand," *W. Post* (October 9, 1910); "Talk of strike by teamsters," *BG* (March 12, 1906); "Italy of Today Not Known by Most of the Italians Coming Here," *BG* (April 10, 1905).

[34] Anna Maria Martellone, *Una Little Italy nell'Atene d'America. La comunità italiana di Boston dal 1880 al 1920* (Naples: Guida, 1973) 126-7.

[35] Bernardy, "Perchè gl'Italiani si addensano nelle città americane" in Frank J. Sheridan, Amy A. Bernardy, Emily F. Meade e Napoleone Colajanni, *Gl'Italiani negli Stati Uniti* (Naples: Rivista Popolare, 1909) 33-40; Bernardy, "Refugium peccatorum," 5-7.

By creating a more responsible tutelage of the emigrant population, Bernardy hoped to also prevent further sullying of the image of Italy abroad: her protest too involved the condemnation of the political class of the Giolitti era for its lack of concern for the education and health of the emigrants.[36] Her work displays a sympathetic awareness of the trials faced by these people—"there's often more tragedy in a single one of these humble lives than in a whole series of volumes," she wrote to Beltramelli[37]—but her primary focus was the defense of Italy's international prestige, marred by their ignorance, their dire poverty, their occasional criminality, and their frequent wretchedness.

This being the case, in her view, a huge responsibility rested on the Italian elites in America, who had a duty to counter the negativity of that country's ever more apparent image of the Italians by presenting an alternative: the refined Italy of the cultured and prosperous classes, the Italy of history, of landscapes, of art. She did not question, but considered ineliminable the presence of such a sharp dichotomy in Italian class structure:

> [M]ay the young people of our embassy and our consulates go out into American society, may they go out and show to the grandsons of the puritan Fathers, to the descendants of Virginian colonels and of northern abolitionists, that old Italy can still produce its gentlemen.... (Bernardy, "Refugium peccatorum," 6)

or again,

> There is so little of superior Italy in America, that that small part labors under a great responsibility: any false step it may take becomes multiplied a hundredfold in that it appears representative of the illiterate mass which is present there, and of the popula-

---

[36] "Lo scandalo del monumento," *Il Marzocco* 16.36 (September 3, 1911): 1.

[37] Bernardy to Antonio Beltramelli, April 11, no year [around 1903-1905], Fondo Antonio Beltramelli, Biblioteca Comunale, Forlí.

tion that lies across the ocean.... (Bernardy "L'emigrazione delle donne," 138)

Bernardy felt herself to be a member of this elite and devoted herself with great diligence to the task of representing Italy to America. She held lectures on Italian art, literature, and history, especially in the cities along the eastern seaboard, and amongst these most frequently Boston, where she became a member of the governing board of the local section of the Società Dante Alighieri, assisting in its reorganization (Bernardy, *Italia randagia*, 237).

But the extent of her work was not limited to her journalism and lectures, she took part in initiatives under the aegis of the Washington embassy, the consulates, and the Italian-American communities of Boston, Philadelphia, New York and Chicago. At the same time she also conducted interviews with well-known Italians and Americans, including Guglielmo Marconi, Eleonora Duse, Theodore Roosevelt and William Taft. Her activities amounted to an intensive campaign to enhance the image of Italy in the United States.[38]

In 1909 and 1911, she met Theodore Roosevelt and William Taft at the White House. In the case of Roosevelt, their interaction was not a typical interview as she was invited only to sit in his office and observe him at work, which allowed only for the exchange of a few phrases. Her report details her impressions of the president's character during this time of silent observation, while he met a dozen visitors pressing their own cases. She took note of the effect of "the Great Teddy" persona on people, his overflowing energy bordering on sheer aggression. She pointed often to his grin "full of teeth," almost a sneer, a rictus, and the moment Roo-

---

[38] Bernardy describes her collaboration with the *Boston Transcript* in *America vissuta*, 445-6; for the articles she published in American magazines, see: "How to see Italy," *Outlook* (April 20, 1907): 890-93; "A New Influence in Music: the Pope," *Good Housekeeping* (October 4, 1904): 379-384; "The Italian Gift of Song: An Interview with Pope Pius the Tenth," *Good Housekeeping* (April 1907): 386-390; "Our Graceful Tyrants," *Good Housekeeping* (July 1908): 33-34.

sevelt acknowledged her with this grimace, seeming to say: "Now, I am going to devour you!" In his case, she creates this insightful portrait of a leader with his charisma on full display, while in the case of Taft, we get the impression of just his imposing physical appearance. He is "a very decent person," but for a political leader this virtue is not enough, he looked bland, almost an insignificant figure, especially in comparison with his "pyrotechnic predecessor." Of course, the fact that he favored restrictions of immigration to the US did not help his image.[39]

The American newspapers also reported on the assignment entrusted to Bernardy in 1907-8 by an Italian Commission, the Commissariato Generale per l'Emigrazione, to investigate the living and working conditions of emigrant women and children in the United States.[40] Originally confined to the Northeastern zone of the country, the inquiry was then extended to the vast area of the midwest and western states. The thorough surveying implied by the project was very different from her usual work as a writer, and was met by an initial reaction of bewilderment.[41] In any case, Bernardy took on this assignment, giving it priority, first asking for a period of leave and subsequently resigning from the College in order to bring it to its completion. These travels took her to the poorest areas of American cities, observing neighborhoods, homes, workplaces, and meetings of Italians in the course of their daily routines. Often she found herself in conditions of discomfort, particularly in the Northwest where she chose to go in winter, wanting to capture the immigrants' living conditions during the more difficult months.

---

[39] Chapter VIII, "I due Presidenti," in Bernardy, *America vissuta*, 165-190.

[40] "What Women Are Doing," *Chicago Daily Tribune* (May 31, 1908); "Miss Bernardy's Work," *NY Tribune* (May 2,1908); "Girl Advises King of Italy," *LA Times* (November 5, 1908); "Good Words for Coast," *LA Times* (April 16, 1910).

[41] Bernardy to Villari, March 28, no year [probably 1907], box. 5, folder 243-4, Carteggio Villari, BAV.

The outcome was two reports of around two hundred pages each, published in 1909 and 1911 in the official bulletin of the Commission for Emigration, a division of the Ministry of Foreign Affairs.[42] And with her main volumes on American society still to come, these works confirmed her status as a specialist of Italian emigration to the States. At the end she declared herself "familiar now with every one of the Italian settlements in America" (Bernardy, *Paese che vai*, 290).

Over a period of some twenty years, she made around forty Atlantic crossings (Bernardy, *Paese che vai*, 6 and 9). Her links with the United States constituted the basis of her activity as a propagandist during the war and in the immediate post-war years. Already in 1916 she offered "to serve, in any way I can, the Fatherland," above all in America.[43] Then for the next two years, beginning in the spring of 1917, Bernardy worked for the "Propaganda Office" of the Italian embassy in Washington, one of the few propagandists attached to the diplomatic apparatus, and the only woman—in fact, she received her salary from the Dante Alighieri Society, a private association, because the law did not permit a woman to be employed in positions of authority within the Ministry of Foreign Affairs.[44] Exploiting her skills and the contacts she had forged in the pre-war years, she worked as a speaker, as a journalist and as a liaison with the Italian-American communities. The

---

[42] Bernardy, "L'emigrazione delle donne e dei fanciulli italiani nella North Atlantic Division, Stati Uniti d'America," *Bollettino dell'emigrazione* 1 (1909) (210 pages) and "Sulle condizioni delle donne e dei fanciulli italiani negli Stati del Centro e dell'Ovest della Confederazione del Nord-America," *Bollettino dell'emigrazione* 1 (1911) (171 pages).

[43] Bernardy to Paolo Boselli, July 20, [1916] and Boselli to Bernardy, July 21, 1916, box 40 "Propaganda di guerra," folder 40 "Amy Bernardy," Fondo Presidenza del Consiglio dei Ministri, Guerra Europea 1915-1918, Archivio Centrale dello Stato, Roma.

[44] Daniela Rossini, *Donne e propaganda internazionale. Percorsi femminili tra Italia e Stati Uniti nell'età della Grande Guerra* (Milan: FrancoAngeli, 2015) 50-58, 93-108.

Boston Evening Transcript, for example, continued to publish her articles and in general maintained a sympathetic attitude towards Italy. Given Bernardy's wide range of qualities—"a keen intelligence, considerable culture, penetrating judgment and a stylish way with the pen"—she served as a precious resource to the Embassy and the Commission and was a vital voice in shaping the two countries' mutual images in a pivotal phase of their relations.[45]

---

[45] Edmondo Mayor des Planches to Egisto Rossi, January 15, 1905, box 175, folder 3964, Fondo Ambasciata d'Italia, Washington 1901-1909.

Italian Americans on Emily Dickinson

Maria Anita Stefanelli
ROMA TRE UNIVERSITY

To the memory of my mother,
Olimpia Gioseffi

An element of Italian culture is identifiable in *patria potestà*, a key legal term in the life of Italians who crossed the ocean as migrants and established themselves in America before 1975, the date of the "Riforma del diritto di famiglia" ('legge n.151/1975').[1] The concept of *patria potestas*, linked to the figure of *pater familias*, comes from Roman law, according to which the male head of the household had "power over his wife, children, agnatic descendants, slaves, and freedmen." It also included, originally, the *ius vitae ac necis,* in other words, "the right to punish by death and always embraced complete control over the limited personal and private rights and duties of all members of the family." (*Merriam-Webster Dictionary* online). With the 1974 reform, "potestà" was entrusted to both parents, although the word itself had become an anachronism, and was replaced in 2006 by "responsabilità genitoriale" (parental responsibility).[2]

People's cultural practices, however, do not automatically conform to established rules, especially those that reduce privileges—in this case, the privileges of the male members of the family, who

---

[1] Family Law Reform, Italian law no. 151/1975.

[2] This was laid down by Italian law no. 54/2006 on the "affidamento condiviso dei figli" (joint care of children) that followed the 1989 New York Convention on the Rights of the Child (which came into force in 1990) and the 1996 Strasbourg Convention (ratified 2003) and that was substantially revised by 'legge n. 154/2013.'

often prefer to disregard such change and assert their authority as head of the family. Before 1975, for example, the husband could decide, by law, where the family would reside, and the wife had to follow suit. With the change in law, the official power of men was diminished. In the home, however, control and surveillance remained and was still carried out by, or on behalf of, the male head of the family; daughters who were no longer minors were kept closely watched until they were married. With marriage, women would again be subject to traditional Italian male ideology. Such 'obligations' again had a kind of equivalence in the Roman *manus maritalis*, which assigned *pater familias* "potestas" over the wife. If a woman stayed single, for instance, she would depend on her father for her education, the potential choice of a husband, financial support and help, in exchange for domestic work which would be demanded (rather than simply being offered by the daughter).

Traditional habits (albeit with regional differences) continued to be tacitly acknowledged; therefore, while specific legal aspects would be challenged in disputes, litigation, or various judicial wrangles, old values remained so deeply rooted in the Italian culture, interiorized by the family, that they often persisted uncontested.

To counter the effects of patriarchy, female members of Italian families often looked for ways of empowerment, and this usually meant finding a way to earn a living, or at least *some* money. An enlightening essay by Mary Jo Bona explores the role of female migrants in the home during the late nineteenth and early twentieth centuries utilizing the filter of Italian American writers who focus on the craftsmanship of sewing. The sewer represented in such scholarship, she writes, "reveals a vision of the world that is fundamentally unjust; she struggles to free herself from powerlessness; and she, or the author as her mouthpiece, links the dual activities of sewing and storytelling melding two forms of expression used by the traditionally powerless. The connection the writers make between sewing and storytelling radicalizes the narrative itself, serving liberatory purposes for the woman who sews and with whom she shares her skills" (Bona 145). The activity itself, however, might eventually secure self-sufficiency.

Cooking was another domestic activity from which single women were hardly exempt. In her autobiography, Diane di Prima has a passage on her—apparently aristocratic, and somewhat prosperous—grandmother Antoinette's homely tasks. After her mother passed away, and being the only girl amongst six brothers and a father, she was expected to oversee the servants and, most certainly, to "plan the menus" for no other reason than being "a very skilled cook." This is how di Prima describes her *nonna's* way of life:

> For all her wealth, she was in a state of serious servitude. Seems my grandmother had six brothers and a father, and her mother had died, and nobody in the family had any intention of letting her marry at all—she was living, it was quite apparent to the men of the household, solely to keep house for them and provide the womanly comforts, however they might have been conceived back then. (We are talking the last decades of the nineteenth century here). [...] When her brothers (and presumably her father [...]) found out that she was being courted—and by such a low-class type as Domenico!—they locked her up in her room. She was their property, clearly, and they weren't about to let the only woman in the house go anywhere. (di Prima 4-5)

In spite of the grandmother—to put it figuratively—being an *istituzione* among first generation Italian emigrants, she was also, somewhat ambiguously, subjected to the male hierarchy. For second and third generation Italian Americans she was often the only one who could speak Italian, or the dialect of her place of origin if she had received no formal education; she was also the one who held onto, and could pass on, family secrets concerning cooking or embroidery. Gradually, with the female offspring of Italian immigrants (several writers among them) having begun to tell their stories, a collective identity began to form the shape of an "all-powerful immigrant grandmother with whom they form a bond" (Romano 107).[3] Whether realistic or not, one such portrait is given in the verse of Maria Fama:

> Nonna Mattia,
> I wrap your apron around me twice
> As I look for cover in your
> Largeness of body and heart
>
> Grant me a portion of your
> Robustness of spirit, great grandmother
>
> Let this apron be my shield
> Let this apron transfer your strong faith
> Your compassion and your courage
> To me, your great granddaughter

"I view Nonna Mattia as a powerful woman, a true heroine," Fama adds in prose (113). A collective creation, the grandmother entered the fictional work of a third generation of Italian writers as the epic ancestress who could provide a consciousness for Italian Americans (many of whom were Americans who hardly spoke Italian) with accepted ethnic roots (Gardaphé 2003, 107).

Besides their culture, migrants to the New World brought with them their character, disposition, virtues and vices, the memory of what they were leaving, and their hopes for the future. They carried across themselves, and, once *in loco*, they longed, or in many

---

[3] Romano lists, among many other women writers, Mary Ann Vigilante Mannino and her book, *Revisionary Identities: Strategies of Empowerment in the Writing of Italian/American Women*.

cases just happened, to become acquainted, or even identify with, the personalities or celebrities of the new land. As to Emily Dickinson—in Camille Paglia's words "the greatest of women poets ... [i]gnored by her own time, ... sentimentalized in her renascence" (623-24)—her genealogical background, meticulously recorded in her poetry, has attracted Italian-American authors whose ancestors would have experienced similar brutality and passion, pain and pleasure, oppression and freedom, violence and survival.

Dickinson was born and bred in Amherst, and it was there that she lived, forming complex relationships with the members of her family and with the eminent literary and religious figures that entered the orbit of her household. She traveled little, read extensively, and her imagination was fecund, luxurious and intense. Her sense of geographical and psychological distance did not prevent her from loving the country's spirit, and Italian American writers reciprocated her esteem with respect and love for her poetry, as well as for her effortlessly acquired independence of mind and spirit.

Various sections follow below, centering on Italian-American writers who embraced the intellectual challenge posed by Dickinson's writings, with the inclusion of Susan Howe, whose half-Irish pedigree and profound appreciation of the poet's insight link her inextricably to those impassioned close readers of Dickinson.

§ SANDRA GILBERT

Since the 1970s, Dickinson has been a favorite author of Anglo-American feminist literary criticism, and was discussed at length in Sandra Gilbert and Susan Gubar's groundbreaking book, *The Madwoman in the Attic*. It was the Italian-American of the two authors, Gilbert, *née* Sandy Mortola, who wrote the chapters "The Aesthetics of Renunciation" and "A Woman—White: Emily Dickinson's Yarn of Pearl," a possible reason being that the two authors made their respective choices following a methodology that consisted in "reading our own lives as well as the texts we study" (Gilbert and Gubar, "Preface" xiii). In the case of Gilbert, she might have read her own life and her own different selves as she was reading Dickinson. One should add that the almost one hundred pages she wrote (where Dickinson gets the lion's share), reveal an obsession with names and naming, the masks Emily wears, and the roles she plays, or does not play, as child, daughter, sister, virgin, wife, spinster ... and Nobody (Gilbert and Gubar, 288).

Could that preoccupation with identity have something to do with Sandra's *italianità* encrypted behind the English surname of her husband, Elliot L. Gilbert?

"I'm Nobody! Who are you?" is the calling card presented in a poem by Dickinson herself which Gilbert uses to illustrate—however ironically—"female self-effacement" versus Whitman's "male self-assertion" (554). Examining in detail the literary consequences of "being Nobody" Gilbert uncovers the range "from a sometimes grotesquely childlike self-image to a painfully distorted sense of size, a perpetual growing hunger, and even, finally, a deep confusion about identity" (555). The critic adds one more sentence that may interest us in our present "re-mapping of Italian America," and that is: "Moreover, being Nobody had worldly consequences, and these may ultimately have been even more serious" (555).

In the case of Dickinson, "being Nobody" meant—among other possible interpretations—being unpublished. Being a woman in society has very often meant "being Nobody"; and "being Nobody," at times, could mean being different owing to culture, gender, sexual preference, or class. Among migrants, "being Nobody" frequently meant, and still means, belonging to a different ethnicity or being without papers, and thus being considered useless or worthless. Thus, one might readily muse if "Italian Americans" transiting through Ellis Island experienced "being Nobody," not being alive? A preoccupation—that of being or not being alive—that Dickinson feels in her poetry.[5]

Like Dickinson, many literary women worldwide have suffered from some sort of identity crisis, and, in a "double-bind" situation, juggle such conflicting roles as being "a woman" or "a poet."[6] Indeed, they could be both *Nobody* and, at the same time, like their male fellow writers, caught in a certain dualism. They may have to face the existential dilemma of a *double identity* when involved, like the Italian American, "in forging an identity out of two competing ways of living and thinking," as Fred Gardaphé puts it (15). However, in the best-case scenarios, Anthony Tamburri, in describing the work of poets of Italian descent, Maria Mazziotti Gillan and Rina Ferrarelli, believes their talent allows them to construct "a double-voiced world that underscores the compound relationship of ethnicity and gender" (xi).

§ HELEN BAROLINI

Proclaiming to be "Nobody" did not prevent Dickinson from creating different identities in her poetry and her letters.[7] In fact,

---

[5] In a letter (April 15, 1862) to Thomas Wentworth Higginson Dickinson asks if her "verse is alive" (Johnson and Ward, L. 260, 403).

[6] Juhasz has explored this theme with reference to Anne Sexton: "To be a woman poet in our society is a double-bind situation, one of conflict and strain. For the words 'woman' and 'poet' denote opposite and contradictory qualities and roles. Traditionally, the poet is a man, and 'poetry' is the poems that men write. The long history of Western literature makes this point painfully clear. It is men who make art, who make books; women make babies. 'Women' are, according to society's rules, very different from 'poets.' A woman's identity is not defined by a profession, such as poet, but by her personal relationships as daughter, sister, wife, mother. Her art (if she presumes to have one) must necessarily conflict with her life. Usually she is pressured, or pressures herself ... to make a choice 'woman' or 'poet'" (1).

[7] Childish personae are a little girl (or boy), a humble Daisy, a small river (Juhasz 7); other personae include wife, daughter (Juhasz 9), Queen, (Juhasz 10) and lover (Juhasz 12).

205

her writings reveal several masks, personae, or *sides* making up the idea, as Helen Barolini calls it in her essay title, "The Italian Side of Emily Dickinson," of the *italicità* [*ante litteram*] of the great poet's diasporic imagination (1994).[8] To support her view, the author of *Umbertina*—the fictional story of an immigrant who achieves economic success for the family while simultaneously becoming a challenge for her granddaughter and great-granddaughter—mentions a 1975 note scribbled in an edition of Dickinson's works by scholar David T. Porter. With reference to the opening lines of poem 1924, "When Etna basks and purrs,/ Naples is more afraid," Porter commented that "Emily Dickinson never visited Italy, and misplaced Mount Etna in Naples; but she was Italian at heart!" (Barolini 2006, 77).[9] Dickinson's wonderment and admiration for Italy (as revealed in poem 80, "Our lives are Swiss") were nourished, according to Barolini, by Mme de Stael's *Corinne, ou l'Italie*, and Elizabeth Barrett Browning's *Aurora Leigh*, with Italy equaling, for the former, "freedom for the superior woman," and for the latter, "My Italy of women." What she could not see from Amherst, Barolini points out, she invents, as in poem 1705:

> Volcanoes be in Sicily
> And South America
> I judge from my geography—
> Volcanos nearer here
> A Lava step at any time
> Am I inclined to climb—
> A Crater I may contemplate
> Vesuvius at Home.

---

[8] *Italicità* rather than *italianità* is the word that Piero Bassetti has been championing for many years with regard to those who are not of Italian descent, but feel, like Dickinson would have felt, a sense of belonging to Italian culture and identity.

[9] That happened during Barolini's research work as residence-writer at Villa Serbelloni, the site of the Rockefeller Foundation's Bellagio Center that fosters cross-cultural and interdisciplinary exchange for the promotion of "the well-being of humanity around the world."

By mentally ascending the mountain to reach the edge of the chasm wherefrom the mystery that dwells in Italy may be pondered, the self acknowledges Italy's visionary potential, its openness, and its freedom. Following in the footsteps of Adrienne Rich's seminal feminist essay, "Vesuvius at Home" (where the use of masks is interpreted as a strategy to conceal power), Barolini elaborates on the idea that Dickinson's "mind [is] capable of describing psychological states more accurately than any poet except Shakespeare" (Barolini 2006, 79). Without resorting to abnormality as a reason or as a justification for not getting married, Barolini values her *slant* stressing (Johnson 1955, poem 1129), her "ambivalence, the teasing switch of genders in her poetic voice, [and] the split between alternate sides of the same person" (Barolini 2006, 80-81). Not unlike the occasional Italian-American migrant woman who defied the tradition of a woman's social recognition being dependent on marriage and maternity and opted instead to take responsibility for her own life, Dickinson empowered her own celibate self—and here I step into Barolini's act of grammatical violence—by "husband-ing" her gift.[10]

§ DANIELA GIOSEFFI, SUSAN HOWE, MARIA MAZZIOTTI GILLAN

"I come from Greek-Albanian-Italian and Polish-Russian-Jewish immigrants, and was born in the twentieth century, but we're both [Emily and I] American women poets of a liberal and rebellious bent," Daniela Gioseffi declares in an interview on the subject of her novel *"Wild Nights! Wild Nights!"* Then she clarifies, "Dickinson was a transcendentalist rebelling against the Puritans, and she made poetry her means of worshipping nature and all creation. I'm a progressive eco-feminist humanist, a Free Thinker, as I believe Dickinson was for her time." She then adds, "[k]nowing her

---

[10] See the use of "husband" as verb (Barolini 1994, 470).

story makes her poetry more accessible to me, and I am enamored of studying the truth of science, too" (Gioseffi 2010b, online).

A liberal, rebellious, independent woman with a penchant for science: these characteristics, Gioseffi emphatically asserts, made her a scholar of Dickinson. Early opposition to the repressiveness of her Italian heritage condemned and isolated her, simply because she was a woman, as she stated: "I grew up always hearing my Italian immigrant father longing for a son. He'd bemoan, 'If only I had a son to carry on the name!' whenever we three sisters upset him" (Gioseffi 2010b). Even if he believed in women's education, so that a girl could grow into a good wife and mother, this did not include college. The slow progress of her time in matters regarding women's emancipation—Daniela was born in 1941, less than twenty years after women's suffrage had been established nationally in the USA—parallels similar struggles in Dickinson's, who was born a hundred and nine years earlier. According to the assumptions of the time, Emily's father believed in education for girls as well as boys, although he also thought that a woman's main concerns should be domestic. He also presided over the type of literature that his children read and would eventually be inspired by. "His heart was pure and terrible and I think no other like it exists," Dickinson confided to her mentor, Higginson, after her father's death (July 16, 1874; Johnson 2: L. 418, 538).

On the other hand, Signor Donato Gioseffi, born in Italy in 1906, had a "deeply passionate nature," and "his ability to empathize with other's sorrow, joy, and longing—even when they were characters in poetic dramas and romantic novels—much inspired," the poet recalls, her future writing (Gioseffi, 2010b, online). His mode of expression characterized by "passionate displays, talk with gesticulation, animated body-language, folksy warmth and informality," did however, as Gioseffi states on the basis of a 1986 study (Robertiello and Hoguet), clash with the "bigotry" of the prejudiced and snobbish society that Italian immigrants had to face "in their attempt to Americanize themselves and assimilate" (Gioseffi 2015). In spite of widespread prejudice and discrimination, Gioseffi succeeded in her career as a writer largely thanks to her father from whom she inherited her love for literature.

One of Gioseffi's favorite facets of Dickinson's multidimensional personality is her "intelligent and progressive mind *as lover of science and scientist*, a thinker who heralded the acceptance of Darwinism to come, and who found spiritual solace in understanding the beauty and wonder of the natural world" (*WN!WN!* online). Volcanoes, the science of which hid various mysteries, whether on the geographical/geological or symbolic level, are functional to her poetry. In one of the three "Master letters" (1861), Dickinson wrote, presumably to the one she loved:

> Vesuvius don't talk—Etna—don't—[Thy] one of them—a sylla-
> ble—A thousand years ago, and Pompeii heard it, and hid forev-
> er—She could look the world in the face, afterward—I sup-
> pose—"Tell you of the want"—you know what a leech is, don't
> you—[remember that] Daisy's arm is small—and you have felt
> the horizon hav'nt you—and did the sea—never come so close as
> to make you dance? (Johnson and Ward 1986, L. 233, 373-75).

Gioseffi quotes the passage, written without line breaks, and reflects on it: "Love, when left unattended or in silence, can explode forth and be felt by the soul. Isn't the volcano Dickinson's symbol for the rage of repressed passion that kept under pressure, like lava, explodes from burning depths?" (Gioseffi 2011, 12). The poet humanizes the volcanoes and the city of Pompeii to create a trope of silence; this serves as a metaphor for repression, which may denote both restraint (one's own choice not to speak) and constraint (somebody else's choice or imposition). Would the poet be referring to the Master rejecting her love through silence and Daisy's [the poet's] passion/despair exploding? Or to the Master being told not to speak while Daisy is telling him how much she would miss him after their parting? Silence can be a choice: like Emily's, who refuses to make a public profession of her belief in Christ as her father would have wished; like Cordelia's, who refuses to speak her love for her father; and like the migrant Italian woman, who chooses to sew to liberate herself from paternal coercion and silent compliance. Yet it can also be an insult to the person who professes love for us. In her seminal work, *My Emily Dickinson*, poet-scholar Susan Howe, who often prefers to juxtapose quotations from literary, cultural and historical essays, or to offer a personal, lyrical aesthetic outpouring rather than extensive comment as critique, quotes the above lines from Dickinson's letter just after inserting in her discussion a line from *King Lear* (Howe 2007, 103). This is where the Fool comments on women's vanity in order to criticize Lear indirectly for being appreciative of his evil daughters' false speeches rather than Cordelia's silence. Howe also used the scanned image of the versified transcription part of the quotation from the Master letter as an epigraph exhibiting the lines in their sigma-like arrangement:

```
Vesuvius   dont   talk  . Etna  .dont  .
they   said a   syllable   one of them
a   thousand   years   ago , and
Pompeii   heard   it ,   and   hid
forever - She   couldnt   look the
world   in   the   face . afterward -
I suppose -   Bashful Pompeii !
Tell you   of   the   want - you
know   what   a   leech   is , dont
you - and   Daisys   arm   is small .
```

[11]

[11] This is the scanned image of one of Dickinson's original "Master Letters" (Johnson, L. 233, 373-375, c. 1861), used by Howe as an epigraph (Howe 1993).

The grapheme associated with the voiceless phoneme it represents makes up a "vision" of silence. The volcano as silence, or repressed talk. "One of the central paradoxes in Howe's work involves the function of silence in poetry, especially poetry by and about women," writes Susan Schultz, adding: "Howe's revision of literary history problematically reproduces women's silences in the text even as it permits their voices to speak through the agency of the reader" (Schultz 21). After all, Dickinson's ambivalent resistance to having her work published goes hand in hand with Howe's challenging of the editors' handling of Dickinson's texts, and, consequently, the violence performed on her output. Not only, in fact, does a question mark still hang over Dickinson's reason for ordering her correspondence to be burned, but also over the posthumous battle for the consignment of the poems to the world as well as the questionable editing of the poet's mercurial textual variants that also gave rise to bitter quarrels between her relations, and eventually legal battles.[12] The question, as one can read in another review of Howe's The Birth-Mark, is that "Emily Dickinson's body of work is, in effect, a manifestation of a much larger American problem: colonization, captivity" until, that is, literary criticism engages in "restoring" the work (Froid online). Indeed this is a problem that Italian migrants and their ancestors had suffered at home during various foreign invasions, with the additional sting of being disparagingly considered "colored," and thus, victims of "the poison of racial hatred" in the New World (Howe in Foster 1990, 164). "How are we such a violent nation? [...] I am trying to understand what went wrong when the first Europeans stepped on shore here" (Howe 164). Maria Mazziotti Gillan, too, as an Italian American woman writer, rejoices in proclaiming in verse the

---

[12] For an introduction to the complex question of the editing, publication and partial destruction or loss of Dickinson's writings, see "Emily Dickinson Museum" Web May 2, 2017 writings.

finding of her voice; her lines sound and look almost Dickinsonian:

> Remember me, Ladies,
> The silent one?
> I have found my voice
> And my rage will blow
> Your house down. (13)

There was the silence of women—like Dickinson's, like that of Italian American women and their descendants—in addition to a pride in one's ancestry, the search for legitimation and official recognition of one's Americanness. But the energy being engaged in what Gillan's book title sums up as *Writing Poetry to Save Your Life: How to Find The Courage to Tell Your Stories* would eventually lead to their voices being heard and becoming thunderous.

Aligning with Howe, Gioseffi asserts that Dickinson's life at home is "a volcano of emotions and passions held in, but released in her poetry" (Gioseffi 2011, 18), and then offers the icon of the poet's life as a "loaded gun" with its "Vesuvian face" "to signify the pleasure of emotional release or ecstasy erupting" (19). The first two stanzas of poem 754 run like this:

> My Life has stood—a loaded gun—
> In Corners—till a Day
> The Owner passed—identified—
> And carried me away—
>
> And now We roam in Sovereign Woods—
> And now We hunt the Doe—
> And every time I speak for Him—
> The Mountains straight reply—

The "loaded gun" has intrigued critics owing to its ambivalence. Is it a metaphorical weapon, or the verbal counterpart of the "slender gun standing on the floor next to portraits of Dickinson judges, generals, governors, and ministers [...] used in killing Indians and wolves," such as we find in a photograph taken in an 1883 Reunion of the "Dickinson family, in Amherst, Massachusetts? The photo shows "a slender gun standing on the floor next to the portraits of Dickinson judges, generals, governors and Ministers—a weapon said to have been used 'in killing Indian and wolves'" (Habegger 4).[13]

The surname of Emily's grandmother, Lucretia Gunn, has led critics to speculate that Emily may have had her ill-tempered granny in mind, whose image she reworks so that Lucretia becomes the sign of the environment in which she grew up.[14] Far from being an idyllic place, the Amherst surroundings were an area of colonialism and extermination, where the rifle was an instrument of defense and offense in the frequent conflicts with the natives, and hunting was a principal source for food (Price 469). In a letter to her son Edward, Mrs. Gunn bluntly described the family activity of the moment: "We are engaged killing hogs to day of course must shorten my letter" (Habegger, Chapter 1). She was a practical grandmother figure just like Maria Fama's Nonna Mattia would be in the following century, the *nonna* whose apron her poet granddaughter imagined wrapping around herself twice as a defensive "shield."[15]

---

[13] The Reunion was attended by the descendants of Emily's paternal ancestors, Nathaniel and Ann Gull Dickinson, who in the seventeenth century had left England for a British outpost in Connecticut with the purpose of practising Puritanism without the interference of the Church of England. Emily does not appear in it.

[14] A seventeenth-century pioneer, Nathaniel Dickinson, is the man who left England (Lincolnshire) for the New World with his wife Anna, about two hundred years before Emily was born to one of his progeny, Edward, the son of Samuel Dickinson, one of the founders of Amherst College and Lucretia Gunn of Montague, Emily's paternal grandmother.

[15] See the poem "Nonna Mattia," above.

Perhaps it was not granny Lucretia who taught Dickinson to sew and cook as many *nonnas* would do in the little Italys where Italian migrants would settle, but she "must have been as proficient with needle and thread as she was with spoon and pot" (Gilbert and Gubar 639), one reads in *The Madwoman in the Attic*. Gilbert, as author of the chapter, makes a point of specifying, "Not all Dickinson's sewing was metaphorical" (639) highlighting women's skills with a needle at the time. Then, the celebrated fascicles are mentioned that—as Bona recalls in her essay on Italian-American women's needlework—"made her a 'highly conscious literary seamstress'" (Gilbert and Gubar 640; Bona 2014, 144), who "knew exactly what she was sewing and why." She copied the completed poems onto sheets of folded stationery, arranged them in groups, and sewed them together into fascicles. It was a neat job, completed with maximum, though entirely domestic, technical finesse, with additional "professional [...] marginal notes that indicate variant readings. [...] It is almost as if, in the absence of editor or printer, Dickinson had both edited and printed herself, like some late-blooming scribe" (640-41). Was she writing for posterity? A posterity, nonetheless, which would not receive her offer as it was, but would question it, and re-shape it. Perhaps because this is an excessive defense of her wish to communicate "on her own terms" (641).[16] This notwithstanding, neither male nor female editors dared to accept her silence as she had wished.

Dickinson's life was a journey through quietness and excitement, rupture and restfulness, frenzy and self-control, in perpetual tension between New England Calvinism, later becoming Congregationalism, and the recognition of its inadequacy to contemporary spiritual experience for one, like Emily, who wished to remain true to herself. Ministers from the Congregational church were regular guests at the Dickinsons' home, and her father, a

---

[16] See also Dickinson 1981.

Yale college graduate, was a strict, domineering figure, who would have preferred his daughter to profess her commitment to the congregation. On her refusal, he asked Reverend Jonathan Jenkins for an appraisal, and received confirmation of Emily's religious integrity (Habegger 542). It would not appear unusual, then, that "she read books her father did not want her to read; she was the only one in the family who did not join the church; she gradually opted out of social life and elected for herself the very unorthodox role of 'Queen Recluse'" (Lindberg-Seyersted 3).

A strict and dominant *paterfamilias* would be the rule among Italian American families. A moving portrait of Gioseffi's immigrant father appears in her "A Memorial Dedication":

He ventured through Isola delle lacrime, "The Island of Tears" [Ellis Island] in 1913, with his mother Lucia La Rosa of Naples, surviving a miserable, but hope filled, journey across the Atlantic on The USS Independence. Though disabled, sickly and poor, he shined shoes and sold newspapers to work his way through degrees from Union College and Columbia University. He was among the first Italian immigrants to achieve honors, a Phi Beta Kappa and Sigma Psi, in the Liberal Arts and Sciences from such societies. Though he spoke no English upon his arrival in the U.S., and was taunted as a "guinea gimp" by his American schoolmates, he was proud of his U.S. Citizenship, achieved in his twenties, and read to me through my youth from Dante, Rabelais, Cervantes and Shakespeare in perfect English, though he also spoke Italian fluently, making me proud of his first homeland. His final words were quoted from Prospero's in "The Tempest": *"The rarer action is in virtue than in vengeance,"* giving me an aesthetic ideal for action as his ultimate philosophy. This paragraph is offered as a tribute to all who share the memory of their immigrant or enslaved parents' struggle in America.

Not unlike the Congregationalist Edward Dickinson, who was born roughly a century before him, Signor Gioseffi used his authority, as American parents did, with intelligence, passing on to his daughter his acquired knowledge of the cultural context in which he lived. It was often recompense with no commercial value, but it was proof enough to have made it.

To his daughter-poet, Signor Gioseffi bequeathed his immigrant tenacity to seek justice and live for poetry—a poetry that is often informed with Dickinsonian references. Going back in her mind to the very beginning of feminine artistry in the Italian language, Gioseffi dedicated a poem to Vittoria Colonna, glorifying the first published European woman-poet who came of age in the sixteenth-century; Colonna is listed among "non-violent activists" along with people such as W.E.B. DuBois, Martin Luther King Jr. and Mahatma Gandhi. A sympathizer of the Reformation and a free spirit, Colonna wrote love poems for her husband while he was away on military expeditions and, after he died, explored religious themes of a somewhat mysterious significance. She was much admired by Michelangelo and entered into a deeply spiritual Platonic correspondence with him. In the two years before her untimely death, she occupied a neutral territory between religious schism and a hoped-for renewal of the Catholic Church, without ever incurring the displeasure of the religious hierarchy. It is no surprise that Dickinson would take an interest in such a noblewoman's life and writings, as is evidenced by an item of ephemera in the archives—a clipping about Colonna from *Scribner's Magazine* dated 1875 (Barolini 2006, 73). This was after her decision to wear white—according to Gioseffi not a virginal or a nunlike garment, but "a commitment to Transcendentalist philosophy, as well as her private rebellion against her father's Puritanical Calvinism" whose followers generally wore black (Gioseffi 2013, online). Not ready to accept the Puritan heritage of unconditional grace and a domineering God, Dickinson's assertive line in poem 528, "Mine—By the right of the White Election!" proclaims, by means of five further supposed possessions, her challenge to the arbitrariness of an uncharted doctrine. In the end, "staying at home" while "Some keep the Sabbath going to Church," as poem 324 discloses, is rewarded with God's sermon and a road that leads to Heaven.

Italy was "the place to go if one wanted to create and fulfill all passionate potential," Gioseffi points out in her review of Barolini's *Their Other Side: Six American Women & the Lure of Italy*. The work focuses on nineteenth and twentieth century women attracted to "Italy's mystic appeal prior to Hollywood's destruction of the idea of the fineness of Italian things and its cruel overemphasis on the Mafia stereotype" (Gioseffi 2006, online). One of the six representative women is Dickinson, who looks at Italy from poem 80, mentioned above:

> Our Lives are Swiss–
> So Still–so Cool—
> Till some odd afternoon
> The Alps neglect their Curtains
> And we look farther on!
>
> *Italy* stands the other side!
> While like a guard between
> The Solemn Alps—
> The siren Alps
> Forever intervene!

Geography here goes hand in hand with psychology, and together, these suggest an ecological ethics, an imagined liveable earth for all. Dickinson was attracted to the free spirit of Italy, and to a way of life there that must have been so different from that of her Calvinist family, strictly observant of the pulpit. In a dialogue between Emily and Clark, the Master in Gioseffi's novel *Wild Nights! Wild Nights!* Emily recites the verse quoted above that "she'd written to hint at her repressed feelings" to which he replies, "I wish you could have come to Italy with me, Miss Emily. Your poetry would flourish there where passion and art are freer to express themselves." And Emily responds, "Yes, Will. I remember Margaret Fuller wrote when she lived in Italy: 'Once I was almost all intellect; now I am almost all feeling. Nature vindicates her rights, and I feel all Italy glowing beneath the Saxon crust" (*WN!WN!*). She then leads him to a secluded bench at the back of the garden. After that, the conversation veers to a critique, on their part, of Mr. Dickinson and Clark's patron who adhere to "Calvin's old Trinitarian doctrines of predestination," while the younger pair expresses progressive views that Emily reiterates in a letter to Austin where she writes, "I'm stunned to think that father has conceded to be "Reborn" as if nature had not born him forth already. It astounds and confounds me. Such faith in Hell's fires frightens me, too." And further down, "I cannot believe in Calvinist predetermination. I prefer the imaginative imagery of Revelation and the study of nature, as Mr. Emerson preaches [...] The volume of Emerson's beautiful poetry he sent me remains my most treasured book" (*WN!WN!*). Emily and Clark's intimate relationship has grown more enthralling after their secret encounter, and, to his excitement and her exhilaration, they agree to a future meeting.

In Dickinson Gioseffi found passion and eroticism, a thing that emerges from the title of her historical novel, taken from line 1 of poem 249, "*Wild Nights—Wild Nights!*" (2010a). Colonel Higginson, misinterpreting the spirit of the lover-speaker, wrote of the poem to his co-editor, Mabel Loomis Todd, in 1891: "One poem only I dread a little to print—that wonderful 'Wild Nights,'—lest the malignant read into it more than that virgin recluse ever dreamed of putting there. Has Miss Lavinia [Emily Dickinson's sister] any shrinking about it? You will understand & pardon my solicitude. Yet what a loss to omit it! Indeed it is not to be omitted" (Bingham 127). Firmly convinced of Ruth Owen Jones' theory that the "Master figure" is recognizable as Professor William Smith Clark, Gioseffi excludes any "portrayal of a religious experience" as the interpretation of the poem. For the author of *"Wild Nights! Wild Nights!"* it is not the reader, but the rigid New England Puritan who deserved to be labeled "malignant"—in fact, the Dickinsons, who "never touched, hugged, or kissed" (*WN!WN!*). Today's reader, in fact, appropriately sees this poem as alive with sexual passion ("Wild Nights - Wild Nights!/Were I with thee/Wild Nights should be/our luxury// [...] Ah, the Sea!/Might I but moor—Tonight—/In Thee!"), the ecstatic declaration of a woman in love who is far from "emotionally detached," and has actually "adopted European styles of kissing and hugging and showing affection" (Gioseffi 2010a, online).

The next section focuses on the only male writer of Italian origin whose work on Dickinson led, like Gioseffi's, to create a fictional Emily. His involvement in Italian-American literature came after the creation of his character for the short novella, "Walt and Emily." Nonetheless, I like to think that the research he engaged into to give shape to his character may have channeled his literary efforts and his steps towards the city of Matera (where he was invited to write a work that became *The Queen of Sassi*) and the Sicilian landscape and culture.

§ PAUL DI FILIPPO

"Italian American writers usually experience the duality of a culture taught at school in English, and the culture (often expressed in the regional dialect of provenance) shared within *la famiglia* at home," Bona explains to her student interviewer at Harvard University on the occasion of a 2011 Colloquium on Italian Americans (Oliverio, online). In the case of Paul Di Filippo (born 1954), a science fiction writer, things developed differently. Italian on his mother's (third generation) and father's side (second generation), his "diluted" acquaintance with Italian culture came from his paternal grandfather, who lived with the family when

Paul was very young. No Italian was spoken at home. His experience of the immigrants' life came from a summer job in the textile mills (where his ancestors had worked) which provided the details for his short science fiction novel, *The Mill* (1991), whose protagonist, he says during an interview, has much in common with himself (Stey Nerd and Paul Di Filippo, online). A fan, and later a successful exponent of fantasy and science fiction, he has been inspired by mainstream authors like Ray Bradbury, Robert A. Heinlein, Isaac Asimov, Arthur C. Clarke, Frank Herbert and Thomas Pynchon, but also by "cult" writers like Robert Silverberg, Clifford D. Simak, Brian Aldiss, Michael Moorcock, Philip José Farmer, John Brunner, Philip K. Dick and J. G. Ballard.

Success came with *Steampunk Trilogy* in 1995. Elements of fantasy, historical fiction, and a good amount of verse are brought into the steampunk hybrid "subgenre," as classified in Ken Gelder's edition of *New Directions in Popular Fiction* under a genre that includes science fiction, which is distinct from some of its "more normative features by tapping instead into specialized subcultural tastes and dispositions" (Gelder 9). Anachronism and progress (a future that did not, however, materialize) overlap, or as the slogan of the steampunk genre has it: "what the past would look like if the future had happened sooner?" In the words of Jess Nevins, a writer-librarian who has written widely on the steampunk subgenre, [17] "The Victorian era is a mirror for the modern period, so it is appropriate for ideological stories for subjects such as feminism, imperialism, class issues, and religion" (8). "Steampunk is aware of its own loss of innocence," Nevins specifies; its writers' worlds are "polluted, cynical, and hard." It "rebels against the system it portrays, [...] critiquing its system of the underclass, its validation of the privileged at the cost of everyone else, its lack of mercy, its cutthroat capitalism" (Nevins 10).

---

[17] He is the author of works on Victoriana and pulp fiction, and accurately detailed book annotations for several comics.

The Trilogy contains a short fiction entitled "Walt and Emily." Dickinson's famous "I never read his book, but was told that it was disgraceful" (25 April 1862, Johnson L. 261, 254) in reply to Higginson's question about Whitman, is turned into her falling in love with the poet; she cannot cope, however, with male-male love, and gives him up in the end. The focus of the work is on Whitman and Dickinson's participation in a spiritualist-scientific expedition to the world beyond in the hope to communicate with Austin and Susan's (Emily's brother and sister-in-law) two aborted children. It draws on the popularity of spiritualism in England and America and the technology inspired by the industrial steam-powered machinery of Victorian times.

The novella deals with a fantasy Dickinson—the way she could have behaved if ... she had bumped into a Walt Whitman having a shower, naked, in the Homestead. Of course, it is fiction; of course Di Filippo moves between the genres he favors—science fiction and *steampunk*—and a new mainstream. The 'punk' element is there, and is identifiable, as he says, in the penchant to discredit the authority, to entertain a nihilistic hope, to use a very personal style that is strikingly unlike the standardized one—all elements welcome in pulp fiction. Throughout the story, quotes from, and connections with the protagonists' real life and works abound. The author has a firm hold on them, and the reader is not allowed to lose track of them either, even within this bizarre and dream-like context. There is no identification of the author with his creatures, nor is there any obligation for him to tell the truth. In a sense, the only obligation is not too far from Dickinson's requirement "to tell all the truth but tell it slant" (as poem 1263 recites). Di Filippo's sense of humor challenges the myth of Dickinson's Platonic relationship with men and of her solitary confinement, thereby granting her an inborn intellectual freedom, a liberated life, a life open to journeys and the appropriation of foreign spaces.

As happens with the *steampunk* attraction-and-disapproval of the Victorian cultural dynamics, Di Filippo is conscious that the past is something to come to terms with, but also something to be revived and changed to stimulate people's minds. His getting involved with his country of origin was probably a consequence of such inclinations, and this bore fruit. In 2012 his journey to Italy took him to Catania, where he met Claudio Chillemi, an Italian science fiction writer from Sicily. It was love at first sight, and this stimulated the two writers to collaborate on a novel about the Majorana case—the mysterious disappearance of young physicist Ettore Majorana after a boat trip to Palermo—which became *Operation Harmony*, a sort of "soft SF" work. Eager to learn "some neat idioms and perspectives inherent in the Italian language," Di Filippo relied on Chillemi's great knowledge of the surroundings of where Majorana had lived, and offered "details of the alternate technology, especially weird music, and also some of the historical twists in the course of the war" (Van Gelber 2014, online). The literary adventure opened the door that had been shut by his parents who wanted to become "good Americans" (Parisi online), as Di Filippo explains, and lose their links with Italian culture. The Italian past comes to the surface, and with it the privilege to restock his writing. The result is a work that combines the memory of ethnic ancestry (with its symbolic "markers") coupled with a belief in one's nationhood; two authors, two languages, and a translator. A new experiment.

It is time for a new re-mapping of the "places, cultures, and identities" of Italian America.

REFERENCES

Barolini, Helen. "Looking for Mari Tomasi." In *Chiaroscuro. Essays of Identity.* Rev. ed. Madison, Wisconsin: U Wisconsin P, 1999. 54-62.

_____. "The Italian Side of Emily Dickinson." In *Their Other Side: Six American Women and the Lure of Italy.* Fordham UP, 2006. 53-82; a slightly different version exists as "The Italian Side of Emily Dickinson." *The Virginia Quarterly Review* 70.3 (summer 1994): 461-79.

Bassetti, Piero. *Svegliamoci italici! Manifesto per un futuro glocal.* Venezia: Marsilio, 2015.

Bingham, Millicent Todd, *Ancestors' Brocades.* New York: Harper and Brothers, 1945.

Bona, Mary Jo. *By the Breath of Their Mouths. Narratives of Resistance in Italian America.* Albany: State U of New York P, 2010.

_____. "A Needle Better Fits? The Role of Defensive Sewing in Italian American Literature." In *Embroidered Stories: Interpreting Women's Domestic Needlework from the Italian Diaspora.* Edvige Giunta and Joseph Sciorra. eds. UP Mississippi, 2014.

Chillemi Claudio. "Interview with Claudio Chillemi." *Acheron* Retrieved May 2, 2017, from https://www.acheronbooks.com/index.php?fc= module&module=smartblog&id_post=55&controller=details.

Johnson, Thomas H. and Theodora Ward, eds. *The Letters of Emily Dickinson,* 3 vols. Cambridge, MA: The Belknap Press of Harvard UP, 1958. (References to letters use L. and the number assigned by the editors).

Johnson, Thomas H., ed. *The Complete Poems of Emily Dickinson.* Boston: Little, Brown & Co, 1960.

Franklin, R. W., ed., *The Manuscript Books of Emily Dickinson. A Facsimile Edition.* Cambridge, MS: Harvard UP, 1981.

Di Filippo, Paul. "The Mill." In *Strange Trades.* Golden Gryphon P: 2002.

_____. *Chasing the Queen of Sassi* (2014). Kindle edition.

Di Filippo, Paul and Claudio Chillemi. *The Horror at Gancio Rosso/Orrore a Gancio Rosso.* Acheron Books, 2015 (English and Italian).

Di Prima, Diane, *Recollections of My Life as a Woman.* New York: Penguin, 2001.

Earle, David, "Conrad Under Wraps: Reputation, Pulp Indeterminacy, and the 1950 Signet Edition of *Heart of Darkness.*" *Studia Neophilologica,* 85: sup1 (2013): 41-57.

Fama, Maria. "La carta parla." In *Breaking Open: Reflections on Italian American Women's Writing.* Mary Ann Vigilante Mannino and Justin Vitiello, eds. West Lafayette, IN: Purdue UP, 2003.

Froid, Dan. "The Birth-Mark: Essays by Susan Howe." *Bookslut* (December 2015). Retrieved May 2, 2016, from http://www.bookslut. com/ nonfiction/2015_12_021335.php.

Gardaphé, Fred. *The Italian-American Writer: An Essay and an Annotated Checklist*. Spencertown: Forkroads, 1995.

_____. "Identical Difference: Notes on Italian and Italian American Identities." In *The Essence of Italian Culture and the Challenge of a Global Age*. Paolo Janni and George McLean, eds. Cultural Heritage and Contemporary Change: 2003. 93-112.

Gelder, Ken. "The Fields of Popular Fiction." In Gelder, ed., *New Directions in Popular Fiction. Genre, Distribution, Reproduction*. London: Palgrave Macmillan, 2016.

Gilbert, Sandra M. and Susan Gubar. *The Madwoman in the Attic*. New Haven and London: Yale UP, 1979.

Gioseffi, Daniela. *Word Wounds and Water Flowers: Poems*. West Lafayette, IN: Bordighera P, 1995.

_____. "Helen Barolini, Their Other Side: Six American Women & the Lure of Italy. A Review by Daniela Gioseffi." *The Montserrat Review*. Drangonfly P, 2006. Retrieved May 2, 2016, from http://www. dragonflypress-ca.com/book-reviews/their-other-side-six-american-women-the-lure-of-italy/.

_____. "*Wild Nights! Wild Nights!*" Austin, TS: Plain View P, 2010a. Ebook.

_____. "Emily and Me." A conversation with Angelina Oberdan, *Sugarmule* 23 (2010b) Retrieved May 2, 2016, from http://sugar mule.x10.mx/23-2.htm.

_____. "Adoration for Italy in Emily Dickinson's Poetry." *i.Italy* (October 2, 2011) Retrieved May 2, 2016, from http://www. iitaly.org/magazine/focus/art-culture/article/adoration-italy-in-emily-dickinsons-poetry.

_____. *The Story of Emily Dickinson's Master: "WILD NIGHTS! WILD NIGHTS!" Emily Dickinson: Lover of Science & Scientist in Dark Days of the Republic*. BookBaby 2013) (abbreviated as *WN!WN!*) Retrieved May 2, 2016, from https://books.google.it/books?id=mKlfDQAA QBAJ&printsec=frontcover&hl=it#v=onepage&q&f=false.

_____. "In Search of a Poetry Community: On Being a Women Writer with an Italian Name in American Literature." *Margento* (April 24, 2015) Retrieved May 2, 2016, from http://artsites.uottawa. ca/margento/en/2015/04/24/daniela-gioseffi-in-search-of-a-poetry-community-on-being-a-women-writer-with-an-italian-name-in-american-literature/. Previously as "Forging into the American Mainstream since the 1970s: On Being a Woman Writer with an Italian American Name." In Angelina Oberdan, ed. and intro, *Pioneering Italian American Culture: Escaping La Vita Della Cucina. Essays, Interview, Reviews, by and about Daniela Gioseffi*. New York, NY: Bordighera P, 2013. 119-30.

Habegger, Alfred. *My Wars Are Laid Away in Books. The Life of Emily Dickinson*. New York: Random House 2001.

Howe, Susan. *The Birth-Mark: Unsettling the Wilderness in American Literary History*. Hanover and London: Wesleyan UP, 1993.

Howe, Susan. *My Emily Dickinson* [1985]. With a preface by Eliot Weinberger. New York: New Directions, 2007.

Jones, Ruth Owen. "'Neighbor—and friend—and Bridegroom—' William Smith Clark as Emily Dickinson's Master Figure." *The Emily Dickinson Journal* 11.2 (2002): 48-85.

Foster, Edward, ed. "Interview with Susan Howe." *Talisman. A Journal of Contemporary Poetry and Poetics* 4 (January 1, 1990): 155-81.

Juhasz, Suzanne, *Naked and Fiery Forms. Modern American Poetry by Women, a New Tradition*. New York: Harper & Row, 1976.

Lindberg-Seyersted, Brita. "Gender and Women's Literature: Thoughts on a Relationship Illustrated by the Cases of Emily Dickinson and Sylvia Plath." *American Studies in Scandinavia* 18 (1986): 1-14. Retrieved May 2, 2016 from http://rauli.cbs.dk/index.php/assc/article/viewFile/1193/1193.

Mannino, Mary Ann Vigilante. *Revisionary Identities: Strategies of Empowerment in the Writing of Italian/American Women*. New York: Peter Lang, 2000.

Merriam-Webster Dictionary (since 1828). Retrieved May 2, 2017 from https://www.merriam-webster.com/dictionary/patria%20potestas?src=search-dict-box.

Nerd, Stay and Paul Di Filippo. "Intervista a Paul Di Filippo" (June 23, 2017). Retrieved September 30, 2017 from http://www.staynerd.com/intervista-a-paul-di-filippo/.

Nevins, Jess. "Introduction: The 19th-Century Roots of Steampunk." In Ann Vandermeer and Jess Vandermeer, eds., *Steampunk*. San Francisco: Tachyon Publications, 2008) 3-11.

_____. *Encyclopedia of Fantastic Victoriana*. Austin, Ts: MonkeyBrain Books, 2005.

Parisi, Nick. "Interview with Paul Di Filippo." *Nocturnia* (December 15, 2015) Retrieved May 2, 2017 from http://wwwwelcometonocturnia. blogspot.it/2015/12/intervista-con-paul-di-filippo.html.

Oliverio, Cecilia. "Italian America: An Interview with Mary Jo Bona." Harvard University (April 20, 2011), youtube. Retrieved May 2, 2016 from https://www.youtube.com/watch?v=seYz7vHgad8.

Price, Bryan D. "Hunting." In Wendy Martin, ed., *All Things Dickinson: An Encyclopedia of Emily Dickinson's World*. Santa Barbara, CA: Greenwood, 2014.

Rich, Adrienne. "Vesuvius at Home: The Power of Emily Dickinson." *Parnassus. Poetry in Review* 5. 1 (1976): 99-121. Reprinted in *On Lies, Secrets and Silence: Selected Prose 1966-1978*. New York, 1979.

Robertiello, Richard C. and Diana Hoguet. *The WASP Mystique*. New York: Donald I. Fine: 1987.

Romano, Ann T. *Daughters of Italy: The Journey of Italian American Women Writers*. Xlibris Corporation, 2010.

Schultz, Susan. "Exaggerated History." *Postmodern Culture* 4.2 (January 1994): 21.

Tamburri, Anthony Julian. *Re-Reading Italian Americana. Specificities and Generalities on Literature and Criticism*. Madison, NJ: Fairleigh Dickinson UP, 2014.

The Bellagio Center. Rockefeller Foundation. Retrieved May 2, 2016 from https://www.rockefellerfoundation.org/our-work/bellagio-center/.

Van Gelder, Gordon, ed. "Claudio Chillemi and Paul Di Filippo, *The Via Panisperna Boys in Operation Harmony*." *Fantasy and Science Fiction* 126.1&2, #711 (January/February 2014). Retrieved September 30, 2017 from http://bestsf.net/claudio-chillemi-and-paul-di-filippo-the-via-panisperna-boys-in-operation-harmony-fantasy-science-fiction-janfeb-2014/.

THE SILVER SCREEN

Guido Trento:
From the "Neapolitan Synecdoche" to Italian American-ness

Giuliana Muscio
UNIVERSITY OF PADOVA

B orn in Naples in 1892, Guido Trento died in San Francisco in
1957, after numerous experiences in Neapolitan, Italian, and
American theatre, radio and film. This varied résumé invites a reconsideration of the issues of cultural identity in relation to language, Italian and Neapolitan culture, and to Italian Americanness, revealing striking differences between the Italian diaspora
on the east and the west coasts.[1] Furthermore Trento's career pos-
es complex historiographic problems, given the scarcity of sources,
often unverifiable and contradictory, and the intricate network of
relations connected with the performer's mobility.

The most relevant part of Trento's film career was actually the
initial one—Neapolitan and Italian—as the multivolume detailed
filmographies edited by Vittorio Martinelli for *Bianco e Nero* document, crediting him with about seventy titles, always as a co-
protagonist with important female stars. In these reviews he was
appreciated for his "sincere," "reliable and laid-back" interpretations, but, quite unexpectedly *Filmlexicon* states that "he did not
have a bright career but [that he] distinguished himself for his innate gentlemanly manner and his scrupulous professional commitment":[2] quite a subdued comment for an actor who had made

---

[1] I address some of these cultural issues in *Napoli/New York/Hollywood., Transnational Film Exchanges Between Italy and US* (New York: Fordham UP, forthcoming).
[2] *Filmlexicon degli autori e delle opere* (Rome: Ed. Bianco e Nero, CSC, 1967). The
only other source in Italian on Trento is a brief profile in Mario Quargnolo, *La
parola ripudiata* (Gemona: Cineteca del Friuli, 1986) 55.

so many important films, and with excellent results. When Trento moved to America his career abroad did not receive any attention in Italian publications, which was by no means a rare occurrence as the Italian press consistently tended to overlook and ignore the work of Italians in Hollywood.[3] This silence is the symptom of a double negation operating transatlantically: the anti-emigrationist and anti-southern attitudes of Italian dominant culture and the wide-spread anti-immigrationist and anti-Italian prejudice characterizing American society in the years before WWII.[4] Unfortunately, this failure to recognize the Italian immigrant stage careers ended up erasing a rich and multifaceted contribution to a budding culture from public discourse. By studying Trento's work in the US, we are able to focus on the mechanisms of the prejudiced erasure of such contributions as well as to discover the articulated history of Italian performance culture in the United States.

Son of a Commissioner of Police born in Naples, Trento started performing on the Neapolitan stage and later in film in this southern metropolis. In order to dispel a commonplace misconception, we should underscore that before WWI and up to the 1920s, the film industry in Naples was a key segment of the then internationally very successful Italian cinema. Since the 18th century Naples was a European cultural capital and it was among the first centers, together with Turin and Rome, to develop a modern film industry, which produced both popular and critically acclaimed films. Indeed, Naples was the place where the first specialized film press appeared in Italy and where other industrial conditions had an early start, with both film theatres and studios

---

[3] On Italians in Hollywood there is only one article, Gianni Puccini, "Italiani nel mondo del cinema," *Cinema* 20, 25 (April 1937): 329-331.

[4] See William J. Connell and Fred Gardaphé, eds. *Anti-Italianism. Essays on a Prejudice* (New York: Palgrave, 2010); on anti-emigrationism in Italy see Emilio Franzina, "Italian Prejudice against Italian Americans," in Muscio, Sciorra, Spagnoletti, Tamburri, eds., *Mediated Ethnicity. New Italian-American Cinema* (New York: John D. Calandra Italian American Institute, 2010) 17-32.

operating since the early 1900s, Neapolitan cinema took advantage of a rich Italian performance culture, characterized by an intense inter-media interaction, which combined music, popular literature, naturalist drama, and film. [6] The *verismo* of the interpretations and a *penchant* for realist *mise en scene*, evident in the frequent use of *plein air* shooting, are often seen as anticipating neorealism, in masterpieces such as *Assunta Spina* and (the lost) *Sperduti nel buio*.

In order to use correctly the adjective "Neapolitan" and account for the characteristics of Trento's film experiences, it must be noted that while "Neapolitan cinema" is often identified with the popular product Elvira Notari and was realized through her company Dora Films (films inspired by the popular novels of Mastriani, Neapolitan songs, and *sceneggiate*),[7] actually, the Neapolitan film industry was also represented by the work of Roberto Leone Roberti (Sergio Leone's father) directing Francesca Bertini, as well as by Giulio Antamoro and Giuseppe De Liguoro, that is, by Neapolitan filmmakers associated with quality products; and Trento was cast in several of their films.

Neapolitan culture was and is a cross of classes, rooted in its diversity of traditions and histories, where the stage, the cinema, the music industry, and popular literature interacted. This amalgamation produced a diversified culture, able to include both high and low expressions, in the harmonious tradition exemplified by the history of *opera buffa* and of the Neapolitan song.[8]

---

[6] On Neapolitan cinema see Adriano Aprà, ed. *Napoletana: Images of a City* (Milan: Fabbri, 1994), especially Vittorio Martinelli's "The Evolution of Neapolitan Cinema to 1930," 29-74; Stefano Masi, Mario Franco, *Il mare, la luna i coltelli. Per una storia del cinema muto napoletano* (Naples: Pironti Ed., 1988).

[7] See Giuliana Bruno, *Streetwalking on a Ruined Map* (Princeton: Princeton UP, 1993).

[8] On Neapolitan culture see Nelson Moe, *The View from the Vesuvius. Italian Culture and the Southern Question* (Berkeley: U California P, 2002), Tommaso Astarita, *Between Salt Water and Holy Water. A History of Southern Italy* (New York: Norton, 2005), Robert Lumley and Jonathan Morris, eds. *The New History of The Italian South:* The Mezzogiorno *Revisited* (Devon, UK: U Exeter P, 1997).

Trento made his film debut in a short produced by Napoli Film in 1913, when he was 21; from there he went on to make several feature films with Napoli Film (or Polifilms) in the studio sets built at Vomero in 1912. While Polifilms was still organized under the direction of Giulio Antamoro, another Neapolitan, Gustavo Lombardo (who had started a distribution company as early as 1904 and created film magazine *Lux* in 1909) expanded his operations internationally and distributed *Cabiria* worldwide, while maintaining a studio in Rome.[9]

In 1915, at the outbreak of WWI, when Trento was the *attor giovane* of Polifilms, he enlisted as a volunteer in the Italian army. In fact, an item in *Motion Picture News* (August 21, 1915, p. 47), in the section "Film news from European capitals," includes his name among the Italian film people who had enlisted on the first day of mobilization, respectively: "Alberto Fassini of Cines, officer of the Royal marine, Comte Antamoro of Polifilm, the *metteur en scene* count Trissino, Guido Trento *artiste de talent*, and from Milano Film Comte Airoldi." The list continued with a litany of aristocratic names. Trento must have appeared as a relevant figure if the journalist chose to mention him in this list of prominent film personalities and members of the upper classes of Italian society. Here, it is worth noting, are the aristocratic origins found in the early days of Italian silent film production. Now often forgotten, Italian film producers in the era of silent cinema invested in films of artistic and literary quality, aiming at both the "nationalization of the masses"[10] and the association of their names with art, not necessarily with commercial success.[11]

---

[9] Mario Franco, *Dalle origini al declino*, in Pasquale Iaccio (ed.) *L'alba del cinema in Campania* (Naples: Liguori, 2010) 243-280, 255-257.

[10] George Mosse, *The Nationalization of the Masses* (New York: Howard Fertig, 2001).

[11] On the cultural attitudes of Italian producers see Giuliana Muscio, "In Hoc Signo Vinces: Historical Films," in Giorgio Bertellini ed., *Italian Silent Cinema. A Reader* (New Barnet, UK: John Libbey, 2013) 153-160.

However, even if Trento had enlisted, his filmography appears to indicate that he did not actually fight the war, but participated in a series of patriotic films made in Naples such as *La fiammata patriottica* by Giulio Antamoro, a short produced by Polifilms, distributed in October 1915, *Savoia, urrah!* by Eduardo Bencivenga inspired by a song by Ferdinando Russo, with star Tilde Kassaj, *Vette del Trentino* (Ignazio Lupi) distributed by Lombardo, and *Guerra redentrice* by Edoardo Bencivenga, all produced by Polifilms Napoli. Therefore, Trento's career highlights the differences between a "Neapolitan cinema," usually identified with a popular product, and the upper-class cultural attitudes of other Neapolitan filmmakers in terms of identity, more "Italian" and patriotic. Indeed, the most patriotic Italian song, *La canzone del Piave*, was composed in Naples by E. A. Mario, the very Neapolitan author of *Santa Lucia Luntana* (as well as of *Tammuriata nera*), and patriotic songs were very popular in Neapolitan *tabarins* after WWI. Notari, too, produced several patriotic films: from the early *Guerra italo-turca tra scugnizzi napoletani* (1912) to *Tricolore* (1913), *Addio mia bella addio ... l'armata se ne va* (1915), *Figlio del reggimento* (1915), *Sempre avanti, Savoia* (1915), and *Gloria ai caduti* (1916). Neapolitan musical expressions and Italian patriotism gave birth to a popular form of nationalism, which constituted a powerful lynchpin in the fragile national identity of the newly born Italian state. This autochthonous metonymic relation between Naples and "patria," combined with the American representation of Italians as southerners, allowed for the creation of the "Neapolitan synecdoche," by which Neapolitan culture ended up representing *Italianità* in the United States, where the southern Italian component of the diaspora was also numerically dominant.

In 1916 Gustavo Lombardo acquired Polifilms and created, in 1919, Lombardo films, one of the major companies in Italian silent cinema, whose star Leda Gys he later married, and where Trento continued to work. In 1928 Lombardo founded Titanus, a glorious film studio that, after WWII, produced several neorealist master-pieces. With this in mind, the interaction between *Napoletanità* and *Italianità* before and soon after WWI needs to be reconsidered in order to avoid identifying southern culture as retrograde. Not-withstanding the prevarication of the Savoia kingdom on the me-tropolis of Naples, even without adhering to the now popular neo-Borbonic revisionism, it is a matter of fact that the economy of the south was damaged by the unification.[12] It is true, conversely, that Naples had a major role in the construction of a modern Italy, and that *Napoletanità* did not diverge from *Italianità*. This observa-tion is particularly pertinent when dealing with Trento's Neapoli-tan career, because he was associated with quality productions and he seems to have identified more closely with the Italian component of his Neapolitan origins.

Trento's work in 1916 was still based in Naples, but after 1917 he started appearing regularly in films made in Milan, Turin, and Rome, with prestigious directors and stars, and from quality liter-ary sources, but he continued making films in Naples too.

In 1918 Trento appeared in the prestigious production of *Frou-Frou* with Francesca Bertini and in the entire serial film *I sette pec-cati capitali* on the seven deadly sins that this silent film diva starred in with various directors. In 1920 he costarred with Vera Vergani in *La paura d'amare* directed by Roberto Roberti, adapted from a work by Dario Niccodemi and produced by Caesar Film in Rome. With such an extensive filmography, Trento might not have been a star, but he was a successful actor, featured in a num-ber of prestigious films with starring roles.

---

[12] Giuseppe Galasso, *Napoli* (Rome: Laterza, 1987) represents the classical inter-pretation of the Neapolitan situation after Unity; Angelo Forgione expressed the new-Borbonic point of view in *Made in Naples* (Naples: Magenes, 2013); see also Pellegrino Nazzaro, "The Mezzogiorno and the Questione Meridionale," in Lu-ciano J. Iorizzo and Ernest E. Rossi, eds., *Italian Americans. Bridges to Italy, Bonds to America* (Youngstown: Teneo Press, 2010) 233-266, 241.

Perhaps it was on the basis of his status in the Italian film industry that in 1922 Trento had the chance to work in two spectacular American productions shot in Rome by Gordon Edwards for Fox Studios: *The Shepherd King* (in Italian, *Re David*) and *Nero (Nerone)*. He interpreted two relevant roles, as King Saul in the first, and as Tullius, a Christian, in *Nero*. American trade papers took notice of him: *The Exhibitor Herald* (April 22, 1922) emphasized how international the cast was, with Italian-American Edy Darclea, Violet Mercerau as the only American, and Nero played by the French Jacques Gretillat, with the remaining roles covered by Russian and Italian actors, including Trento and Sandro Salvini (Tommaso Salvini's grandson). This review of *Nero* emphasized the production value, mentioning the use of twenty-six cameramen and 60,000 extras in a single scene; and that "an entire city built at the outskirts of Rome was destroyed in the filming of one scene." It also mentioned "riots of disgruntled workmen who had failed to obtain employment with 'the rich Americans.' So serious did one of these riots became, that it is stated, both police and mounted troops were called out to suppress it, and a detachment of troops was thrown about the American Embassy to prevent an additional demonstration." It is noteworthy how, in reporting Italian socio-political tensions, American film journalists regularly ignored the political implications of the "disorder," and quoted it to emphasize the difficulties production met because of Italian endemic "disorder." Italian and American film histories have not paid any attention to the prejudiced attitudes journalists from both nations exhibited in discussing the twelve silent American film productions in Italy—Italians ignoring them or representing Americans as uneducated barbarians, and Americans praising Italian crafts and artistic showmanship, but always stressing the crowds' unruly behavior.[13] These attitudes contributed to both

---

[13] See Giuliana Muscio, "Il Grand Tour cinematografico: produzioni americane in Italia negli anni Venti," in Michele Canosa ed., *A nuova luce. Cinema muto italiano.*

erasing the relevance of the American film experience in Italy (thus also hiding the role fascism played in it) and to canceling the memory of a past in which Italian cinema dominated the world markets with its historical spectacles.

An American review of *The Shepherd King* stated that Trento as Saul "gives a very good character study of the king, whose jealous fears, as he realizes his rapidly declining power, re-act upon him for his own downfall."[14] Pictures of Trento as Saul accompanied some of the reviews and hence made him known to American audiences. In *The Exhibitor Herald* (October 13, 1923), the reviewer praised the mostly Italian cast of *Nero* and added: "Guido Trento as Tullius was the handsomest man I have ever seen on the screen." Perhaps an exaggerated comment, but in the era of Rudolph Valentino, Italian male beauty was quite appreciated in the U.S.; nonetheless, an appreciation of the Italian aesthetics and beauty did little to curtail the strong anti-Italian prejudice.[15]

After working with Trento on these two Roman sets, it is not surprising to learn that director Gordon Edwards invited him to Hollywood, where the Neapolitan actor moved in 1924. Actually, 1924 is the year when several actors from Italian silent cinema like Lido Manetti, Luciano Albertini, Agostino Borgato, and Eugenio De Liguoro made the trip to Hollywood, but Albertini soon left for Germany and De Liguoro for Latin America, while Manetti died in a mysterious accident; only Trento stayed on.

In a sense, this artistic diaspora parallels Italian migration, characterized by the enormous rate of returns (68%) but also by its

---

I (Bologna: Cleub, 2000), 89-102. *Pictures and the Picturegoer*, March 1925.

[14] On the contradictory relation of the American audience with Valentino see Silvio Alovisio, Giulia Carluccio, *Rodolfo Valentino. Cinema, cultura, società tra Italia e Stati Uniti negli anni Venti* (Torino: Kaplan, 2011).

[15] On Italian emigration see Mark Choate, *Emigrant Nation. The Making of Italy Abroad* (Cambridge: Harvard UP, 2008) and Donna R. Gabaccia, *Italy's Many Diasporas* (London: U College of London P, 2000).

multi-directionality[17]—but it also deeply differs from it because 1924 is when quotas were enforced and the flow of Italian emigrants to the US almost stopped, while Italian artists and performers could always enter the US, without the need of a visa. In fact the history of the Italian diaspora and that of the Italian "travelling players" correspond only in part: Caruso and Valentino were popular in the worse times of the anti-Italian prejudice. The divarication between these two histories emphasizes the absolute value attributed to the Italian performer in US culture, at any time.

1924 was also the year in which Fascism became a regime, but these artists never claimed this new form of government as a motivation for leaving Italy. Professional, industrial motivations seemed more relevant to explain this diaspora, because in the period from 1922 to 1930 the number of Italian film productions was the lowest ever.

In the U.S., *The Motion Picture Herald* (April 1924) mentions Trento in a credited role in the cast of *It Is the Law* that Edwards adapted from a drama by Elmer Rice, whose protagonist was Italian American Mimi Palmeri. Although a prestigious film, widely discussed and reviewed, Trento's name never appears in the articles, even if he had a credited role. This was the last film Edwards directed, unexpectedly dying of a heart attack, and as a result Trento was suddenly left without a sponsor.

This might be why in July 1924 Trento was in San Francisco and joined the Italian immigrant stage, working with the Pisanelli company at Teatro Alessandro Eden (Estavan, 68-69). The immigrant stage in San Francisco was different from the one on the East Coast, given the regional diversification of the Italian diaspora in California, especially compared to the concentration of southern

---

[17] Lawrence Estavan, *The Italian Theatre in San Francisco* (San Bernardino: Borgo P, 1991) 68-69. Earlier on the San Francisco stage had also seen the relevant experience of Tina Modotti, and Frank Puglia, who both went to Hollywood in 1920, and of Ines Palange, soon to interpret Tony's mother in Hawks' *Scarface*.

Italians typical of the East Coast. In addition to the classics and popular dramas, the immigrant stage proposed a varied *repertoire* in Italian, with a change of show every night that valorized the versatility of Italian performers and was appreciated also by American audiences. Although *Signora* Pisanelli was Neapolitan, the popular tradition of the Tuscan mask of Stenterello was prominent in northern California, unlike the East Coast, which was dominated by the Neapolitan traditions of *sceneggiate* and *macchiette*.

From a cultural point of view, the Teatro italiano in San Francisco was more ambitious than the popular New York immigrant stage, prodded as it was by Italian newspapermen like Ettore Patrizi, the influential nationalist director of *L'Italia*, and supported by a class of *prominenti* who wanted to extoll their own culture and presence as a successful Italian diaspora (as in the case of food companies such as Del Monte and Ghirardelli, or of the wine producers, or as the Giannini brothers, founders of the Bank of Italy, which became Bank of America). Also in 1924 Eleonora Duse performed Ibsen's *Spettri*, Praga's *La porta chiusa*, and D'Annunzio's *La città morta* in San Francisco. And while Trento was on stage at the Eden, Silvio and Ester Minciotti interpreted both Shakespeare and Dumas at the Liberty theatre. In fact "with a delightful facility the actors leaped from one company to another, slipped from operetta to melodrama, and from farce to tragedy. They were true Italian actors" (Estavan, 71). (In the post-WWII era the Minciottis played relevant roles in Manckiewicz' *House of Strangers*; Esther Minciotti interpreted *Marty*'s mother in the eponymous Oscar-winning "American neorealist" film.)

The Teatro Italiano in San Francisco seemed to decline after 1928, but radio offered enough work to the immigrant performers, and this is where Trento most likely went, experimenting with his voice and his diction.

In the 1930s, famous dramatic actress Mimi Aguglia launched an intense program of Teatro Italiano, sponsored by the San Francisco *prominenti* and Fascist intellectuals like Patrizi, proposing Pirandello and D'Annunzio and elevated dramas, supported by "a few Americans and ... [the] Dante Alighieri Society, the Italy-American society, the Cenacolo Club, the Figli d'Italia."

But by 1928 Guido Trento was back in Hollywood, working in *Street Angel*, a key silent film by Italian American Frank Borzage, set in Naples, where the spiritual values of the characters fuse with a simple Catholicism, and the streets of the southern city are not conventionally picturesque. In the film, Trento had a relevant role as a policeman and appeared with other Italian performers, like Henry Armetta in the role of the circus manager, and Gino Corrado and Alberto Rabagliati in minor parts. Trento played a sergeant, initially tricked by Angela (Janet Gaynor) and by Mascetto (Armetta) who hid her in the circus bass drum while the *carabinieri* were chasing her. The sergeant keeps looking for her in a persecutory mode, often appearing as a long expressionist shadow on the walls of the city. He finally captures her in the very moment she has conquered happiness with naïve painter Gino (James Farrell) but takes pity of the poor girl and waits for her to let her spend a last hour with her man. While Trento has a notable screen time (about ten minutes overall) and several close ups, his performance is not as "picturesque" as Armetta's Italian character; on the contrary, he is restrained and offers an interpretation quite mature compared to the stereotypes that were ever-prevalent in 1928. However, Italian censors did not accept this representation of a "sordid" Naples and the ridicule of the *carabinieri*, and they thus cut most of Trento's scenes from the Italian version, which explains why Italian critics never discussed Trento's relevant role and performance in *Street Angel*.

The original musical accompaniment for this silent film used *O sole mio* as a symbolic tune for the two lovers, who whistle it to communicate their deep nostalgia when they are separated.[19] During this period several American films set in Italy (not exclusively those set in Naples, as in the case of Lubitsch's *Trouble in Paradise*, which is set in Venice)[20] utilized this popular song as representative of Italy, further contributing to the construction of the "Neapolitan synecdoche" and the identification of the Italian diaspora with Neapolitan culture.

Trento did not abandon his Hollywood dream and appeared in *The Charge of the Gauchos* (Albert Kelley, 1928) entitled also *Una nueva y gloriosa nacion*, actually an Argentinian-American film, whose title was inspired by a line of the Argentinian national anthem. The cast included Francis Bushman, Henry Kolker, and Gino Corrado (the Italian actor who played more bit roles in Hollywood than anybody else). It was a notable transnational experiment revealing another area for cultural interaction with the Italian diaspora — this time in Latin America. Usually overlooked and mentioned briefly in the discussion of the coming of sound, this conjuncture takes for granted that for somatic and linguistic reasons Italians were well suited to play Latin American characters or interpret films in Spanish. With the ample possibilities to cast instead Mexican performers in these roles, it is again a compliment to the versatility of Italian performers if they were used in these instances.

No credits exist for Trento in D.W. Griffith's *Lady of the Pavements*, but a picture from the set of *Photoplay* (July 1929) shows him mid-scene "with Jetta Goudal in his arms." Within the next year, he also played an uncredited role in *The One Woman Idea* (*Il*

---

[19] The song was composed in 1898, lyrics by Giovanni Capurro and music by Eduardo Di Capua, written when he was playing in an orchestra in Odessa — transnational from its very birth. Actually it was played instead of the Royal March at the Anversa Olympics of 1920.

[20] On *Sei tu l'amore* see Quargnolo, *La parola ripudiata*, 32.

velo dell'Islam, Berthold Viertel, 1929). Subsequently, however, his career fell into decline.

When it became evident that sound was here to stay, it proposed new challenges to Italian performers who had emigrated recently. Sound introduced the issue of language and accent, both in the immigrant community and in Italy, where Mussolini imposed Italian dubbing on all foreign films.

Legend has it that, in 1929, Trento had the idea of making a film with Italian dialogue for both the immigrant and the national market, where the talkies had just begun to appear in English but no film in Italian had yet been shown.[21] Trento and Alberto Rabagliati, who had met on the set of *Street Angel,* toured California in an old Ford in search of financial backing for their project, trying to convince the numerous winemakers of Italian origin to contribute, and, in the end, be able to finance the Italotone Film Production. Joining here the two primary Italian, economic activities in California (*spettacolo,* or film and stage traditions, and winemaking), they thus formed an innovative organization of businesses and hence created a system that would supply the immigrant community with both Italian products and entertainment.

Variety offered a "reasonable" estimate of the cost in 75,000 dollars, Quargnolo suggested 100,000: indeed, from the few surviving stills—the film is lost—*Sei tu l'amore?* was not a small production, with dance numbers and fancy costumes. The direction of the film was entrusted to Alfredo Sabato, an actor who had had a career in the silent film (Quargnolo, *La parola ripudiata,* 32). He was credited as a "technician" in *Street Angel's* Settings Section, but *Sei tu l'amore?* is his only credit as director.

---

[21] Sabato interpreted A *Time to Love* (Frank Tuttle, 1927), a farce with Raymond Griffith and William Powell, where Neapolitan aristocrat Mario Carillo (Caracciolo) also appeared as a duelist, and in Borzage's *The River* (1928) at Fox, with Charles Farrell and Mary Duncan.

Italian sources attribute to Rabagliati a more relevant role than he actually played in this project, while American sources document that the initiative was mostly Trento's and Sabato's. An article in *American Filmograph* (June 7, 1930) reads: "'First Italian Talkie Produced Here.' At the Tec-Art studios the first all-Italian talking picture is being made. Louise Caselotti [at the time a successful opera singer] and Rabagliati, and such well-known Hollywood character actors as Henry Armetta, Miss Ines Palange, Mario De Dominici, August Galli and Luigi Colombo ... the scenario was written by Guido Trento and Alfred Sabato, the latter is also directing. The release is independent except in the Italian speaking countries where arrangements for distribution are now being perfected."

In addition to Rabagliati and the beautiful contralto Luisa Caselotti, *Sei tu l'amore?* cast other Italian immigrant performers: direct contact with Hollywood and its professionals permitted a faster and more competent reaction to the introduction of sound.

Sei tu l'amore? is the story of three men (Galli, Armetta, and De Domenicis), who support a young milliner (Caselotti), an apparently *coquettish* character, opening an elegant shop, allowing her to climb the social ladder. After some comic misunderstandings, painter/architect Mario (Rabagliati) declares his love and marries her. The source of the film was a play by Piero Mazzoletti, adapted by Trento, performed in Italy by the prestigious Menichelli-Falconi company, in 1925. It was a popular recent play of Italian bourgeois theatre, centered on a working girl and her aspirations for upward social mobility, suitable for an American narrative. Curiously enough, in *Street Angel* (on whose set most of these performers met) Borzage had represented Angela as a typical pathetic Italian character, while Trento and colleagues proposed a modern Italian girl, self-employed and with a taste for fashion. *Sei tu l'amore?* was a strange cultural mix: a piece of Italian cinema produced in Hollywood, thematically anticipating the "white telephones," a (modern) musical comedy very different from the Italian film-*sceneggiate* made in the same years in New York.

American reviews were positive. *Variety* also mentioned a contemporary distribution in Italy, "through Pittaluga," the main film producer/distributor in the country at the time, but it did not happen: Rabagliati took a print of the film to Italy on the transatlantic liner *Biancamano*, travelling third class.

From a chronological point of view, *Sei tu l'amore?* was the first film from the U.S. with Italian dialogue, and, in some Italian cities, one of the first talkies ever to be screened. In Italy it was received as a curiosity, and with a touch of mockery for the accents of some of the actors, in particular "the terrible accent of Armetta, one of those artists that for decades lived in America—recalled some Italian critics—and only remembers some phrases in dialect."[22] This comment parallels subsequent Italian criticism of the dubbing made in the U.S., expressing irritation towards the regional accent of the Italian immigrant performers who gave voice to these translations; an irritation that grew stronger when sound ceased being new and the Italian public had become used to the unaccented dubbing done in Italy. Behind this "irritation" there was the uneasiness towards the forgotten and negated cultural experience of Italian emigration, that in making itself *heard*, provoked a distancing, full of guilty feelings. However, while the Hollywood-made *Sei tu l'amore?* was distributed and reviewed in Italy, there is no trace of all the "Neapolitan" films made on the East Coast in Italian film criticism or historiography.

---

[22] He appeared in *No dejes la puerta abierta* (Frank Tuttle, 1933), a Fox remake of the musical comedy *Pleasure Cruise* where he was in the featured role of Mr. Delfi and *La ciudad de carton* (Louis King, 1934) with Antonio Moreno, a metafilm on Hollywood which cast also Francesco Maran from Trieste; *The Gay Senorita* (Arthur Dreyfuss, 1945) was not a Spanish version but a film for the Latin markets, made at Columbia, dramatizing the local (re)appropriation of an Olvera-like street in Los Angeles as a cultural space.

Even though the experiment seemed successful, it did not have a follow-up. The press announced that Italotone was going to produce also films in Spanish, but the company as such did not appear again in film credits. This move towards Spanish-speaking countries would have been motivated by the fact that the Italian market was too small to justify this investment, while the Italian community in Latin America not only constituted a large audience, but had enjoyed the experience of the Italian "travelling players" in the past. Sabato for instance went on working in Spanish versions.[23] Trento too participated in the Hollywood experiments of the multiple language versions, that is, versions of the same script, on the same set with the same costumes, interpreted by different national casts. In *Il grande sentiero*, the Italian version of Walsh's *The Big Trail* with John Wayne,[24] the cast included Franco Corsaro in the Wayne's role, Luisa Caselotti, Frank Puglia, and Agostino Borgato. Trento played the key-role of the antagonist, a vicious westerner. He also interpreted the role of the prison warden, originally played by Wilfred Lucas, in *Pardon US*, the first feature film for Stan Laurel and Oliver Hardy, in the Italian version, *Muraglie*. According to Quargnolo he also worked at dubbing at Fox. Trento's last film credit is the Count of Marsay in the mystery *Secrets of the French Police* (Edward Sutherland, 1932), produced by David O. Selznick, who would go on to produce *Gone with the Wind* and Alfred Hitchcock's *Spellbound*.

After the early 1930s either something went wrong in Trento's American film career or he made the decision to leave the film industry. He moved to San Francisco, where he performed on Italian radio, which was then quite "fascistized," with a notable in-

---

[23] Giuliana Muscio, "Come *The Big Trail* divenne *Il grande sentiero* e *Men of the North* divenne *Luigi la volpe*," in Anna Antonini ed., *Il film e i suoi multipli* (Udine: Forum, 2003) 105-114.

[24] Stefano Luconi, Guido Tintori, *L'ombra lunga del fascio* (Milan: M&B, 2004).

vestment on the part of the regime in the nationalization of "Italians abroad."[25]

After December 1941, purges, arrests, and deportations hit hard Italian radio stations, several of which were shut down. Journalist Ettore Patrizi was "relocated" from San Francisco to Reno, Nevada, and Guido Trento was arrested and imprisoned in the Missoula camp.[26]

Information on forced repatriation, or internment, of Italians from radio and film is still vague, because this humiliating experience generated such shame in the community that it is rarely mentioned in biographies. Executive Order 9066 (Feb 1942) authorized the internment or repatriation of German, Italian, and Japanese Americans and has only recently received due historical attention. While some historians minimize the issue because these measures involved a small number of Italians and were never as drastic as those applied to Japanese Americans, silence about these punitive regulations, which affected people's lives without trials and in total secrecy, cannot be accepted: the shame should not fall on the immigrant community but on a system that lost respect for the democratic process and rule of law.

Trento's story was part both of the modern synergies created by the immigrant community on stage, in radio, and film, and of the processes Hollywood elaborated in the representation of ethnicity and nationality. He represents the "Neapolitan synecdoche" in a particular way, which emphasizes the ability of Neapolitan culture to appear as high and low, combining nationalism and regionalism, while it stresses identification with Italian culture and

---

[25] Trento is mentioned in Rose D. Scherini, "Executive Order 9066 and Italian Americans: The San Francisco Story," in Gloria Ricci Lothrop, ed., *Fulfilling the Promise of California* (Spokane, WA: California Italian American Task Force, The Arthur Clark Company, 2000) 215-230, N.8, 229.

[26] Laurence DiStasi, ed., *Una storia segreta. The Secret History of Italian American Evacuation and Internment during World War II* (Berkeley: Heyday Books, 2001).

patriotism from the enlistment in WWII to the linguistic and cultural identification as an Italian abroad, with the important achievement of making the first "All talking, All singing" Italian film in Hollywood.

Trento's interment in Missoula is not only a tragic event, but it represents the very moment in which the issue of language and national identity became a moral choice for several immigrants. Furthermore, the prohibition to speak "the enemy's language" forced the loss of speaking Italian at home, and therefore created a huge gap in the cultural identity with one's country of origin.

The mystery remains about what happened to Guido Trento between 1932 and 1941, but the drama of the internment in Missoula is enough to explain why his career has not been acknowledged within Italian American culture, which he helped build. Ignored in Italy because he had left it for Hollywood, he was imprisoned in 1941 because he was too "Italian" for Hollywood.

Italian American G.I.s in Hollywood World War II Movies

Matteo Pretelli
UNIVERSITY OF NAPLES "L'ORIENTALE"

INTRODUCTION

During March of 1944 a ferocious war was being waged in the Pacific with American troops attempting to ground down the Japanese resistance. In Brooklyn, New York, Private Salvatore Scalare's mother and fiancé spent a relaxing afternoon at the movie theater. Before the beginning of the screening, a newsreel showed a group of American soldiers taken as POWs by the Japanese and among them they recognized Salvatore. This no doubt caused them a great deal of surprise, as they were not aware that Salvatore had been imprisoned. A few days later, the moviegoers Luca and Antonietta Cavalluzzi—two immigrants from Bari (Italy) residing in Mount Vernon, New York—watched a combat movie that recounted the fierce Battle of Tarawa in the Pacific. Surprisingly enough, among the combatants they could identify their son Joe.[1]

Scalare and Cavalluzzi's relatives were among the nearly ninety million Americans who weekly attended movie theaters across the country, a leisure activity that became a communal viewing experience that shaped Americans' attitude towards their country's war effort (Ramsay 38-39). Seeing American servicemen of Italian origin was not altogether rare as their number in the U.S. armed forces was in the order of hundreds of thousands. Despite

---

[1] "Riconoscono il loro caro in un film nipponico," *Il Progresso Italo-Americano* (17 March 1944): 5; "Il sergente Joe Cavalluzzo appare ai suoi sullo schermo da un bivacco di Tarawa," *Il Progresso Italo-Americano* (20 March 1944): 3.

this, historians so far have paid scant attention to the war experience of Italian Americans, the largest ethnic group present in the U.S. armed forces during World War II according to military historian Thomas Bruscino (Bruscino 58). The little attention given to this subject by few scholars (Belmonte; LaGumina; Luconi; Mormino; Patti) has focused on particular aspects of the stories of these soldiers, individuals born in the United States to Italian parents who were sometimes called upon to fight in the land from where their relatives had departed. This lack of attention may be due to a greater historiographical interest in the topic of Italian-Americans' deprivation of civil liberties during wartime, the result of the American government heightened suspicion of espionage even leading to the internment of some Italian Americans. Immediately after the Untied States' entry into World War II, indeed, around 600,000 Italians not yet naturalized as American citizens were branded as 'enemy aliens' (a status removed on 12 October 1942) and subjected to many restrictions of their private liberties (Fox; Tintori; DiStasi 2001 and 2016). Against this backdrop, Italian Americans widely proved their allegiance to the cause of the United States by enlisting and fighting on all fronts. This war experience is told by a good amount of testimonies made up of memoirs and oral interviews. In addition, the Italian press in the United States—in particular *Il Progresso Italo-Americano*, the daily newspaper published in New York and distributed nationally—recounted the daily stories of these servicemen, described their bibliographical sketches, and even offered lists of those who were killed in action, wounded, or taken prisoners by the Axis forces.

This study aims to analyze the presence of Italian American servicemen in World War II movies produced by Hollywood from the time of the war onwards. After an analysis of the function of ethnicity in Hollywood's war movies, the essay will look at the Italian servicemen being identified in a surveyed sample of motion pictures. Particular attention will be paid to a few overlapping issues, namely Italian American ethnicity, diffused American patriotism, and the servicemen's ties to the institution of family and gender relations.

HOLLYWOOD, THE "JUST WAR," AND ETHNICITY

In terms of methodology, in order to identify characters of a marked Italian background I referred to the study of scholar Jeanine Basinger, who has analyzed hundreds of war movies (Basinger 2003). This current study has established twenty-two Hollywood movies in which Italian American soldiers can be clearly distinguished. The sample includes war films (produced during the years of the war or afterwards) of different typologies, whose plots are often extracted from novels:[2] mostly combat films, such as *Sands of Iwo Jima* (1949), which stars John Wayne, or Steven Spielberg's internationally-acclaimed *Saving Private Ryan* (1998); movies set in the Hawaii Islands, such as *From Here to the Eternity* (1953) with Frank Sinatra; non-combat movies such as a *Bell for Adano* (1945); movies with flashbacks to the war and the experiences of soldiers, as in the case of *The Godfather—Part I and II* (1972 and 1974). In addition, Italian American G.I.s are present in the miniseries *Band of Brothers* (2001) and *The Pacific* (2010), both produced by Steven Spielberg and Tom Hanks.

In the United States, the entire population was mobilized to endorse the cause of democracy and the push for victory (Blum; Bruscino). Hollywood made no exception, since the cinema industry was co-opted to facilitate the spread of propaganda at home and abroad. Mutual interests strengthened the relationship between Franklin Delano Roosevelt's administration and the cinema moguls, so much so that the former relaxed anti-trust legislation and worked to reduce import tariffs on American movies set in foreign countries. In return, Hollywood fully embraced patriotism and endorsed Washington in order to promote a positive image of

---

[2] On WWII soldiers' writings see Bodnar.

the United States around the globe (Bennett 18-19). The collaboration was so tight that the Office of War Information—the agency in charge of services of information and propaganda in and outside the United States—published a *Government Information Manual for the Motion Picture Industry*, a handbook intended to drive wartime movie production, while Hollywood could access aircrafts or background actors (Winkler; Muscio 1050-1051; May, 142). According to the scholar Todd Bennett, this mutually beneficial scenario was instrumental in Hollywood becoming "fully American" and a symbol of the United States (Bennett 16).

Ethnicity played a pivotal role in displaying World War II as the "just war," a conflict intended to destroy the totalitarian regimes in Europe and Asia and affirm the dominance of democracy globally.[3] The genre of combat movies, in particular, featured military units in which the ethnicity of soldiers is easily identifiable. While the New Deal era re-evaluated the role of ethnic groups, during WWII, ethnicity within the military became a central trope and was utilized to portray harmony in American society. Thus, the ethnically diverse platoon evident in many movies served as a microcosm of an American society united in pursuit of victory. According to Richard Slotkin, WWII combat films signaled a shift from a white America towards multiethnic and multiracial discourses (although African Americans were not screened, given the fact they had been obliged to fight in segregated units) (Slotkin 470, 489). Nevertheless, patronized hierarchies persisted, because leaders with Anglo-Saxon somatic traits usually led the group. Postwar war movies, however, nuanced this aspect and the leadership's infallibility does not go unquestioned anymore, and the platoon's harmony is not taken for granted (Muscio 1059, 1061, 1068, 1070).

In regards of combat films, scholar Jeanine Basinger (1998) categorizes them periodically: during World War II, movies had pat-

---

[3] For the American view of European totalitarianisms see Alpers.

riotic goals aimed "to help the audience to get behind the war and set aside their doubts and fears;" after 1949 there was a resurgence in war movies, produced in a phase of "earned national pride"; the 1960s, furthermore, saw a celebration of war through the epic recreation of major battles; the last category, starting from the late-1990s, featured more critical, candid portrayals of the war, including movies like *Saving Private Ryan*, *The Thin Red Line*, and *U-571* (Basinger 1998). Generally, interest for war movies is further fostered through TV shows, documentaries, books, and has a main impact on the construction of collective memory of wartime (Basinger 1998; Eberwein).

Despite the inclusion of different ethnicities within the American combat unit in war movies, many still reiterate traditional ethnic stereotypes such as the drunk Irish, the Italian Latin-lover, and the whining Jew (Muscio, 1061; Slotkin, 469-470). Through a full survey of all U.S. combat films relating to WWII, the scholar Jeanine Basinger states how:

> The group is made up of a mixture of ethnic and geographic types, most commonly including an Italian, a Jew, a cynical complainer from Brooklyn, a sharpshooter from the mountains, a Midwesterner (nicknamed by his state, 'Iowa' or 'Dakota'), and a character who must be initiated in some way (a newcomer without battle experience) and/or who will provide a commentary or 'explanation' on the action as it occurs (a newspaperman, a letter writer, an author, a professor). (Basinger 1998)

Italian ethnicity is neatly identifiable in motion pictures produced at least until the 1950s. Soldiers have Italian-sounding surnames and Mediterranean somatic traits, such as dark-skinned faces or greased-back hair, and are often associated with Italian language or dialects. The usage of the native language is in any case accompanied by a full command of accent-free English, a capacity that discloses how these people mirrored young people born and raised in the United States. According to the 1920 U.S. census, they were mostly part of a second generation that outnumbered the generation of their parents that had arrived from Italy. Educated in American public schools and accustomed to the consumerist model of the American way of life, this second generation still retained features of the native culture, but inevitably perceived themselves as "American." This feature is clearly understandable by reading writings of those who took part in the conflict (Belmonte; Orsi).

Italian ethnicity is particularly accentuated in movies starring Wally Cassell—born in Sicily as Osvaldo Castellano—as Private Dondaro in *The Story of G.I. Joe* (1945) and as Marine Ben Regazzi in *Sands of Iwo Jima* (1949). Both characters are clearly identifiable as Italian by their bizarre comic caricatures. Ben Regazzi, in particular, is a sociable person, very friendly to his comrades and appreciated by all components of the multiethnic platoon, which also includes two Irish brothers and a Greek. Regazzi embodies some stereotypes associated with the Italian American since the beginning of American silent cinema, such as the tendency to get drunk and obsess over women (Casaregola, 116; Bondanella). Likewise, in *From Here to the Eternity*—a 1953 multi-award winning movie that received twelve Oscar nominations—the Italian American soldier Angelo Maggio (played by popular singer Frank Sinatra) is funny, easygoing, proud, stubborn, and prone to get drunk and dance. Consequently, he is subjected to ethnic prejudice by Sergeant "Fatso" Hudson, who labels Maggio in derogatory terms as "wop," "Little Mussolini," and "tough monkey" (Bondanella 35-37).

In terms of stereotypes, Italian American servicemen are also often depicted as boastful. It is definitely the case of abovementioned Ben Regazzi, who—in talking to a group of Marines—credits himself with the killing of thirty-two Japanese enemies and blames the fact he had not received any reward because he "got enemies in Washington." Boastfulness is then associated to a

Macho culture traditionally bound to the Italian people and Italian American servicemen are not exempt. While Regazzi and Maggio repeatedly express their appreciation for ladies, Private Colucci in *Eight Iron Men* (1952) constantly sexualizes women in his dreams. In a sort of hilarious and paradoxical context, in *The Story of G.I. Joe* (1945) in a mix of English and Sicilian dialect Private Dondaro seduces a young Sicilian lady just in the midst of a battle. Nonetheless, the image of Latin lover Italian American serviceman is longstanding, and can be seen in more recent movies with characters such as Sergeant Ruffelo in *Yanks* (1979), Private Mazzola in *U-571* (2000), and Private Fusco in *Pearl Harbor* (2001).

After the 1950s, the ethnicity of the Italian American soldiers is gradually downplayed, and it is more difficult to distinguish them from their comrades. They may still be recognized, however, from their Italian-sounding surnames, explicit reference to their background, Catholic crucifix necklaces, or the utilization of idiomatic expressions such as "capisc" (understand?), as is the case for Private Caparzo in *Saving Private Ryan* (1998). The reason behind this shift can be accredited to an "ethnic revival" that led many ethnics to revalue their background in the late 1960s. Many ethnic groups of European descent worked to improve their image, attempting to eliminate older negative stereotypes, as in the case of Italians who lobbied to ban the words "Mafia" and "Cosa Nostra" from the media. With this in mind, Hollywood may have decided to reduce ethnic characterization, especially comic representations (as in the cases of Regazzi and Maggio), in order to avoid potential retaliations.

PATRIOTISM

Despite the fact that in a few movies Italian American servicemen might appear undisciplined or unruly, they often appear as the highest expression of American patriotism. All of them fight with vigor, devotion and the spirit of sacrifice, and on some occasions they carry out heroic deeds that save their comrades. For instance, in the midst of a battle to reach the top of a hill in *Sands of Iwo Jima*, Regazzi leads a tank towards his companions and allows the platoon to accomplish the mission. In *Eight Iron Men* (1952), Private Colucci is a soldier that shirks many of his tasks; nevertheless he will be the one to destroy an enemy machine gun that threatens the lives of his peers. In *The Purple Heart* (1944), Lieutenant Angelo Canelli (played by Italian American actor Richard Conte)[4] is one of the few American airmen taken as a POW in Japan. Perfectly American in style and accent, before the war Canelli was an aspiring student of art who was destined to study in Italy and fulfill his father's dreams of becoming a modern "Michael Angelo." Canelli's projects were frustrated by the fact that Italy had entered the war on the "wrong side," thus, unbeknown to his parents, he enlisted voluntarily in the U.S. air corps because he wanted to fight "the thing that had spoiled my father's dream."

Americanism is also particularly marked in the Campaign of Italy in which many Italian American servicemen took part. In *A Bell for Adano* (1945), Major Joppolo is the military administrator of the fictional Sicilian city of Adano. Thanks to his knowledge of the Italian language and culture, he is able to approach the local population whom he conquers through a fair and equal administration that boosts the image of the United States as a land of democracy. Additionally, Joppolo pays respect to the local necessities and traditions, marking a shift away from the Fascist tyranny of the past 20 years that had ruled over citizens' lives.

Undoubtedly, Marine Sergeant John Basilone—a main character of the TV miniseries *The Pacific* (2010)—embodies the highest degree of American patriotism for an Italian American service-

---

[4] Born in New Jersey as Nicholas Peter Conte, Richard Conte was an actor on Broadway throughout the 1930s, and in 1942 signed a contract with Twentieth Century Fox (Aste 389). Besides Canelli in *The Purple Heart*, he played the role of an Italian prisoner of war in *A Bell for Adano*.

man. One of the few Marines awarded the Congressional Medal of Honor for his service in World War II, Basilone was killed in action during the Battle of Iwo Jima. Before his death, he toured the country on behalf of the U.S. military authorities, promoting the sale of War Bonds. He was "sold" to the public as an exemplary figure of an "ordinary" American (child of an immigrant family) that had come to the fore on account of his "specialness" and exceptional military capacities, as demonstrated in the fight against the Japanese (Frontani). In *The Pacific* (2010), Basilone is presented as exemplary in terms of his dedication to the war cause, as well as his heroism and altruism. Nonetheless, even the miniseries does not hesitate to reproduce stereotypes associated to Italians, as Basilone is still portrayed as a playboy personality.

Generally, the image of patriotic Italian American soldiers is prevalent against the backdrop of negative stereotypes to which they had been subjected in ordinary life and in cinema (Connell & Gardaphé). However, once in a while these stereotypes resurge. In *Eight Iron Men* (1952), Private Collucci is often portrayed carrying a knife in his hands, inevitably recalling the typical image of the aggressive Italian immigrant portrayed by magazines and crystallized in American popular culture. In *Sands of Iwo Jima* (1949), a soldier with Anglo-Saxon physical traits teaches Regazzi how to properly fold an American flag, recalling the supposed "inferiority" of Italian ethnics. In *Brass Target* (1978), Major John De Luca—in early postwar Germany called to investigate the disappearance of a gold-loaded train—reiterates old-fashioned stereotypes by stating "I am a Sicilian, to me everything is conspiracy." In *The Big Red One* (1980), on a ship leading U.S. troops from North Africa to Sicily one of his peers taunts Private Vinci for his Italian ethnicity, belittles his masculinity, and advises him to drink his "dago red" (Italian wine) and sing *O sole mio*. Projecting again the image of hot-blooded Italians, Vinci overreacts by placing his rifle in the soldier's mouth and starts to sing the Neapolitan song, with the rest of the group joining him. This scene is emblematic of Holly-wood's attempt to portray the harmony between the different eth-nicities in the American platoon, as all of the soldiers ultimately share the aim of victory in war. In the world-renowned movie *Saving Private Ryan* (1998), we find such a balance. In a scene where a bag of dog tags is searched, symbolic of those killed-in-action, a member of the platoon calls those with Italian surnames "guin-eas." But the portrayal of Italian Americans does not begin and end with this incident, instead the movie features the story of Private Adrian Caparzo (played by Vin Diesel) who is unquestionably a competent member of the platoon and is not subject to any dis-crimination. Moreover, he is eventually portrayed as a hero fol-lowing his death whilst attempting to save a girl.

FAMILY AND GENDER RELATIONS

Maybe unsurprisingly, family has a great impact on Holly-wood's portrayal of Italian American soldiers. According to the scholar Ilaria Serra, in American cinema, Americans of Italian back-ground have been often depicted in their household to the extent that

> [t]he predominance of the family as a narrative unit is part of a larger tendency in American cinema. In the majority of Italian American films, however, the family is not only a cue for come-dy or simple wallpaper, it is indeed a constitutive part of the narration. (Serra 197)

Angelo Maggio has a typical American family of Italian de-scent with many siblings and a sister whose "honor" has to be de-fended against Sergeant "Fatso" Hudson's vulgar references. At the beginning of *A Walk in the Sun*, Italian American Private Rive-ra is introduced as willing to build a family with a wife and many children, thus recalling the "holiness" of the family institution in Italian American culture. In *To Hell and Back*, during the occupation of Naples, Private Valentino leaves his comrades temporarily to visit his relatives and bring them gifts, fulfilling a promise made to his mother. In fictional terms, Valentino shares the practice of traveling to the ancestral town undertaken by many Italian American G.I.s during World War II. These trips had a strong emotional impact on both the soldiers and their relatives, and facilitated relations between the local people and the American occupiers. The practice became such a regular occurrence that *Il Progresso Italo-Americano* periodically published stories about Italian American soldiers coming face-to-face with their ancestral roots.

The family household is also the natural setting for Italian Americans in *The Pacific* (2010) and *The Unbroken* (2001), the latter a movie that recounts the unusual story of Louis Zamperini, an American Olympic athlete that was imprisoned by the Japanese in WWII. While Zamperini's mother is held in high regard by the neighborhood for her respectability, Basilone's family is a paradigm of the American patriotic household in which all members accept the loss of their son. In one of the final scenes of *The Pacific* (2010), the delivery of John's Medal of Honor to his family by his wife Lena (an Italian American Marine Sergeant as well) celebrates the unity and sacrifice of the family on behalf of the highest goal, victory for America.

Nonetheless, war and due allegiance may cause division in Italian American families, as is evident with perhaps the most famous cinematic one, the Corleone family of Francis Ford Coppola's *The Godfather*. In the final scene of the second episode, all siblings are sitting by a table waiting to celebrate their father's birthday. Conversation turns soon to the breaking news about the Japanese attack on Pearl Harbor and the increasing number of enlistments. Sonny, the oldest brother, belittles all enlisting volunteers by describing them as "saps risking their lives for strangers" and points out that "blood comes before the country." Michael, the youngest brother, contests Sonny's words that reflect their father's and announces that he has quit college in order to enlist in the Marines. According to Robert L. Fleeger, Michael is "a clearly ethnic but assimilated veteran who identifies with 'American' traditions" (Fleeger 194). On the contrary Sonny, who tries to punch his brother, reiterates values of his father's generation that are bound to the ancestral culture of the Old Country. In other words, the 1930s saw a generational clash as Italian American parents struggled to come to terms with the new, more Americanized identity and customs of their children (Orsi).

Italian American relations with the Italian people were greatly facilitated by encounters with local women, a point reiterated by the fact that around a third of all American male citizens that married Italian women in this period were of Italian origin (Varricchio 146). Italian Americans served as a cultural bridge between Italians and Americans as they spoke Italian, knew the local culture and could easily interact with the local population. All Hollywood's movies set in Italy screen Italians and Italian Americans as belonging to a sort of "enlarged family" made up of warm exchanges. Overall, Italian Americans retain their American identity, but in Italy it can be somehow fluid and shifting. A case in point is Private Tranella in *A Walk in the Sun* (1945), who is called to translate the interrogation of two Italian defectors. When it is revealed that the Italians originally come from Tranella's father's hometown, he leaves behind his "American" composure and starts to gesticulate obsessively, defending the honor of the Italian people.

CONCLUSIONS

Why is the presence of Italian American servicemen so prominent in war movies, and why have they, on the whole, been portrayed as true, patriotic Americans? Other ethnicities that were linked to the Axis Powers of WWII do not seem to have received the same benevolence. American servicemen of German background, for example, appear to have been portrayed poorly on the big screen. In *U-571* (2000), Seaman Wentz asks his superiors not to disclose his German ethnicity for fear of being hated by his comrades. In TV miniseries *Band of Brothers* (2001), one of the German soldiers captured by the Americans reveals that he is originally from Astoria, New York, and was drafted by the German army after he returned to the fatherland with his parents. His connection to the United States and apparent innocence do not save him from an illegal execution together with other German prisoners of war. In the psychedelic movie *Inglorious Basterds* (2009), Quentin Tarantino fictionally utilizes a German-speaking unit of Jewish Americans to create chaos in Nazi Germany. Their task is to kill as many Nazis as possible, while their "trademark" is taking their victims' scalps as souvenirs, or making incision of swastikas on prisoners' foreheads. A partial reconciliation with German-ness happens when former German soldier Hugo Stiglizt, murderer of many Nazi officials, joins the group. However, although Stiglitz is now on the "right" side of the war, his truculent face recalls again a negative perception of German-ness. At the same time, Japanese Americans, most of whom were imprisoned during WWII across the U.S., are far from being depicted in movies as beneficial to the country's war efforts. John W. Dower described how, contrary to the Germans, the Japanese were utterly dehumanized by American servicemen as they were considered racially inferior to the point that they were perceived as subhuman, likened more to rats, reptiles, or insects (Dower 77-93). Thus, while Germans were seen as efficient and obedient and there was potential to draw distinction between Nazis and "Good Germans," the Japanese were only cruel, lowly, and deserved to die (Doherty 282; Muscio 1064). In other words, an enemy aimed to impose a racial superiority through cruelty (Slotkin 480, 484). However, the contribution of a Japanese American battalion in the 442nd Regimental Combat Team to the U.S.'s war efforts in Europe was portrayed in positive terms in Robert Pirosh's 1951 movie *Go for Broke!*. The motion picture aimed to demonstrate the patriotism of Americans of Japanese descent, according to Thomas Doherty, "in service to the emperor, the native tenacity of the Japanese was fanaticism; in service to Uncle Sam, it was exemplary devotion to duty" (Doherty 147). Such an approach may have been the result of the Cold War climate of the time, when the U.S. found in Japan an ally to counter the rising of Communists in China. Indeed, in the same year of the movie's release, the two countries signed a peace treaty officially ending the war tensions.

The Italian people never received such negative treatment by Hollywood. In his study, the scholar Thomas Guglielmo points out how in motion pictures and popular literature Italians were "forgotten enemies," in the sense that they were not described as true enemies, but rather as easy-going bunglers, craven soldiers, jovial, good, and loyal people, sympathizers of the United States, loathing militarism, and victims of Mussolini and fascism (Guglielmo 5-22).[5] In his propaganda movie *Why We Fight*, commissioned by the Department of Army, Italian American filmmaker Frank Capra offers again a more benevolent portrait of the Italian people than the Germans and Japanese, and attempts to reverse many of Hollywood's traditional Italian stereotypes (Cavallero; Buchanan 224).

Given this scenario, Hollywood could not have projected a negative image of the many Italian Americans who had fought for democracy. Their prominence on screen might merely be the result of the undeniably large numbers who took part in the war, forming a significant part of America's multiethnic platoons. Secondly, Italian Americans constituted an important political lobby for Roosevelt's electoral coalition and they had demonstrated to be

---

[5] The most exaggerated depiction of Italians in WWII probably comes from *What Did You Do in the War, Daddy?* (directed by Blake Edwards, 1966). In this comedy, set during the occupation of Sicily, Italians are portrayed as happy-go-lucky pranksters, drinkers, and partygoers, and whilst they fraternize with the Americans, the Germans are shown as the real enemies.

one of the most loyal ethnic groups to the American cause. Lastly, it may also be important to note that the apparent jovial nature of Italian Americans in the movies might be a narrative tool, intended to lighten the heaviness imposed by dramatic scenes of conflict.

FILMOGRAPHY

Combat and non-combat movies set in World War II and produced during World War II

So Proudly We Hail! (directed by Mark Sandrich, 1943, set in the Philippines).

The Purple Heart (directed by Lewis Milestone, 1944, set in Japan).

A Walk in the Sun (directed by Lewis Milestone, 1945, set in Italy).

A Bell for Adano (directed by Herry King, 1945, set in Italy).

The Story of G.I. Joe (directed by William Wellman, 1945, set in Tunisia and Italy).

Combat and non-combat movies set during World War II and produced after World War II

Sands of Iwo Jima (directed by Allan Dwan, 1949, set in Japan).

Eight Iron Men (directed by Edward Dmytryk, 1952, set in Italy).

From Here to the Eternity (directed by Fred Zinnemann, 1953, set in Hawaii Islands).

To Hell and Back (directed by Jesse Hibbs, 1955, set in North Africa, Italy, France).

The Pigeon that Took Rome (directed by Melville Shavelson, 1962, set in Rome).

The Thin Red Line (directed by Andrew Marton, 1964, set in Guadalcanal, Solomon Islands).

The Bridge at Remagen (directed by John Guillermin, 1969, set in Germany).

Castle Keep (directed by Sydney Pollack, 1969, set in Belgium).

The Godfather — Part II (directed by Francis F. Coppola, 1974, set in the United States).

The Big Red One (directed by Samuel Fuller, 1980, set in North Africa and Europe).

Saving Private Ryan (directed by Steven Spielberg, 1998, set in Normandy).

U-571 (directed by Jonathan Mostow, 2000, set in the Atlantic Ocean).

Pearl Harbor (directed by Michael Bay, 2001, set in Hawaii Islands).

The Unbroken (directed by Angelina Jolie, 2014, set in the Pacific Theater and Japan).

Yanks (directed by John Schlesinger, 1979, set in England).

Non-combat movies set after World War

Godfather — Part I (directed by Francis F. Coppola, 1972, set in the United States).

Brass Target (John Hough, 1978, set in Germany).

TV miniseries

Band of Brothers (directed by Steven Spielberg and Tom Hanks, 2001, set in the European Theater).

The Pacific (directed by Steven Spielberg and Tom Hanks, 2010, set in the Pacific Theater).

Bibliography

Alpers, Benjamin L. *Dictators, Democracy, and American Public Culture: Envisioning the Totalitarian Enemy, 1920s-1950s*. Chapel Hill-London: U North Carolina P, 2003.

Aste, Mario. "Movie Actors and Actresses." In *The Italian American Experience: An Encyclopedia*. Salvatore LaGumina et al., eds. New York: Garland, 2000. 387-395.

Aversa, Alfred Jr. "Italian Neo-Ethnicity: The Search for Self-Identity," *Journal of Ethnic Studies*, 2 (1978), 49-56.

Basinger, Jeanine. "Translating War: The Combat Film Genre and *Saving Private Ryan*," *Perspectives on History: The Newsmagazine of the American Historical Association*, October 1998, available at https://www. historians.org/publications-and-directories/perspectives-on-history/october-1998/translating-war-the-combat-film-genre-and-saving-private-ryan.

Basinger, Jeanine. *The World War II Combat Film: Anatomy of a Genre.* Middletown: Wesley UP, 2003.

Belmonte, Peter L. *Italian Americans in World War II.* Charlestone: Arcadia, 2001.

Bennett, M. Todd. *One World, Big Screen: Hollywood, the Allies, and World War II.* Chapel Hill: U North Carolina P, 2012.

Blum, John Morton. *V Was for Victory.* San Diego: HBJ Book, 1976.

Bodnar, John. *The "Good War" in American Memory.* Baltimore: Johns Hopkins UP, 2000.

Bondanella, Peter. *Hollywood Italians: Dagos, Palookas, Romeos, Wise Guys, and Sopranos.* New York-London: Continuum, 2006.

Bruscino, Thomas. *A Nation Forged in War: How World War II Taught Americans to Get Along.* Knoxville: U Tennessee P, 2010.

Buchanan, Andrew. "Good Morning, Pupil! American Representations of Italianness and the Occupation of Italy, 1943-1945," *Journal of Contemporary History* 43.2 (2008): 217-40.

Casaregola, Vincent. *Theaters of War: America's Perception of World War II.* New York: Palgrave, 2009.

Cavallero, Jonathan James. "Redefininig Italianità: The Difference Between Mussolini, Italy, Germany, and Japan in Frank Capra's 'Why We Fight'." *Italian Americana* 22.1 (2004): 5-16.

Connell, William J. and Fred Gardaphé, eds. *Anti-Italianism: Essays on a Prejudice.* New York: Palgrave, 2010.

DiStasi, Lawrence. *Una Storia Segreta: The Secret History of Italian American Evacuation and Internment During World War II.* Berkeley: Heyday Books, 2001.

DiStasi, Lawrence. *Branded: How Italian Immigrants Became 'Enemies' During World War II.* Bolinas: Sanniti Publications, 2016.

Doherty, Thomas. *Projections of War: Hollywood, American Culture, and World War II.* New York: Columbia UP, 1999.

Dower, John W. *War Without Mercy: Race and Power in the Pacific War.* New

York: Pantheon Books, 1986.

Eberwein, Robert. *The Hollywood War Film*. Malden: Wiley-Blackwell, 2010.

Fleeger, Robert L. *Ellis Island Nation: Immigration Policy and American Identity in the Twentieth Century*. Philadelphia: U Pennsylvania P, 2014.

Fox, Stephen. *The Unknown Internment. An Oral History of the Relocation of Italian Americans during World War II*. Boston: Twayne, 1990.

Frontani, Michael, "Becoming American: 'Manila John' Basilone, the Medal of Honor, and Italian-American Image 1943-1945." *Italian American Review* 4.1 (2014): 21-52.

Guglielmo, Thomas. "The Forgotten Enemy: Wartime Representations of Italians in American Popular Culture, 1941-1945." *Italian Americana* 18.1 (2000): 5-22.

Hake, Sabine. *Screen Nazis: Cinema, History, and Democracy*. Madison: U Wisconsin P, 2012.

Jacobson, Matthew Frye, *Roots Too: White Ethnic Revival in Post-Civil Rights America*. Harvard: Harvard UP, 2006.

LaGumina, Salvatore J. *The Humble and the Heroic: Wartime Italian Americans*. Youngstown: Cambria Press, 2006.

Luconi, Stefano. "Italian Americans and the Invasion of Sicily in World War II." *Italian Americana* 25 (2007): 5-22.

May, Lary. *The Big Tomorrow: Hollywood and the Politics of the American Way*. London: U Chicago P, 2000.

Mormimo Gary R. "It's not Personal, It's Professional: Italian Americans and World War II." In *The Impact of World War II on Italian Americans, 1935-Present*. Gary R. Mormino, ed. New York: American Italian Historical Association, 2007. 11-19.

Muscio, Giuliana. "Hollywood va in guerra, Storia del cinema mondiale." In *Gli Stati Uniti*. Vol. II. Gian Piero Brunetta, ed. Turin: Einaudi, 2000. 1049-1088.

Orsi, Robert A. "The Fault of Memory: 'Southern Italy' in the Imagination of Immigrants and the Lives of Their Children in Italian Harlem, 1920-1945." *Journal of Family History* 15.2 (1990): 133-147.

Patti, Manoela. *La Sicilia e gli Alleati: Tra occupazione e Liberazione*. Rome:

Donzelli, 2013.

Ramsay, Debra. *American Media and the Memory of World War II*. New York-London: Routledge, 2015.

Serra, Ilaria. "Italian-American Cinema: Between Blood Family and Bloody Family." In *Mediated Ethnicity: New Italian-American Cinema*. Giuliana Muscio et al., eds. New York: John D. Calandra Italian American Institute, 2010. 189-224.

Slotkin, Richard. "Unit Pride: Ethnic Platoons and the Myths of American Nationality," *American Literary History* 13.3 (2001): 469-498.

Tintori, Guido. "New Discoveries, Old Prejudices: The Internment of Italian Americans during World War II." In *Una Storia Segreta: Italian American Evacuation and Internment during World War II*. Lawrence DiStasi, ed. Berkley: Heyday Books, 2001. 236-249.

Varricchio, Mario. "Il sogno e le radici: nostalgia e legami transnazionali delle spose di guerra italiane." In *Lontane da casa: Donne italiane e diaspora globale dall'inizio del Novecento a oggi*. Stefano Luconi & Mario Varricchio, eds. Turin: Accademia UP, 2015. 115-148.

Winkler, Allan M. *The Politics of Propaganda: The Office of War Information 1942-1945*. New Haven: Yale UP, 1978.

"Unhomely" Domesticity in Nancy Savoca's *Household Saints* and *Dirt*

Sabrina Vellucci

ROMA TRE UNIVERSITY

In a seminal essay entitled "The World and the Home," Homi Bhabha called attention to "the deep stirring of the 'unhomely'" (141). In what he defines as "unhomely moments," "the intimate recesses of the domestic space become sites for history's most intricate invasions. In that displacement, the border between home and the world becomes confused; and, uncannily, the private and the public become part of each other, forcing upon us a vision that is divided as it is disorienting" (141). A paradigmatic colonial and post-colonial condition, the "unhomely" also resonates in fictions that deal with intersecting differences in a range of transhistorical contexts. It is, therefore, through this lens that I will examine the depiction of domesticity and domestic labor in *Household Saints* and *Dirt*, released respectively in 1993 and 2003, by Italian-Argentinian-American director Nancy Savoca. My purpose is to show how, in both movies, the unhomely is used to reflect on the gendered nature of housework and on the characters' complex negotiations between different cultures, generations, and between the private and the public sphere. In both films, the question of gendered domestic labor is compounded with issues of ethnicity, class and – particularly in *Dirt* – citizenship, revealing the ambivalent outcomes of the irruption of the "world" in the home.

Based upon Francine Prose's 1981 novel by the same title, Nancy Savoca's *Household Saints* tells the story of three generations of Italian Americans in New York's declining Little Italy of the 1950s through the 1970s. The film begins at a family gathering set in the present, where younger family members ask their elders about the old neighborhood. As the grandmother begins to tell the story of the Santangelos and their "miracle sausages," the film flashes back to 1949 and narrates the fateful marriage of Catherine and Joseph. The first half of the movie focuses on the confrontation between Catherine and Carmela, Joseph's Sicilian mother. While Catherine is skeptical of religion, the widowed matriarch is a first-generation Italian immigrant who believes in curses and the evil eye, and habitually converses with the Virgin Mary and the saints, as well as with her dead husband. In these passages, the domestic space functions as a claustrophobic setting that also symbolically epitomizes Catherine's entrapment within a pre-existing gendered plot.[1]

In the middle section of the film, the apartment's gloomy atmosphere, together with the distress experienced by Catherine, is dispelled by Carmela's unexpected death. As a variation on the magic realistic tone that enlivens the first part of the film, or perhaps an ironic allusion to the miracles that are part of Carmela's belief system, Savoca clusters three events, Easter Sunday, Catherine's recovery after a miscarriage, and Carmela's demise into a single sequence, which is immediately followed by Catherine's transformation into a modern woman of the fifties. By taking over the

---

[1] In her analysis of Savoca's first film, *True Love* (1989), Veronica Pravadelli identifies the correlation of visual claustrophobia and female subordination, that the director conveys by having the protagonist (significantly named "Donna" — Italian for 'woman') appear "both visually and narratively trapped": "In *True Love* [...] the Italian-American community is represented as a closed and autonomous world. Italian Americans seem to live in a 'parallel' universe: no integration or contamination exists between 'Americans' and 'Italian Americans.' More specifically, the Brooklyn community depicted by Savoca [...] is quite static and impermeable to change [...]. But the neighborhood is not simply static: for women and younger people, the closed world inhabited by the community is truly claustrophobic" (172).

responsibility for preparing the sausage that has made the San-tangelo's business successful, giving birth to Teresa, and, further still, flouting old Italian/American superstitions, Catherine claims the power to determine her own life.

As the conflict between an urban Italian/American neighbor-hood in decline and the developing suburbs of the post-war peri-od looms in the background, Catherine seems the best-suited char-acter to deal with the resulting pressures and changes. Her work "both within and beyond a strict domestic sphere" drives the fami-ly out of an isolated ethnic existence and into an assimilated, mid-dle-class American culture (Ruberto 171). Yet, as Laura Ruberto observes, *Household Saints* questions whether "the movement of Italian Americans into a consumerist middle-class life in the 1950s and 1960s helped liberate Italian/American women from Old-World patriarchal constraints or merely reinstituted those con-straints within a dominant non-ethnic environment" (170). In-deed, as Irena Makarushka remarks, "Savoca resists the notion that traces of the tradition into which one is born can be made to disappear by mere [...] cosmetic changes" (86). Catherine's desire to eradicate the superstition that plagued her early married life is challenged, and her rationalizations are further nullified by the life and "sainthood" of her daughter, Teresa.

From early childhood, Teresa believes that her purpose in life is to serve God in self-effacing ways. She eventually finds her vo-cation in high school, when she is awarded a book on Saint Thérèse of Lisieux. Also known as the "Little Flower," Thérèse de Lisieux was the French nun whose convent life consisted of very ordinary chores that inspired generations of Catholic schoolgirls. Thus, Tere-sa sets herself to zealously scrubbing stairs and floors and refusing to eat dinner. Like her grandmother, she has visions and visita-tions. Yet, unlike Carmela, Teresa ends up in a mental hospital run by nuns, where she mysteriously dies leaving behind her signs that many, in the Italian/American neighborhood, read as miracles. In fact, Teresa seems to literally embody Marcus Lee Hansen's "principle of third-generation interest," which states that "what the son [or daughter] wishes to forget the grandson [or granddaughter] wishes to remember" (9).

The process of third-generation ethnic rediscovery is symbolized visually in a shot that frames Teresa as Carmela's reincarnation, in one of what I would call the film's "unhomely moments." In this scene, we watch Teresa as she wakes up in the middle of the night to the smell and sound of sausages roasting on a pan and heads for the kitchen saying to herself, "I know what this is. This is a test" (she had indeed engaged in a prolonged fasting both to purify herself on her way toward becoming a bride to Jesus and as a protest against her father's refusal to let her join the Carmelites). While we are made to believe that the cooking of the sausages awakens Teresa, we see that it is actually she who is doing the cooking, as the close-up shows us her dark hair and white night gown, while the hand that is holding the pan and fork is clearly the hand of a younger person. Yet, as Catherine, also awakened by the sounds, appears at the kitchen doorway, in the place of Teresa we see for a moment Carmela, who is also wearing a white night gown and from behind looks like Teresa. It is only when she turns around and looks back at Catherine that we recognize her. As the scene switches from the over-the-shoulder shot of Teresa cooking to Catherine in the doorway, we see that Catherine, momentarily, sees Carmela, who actually turns toward her with a most ambiguous silent look. Immediately after, we have another close-up of Catherine, who is still in the doorway but now sees Teresa at the stove: she has given in to her hunger and is stuffing herself with the cooked sausage.

In light of Hansen's theory of the "third-generation interest," Catherine's position is most revealing, not only because, in keeping with the anti-realistic nature of the scene, Catherine appears on a threshold, in a liminal position, suspended between dream and reality, superstition and objectivity. Most significant, the apparition of Carmela reminds the viewer that Teresa and Carmela are made of the same cloth, both are very religious and believe in the many visions they have. Unlike Catherine, both subscribe to principles that make them look anachronistic with respect to contemporary U.S. culture. The fact that Catherine remains in the doorway and does not enter the kitchen until Teresa reappears underscores the distinction between her and Carmela, and solidifies the connection between the first (Carmela) and third generation (Teresa). Only these two—grandmother and granddaughter—can be in the kitchen at the same time. Catherine cannot enter until Carmela is gone. The connection is further emphasized by the resemblance of the white nightgowns that Teresa and Carmela are wearing, whereas Catherine's nightgown has a print design on it. The simplicity of the white nightgown (old world, religiously restrained) is set up against the ornate nightgown (new world) that Catherine wears. In any case, Carmela's uncanny apparition at the stove disrupts what is supposed to be a cozy atmosphere of everyday habitual practices and environments, and further highlights that for the woman homemaker the home has always been marked by profound ambivalence.

At the end of the film, as we go back to the initial scene set in the present, the grandmother concludes her story underlining the relationship between domesticity and spirituality and asserting that Teresa "saw God in her work." Yet, her daughter, with a baby in her arms, offers another perspective. She says: "I could name a list of women as long as my arm who went crazy cooking and cleaning and trying to please everybody." Thus, the film sets up another generational contrast: dismissing any supernatural explanation of the events, the younger generation critiques domesticity and unwaged household labor as defining elements for women. Indeed, the actual set up of the three generations is telling. On the one side of the table, the daughter, granddaughter and great-

Makarushka argues that the film's critique of traditional gender norms begins at the outset of the film, when the grandfather cajoles her wife to recount the story correctly and takes the stage to tell his version of the events. "The grandfather's usurpation of his wife's power to tell the tale confirms the cultural silencing of women and the politics of patriarchy" (Makarushka 84) – however, it must also be noticed that when the film returns to the present, in the movie's last scene, it is the grandmother who is narrating the story. Arguably, this structuring encourages viewers to be mindful of the narrator's biases—a stance that seems especially appropriate when we consider Savoca's propensity for targeting gender norms and inequalities in her films.[2]

To be sure, throughout the narrative, we see female and male characters who do not fit neatly into their environment and who resist gender norms. Toward the end of the film, Joseph acknowledges Catherine's freedom and allows himself "to take on the 'feminine' role of the emotional and distraught parent" upon Teresa's death. In contrast, Catherine "resists traditional religious and ethnic signifiers and projects a coolness and rationality culturally attributed to male behavior" (Makarushka 90-91). They are, as Savoca has said, trying to perform roles that "are like ill-fitting clothes." As a matter of fact, in order to find happiness, Joseph and Catherine must reject the neighborhood's superstitious beliefs and some of its cultural norms (Cavallero 86-87). Indeed, if, on the one hand, the frame narrative set in the 1990s constructs the central section as a legendary tale, on the other hand, the juxtaposition between the two sections allows the viewer to see high-

---

[2] While my reading does not support this interpretation, Jonathan Cavallero notes that the women characters in the scene—both the grandfather's wife and his daughter and granddaughter who are listening to the story—"accept this turn of events without protest. If Savoca is targeting the grandfather's dominance of the situation, she may also be targeting the women's acquiescence to and complicity in such dominance" (86).

ly valued myths for women in Italian/American culture, such as domesticity and saintliness, for what they are, stressing their fictitious if not pernicious nature. Therefore, ultimately, the juxtaposition reveals that the legend has lost its charm, and the effect is rather the uncovering of the fallacies of a system of belief that appears to be no longer tenable.

Nancy Savoca has been critical of her Italian/American background—a culture that she sees as providing a strong sense of identity while also limiting one's individuality and opportunities. Thus, in her films characters constantly step in and out of the constructed ethnic worlds "in order to focus the audience's general attention on [...] *transcultural* processes" (Camaiti Hostert 142). Savoca's mixed ethnic roots are complicated by her family's frequent moves before and during her childhood, and by an experience of immigration that is different from the typical pattern. Her father was born in Sicily, but he was raised in Argentina, where he met his wife, and it is from this country that her parents migrated to the U.S., just before she was born. Once in the U.S., her family settled into a working-class existence in the Bronx, New York, "where financial and social pressure made their day-to-day existence tumultuous and tenuous. 'Every couple of years,' she remembers, '[my parents] would say, 'I can't take it here anymore. We gotta leave'."[3] When Savoca was five, her family actually did return to Argentina, but soon after moved back to the U.S. The uncertainty that characterized Savoca's upbringing inflects her films and, in connection with the experience of migration or of a compelled moving back and forth between different countries of the American continent, is especially relevant to the story narrated in *Dirt*.

In contrast to *Household Saints*, where both the isolated nature of the ethnic neighborhood and the constrictions of domesticity

---

[3] Interview with the author, March 17, 2008 (Cavallero 77).

confine female characters, *Dirt* features a protagonist who is forced to negotiate an ever-changing transnational context through domestic labor. This independent film tells the story of Dolores del Rosario, an undocumented Salvadoran immigrant, who earns a living cleaning the homes of affluent people in Manhattan's Upper East Side. Dolores is often framed as she moves in a world of luxury that stands in stark contrast to her own one-bedroom apartment in a predominantly Latino neighborhood in Queens, where she lives with her husband Rodolfo and her teenage son Rudy. Like her, they are both undocumented. Rodolfo has recently lost his job, so Dolores must struggle even harder to earn a living as she is also sending money back to El Salvador for the construction of their house.

In this respect, Dolores's situation recalls a common practice during the historic period of Italian immigration to the United States, 1880-1924. Throughout these four decades many of the Italians who emigrated to the United States sent money back in the form of remittances and, according to available statistics, approximately fifty percent of them returned to Italy after having accumulated the necessary funds in order to build a better life for themselves back in Italy (Choate 72-100, *passim*).[4] Hence, Dolores and her husband's desire to return to El Salvador is not much different from what Italian immigrants to the U.S. experienced dec-

---

[4] See also what Nancy Foner writes, looking at these transnational ties and practices from a wider perspective, that is, over a period of time that extends to the 1990s: "Italians often sent funds home to purchase land and build houses with the goal of returning. And many did return. Some were 'birds of passage,' going back and forth between Italy and the United States, which Italian migrants often referred to as 'the workshop.' Other Italians went home for good. According to official statistics, return rates were actually higher at the beginning of the twentieth century than at the end; in the first two decades of the twentieth century, thirty-six of every one hundred immigrants entering the United States left, whereas between 1971 and 1990, the number was twenty-four out of one hundred" (2484).

ades before.[5] It is thus through the lens of such historical resonances that we can also read the works of filmmakers, writers, and
artists who, like Savoca, are of dual cultural heritage, and, by virtue of their complex positioning, are possibly more prone to detect
and register such similarities across time and space.[6]

Dirt features three flashback sequences in which Dolores recalls her dangerous voyage across the U.S.-Mexico border with
her son. These scenes, characterized by darkness and tension, are
set apart from the rest of the narrative by means of formal features
such as their "abrupt appearance, visual shakiness, skewed an-
gles, limited vision," all of which convey "an overpowering sense
of fear, uncertainty, anxiety, and 'liminal panic'" (Marciniak 351).
In one of these memories, the experience of border crossing is
linked to the idea of asphyxiation. We are shown Dolores holding
a small Rudy in her arms as they occupy a narrow dark space inside a truck. Rudy gasps for air and various voices off-screen are
heard saying "Lift him up to the window. [...] There's no air coming in. [...] Breath! [...] Breath, Rudy. Rudy, please. Breathe! He is
turning blue! He is fainting! What do we do? [...]." Refusing sentimental display or emotionality on the part of Dolores in the act of
remembering or in her present awareness of the precariousness of
her and her son's life, *Dirt* represents the experience of border
crossing "as a psychically lingering, unhealable wound, a wound
that evokes a very material sense of the border and its continuing
return" (Marciniak 351). More than other films by Savoca, *Dirt*
confronts the threat of physical and symbolic dislocation, the

---

[5] A reminder of the importance of seeing the similarities between the past and
the present, what we witness in today's Italy, where arrivals of migrants and refugees are everyday—and, most often, dramatic—occurrences, calls to mind the
turn-of-the-century departure of more than one hundred years ago.

[6] For an in-depth chronicle of Italians leaving for Canada, see, for example, Eugenio Balzan's 1901 articles, that he wrote as he accompanied them to North
America. The discussions we hear today about migration to Italy echo to a great
extent what Balzan had chronicled more than one hundred years ago.

traumas associated with relocation, assimilation, financial insecurity, and the numbing effects these situations can have on the characters' emotional lives.

As the plot progresses, Dolores's life seems to gradually unravel. She loses two of her best paying jobs and has to cope with the sudden death of her husband, who is killed on a construction site. With the help of friends, Dolores collects enough money to take Rodolfo's body back to El Salvador. However, after burying him and realizing that there is no future for her or Rudy in that country, she sells the "dream house" they have built with all their hard earned savings to buy two counterfeit passports and return to the U.S. The film thus contradicts what in the past was considered a successful end, the return to one's own homeland. The fact that this is not the case for Dolores can be read as a kind of historical paradox. She is no longer the El Salvadoran she was before she left. Her stay in the U.S., regardless of the challenges and difficulties, has changed her; she has her mind set on other goals, which no longer include El Salvador but, rather, life in the U.S. Through her initial migratory act, her sense of self has now been altered, and, in keeping with the proverbial statement, Dolores is no longer able to "go home" — she no longer sees her future in her native country. This is made especially clear in a scene in which, after the funeral in their small village, Dolores is shown lying on a hammock, while women in the adjoining room comment on the extent of her change since she left for the USA. To them she looks thinner and "more independent," and even though "she does not wear pants," because Rodolfo "took care of her, so she didn't have to become one of 'those,'" they disapprovingly observe that she smokes cigarettes (and as they talk, Dolores slowly turns her head, takes a cigarette from a small table, lights it, and starts smoking). Like Catherine in the scene of the stove in *Household Saints*, Dolores is shown here as she occupies a liminal position. The hammock is placed in a lobby, at the intersection between two different rooms peopled respectively by men sitting around a table and women talking and performing various tasks. While the scene opens with an old woman all dressed in black kissing Dolores on her forehead and telling her soothingly: "Now you are at home. Rest. Rest, I am going to take care of you," Dolores appears completely detached from her environment, she has clearly become an outsider. Soon after this episode, Dolores decides to go back to the U.S. One morning, at daybreak, she wakes Rudy up telling him: "We are leaving. We are going home." Even conceding that in this passage Dolores is using the word "home" from Rudy's perspective, it is clear at this point that home is no longer in El Salvador for Dolores either, as it has never been for Rudy. He has grown up in New York and has no memory of El Salvador. In a previous scene, before Rodolfo's death, when Dolores reminds him that they are planning to return "home" and that El Salvador is "his country," Rudy bursts out: "And who says I am going back to that stupid place? No, that's your country. I don't remember nothing about that place and I'm never going back there!" As Katarzyna Marciniak notes, one of the painful "clashes" foregrounded in *Dirt* is the generational difference between Dolores and Rudy, whose "transnational liminality is navigated by complex feelings of rage that, as a teenager, he can hardly control or comprehend" (351).

Following an excruciating cross-examination by a USA embassy employee, Dolores and Rudy do not succeed in getting tourist visas to return to the United States. As a result, their only recourse is to buy two counterfeited passports, which finally allows them to come back "home"—a word that, by the end of the film, acquires an entirely new meaning for Dolores. It is difficult, however, not to detect the bitter irony, if not outright disillusionment, in the ending. Not only does Dolores end up working for the horrible woman who, at the very beginning of the film, had yelled at her for momentarily leaving garbage in the hallway, who had threatened to use her influence to have Dolores fired from her job in the building, and who keeps patronizing her, but the film also concludes with Dolores's voice-over commenting on the fact that in the U.S. there is an endless supply of work—that is of dirt—for her to take care of.[7]

Dolores's depiction in *Dirt* patently undermines stereotypical portrayals of the Latina maid. As one of the film's favorable reviews suggests referring to the 2002 blockbuster *Maid in Manhattan*, "This is no J-Lo fantasy" (Scheib). Indeed, the character of the Latina maid is constantly featured in mainstream cinema, but she regularly appears as a marginalized other, and her personal story is rarely engaged[8] (Padilla 54). Also, viewers are seldom informed of the historical context of immigration that conditions her citizenship and employment status in the United States. *Dirt* focuses precisely on this missing background. Its originality resides in the fact that, with great poise and nuance, the film "pulls the abjected and marginalized characters out of the peripheries where they are typically placed and makes their lives the central focus of the diegesis" (Marciniak 350). Most importantly, the film prompts questions regarding a gendered immigrant labor force that is a significant element of the U.S. economy and, as Yajaira Padilla states, "provides insight into the construction of emergent and overlooked

---

[7] In her analysis of the ways in which removing other people's dirt by immigrant workers intertwines with gendered and racialized processes of social abjection, Marciniak identifies "a conceptual correspondence between garbage and the cultural renditions of foreign others" and highlights the ways in which "the concept of 'dirt' gets transposed onto the cleaners suggesting that those who clean dirt are themselves disposable bodies, only useful and tolerable as long as they cohere the messy lives of 'legitimate' and properly 'clean' natives" (337).

[8] A notable exception is represented by the documentary *Maid in America* broadcasted on PBS in 2005 and directed by Anayansi Prado. As Gabiola writes, this film "is a good example of the global and transnational phenomena invested in the mobilization of female bodies in search of a better life." Based on the lives of Telma and Eva, two Mexican women, and Judith, a Guatemalan mother, "the documentary attempts to reflect the social injustices and sacrifices undergone by these women who have to survive in the new cultural scenario" (119).

transnational Latino identities [...] whose cultural and economic ties to [their country of origin] are shaping their very incorporation into the United States" (54). Hence, the above-mentioned framing of Dolores underscores her status of suffering at the hands of a system that appears to have no compassion at all for the outsider and that hypocritically excludes the clandestine foreigner while capitalizing on her useful work.[9] As Mona, Dolores's Dominican colleague and friend, bitterly remarks, noticing the signs of sympathy that, after Rodolfo's death, Dolores eventually receives, "Why does it take a disaster for people to act human?" The fact that a person in Dolores's position has to suffer terrible losses for people to show some compassion is revealing of the continuing hostility that immigrants must face in their adopted countries, in the years 2000s as it was a century before, sometimes even from people who have been in the same predicament at an earlier time. Such framing goes hand in hand with her name, Dolores del Rosario: literally, the "pains" of the "rosary," a symbolic Mount Calvary that she must endure in her attempt to build a better future for herself and her family.

In the film's initial scene, we are immediately introduced to Dolores, a forty-something, petite woman with long dark hair and brown eyes, emerging from a crowded subway exit in Manhattan and trying to make her way among taller and bigger people who, mostly going in the opposite direction, bump into her without noticing her or apologizing. In this as in several subsequent scenes, the camera focuses in on Dolores's facial expression, showing a mixture of circumspection, distress, and determination. Both the close-ups on her face and the counter-shots illuminate and emphasize her perspective, capturing her anxiety and frustration as

---

[9] As Marciniak pointedly remarks: "many who experientially brush against discourses of (il)legality, already realize that the useful clandestine foreigner is not only tolerated but, in fact, structurally factored into the global economic system itself" (353).

well as her steadfastness, and creating a sense of intimacy between her and the viewer that lasts throughout the film.[10] The film's exploration of Dolores's experiences and view "from below" also foreground the theme of invisibility—one of the most harmful consequences of being an undocumented immigrant—which is repeatedly evoked through Dolores's dread whenever she sees a policeman, her requests that employers always pay her cash, her unwillingness to provide her address or phone number, and her extreme discretion. As the caption on the film's poster announces: "she lives her life without leaving a mark."

Accordingly, Dolores is often framed alone, as she seldom sees her employers and simply follows the orders they leave in handwritten notes. Even in her exchanges with them, her subordination is visually rendered by the lower position she occupies on the screen. Close-ups show her applying cleaning products on bathtubs and toilets, picking up dirty clothes strewn on the floor, scrubbing glasses, and so on. Indeed, while the film details Dolores's cleaning routines, "it sutures its audience repeatedly into the rhetoric and imagery of garbage and dirt linked to racialized structures of oppression" (Marciniak 350). Likewise, her clothes and the mass-produced T-shirts she wears stress her working-class status and effectively call to mind another form of gendered immigrant labor—that of the maquiladora industry (Padilla 51). The scenes that portray Dolores moving around luxurious apartments in Manhattan's Upper East Side, filled with expensive furniture, stand in stark contrast to those depicting Dolores's impoverished

---

[10] It may be worth recalling what Mary Ann Doane writes with regard to the use of the close-up in U.S. cinema: "As Eisenstein and others have pointed out, the concept is inflected differently through its varying nomenclature in different languages. [...] In the American context, [the close-up] is conceptualized in terms of point of view, perspective, the relation between spectator and image, the spectator's place in the scene, and an assumed identification between viewer and camera" (92).

neighborhood and her modest dwelling. The narrative thus sets the stage for a series of emotional and symbolic clashes that document the profound disparities existing between the wealth of Park Avenue's inhabitants and the undocumented workers whom they employ to attend to the domestic chores.

Recalling Amy Kaplan's notion of nineteenth-century "Manifest Domesticity," which "turn[ed] an imperial nation into a home by [...] colonizing *specters* of the foreign that lurk[ed] inside and outside its ever shifting borders" (203), Padilla affirms that the Salvadoran immigrant is often construed as a "domesticated" *Other* whose stereotypical portrayal re-enforces the status quo. Such a domestication entails a disavowal of key historical realities in order "to facilitate a less critical and, therefore, more 'consumable' [...] representation of the Latina foreign laborer" (Padilla 46). Her stereotypical portrayal is "suggestive of the need to 'domesticate' all foreign subjects—those alien elements who reside in the U.S. 'home' and are integral to the U.S. economy, but who must nevertheless, remain inferior" (Padilla 46). In contrast to such domestication, *Dirt* foregrounds the experience of border crossing—both in flashbacks of the journey that, twelve years earlier, almost cost Dolores and her son their lives, and in the subsequent crossing that finally grants them "legal" status—as well as in the many similar experiences narrated by other characters from Dolores's working milieu.

Also, looming in the background is the topic of El Salvador's bloody civil war, as in the passage showing an exchange between Dolores and Mrs. Cambridge, an elderly rich white socialite. During a job interview, as they walk through multiple rooms, the latter ushers Dolores into one that has been turned into a photo gallery since her son left. In a medium shot, the camera shows the walls entirely covered with pictures, some of which portray Mrs. Cambridge herself alongside important public figures such as Hillary Clinton and Barbara Bush, whom the lady has had "the good fortune to meet due to [her] charity work," as she explains to Dolores. Immediately afterwards, in eloquent close-ups, we are shown pictures of a completely different nature taken by her son in different parts of the world. The photographs that Mrs. Cambridge has kept from "Jack's collection" depict crying children, prisoners of war, suffering, privation, violence, death. Commenting on this section of the gallery, Mrs. Cambridge says: "Such tragedy. I think that our country is only now beginning to understand such tragedy. Don't you, Dolores?" After a short pause, she seems to realize for the first time that Dolores may actually belong to one of those unidentified countries that her son immortalizes. She asks: "Actually, what country are you from?" Following Dolores's answer, "From El Salvador," she states, "Well, you understand tragedy, then, don't you?" After a brief, embarrassed silence, Mrs. Cambridge casually changes topic and says to Dolores: "Well, let me show you where the bathroom is." The anticlimax of this moment, and the irony underlying the whole scene, point to the radical differences between the two women. While Mrs. Cambridge collects and displays images of trauma, the viewer is made aware that Dolores may be intimately familiar with such experiences of horror (the episode occurs at the beginning of the film, before we actually learn Dolores's story). Thus, while it can be assumed that Dolores has experienced horror and tragedy first-hand, the upper-class socialite contains them in her photo gallery and, interposing a safe aesthetic distance, finds them "just so inspiring."

Accordingly, if on the one hand, the Salvadoran immigrant can be viewed as a "domesticated" *Other* who re-enforces and perpetuates the status quo, on the other hand, domesticating the Salvadoran immigrant "entails a necessary disavowal of the past" (Padilla 46). Such a disavowal cannot avoid the return of that which has been repressed. In this shot the "unhomely" creeps up in the silence following Mrs. Cambridge's rhetorical question to Dolores —"Well, you understand tragedy, then, don't you?"—, which conjures up the suppressed specter of a brutal war within a comfortable, lavishly furnished U.S. house. The incident reminds us that the civil war that ravaged El Salvador from 1980 to 1992 was a key factor in Salvadoran migration to the U.S. In this war the United States played a key role, sending millions of dollars to help support El Salvador's oppressive government in their fight against "the communist threat" (Padilla 46-47). Such involvement of the United States caused many immigrants to be denied asylum precisely because they were not recognized as 'political' refugees. The passage suggests that the war persists as a key historical aspect of Dolores's background and alludes to the new forms of persecution immigrants suffer because they are undocumented (Padilla 53).

Being undocumented is in fact a key element that divides the Latino groups in the film. *Dirt* shows that distinctions based on citizenship are not always cause for tension – Dolores's friends are from the Dominican Republic, Jamaica, Puerto Rico, Italy, and Ireland. But the film showcases the difference based on class between her and the Ortegas—the upper-class Latino family she has worked for over a nine-year period and who eventually fires her because her illegal status is incompatible with Mrs. Ortega's decision to run for Congress on an anti-illegal alien platform. Such distinction in class is further buttressed by the hypocrisy of the Ortegas precisely because Dolores's firing is due to her illegal status. Ironically, the person who fires her has done so in order to run for congress, the one place where Dolores's and most other undocumented workers' plights could be remedied. Both the afore-mentioned pretense and a paradox of desired place (i.e., Congress) clamor loudly.

Dolores's representation also takes shape through these intersections, all of which call attention to the importance of immigrant and transnational ties in the definition of Salvadoran-American and Latino identities. *Dirt* stresses how, by showing that characters from diverse backgrounds face similar struggles, Savoca lays the foundation for a new community that is based on shared experiences of gender and class rather than just ethnic or regional identity. As she affirms in an interview: "To me the greatest thing a movie can do [...] is to tell you a story that takes place in Iran about an Afghani immigrant on a construction site, and then make you realize 'oh my gosh but I know who that is.' Even if it is an Afghani in Iran, 'I know who that is'" (Serra 7).

Consequently, the transnational dimension of Dolores's life as a Salvadoran *doméstica* "does not suggest an image of an easily 'domesticated' or incorporated subject" (Padilla 54). In the first part of the film, Dolores and Rodolfo's hope is to finish building their house in El Salvador so that they can return to settle there and make a living by opening a small grocery store. They are determined to prosper in the U.S., yet their ultimate goal is to return to the place they consider home. As a matter of fact, the remittances and their investments in property in El Salvador are transnational enterprises that help to fulfill their "American Dream" elsewhere (Padilla 54). Hence, if on the one hand *Dirt* problematizes the myth of the return to one's origins, on the other hand it complicates the assimilationist discourse of the "American Dream." Most important to our discussion, the film shows how Dolores is capable of defining herself not only through her refusal to forfeit her cultural ties and Salvadoran identity, but also through her hard labor and the relationships she establishes in her workplace. In so doing, the film further connects women, work, and consciousness in more than one national territory.

As an American writer-director of dual Argentinian and Italian heritage, Savoca builds her filmmaking on the questioning of such notions as "ethnic identity" and "culture," while also affirming the importance of valuing one's background and resisting assimilation. Her willingness to see working-class women as empowered individuals whose actions help to shape the culture they inhabit counters ethnic stereotypes. In both *Household Saints* and *Dirt*, she does not offer a single perspective on either Italian/American women or Latinas and recognizes, instead, the divergent causes and effects of migration and assimilation on the everyday life of the characters. Savoca's films also show that the question of self-representation is complicated by the often troubled relationship women maintain with their culture of origin and the dominant U.S. culture. As Edvige Giunta suggests, for women authors designations such as that of "Italian American" should not be used "as a rigid epithet, but, rather, as a problematic term for a diverse group of authors who adopt and challenge ethnicity and envision it as a [...] mutable terrain for creative and political inquiry" (Giunta 18). *Household Saints* and *Dirt* offer further evidence that women inhabit Bhabha's interstitial space between "private and public, past and present, the psyche and the social" (148) and that it is from there that their stories must be told, showing the conflicts, questioning all dualisms, and still attempting to bridge "the home and the world."

WORKS CITED

Balzan, Eugenio. *L'emigrazione in Canada nell'inchiesta del «Corriere» 1901.* Renata Broggini, ed. Milan: Fondazione Corriere della Sera, 2009.

Bhabha, Homi. "The World and the Home." Third World and Post-Colonial Issues. *Social Text* 31/32 (1992): 141-153.

Camaiti Hostert, Anna. "Gender and Ethnicity in Italian/American Cinema: Nancy Savoca and Marylou Tibaldo-Bongiorno." In *Mediated Ethnicity. New Italian American Cinema.* G. Muscio, J. Sciorra, G. Spagnoletti, A. J. Tamburri, eds. New York: John D. Calandra Institute, 2010. 141-148.

Cavallero, Jonathan J. "Nancy Savoca. Ethnicity, Class, and Gender." In *Hollywood's Italian American Filmmakers: Capra, Scorsese, Savoca, Coppola, Tarantino.* Urbana, IL: U Illinois P, 2011. 77-98.

Choate, Mark I. *Emigrant Nation: The Making of Italy Abroad.* Cambridge, MA: Harvard UP, 2008.

Doane, Mary Ann. "The Close-Up: Scale and Detail in the Cinema." *differences. A Journal of Feminist Cultural Studies* 14.3 (2003): 89-111.

Foner, Nancy. "Engagements Across National Borders, Then and Now." *Fordham Law Review* 75.5 (2007): 2483-2492.

Gabiola, Irune del Rio. "Globalizing the Care Chain: Representations of Latinas in *Maid in America.*" *Chasqui* 42.1 (May 2013): 119-130.

Giunta, Edvige. *Writing with an Accent. Contemporary Italian American Women Authors.* New York: Palgrave, 2002.

Hansen, Marcus Lee. *The Problem of the Third Generation Immigrant.* Rock Island, Ill.: Augustana Historical Society, 1938.

Kaplan, Amy. "Manifest Domesticity." In *No More Separate Spheres!* Cathy N. Davidson and Jessamyn Hatcher, eds. Durham: Duke UP, 2002 [1998]. 183-207.

Makarushka, Irena. "Tracing The Other in *Household Saints.*" *Literature and Theology* 12.1 (1998): 82–92.

Marciniak, Katarzyna. "Foreign Women and Toilets." *Feminist Media Studies* 8.4 (2008): 337-356.

Padilla, Yajaira M. "Domesticating Rosario: Conflicting Representations of the Latina Maid in U.S. Media." *Arizona Journal of Hispanic Cultural Studies* 13.1 (2009): 41-59.

Pravadelli, Veronica. "The Difficulty of Gender in Italian-American Culture: Gender and Ethnic Identity in *True Love, Little Kings,* and *Puccini for Beginners.*" *Mediated Ethnicity.* In *New Italian-American Cinema.* G. Muscio, J. Sciorra, G. Spagnoletti, A. J. Tamburri, eds. New York: John D. Calandra Italian American Institute, 2010. 171-179.

Prose, Francine. *Household Saints. A Novel.* New York: Open Road, 2013 [1981].

Ruberto, Laura E. "Where Did the Goodfellas Learn How to Cook? Gender, Labor, and the Italian American Experience." *Italian Americana.* 21.2 (Summer 2003): 164-176.

Savoca, Nancy. Dir. *True Love.* USA, 1989.

_____. Dir. *Household Saints.* USA, 1993.

_____. Dir. *Dirt.* USA, 2003.

Serra, Ilaria. "An Interview with Filmmaker Nancy Savoca." *Florida Atlantic Comparative Studies* 8 (2005-2006): 7.

Re-Mapping Generations

Vito Zagarrio
ROMA TRE UNIVERSITY

OF FAMILY AND ROOTS

Reflecting on a recent film by Francis Ford Coppola, I am again considering the term Italian-American (with the hyphen, to emphasize the equal standing of both the Italian and American identities) and the complex social, political, and psychological effects of the Italian identity in relation to generational change and the passing of time.[1]

In his penultimate film, *Tetro* (2009, released in Italy as *Segreti di famiglia*), a dark, disturbing film, "tetro," the nickname of the main character, is Italian for "dreary" and suggests as much for the movie itself, which can be analyzed in a number of ways: from the perspective of the meta-linguistic (like many of Coppola's films, a re-

---

[1] See, V. Zagarrio, "F.C. - F.C., ovvero: Italian American Dream dal film muto alla television," *Cinema e Cinema* 38 (Jan-Mar 1984), later in "Cronache parlamentari siciliane," *Il cinema e la Sicilia*, 1990 (as "L'americano di Bisacquino"). See my essay, "Immaginari italoamericani. Generazioni, generi, genders," in *Scene italoamericane. Rappresentazioni cinematografiche degli italiani d'America*. Anna Camaiti Hostert and Anthony Julian Tamburri, eds. (Rome: Luca Sossella, 2001); in English as "The Italian American Imaginary: The Imaginary Italian American: Genres, Genders, and Generations," in *Screening Ethnicity. Cinematographic Representations of Italian Americans in the United States*. Anna Camaiti Hostert and Anthony Julian Tamburri, eds. (Boca Raton, FL: Bordighera P, 2001. See, also, my following books: *The Un-Happy Ending. Re-viewing the cinema of Frank Capra*. New York: Bordighera P, 2011); *Frank Capra. Il cinema americano tra sogno e incubo* (Venice: Marsilio, 2009); *Non solo Hollywood, Percorsi e confronti del cinema centenario* (Foggia: Bastogi, 1996); *Francis Ford Coppola* (Milan: Il Castoro, 1995); and *Frank Capra* (Milan: Il Castoro, 1995).

flection on cinema, on television, and on media; constructed in a self-reflexive manner, the story within the story); from the psycho-analytic perspective (the "secrets of the family," hidden, irreconcilable conflicts of the fundamental unit of society, the nuclear family); from the perspective of genre films (a hybrid of family drama, melodrama, and coming-of-age story); from technical points of view (a "formalist" film and what one could call "expressionist" based on the contrasting black and white and color scenes and the claustrophobic scenography); and finally from the perspective of identity.

Actually, Tetro is short for Tetrocini, an obviously Italian surname that once again shows Coppola coming to terms with his roots. Here is the plot: the almost eighteen-year-old Bennie goes to Buenos Aires to visit his big brother Angelo who he has not seen in more than ten years. The brother, it is discovered, is in a psychiatric hospital and had broken off all ties with the family. In fact, Angelo now goes by Tetro because of his difficult relationship with his father, Carlo Tetrocini, a world-renowned orchestra conductor. Tetro lives in Boca with his girlfriend, Miranda, working in a small theatre as a light technician, and allows Bennie to stay for a few days, enough time for the repairs on a cruise ship where Bennie works as a waiter to be completed. Although before parting ways, Tetro left a letter for his younger brother and promised that one day he would return to rescue and take care of him, no longer wanting a relationship with the rest of his family. One day, Bennie finds amongst Tetro's writings an unfinished play, and having grown up with the myth of his big brother and his literary genius, he decides to complete it and submit it to a festival (though Tetro never intended to have it published). When Tetro finds out, he is furious, but Bennie claims that the play was also his story and thus decides that the play be produced in a theater. All of this forces Tetro to confront the reasons for breaking away from the family, and in the end revealing the secret he has hidden behind for years: the trauma that has plagued him is the death of his

mother, the melodramatic peak of the film, which is accompanied
by the disturbing Oedipal revelation, with Bennie not just being
Tetro's half-brother but also his son. This spectacular turn of events
is resolved during a disturbing and nonrealistic postmodern live
broadcast.

The film is set in Argentina but the last names make it clear
that we are talking about the Italian community in this country;[2]
and anyway all of the melodramatic and operatic resonances are
steeped in Italian sources. Moreover, many parts of the film recall
the director's own life: two brothers who were conductors of or-
chestras resemble Coppola's father and uncle who were both musicians; children who grow up in the shadow of their father's great
artistry might refer to his own children; Roman and Sofia; the decision to liberate oneself from a much renowned name like Nico-
las Cage did, Coppola's nephew; an accident where a loved one
loses their life, in the film it is Tetro's mother while in reality it is
the oldest son of Coppola, Giancarlo, who died in a boating accident. Furthermore, Coppola claims to have shared in the movie

---

[2] A notice on the web in 2013 announced that Coppola was working on a film
about a "traditional" Italian-American family: "*Francis Ford Coppola Returns to
Italian-American Family Dramas With New Film*: Hey, it certainly sounds better
than *Twixt*. THR reports that Francis Ford Coppola is readying a new feature that
should appeal to more of his traditional fanbase. The film is currently untitled,
but the outlet reports that 'it will chronicle an Italian-American family and span
from the 1930s to the 1960s.' The project is also described as 'a coming-of-age
story that focuses on a boy and girl in their late teens.' While details are obviously slim as of now, The Wrap's Jeff Snider also tweeted today that 'Dance will be a
key element in the new Francis Ford Coppola movie. That's all, folks.' So that's
... something. Oh, is this going to be a new *Dirty Dancing*? Is that it? Coppola is
currently writing the screenplay himself, and while the project has no firm studio
commitments (despite having offices on the Paramount lot), a pair of casting
directors have already been brought on (Courtney Bright and Kate Erbland)."
The film was never made, but the announcement underscores Coppola's obsession with the Italian-American family.

the dynamics between his father and uncle and then between his father and himself.

Accounting for the distressful events, the origins of the complex psycho-family developments that arise in this film work heavily on the unconscious mind. And it is amongst this backdrop that I would like to reflect upon Italian Americana across generations and the representation of Italian Americans by different ethnicities, as in the case of the films by the African-American director Spike Lee.

CAPRA AND COPPOLA: GENERATIONS JUXTAPOSED

As is obvious, this is also a generational problem: the generation that fled from Italy and draws on the American Dream and the second generation that knows Italy as a mythical land, placed at the center of their imagination.

Now aiming to compare Coppola to the well-known proponent of Italian emigration in America, Frank Capra, we can observe two methods and two opposing stories from Italian American directors. One director is at the beginning of cinema, when film was taking its first steps and all possible innovations and outcomes were possible, the other when cinema was at the end of this road, when movies were part of a larger, more complex, erratic universe, moving from silent film to television and from electronic to digital. And through all of this there is a red thread joining the many generations, connecting the starting point to our current point of arrival, it is the Italian American roots, or more exactly the relationship between the American myth and the myth of the Mediterranean, between integration and returning to the origins.

On the one hand, there is Capra, a Sicilian from Bisacquino, the workhorse of our cinematic nationalism. In the 1930s, Frank Capra was exalted by Sicilians and Italians as a national treasure. Capra reiterated and demonstrated the "Italian superiority" in cinema at all levels from technique to poetry. In 1934, the year the Directorate-General for Cinematography was founded—marking the beginning of the Luigi Freddi era as head of Italian cinema under Fascism—magazines opened their special issues dedicated to the cinema, featuring Frank Capra as the prototypical Italian director. And it was the magazine *Quadrivio*, directed by Luigi Chiarini, that pointed to the work of Capra during a period where the regime was restructuring its public facilities in the model of the New Deal and the Hollywood studio system. Most importantly, at its inauguration (April 25, 1937-XV), Cinecittà praised Capra and dedicated a special dossier to the great Italian-American director, "It was natural that a dossier be dedicated—on the occasion of the birth of this city of cinema—for the past, present, and future of Italian cinema, a thoughtful, comprehensive study of the Sicilian, Frank Capra, justly regarded today as the greatest director in the world." The critical essay by Emilio Cecchi and Gramantieri's biographical entry on the film director wanted to present a dazzling homage to cinema, to the popular and luminous figure of the Italian artist, "one of our most worthy representatives of our art abroad." At a time in which Benito Mussolini boasted that New York was the largest Italian city (because of its one million Italian immigrants), Capra could rightly be considered as the greatest Italian director, even though there are such directors as Alessandro Blasetti, Augusto Camerini, and Raffaello Matarazzo, who worked and created in Italy.

Now, what role does Capra play in this reversal of the American myth and Italian pride? None in the local and provincial chauvinism of Italians! In fact, Capra—Gian Piero Brunetta also wrote about his role in a review dedicated to *Little Italy*—detaches himself from his Italian roots in particular ways, rejecting the Italian primordial mother. Now he was led by the Statue of Liberty, whom he met in all her majesty in 1903 when upon their arrival his family flooded the land with gracious kisses. Italy then signified poverty, close-mindedness, and death; while America sought new horizons, unlimited possibilities, opportunities for everyone, and social mobility. "I hated being poor. Hated being a peasant. Hated being a scrounging news kid trapped in the sleazy Sicilian ghetto of Los Angeles. My family couldn't read or write. I wanted out. A quick out. I looked for a device, a handle, a pole to catapult myself across the tracks from my scurvy habitat of nobodies to the affluent world of somebody." These are the first words from the foreword of *The Name Above the Title*, the autobiography of Capra. They are words of love surrounded by tragedy and misery.[3]

Looking back at it, the first chapter contains the only "scenes" of Capra in Sicily and Italy for a movie never realized (or only "realized" after many generations by Coppola) on the lives of Italian Americans and on Sicilian roots, chock-full of episodes, narrative sequences, and short film plots more than personal memories. These first pages are a little jewel of popular literature (regardless of how truthful they are), following the chronicling of an arrival in a village, a letter from Ben, a son's loss of faith, the anxious anticipation that the letter causes amongst the illiterate of Bisacquino. Ben's adventures are described in flashbacks, from Palermo to Los Angeles, passing through New Orleans, San Francisco amidst flight, abductions, and a variety of fights. The journey to America across turbulent seas tells the story of his mother, Saridda, the only one with the courage to brave the unknown and arrive thousands of miles later in Los Angeles. The early years of Frankie's life, described in a moving realism, filled with a mix of languages and dialect cues, as when young Frank returns home desperate and crying on his mother's lap and she tells him: "Coraggio, figlio, coraggio." And the observation in which Frank, trying to make ends meet, gives private lessons to a rich person, "The rich have it all, but accomplish little; and, had Baldwin been born a poor boy in New Orleans or Memphis, he might have become one of our

---

[3] See, Frank Capra, *The Name Above the Title, An Autobiography* (New York, Macmillan, 1971).

great jazz musicians," gives us a moral and populism typical of Capra. And a very cinematic final episode, essential to understanding Capra's approach to *italianità*, in which the mafia boss of a syndicate of Sicilian smugglers, Tuffy, offers a young Frank work and "dirty" money, playing into the stereotype, only to have Frank throw the money back in his face.

There is another strange *scene* demonstrating how seductive the stereotypical Italian American identity is, which is based on the subject matter of Francisco Motta Flores and Antonio De Sousa Duarte's novel, *Frank Capra non era un mafioso*.[4] A curious mixed genre piece of literature, the book moves between historical pamphlet and pure fiction, and its two authors tell four stories that happened or could have happened with Capra at its crossroad. The other key characters include Vito Cascio Ferro, founder of the mafia, Joe Petrosino, the well-known detective, who also found his life recreated in fiction and comics, and finally Enrico Caruso. These four Italians have had to deal with America and its myth that are themselves mythical and emblematic of certain Italian stereotypes, and to these stereotypes the book is a slave. While the idea is beautiful, the story does not fulfill its ambitions. Taking on Capra's story by borrowing from his autobiography, which was already fictionalized, only renders it increasingly unreal. And the other stories that circle around Capra oftentimes feel forced, as when it is casually described how the mafia boss and Capra's emigrating family are sitting opposite one another on the transatlantic ship "Germania," worlds apart but both bound for a future notoriety in the United States.

However, I want to cite a passage that reflects on Capra's filmography: Mike Pinderello—a former employee of Petrosino who then worked at Columbia carrying projectors and electric cables—

---

[4] Francisco Motta Flores, Antonio De Sousa Duarte, *Frank Capra non era un mafioso. Una storia sul cinema, cosa nostra e l'invenzione dell'american dream* (Rome: Cavallo di ferro, 2009).

was invited by Frank Capra(!) and asked for his opinion on his movies. Here we are in the days of his film *Lady for a Day*, "those films," replied the shrewd former detective, "are well done, enchanting and entertaining. To those who've seen them, they won't give you an ulcer or a headache, you'll sleep without worries, and, better still, after two days, no one remembers [...] I was a detective. I was trained to read what was not written, to see what others did not see [...] The problem with those films, that is with your films, is that they don't reveal your past. You're from Sicily. Probably from a large family [...] Suddenly you start making films. Dollars begin to roll in and the survival instinct imposes itself on the immigrant, on the creator of these films. No risks. Fine, everything is well done, all in its right place. But cinema is what Ford, Vidor, and Chaplin do: the cinema of those who put all of themselves in play. Instead, Mr. Capra does not shock. Some shaking, maybe a bit of teasing, and the right amount of laughs." Apart from the improbability of the situation, this dialogue stems from all of the recent criticism flung at Capra: the non-authorial, the ideological "marzipan," and Italian-American neuroses.

Let's go back to Capra's work. In the long career and in many Capra films, Italy and the Italian are close to non-existent. Refused, removed, forgotten in an effort to emerge, to free oneself, to become "American," to be one of them. The odd exception is the youthful film, *La Visita Dell'Incrociatore Italiano LIBYA a San Francisco*, a documentary from 1921, completed shortly before his directorial debut, which sheds new light on previously considered settled decisions about our ethnic and national "identity." It was often insisted that signs of Italian origins be removed. True as that might be, this early documentary is a lavish look into the Italian-American community. Commissioned by the Italians of San Francisco, the film tells the story about the arrival at the Golden Gate (which does not yet have its famous Bridge) of the battleship *Libya*. With exacting precision, Capra discusses boats (including "the movie boat" in a meta-twist and, a little narcissistically, the director shows himself and his crew), they go out to sea to meet the ship and are warmly welcomed by the crew. There is a great party gathering many from the local Italian-American community. The heart of the story is this community, "the Italian Virtus Club," and the director strives to bring out what it means to be Italian in San Francisco. The Bank of Italy, which would play a key figure in Capra's future career; the banker Giannini (to whom Ed Buscombe would dedicate a famous essay);[5] the sports club, with the certain inclusion of soccer; the banquet hall from where emerge VIPs, ladies, and the local seductress; and the final go-around, repeated *ad infinitum*, where the entire party parades around in circles. All in all, it is a moving portrait of an age, interesting from an anthropological point of view, an important historical document, an archive of unique images (the faces of people, the movements of bodies, the reactions to being in front of a camera), shot already with particular directorial sensitivity, and even a fairy tale, one of many from Capra's career. Here it is the tale of the "Italian dream" and all of the utopias that are contained in the magical passage along the Libya that looks so much like Fellini's Rex from *Amarcord*. And among other things, the Libya refers to Italy's colonial dreams, and perhaps, in this one can see the foundations of Fascism being laid and how, in a few months, there will be his "March on Rome." The looming Fascism is perceived in smells, like the emphatic signs at the beginning and at the end of the film with the Libya as the traveling strip of their homeland, or the slip, "With Italy, with the navy, with the Libya!"

After this debut, Italy almost disappears from Capra's films. While there are many situations that are open to recollections of his own origins and those of his family, such references are always

---

[5] See, E. Buscombe, "Notes on Columbia Pictures Corporation 1926-41," *Screen* 16.3 (1975): 65-82.

masked and integrated into a more familiar American model. For example, in *The Younger Generation*, an important film in the transition between silent film and "the talkies," the plot revolves around a poor family from the Lower East Side of Manhattan, but here it is a Jewish family, even if the mother resembles the Sicilian women of Coppola.

Among the few exceptions: the only traceable Italian from the "classic" films of Capra is Mr. Martini, the good neighbor and bartender, the man Jimmy Stewart helps to buy a house in *It's A Wonderful Life*. And the only Italian cultural reference is in the same film, when in Mr. Martini's bar, we hear a Neapolitan song, *Santa Lucia*. But it is only a fragment that will be upended into the nightmare of George Bailey's "dream," and Martini's "Italian" bar will become a place of perdition and corruption.

Then, and we are already in the downturn of Capra's career, there is Frank Sinatra in *A Hole in the Head*; not only does he portray an Italian-American character but Sinatra himself is also an icon of Italian Americana. In the film he plays a down-and-out loser with a tenderness about him, far from the usual Italian stereotype of the volatile but vivacious temperament.

Another exception is a political case with the representation of Italy in *Why We Fight*. This is a series of war documentaries that Capra declared as propaganda in favor of the Allies. Capra, here, makes direct contact with his distant homeland and describes it as the "enemy." In *Prelude to War*, he associates Mussolini with Hitler and the Japanese emperor, and portrays the Italian boot as the dominated symbol of Roman Fascism borrowed from the ruling regime. Capra stresses, as he will do obsessively after the war in times filled with witch hunts across the country, his patriotism and devotion to America. When not the enemy, Italy is still far off, remote.

Why this "removal" of roots? I had to ask Capra himself in an interview in 1982. "I never did," Capra explains, "movies that did not have an American background, even when they were developed in China or in Tibet. I have often thought about making movies in Europe, in France or Italy. But then I would say to myself: I don't know the French, I don't know how they think, how do they speak when they talk casually, what words do they use in real life. And regarding Italy, I was only six, what roots could I have? I don't remember anything from before, because when we left from Palermo and arrived on the open sea, it was such an incredible thing that all previous memory vanished. That is the moment of origin. From there my memory begins, as part of the ship. Before that grand ship, I don't remember anything before. And I said, when I returned to Bisacquino, three years ago, I don't feel any emotion. I don't recognize anything here."[6]

The "dismissal of Italy" is confirmed in his autobiography when in a letter to Benny, there is a clear message from Mr. Orsatti, the Italian American who helped the young Capra: "And, Orsatti added, if the Capra family wished to see Ben again they would all have to come to Los Angeles, because Ben says he is never coming back to Sicily." Thus, to Sicily, he does not return. The true homeland is American, "Los Angeles—America, America!" the Capra family cheers, like a character from Joseph Roth's *Hotel Savoy*. But here there is no central European catastrophe, no purifying fire. He leaves Sicily behind him, alone, miserable and desperate.

Yet, desperate but beautiful, Sicily is loaded with original myths, and it returns, some generations later, through Coppola. By the time Coppola begins his studies at UCLA, many prejudices have been placed on Italians and this prepares him to become one of the leaders of New Hollywood. Like Capra, he aspires to have "the name above the title," representing with power "the director as superstar," as quoted in the title of the book by Gelmis,[7] where the director was no longer the anonymous craftsman but the au-

---

[6] V. Zagarrio, *Frank Capra*, cit.

[7] R. Gelmis, *The Film Director as Superstar* (London: Secker & Warburg, 1971).

teur. Again like Capra, the motivation is the desire to reclaim the ability to play: Capra had a father, Salvatore, who was an illiterate farmer, his revenge on the world was to study, to become someone. Meanwhile, Coppola had a father, Carmine, who had never broken through, remaining the anonymous shadow figure, a flute player in Toscanini's orchestra. His vengeance then is the familiar appeal against the frustrations of his father, and the generational rebellion against taboos and anti-Italian prejudice: Coppola's Oedipal battle versus Capra's inferiority complex. But even more so, theirs is the fight for survival in America, for Capra as much as for Coppola, to confront and emerge as the American Dream.

Following a generational trend, Coppola discovers his roots; the first steps were through the family archive, the name of his mother and father, Italia and Carmine. Then there is the mature exploration of Italian culture through cinema and his great admiration for Bernardo Bertolucci. In this way, "the Italian" becomes a recurring figure in his films, both in the narrative system and in the cast and crew. "The Italian" is seen on the one hand with the usual traditional deformations (the Sicilian Mafioso, the man of honor, manly and paternal, and spaghetti, which Coppola had commissioned and sent to the Philippines during the shooting of *Apocalypse Now*). On the other hand, the Italian is seen with admiration for its "humanistic" ability to combine the poetic and technical, hence the decision to hire Vittorio Storaro for *Apocalypse Now* and Nino Rota for music in *The Godfather*, both having previously worked for Bertolucci and for Federico Fellini, respectively. Rota and Storaro quintessentially represented Europe.

"The Italian" also is the image of the marginalization of a minority. Coppola has an ambiguous attitude towards his peers, somewhere between absolution and condemnation. In *The Godfather II*, there is a thoughtful analysis of the Mafia that ends in absolution, and there is also a more general accusation made against Italian Americans, their ways, their presumptions, and their flashy clothes. At the beginning of the movie, when the Nevada senator tries to challenge Michael Corleone, like Mario Puzo, Coppola does not shy away from the popular stereotype of Italians and instead, here, he elevates them. The Italian Americans of *The Godfather* are both loving family members and bloody assassins. They are respectful advocates of morality within their clan and vigorous lovers. But he turns these stereotypes into myths when Tom Hagen, Michael Corleone's brother-in-law and family lawyer, goes to the high security prison to confront mob boss Frank Pentangeli (who has betrayed the family) and suggests suicide. But the suggestion is not made explicitly or with brute force, instead through rhetoric, recalling the stories of traitors in Ancient Rome and how honor remained intact for their families if they committed suicide after a failed revolt.

In Coppola, the image of "the Italian" then becomes the condensation of myths and human rituals, often associated with the image of the party throughout *The Godfather* saga but also in a subliminal section of the American-themed film *The Rain People*, a small, early, extraordinary film by Coppola. In a brief flashback, Natalie, the protagonist, recalls her wedding, a tarantella, the dance of newlyweds.

One could say that Coppola's relationship with Italy is similar to his Oedipal relationship with his father, but using the symbolic means of cinema the director tries to kill, ritually but unnecessarily. Consider the paternal figure of Kurtz in *Apocalypse Now*, killed by Captain Willard in an arcane ritual, recalling the ancestral act of sacrificing the calf. This also brings to mind Vito Corleone's paternal figure (as also portrayed by Marlon Brando) in *The Godfather*, who is succeeded by his more cynical, though more educated son, Michael. Through this, one can understand Coppola's attraction to Bertolucci and the Oedipal complex at the core of much of his filmography. But even for Capra, if we continue this comparison, there is this intergenerational confrontation. As in the previously mentioned *The Younger Generation*, where the relationship between father and son explodes. The father is an old Jew of the Lower East Side bound to the family and its values, while the son, on the other hand, rejects tradition and cynically tries to climb the social ladder and move to the Upper East Side. But in the end, he finds himself all alone. In short, it appears that Capra sticks with the father where Coppola sides with the son.

There is a moment in which these two filmmakers (two generations of Italian Americans that nearly bookend two major moments in the history of cinema) meet in a direct way. Francis Ford Coppola draws directly on the large themes of Frank Capra, he identifies with Capra and his heroes, most particularly in his film *Tucker*. It is as if Coppola wanted to rehabilitate the universe of Capra, enhancing the mediocre aura of this character/symbol, and substituting the moderate with tension and an aesthetic system. Capra is reinterpreted through "New Hollywood" styling; the "mild" style of the Sicilian craftsman is reconsidered in an elevated form with a touch by the auteur. This is Coppola's debt to Capra: the protagonist, Preston Tucker, recalls the epics of Jefferson Smith and George Bailey, small heroes fighting against a corrupt world, in the name of the American dream. And the dream of Coppola, which resonates with Capra's utopia, is also the greater purpose of cinema, from both production and artistic perspectives, and it is a challenge Coppola can win, in the moment, but it is destined to fail. In the same way that Tucker falls to the big auto companies, Coppola, too, was devalued by the major Hollywood studios. In the American movie machine, so standardized, Coppola was consistently pressured to reject independent and creative production. And though he responded with the grand, ambitious project of Zoetrope, a system more creative and democratic, the result was an economic failure and a return to a major studio contract was needed in order to continue producing films on a large scale.

Through *Tucker*, Coppola pulls the threads of the American Dream and ties together the hopes and frustrations of two generations of Italian Americans: those who left the homeland, denying their roots, like Capra, and those who regained ancestral places and ambitions, like Coppola. The biographical tale of Preston Tucker and his attempt to go head to head with the big automobile manufacturers is mixed and blended with an autobiographical statement from Coppola, private and collective memory intertwined, and a social parable (the car being a grand metaphor for industrial society and capitalism). Moreover, the film is bracketed by two visions of reality: the chaotic opening credits, flashy and engaging, and those of the end credits, restrained and immortalized, with photographs of the real life Preston Tucker (whose story the film was based on). The viewer is given a chance to reconsider the events of the film just seen in a more thoughtful way.

In short, Frank Capra and Francis Ford Coppola are on opposite sides of a historic moment that spans the twentieth century, but their positions are not opposing. In fact, they are complementary and are part of an era of generational transitions. Whereas Capra embodies the need for integration of the first generation of immigrants without apparent nostalgia, with anger, and with an aggression dictated by generations of misery, Coppola represents a more detached recuperation, a rediscovery of one's roots, by a generation of the young and intellectual. Both filmmakers share a kind of Italian complex, inferiority and superiority together.

Scorsese And The Others

When considering modern American cinema and movie stereotypes from the seventies to today, it is impossible to avoid the Italian Americans of Martin Scorsese, especially those who populate *Goodfellas* and *Casino*. Scorsese confronts the stereotypes of Italian identity, not only in his latest but throughout his career: from *Mean Streets* and *Raging Bull* to his youthful shorts *Italianamerican* and *American Boy*, where the director puts his life and family into the mix.

The Italian family is the basis for Scorsese's beautiful homage to Italian cinema, *My Voyage to Italy*, a title that recalls a film close to his heart, *Viaggio in Italia* by Roberto Rossellini, but is also a move to travel back through memory, a personal diary within his own autobiography of an investigation into the history of film. The nostalgia for the Little Italy of his origins, for the neighborhoods of his family of immigrants from Polizzi Generosa, is married to a nostalgia for the grand tradition of Italian cinema, particularly Neorealism. Rossellini is a central figure in this long journey, a director who belongs to part of Scorsese's cinematic family. Placing himself in the old Italian American neighborhoods and recovering found footage of his family, Scorsese ventures through Italian cinema, investigating its influences and its legacies.

This filmmaker's tribute and self-reflexive review of the history of cinema seems to be a familiar approach to Italian American filmmakers and their personal filmographies. For example, Brian De Palma's *Blow Out* is a clear homage to Michelangelo Antonioni's *Blowup*; Michael Cimino's *The Sicilian* is an attempt at a Hollywood remake of Francesco Rosi's *Salvatore Giuliano*; and more recently, we have Abel Ferrara's own passionate homage to Pier Paolo Pasolini. They cannot help but confront themselves with these predecessors. These are the ancestors, the progenitors, and initiators of their family saga in America, as well as the founding fathers of the national cinema.

Like Scorsese, as we have seen with Coppola, Italian American directors have taken account of their origins through the medium of film and with strong emphasis on the history of Italian cinema. It is not just a matter of "representing" the image of the Italian American or the country of origin, instead these directors have used the tool of cinema to reflect and analyze their stories, and through this self-reflexivity many generations are then able to share and reconsider what it means to be Italian and Italian American.

PERSPECTIVES & PROPOSALS

Italian American Studies in the Italian University System: Current and Future Perspectives

Margherita Ganeri
UNIVERSITY OF CALABRIA

This essay will not deal with the state of the art of Italian American Studies in Italy. Though it is worth underlining that this field of study is relatively young, as it emerged about three decades ago, over the last few years it has increasingly affirmed itself as one of the most interesting areas of research.[1] The growth of Italian American Studies has been coterminous with the affirmation of U.S. Italian Americans' public identity, as the documentary *The Italian Americans*, produced by PBS at the beginning of 2015, best exemplifies.[2]

In this essay, I shall reflect on the opportunities that may arise from introducing Italian American Studies within the Italian university degree programs or curricula and on the possible and desirable ways through which this may occur. Such a discourse cannot but take its cue from the observation that they are practically

---

[1] In the "Preface" to the first edition of the anthology *From the Margin. Writings in Italian Americana*, the editors Anthony Julian Tamburri, Paolo A. Giordano, and Fred L. Gardaphé affirm that the extent of these studies in the United States in the 1980s was very limited (West Lafayette, Indiana, 2000 [1991]) xiii-xiv. As far as Italy is concerned, I provided an overview of the state of the art of Italian American Studies in "The Broadening of the Concept of 'Migration Literature' in Contemporary Italy," *Forum Italicum* 44.2 (2010): 437-451. This essay is included also in the book: Margherita Ganeri, *L'America italiana. Epos e storytelling in Helen Barolini*, (Arezzo, 2010); and in its English translation (Fano-PU, 2015).

[2] Written and produced by John Maggio, narrated by Stanley Tucci.

absent from the national educational curricula.[3] However, this gap will almost certainly be filled due to the growing expansion of the research in the field and to the increasing cultural exchanges among international universities.

Given their intrinsic cross-disciplinary nature, Italian Americana appears as a dynamic field, which brings together scholars from many disparate research areas and geographical locations. If cultural exchanges constitute the means through which the humanities can progress, Italian American Studies, more than any other discipline, is located at the crossroads between disciplines and cultures. Any discourse on the opportunity to include them within the national university system has to start by acknowledging their transnational character, which in turn results in a multiplicity of common interests and advantages. Italian scholars need their American counterparts to come and teach in Italy and require their help to design new academic programs. American scholars, on their part, need to remain continuously informed as to what concerns the evolution of Italian national culture because this constitutes a fundamental part of their future research and of their mobile and dynamic constructions of "Italianità." Indeed, their "Italianità" is the essential component of that *hyphenated* identity that is the pivot of this field of studies.

Thus, cultural exchanges are the lymph that provides nourishment to both Italian and American scholars, because these exchanges allow the latter to construct and pursue some common cultural and identity research interests. And such interests can ac-

---

[3] No scientific area or discipline in the Italian university system is solely or only partly devoted to Italian American Studies. As a result, there are no teaching positions available in this field. The only existing position, now held by Francesco Durante, is available at Suor Orsola Benincasa University, a private institution in Naples. In the public university system, the only compulsory and complete course for Master's Degree students takes place at the University of Calabria and has been running since the academic year 2014-2015. More information on this program will be provided later in the article.

tively aid in the building of a bridge to connect the two sides of the ocean, and also different parts of the world.

More generally, the theme of diasporic identities is among the most relevant for the future of humanities research: on the one hand, the global diasporic movement has never been so dramatic and intense as in the last decades; on the other hand, the very notion of diaspora is grounded in the idea of mobile and multifaceted knowledge which in turn is an expression of the global socio-cultural dynamics.

During the three-day Bellagio workshop held in March 2014 at the Rockefeller Foundation Center,[4] participants shared a sense of being part of a new and important enterprise. It was the feeling that a momentous event was taking place. Eighteen scholars from the U.S. and Italy met to discuss strategies for the introduction of Italian American Studies in the Italian university curricula. The conference was the first ever of its kind, and it marked a turning point. Indirectly, this conference also proved that before 2014 the field of Italian Americana was completely absent from Italian teaching programs. What has been done in the two years following the conference and what could be done in the next years? The following observations reflect my personal experience at the University of Calabria, where a new academic program in Italian American Studies has been established. This program is, as far as I know, the first and the only of its kind in the Italian public university system.

---

[4] The conference took place on March 4-6 2014, in Bellagio (CO), at the Rockefeller Foundation. Organized by the John D. Calandra Institute (Queen's College, City University of New York), the conference was attended by some of the U.S.'s most recognized scholars in the field and by some leading Italian scholars of American and Italian Studies. The proceedings are in the volume: Anthony Julian Tamburri and Fred L. Gardaphé, eds., *Transcending Borders, Bridging Gaps. Italian Americana, Diasporic Studies and the University Curriculum* (New York: John D. Calandra Italian American Institute, 2015). And, in Italian, in the section *Officina*, of the journal *Palinsesti. Quaderni del Dottorato internazionale di Studi Umanistici—Università della Calabria* 3 (2015): 21-179.

First of all, let me offer readers a brief description of this program. Originally, the aim of our project was to create a research center in the Department of Humanities, together with other Departments. However, the project took a different direction. Considering the potential impact of a research center in our national system, we realized it would not have been very significant, especially considering the difficult financial situation of all Italian public universities, including ours. And it was this consideration that led to the institution of a new teaching program. To develop a research center that may have considerable impact is an extremely difficult task, even more so if funds are not available. Furthermore, a research center is more oriented towards the academic community of scholars and professors than that of students. After diligent deliberation, we were convinced that the best way to introduce the field of Italian American Studies in our system would be to work on curricula and teaching, to make it a compulsory component of the students' academic career. Of course, research was an important aspect of this project but the goals are significantly different than those that are pursued in terms of curricula.

In the academic year 2014-15 a full 9-credit course was launched as part of the Master's Degree in Modern Philology, called "Cultura e Letteratura italiana Americana" (CLIA) [Italian American Culture and Literature]. The course is in English and lectures are held by a number of visiting professors from the United States who teach for a period varying between one and two weeks.[5] The course was made possible thanks to an agreement signed with the

---

[5] In the Italian public university system, teaching disciplines are divided, on a national level, into clearly separated sections, the so-called "settori scientifico-disciplinari" [scientific disciplinary sections]. Instructors and professors are obliged to teach courses that fit in their proper section, and because all the courses offered must have formal designations of at least one sector, the one of the instructor is chosen subsequently. Since the CLIA course is something totally new, we did the reverse at UniCal: because my scientific sector is L-Fil-Let-11 Contemporary Italian Literature, the CLIA course falls within it.

City University of New York, and to the huge (also organizational) support coming from Anthony Julian Tamburri and Fred L. Gardaphé. Both scholars had already been guest professors in my Contemporary Italian Literature for the Master's Degree in Modern Philology in the academic year 2013-14, teaching a 12-hour series of lessons each, offered in Italian, on Italian American cinema and literature respectively.

The first edition of the CLIA course, held in English, started in October 2014. It was an immediate success (with 34 registered students) and in the next year became mandatory. With this tide of enthusiasm and interest, it is in the process of becoming one of the cornerstones for a new curriculum available within the Modern Philology Master's Degree, with the aim to host other courses on Italian Diaspora in the future.

The curriculum, called "Italian Studies," offers all of its courses in English; with the hope that in the future such a course will be autonomous, and may be turned into a Master's Degree program targeting international students who wish to specialize in Italian Studies. Such a degree program would offer a significant number of courses focusing on the Italian communities in the world and their culture, on the theoretical approach to Diaspora Studies, and, to a lesser extent, on post-colonial studies.

In its second edition, the CLIA course had 43 registered students, and by the third, which began on October 3rd, 2016, the course had 56 registered students. There have been several requests to write Italian American Studies related dissertations, and at the end of the 2016, the number of dissertations written or in progress, relating to the field, were 19; an incredible result only two years after the launch of the course, considering the average numbers of master's thesis in other most popular disciplines are around four to five a year. Our goal for the forthcoming academic years is to run courses on virtually all Italian diasporic cultures in the English-speaking world, including Italian-Canadian, Italian-

Australian, and so on. Then, in the following stages, we will also include courses that focus on Italian communities in other countries and languages, starting with Latin America, most notably Argentina and Brazil.

In conjunction with CLIA, a specialized advanced program, "Italian Diaspora Studies Summer Seminar," has been launched to a closed number of post-doctorate students, academics, and international lecturers. The program is based on a collaborative partnership between the University of Calabria and the John D. Calandra Italian American Institute. Over three weeks, the Seminar includes six full courses held by leading scholars in the field and some additional guest speakers. A series of guided visits around the region are also included as an integral part of the study program. This program is now in its second edition and it is meant to become a permanent institution, running potentially every year. This is the one and only training course available worldwide that prepares and mentors potential educators in the field of Italian Diaspora Studies.

The creation and launch of these new programs entailed a tremendous amount of work; however, there is a lot of enthusiasm for having devised something new, topical, and cutting-edge. Of course, there are still some difficulties that need to be overcome, especially from a financial point of view. Several U.S. institutions and associations funded a number of scholarships; yet, greater financial resources will be necessary in the future to keep these courses running, in order to pay for the costs of visiting professors and to finance the mobility of the student, both incoming and outgoing. Moreover, if the costs of these courses are relatively low, considerably higher funds are required to create an equipped study center and a specialized library at the University of Calabria.

Now I would like to go back to discussing the intentions at the heart of these projects. Our aim was the inclusion of Italian American Studies within those curricula designed for the training of teachers and scholars of Humanities and Literature in Italy. I have written extensively on my support for the introduction of Italian America Studies into the Italian university system, not only as a part of American Studies, but also, more fruitfully in terms of curricula developments, as an integral part of Contemporary Italian Literature Studies.

Contemporary Italian Literature is a scientific sector that covers the second part of the nineteenth century, starting with Italy's Unification. The Great Migration, as it is well known, became a significant phenomenon after the Unification, depending mostly on post-Unification national politics. Massive migratory flows, whose complexity will not be discussed here, have characterized Italian national history, both before and after Unification. These flows are still ongoing today, as a great number of Italians, especially graduates, are forced to emigrate in search of more favorable working conditions. Thus, emigration was and continues to be an essential quality and distinctive issue in Italian history and should be reflected accordingly. Begging the question, why have emigrant writers been left out of the Italian canon if migration has been such a well-documented and critical facet of Italian history?

Why have so many teachers willfully ignored the numerous pages on the topic written by authors such as De Amicis, Pascoli, Capuana, Maria Messina, Pirandello, Sciascia, Corrado Alvaro, among others? The phenomenon of emigration and the cultural forms that it brought about have been systematically ignored by academia nationally.

The study of literature through a transnational theoretical perspective is now very common; as a result, it is no longer viable to study Italian literature ignoring European and world literatures. Likewise, the study of Italian writers abroad and of their descendants should no longer be ignored.

Italian Studies are condemned to disappear if they aren't able to renew themselves, discovering their place in a global context.

And it is my opinion that the most effective way to do so is to open up to and work with their diasporic communities. Such an influx can prove vital for the survival of Italian studies. Furthermore, the intersection between Italian Studies and Italian American Studies does not originate in a series of arbitrary comparisons but on actual and objective historical facts.

Why shouldn't Italian American authors be considered part of the Italian literary canon? The longstanding response has been that they already belong to other literatures, American, Canadian, Argentinian, Brazilian, and so on and so forth. Additionally, they do not write in Italian. However, this is not always the case. For example, in the case of the United States, the first volume of the majestic anthology *Italoamericana*, edited by Francesco Durante, and covering almost a century of history and literature until 1880, includes only texts written in Italian.[6]

Until the end of the 1930s writers were keen on using their native language. For many years and, still to present day, many writers continue to be bilingual, as is most notably the case with the great Joseph Tusiani. Why shouldn't those authors who write in Italian, not be included in the Italian literary canon, if the quality of their work is deserving? But I would still go another step further, bilingual writers and even those who write only in English should be included not just in the literary histories of the United States but in the Italian ones, given their double cultural identity.

I have maintained for some years that writers like Mario Puzo, Pietro di Donato, John Fante, or and Helen Barolini, should be included in both the American Studies university syllabi and in

---

[6] Francesco Durante, ed., *Italoamericana. Storia e letteratura degli italiani negli Stati Uniti* (Vol. I [1776-1880], Milan, 2001; Volume II [1880-1943], Milan: Mondadori, 2005). The second volume has been translated in English: Francesco Durante, edt., *Italoamericana. The Literature of the Great Migration, 1880-1943*. General Editor of the American Edition: Robert Viscusi; Translations Editor: Anthony Julian Tamburri; Bibliographic Editor: James J. Periconi (New York: Fordham UP, 2014).

Contemporary Italian literature ones, through either their translations or by teaching classes in English, as it occurs in many universities, and will continue to occur with greater frequency.

Is Cioran a Rumanian or a French writer, is Conrad a member of Polish or British literature, is Camus French or Algerian? There has been a large debate on each of these prominent writers, and the answer is always that they have both identities.

Moreover, translations have always been an integral part of the teaching of Literature. How many people are reading Tolstoj and Dostoyevsky in Russian outside of Russia?

Two writers that have been very influential in my life and for my research are Flaubert and Proust. And, I must admit, I have read them only in translation. My knowledge of French is too poor to read them in the original. Why should I be ashamed of it? That doesn't mean I haven't appreciated or understood them. Translation is a precious tool to World Literature, and, especially in our global context, we need to place it at the core of our teaching and researching practices.

My goal is to integrate the vast repertoire of Italian Diasporic Literatures with that of Contemporary Italian Literature within the curricula offered at the University of Calabria. I am convinced that Italian American Studies should be affiliated with Italian Studies. This is particularly true when dealing with curricula developments. Italian Diasporic Literatures should become a recognized part of Italian Literature. Every history of Italian Literature should include at least some of the most important writers from the most important literatures produced by Italians abroad, even when they are written in different languages. How could we pursue any transnational perspective, which is so celebrated today, without considering the Italians abroad?

Fred Gardaphé often writes that the future of Italian American Studies is in Italy, and I am sure he doesn't mean that this future is only in the field of American Studies in Italy. Moreover, I think

Gardaphé believes that Italian Americans, not only scholars, need to be continuously updated on the Italian culture to keep their hyphenated identity alive.[7] Building a transnational network of scholars and a series of cooperative programs is the key to this future; the exchange of scholars and students is another.

A general study of Italian Diaspora should be pursued rather than limiting ourselves to the field of Italian Americana. I am convinced that Italy offers the opportunity to study the different diasporic cultures and literatures of Italian origin as a potentially unified phenomenon, to adopt a comprehensive and comparative perspective, which promises to be very fruitful and stimulating for every culture involved. In order to succeed, all the Italian academicians interested in the field should connect and collaborate with colleagues of different fields and geographical locations. It is crucial that we know what the others are doing or would like to do in order to cooperate and build a common ground that encompasses an ever-expanding dialogue. Associations and periodical meetings should help develop the idea of a national plan aimed at including Italian Diaspora Studies in our university curricula.

We are in a global world where cultural and linguistic integration has become a necessary requirement for the educational system. Just as migration is a central issue in the political agenda, scholars and teachers must start to address the crucial question of migration literature. I talk about literature because it is my field, but there is no limitation to it in regard to other cultural expressions.

In the last three years I have been asking myself why the CLIA course has been so successful among the students at University of Calabria. Are they specializing in American Studies? No, only a few are. The large majority are students from the Italian Studies

---

[7] Fred L. Gardaphé, *Italian Signs, American Streets: the Evolution of Italian American Narrative* (Duke: Duke UP, 1996) in Italian as, *Segni italiani, strade americane: l'evoluzione della letteratura italiana americana* (Firenze: Franco Cesati Editore, 2012).

program. So, why are they interested? The answer is that living in a region with a very high rate of unemployment, Calabrian graduates know that they will have to emigrate at the end of their studies, or they will be stuck with a very limited future, especially those who graduate in the humanities. Such a negative situation turns out to be very positive for Diaspora Studies: the Calabria region and the young students at the University of Calabria, offer an ideal setting for the birth of a course of studies on Italian Diaspora. It fits perfectly well in the local context.

For our part, we are convinced that we have launched a program with a strong cultural significance, and not only for the geographic area where the University of Calabria is located. Calabria has been a place of passage, of departures, of landings, of settlements and colonies, from as far back as the Magna Graecia, and the tradition has stuck. Emigration has left a deep mark on the history of the region. But this is true also for other parts of Italy. Since migration has been a predominant phenomenon for the entire nation, particularly in the years after Italy's Unification, we strongly believe that programs centered on and reflective of Italian migrations will have considerable impact everywhere in the country, both within and beyond academia. The perspectives and promises arising from international cooperation in various fields of knowledge related to Diaspora studies have an ethical and social purpose that goes well beyond any self-referential conceptualization of culture. If the ultimate objective of building new curricula is to promote civilization and social progress, the study of Italian Diaspora serves this cause very well, and not only on a national, but also on a transnational level.

Military Nationalism and the Re-elaboration of Ethnicity: Italian Americans and World War I

Stefano Luconi

UNIVERSITY OF GENOVA

This essay analyzes how the patriotic discourse surrounding World War I contributed to redefining the identity of both Italian newcomers and their progeny in the United States. Specifically, it discusses how nationalistic rhetoric helped the immigrants from Italy and their children supersede their initial localistic self-perceptions and develop a sense of affiliation shaped by their mutual Italian ancestry, which, however, was not impervious to the consciousness of being part of the larger American society. The latter hardly survived in the early postwar years and the former ended up prevailing.

PREWAR LOCALISTIC ALLEGIANCES

The belated achievement of Italy's political unification, a process that began in 1861 and was not completed until the end of World War I, let the population of this nation long retain an intense feeling of loyalty toward the local community—be the latter the native region, province, town, or even village—and reveal a rather weak attachment to their country as a whole.[1] The Italian expatriates from different geographical backgrounds, too, generally failed to think of themselves as members of the same nationality group upon disembarking in the United States at the turn of the

---

[1] Luigi Manconi, "Campanilismo," in Guido Calcagno, ed., *Bianco, rosso e verde: L'identità degli italiani* (Rome and Bari: Laterza, 2003) 36-42.

twentieth century. One of them observed that, "for me, as for the others, Italy is the little village where I was raised."[2]

The notion of the recently-established Italian state as a hostile entity that had instigated their exit because it was unable to provide for its people and had confined itself mainly to imposing levies and drafting young men into the army further prevented immigrants from developing a national identity. To many expatriates such as Antonio Pierro, a native of Forenza in the province of Potenza, "Italy meant taxes and conscription."[3]

The dynamics of the resettlement overseas further strengthened insular allegiances. As the newcomers arrived in the United States primarily by means of chain migration based on family and village connections, they gathered together along lines of subnational affiliations that reflected their diverse local backgrounds in the native land. As author Richard Gambino has remarked, "Italian-American neighborhoods were indeed clusters of transplanted towns of the Mezzogiorno."[4] Specifically, Italian vice-consul Luigi Villari pointed out about New York City's so-called "Little Italy" in 1912 that

> some neighborhoods are inhabited exclusively by newcomers from a given region; we can find only Sicilians in a street, only people from Calabria in another street, and immigrants from Abruzzi in a third one. There are even streets where only individuals from a single town live: a colony from Sciacca here, a colony from San Giovanni in Fiore there, a colony from Cosenza somewhere else.[5]

---

[2] As quoted in Phyllis H. Williams, *South Italian Folkways in Europe and America: A Handbook for Social Workers, Visiting Nurses, School Teachers, and Physicians* (New Haven: Yale UP, 1938) 17.

[3] David Laskin, *The Long Way Home: An American Journey from Ellis Island to the Great War* (New York: Harper Collins, 2010) 104.

[4] Richard Gambino, *Blood of My Blood: The Dilemma of the Italian Americans* (Toronto: Guernica, 2003) 110.

[5] Luigi Villari, *Gli italiani negli Stati Uniti d'America e l'emigrazione italiana* (Milan: Trevis, 1912) 216.

Subnational divisions extended to social life as well. The Order Sons of Italy in America, a mutual aid society that became the largest and most influential Italian-American ethnic organization nationwide, welcomed individuals of Italian descent regardless of their, or their parents', place of origin in the mother country.[6] Yet, despite this case and a few other exceptions, most Italian-American fraternal associations initially admitted only those immigrants who had come from a specific geographical district and denied membership to fellow countrymen who had been born elsewhere. The qualifying area could be as large as a whole region, but it was often as narrow as a town or a village. For instance, only individuals born in Castrogiovanni and the province of Caltanisetta as well as their offspring were entitled to join Philadelphia's Società di Mutuo Soccorso fra Castrogiovannesi e Provinciali.[7] As an immigrant aptly argued, social grouping in the Italian-American settlements usually "reflected the older historic disunity of Italy."[8]

Ethnic discrimination helped prevent Italian immigrants from identifying with their native country. The awareness that Italy ranked among the most backward of European states by Anglo-Saxon standards in the eyes of the US establishment, despite the cultural enthusiasm of the previous generation of American Grand Tourists,[9] curbed the development of a national consciousness among

---

[6] Jennifer M. Guglielmo and John Andreozzi, "The Order Sons of Italy in America: Historical Summary," in Jennifer M. Guglielmo and John Andreozzi, eds., *Guide to the Records of the Order Sons of Italy in America* (Minneapolis: Immigration History Research Center, 2004) XIX-XXX.

[7] "Regolamento," 9, Papers of the Società di Mutuo Soccorso fra Castrogiovannesi e Provinciali, box 1, folder 1, Balch Institute Collection, Historical Society of Pennsylvania, Philadelphia.

[8] Federal Writers' Project of the Works Progress Administration for the State of Rhode Island, *Rhode Island: A Guide to the Smallest State* (Boston: Houghton Mifflin, 1937) 99.

[9] John Paul Russo, "From Italophilia to Italophobia," *Differentia* 4.6-7 (Winter-Fall 1994): 45-75.

the expatriates and induced the newcomers to disavow their Italian roots, encouraging them to emphasize their regional heritage. Yet the spread of jingoistic feelings after the outbreak of World War I contributed to the demise of the immigrants' localistic allegiances.

THE RISE OF NATIONALISM

Anarchists, socialists, and other Left-wing radicals from Italian background opposed their motherland's entry into the military conflict and antagonized the subsequent participation of the United States in the war. In early 1915, for example, a Socialist immigrant named his daughter Pace to stress his own commitment to the retention of neutrality by both his native and adoptive countries.[10] Anarchist Carlo Tresca stood out among the staunchest foes of the war and, between March and May 1916, embarked himself on a propaganda tour in California's Italian-American communities to discourage his fellow ethnics' enlistment in the Italian army.[11] After the United States entered the conflict in 1917, the Italian Socialist Federation of North America stuck to the St. Louis Resolution of the Socialist Party of America that proclaimed "its unalterable opposition to the war."[12]

However, although they proved to be very vocal, these radical activists also turned out to be a small minority. Some of them, such as Edmondo Rossoni and Domenico Trombetta, both former members of the anarcho-syndicalist Industrial Workers of the World, even switched side. The experience of anti-Italian discrimination resulting from the lack of trans-ethnic solidarity within the

---

[10] Helen Barolini, *The Dream Book: An Anthology of Writings by Italian-American Women* (Syracuse: Syracuse UP, 1985) 300.

[11] Nunzio Pernicone, *Carlo Tresca: Portrait of a Rebel* (New York: Palgrave, 2005) 87-88.

[12] Elisabetta Vezzosi, *Il socialismo indifferente: Immigrati italiani e Socialist Party negli Stati Uniti del primo Novecento* (Rome: Edizioni Lavoro, 1991) 167-68. The quote is from "The Socialist Party and the War," in Alexander Trachtenberg, ed., *The American Labor Year Book, 1917-18* (New York: Rand School of Social Science, 1918) 50.

US labor movement led them to the field of nationalism and to advocate Italy's entry into the war.[13] Specifically, after Rossoni's interventionist wishes had been fulfilled, he resigned the editorship of the neutralist and anti-militarist *Il Proletario*—the mouthpiece of the Italian Socialist Federation of North America—and established a newspaper of his own, *L'Italia Nostra*. From the latter's columns he celebrated the Italian soldiers' alleged heroism in the battles against the Austrian troops from September 1915 to March 1916, when he left the United States for Europe to enlist in the Italian army, although he never made it to the frontline and his services were almost exclusively for propaganda purposes.[14] The radicals who yielded to chauvinism and became war-mongers also included women such as Socialist émigré and poetess Bellalma Forzato Spezia, who contributed to the New York City-based jingoistic weekly *Il Cittadino*.[15] Although she wrote a women's column called "Problemi femminili" (female problems) for this newspaper, Forzato Spezia managed to intertwine her suggestions for the treatment of adipose tissue or a happy marriage with appeals urging Italian-American mothers to be strong and not to interfere with their sons' participation in "the titanic struggle" against the "Teutonic virus."[16]

Indeed, regardless of their political orientation, in the aftermath of the outbreak of World War I and in the wake of Italy's entry into the conflict, many Italian immigrants revealed patriotic sentiments that induced the newcomers not only to support the martial efforts of their motherland but also to re-calibrate their own identity. As a result, they dropped their previous localistic

---

[13] John P. Diggins, *Mussolini and Fascism: The View from America* (Princeton: Princeton UP, 1972) 87, 112.

[14] John J. Tinghino, *Edmondo Rossoni: From Revolutionary Syndicalism to Fascism* (New York: Peter Lang, 1991) 65-73.

[15] Marcella Bencivenni, *Italian Immigrant Radical Culture: The Idealism of the Sovversivi in the United States, 1890-1940* (New York: New York UP, 2011) 146.

[16] Bellalma Forzato Spezia, "L'ora del sacrificio," *Il Cittadino*, October 4, 1917, 2.

allegiances, extended their sense of belonging, and came to think of themselves as Italians.

Ethnic leaders and associations as well as the Italian-language press celebrated Italy's declaration of war on Austria on May 23, 1915, with bombastic rhetoric and mobilized to back the military machinery of their ancestral country.[17] The only exception was the Italian-American community in Tampa, Florida, because of the high concentration of anarchists and other Left-wing radicals, mostly political exiles who had fled the repression of the Sicilian *fasci* (workers' leagues) in 1893.[18] This massive campaign contributed to persuading the rank and file members of the Little Italies that they had something in common despite their different places of origin in their native land. In addition, after being victims of stereotypes and intolerance in their host society because of their ethnic heritage, Italian immigrants and their children became aware that their national origin was no longer a liability from which they had to distance themselves as soon as the United States entered the military conflict against Germany as an "associate power" at the side of Italy in 1917, on April 6. For example, the Providence-based and Italian-language weekly *L'Eco del Rhode Island* pointed out that "our hearts rejoice because Americans have begun to appreciate us as they are enthusiastically rallying to

---

[17] Ernest L. Biagi, *The Purple Aster: A History of the Sons of Italy in America* (New York: Veritas P, 1961) 137; Humbert S. Nelli, "Chicago's Italian-Language Press and World War I," in Francesco Cordasco, ed., *Studies in Italian American Social History: Essays in Honor of Leonard Covello* (Totowa, NJ: Rowman and Littlefield, 1975) 66-80; Sergio Bugiardini, "L'associazionismo negli Usa," in Piero Bevilacqua, Andreina De Clementi, and Emilio Franzina, eds. *Storia dell'emigrazione italiana: Arrivi* (Rome: Donzelli, 2002) 571; Christopher. M. Sterba, *Good Americans: Italian and Jewish Immigrants during the First World War* (New York: Oxford UP, 2003) 133-52.

[18] Gary R. Mormino and George E. Pozzetta, *The Immigrant World of Ybor City: Italians and Their Latin Neighbors in Tampa, 1885-1985* (Urbana: U Illinois P, 1987) 155.

support Italy."[19] Likewise, *Il Progresso Italo-Americano*, a daily print-ed in New York City and the most authoritative Italian-American newspaper in the country, expressed its enthusiasm because "the same cause unites both nations", the United States and Italy.[20] It also welcomed Washington's participation in the conflict as "an opportunity to demonstrate our loyalty to this country in words and in deeds."[21] Similarly, *Il Cittadino* rejoiced when, on the occasion of the visit of an Italian military delegation to the United States in 1917, such leading mainstream dailies as the *New York Times* and the *World* celebrated Italy's heroism and commitment to democracy. "These words," remarked *Il Cittadino*, "pay us back with interests for our previous pains" resulting from ethnic intolerance and bigotry. The newspaper added that such a change of U.S. attitude towards Italy would also benefit the Italian Americans, as the latter had become "the increasingly relished guests of this Nation which is our friend and ally."[22]

The mission of the Italian delegation, aiming at securing greater military and political support for Rome's war efforts on the part of the United States, was eventually unsuccessful.[23] Yet, its outcome was of little concern to *Il Cittadino*, which interpreted its role primarily in terms of ethnic redress for Italian Americans. The proclamation of June 21, 1917, as "Italy Day" by New York State's Governor Charles S. Whitman also made *Il Cittadino* proud because it was a gesture of acceptance for Italian Americans.[24] When

---

[19] "Italiani alla riscossa," *L'Eco del Rhode Island*, June 8, 1918, 1.

[20] "I nostri renitenti," *Il Progresso Italo-Americano*, April 8, 1917, 6. For *Il Progresso Italo-Americano*, see Bénédicte Deschamps, "De la presse 'coloniale' à la presse italo-américaine, le parcours de six périodiques italiens aux États-Unis (1910-1935)" (Ph.D. dissertation, University of Paris VII, 1996) 66-69

[21] "L'eco italiana del messaggio di Wilson," *Il Progresso Italo-Americano*, April 3, 1917, 6.

[22] "L'arrivo della missione italiana," *Il Cittadino*, May 24, 1917, 1, 4 (quote 4).

[23] Liliana Saiu, *Stati Uniti e Italia nella Grande guerra* (Florence: Olschki, 2003) 100-18.

[24] "Italy Day," *Il Cittadino*, June 21, 1917, 1.

Charles Evans Hughes—a former associate justice of the U.S. Supreme Court and the 1916 Republican presidential candidate—urged US governors and mayors of large cities to celebrate the third anniversary of Italy's entry into the war on May 24, 1918, Italian Americans hailed his incitement as evidence that they were no longer perceived as aliens and outcasts in their adoptive society.[25]

By the same token, once Italian-American Congressman Fiorello H. La Guardia's exploits while in command of a U.S. Air Force unit on the Austrian front became known, an immigrant with a brother in the Italian army congratulated him on his remarkable contribution to the improvement of the reputation of "our inspiring Latin race" in the United States.[26] A similar recognition came to La Guardia from New York City's Garibaldi Lodge of the Order Sons of Italy in America.[27]

A few years earlier, in 1912, Italy's military victory over the Turkish Empire and her seizure of Libya had failed to trigger off significant enthusiasm in the Italian-American communities.[28] On that occasion, the stigmatization of Italy's war of aggression by the administration of President William H. Taft and the censures of Rome's scramble for colonial possession in the only section of Mediterranean Africa which was not under European control on the part of a few US commentators had prevented many immigrants from identifying with their native country because their motherland's foreign policy had been subjected to disapproval in

---

[25] Peter G. Vellon, *A Great Conspiracy against Our Race: Italian Immigrant Newspapers and the Construction of Whiteness in the Early 20th Century* (New York: New York UP, 2014) 114-15.

[26] F. Dugena to Fiorello H. La Guardia, September 2, 1918, Fiorello H. La Guardia Papers [hereafter FLGP], reel 45, box 65, folder "World War I Papers," New York Public Library.

[27] Stefano Miele to La Guardia, April 24, 1918, FLGP, reel 45, box 65, folder "World War I Papers."

[28] Salvatore J. LaGumina, *Long Island Italian Americans: History, Heritage, and Tradition* (Charleston: History P, 2013) 42.

America.[29] Such criticism, however, was temporarily dropped as the United States and Italy joined forces against the German Empire in 1917. The removal of this drawback eventually manage to sweep away any inhibition Italian Americans had felt about associating themselves with their motherland. As the U.S. press extolled their nation's "civilization" and its "warlike virtues" on Italy Day, Italian Americans felt a "stronger" and "more cohesive" community.[30]

WARTIME MULTIFACETED PATRIOTISM

After yielding to nationalism, the immigrants became so confident that they freed themselves from any previous restraint in showing both their attachment to Italy and the backing of their motherland's specific goals. Until the mid 1910s, organizations such as Hull House, the settlement house Jane Addams had established in Chicago to facilitate the social accommodation of the members of foreign-born minorities, drew upon episodes of struggle for independence of single European nations, including Italy's *Risorgimento* (namely the fight for the country's political unification), to encourage the city's diverse immigrant groups to cherish their own ethnic heritage.[31]

Conversely, at wartime, the call for one-hundred-percent Americanism replaced the previously perception of American society as a melting pot.[32] "America wants no more Little Germanys or Little

---

[29] Marco Rimanelli, "United States-Italian Diplomatic Relations, 1776-1945," in *The Italian American Experience: An Encyclopedia*. Salvatore J. LaGumina et al., ed. (New York: Garland, 2000) 650; John A. DeNovo, *American Interests and Policies in the Middle East, 1900-1939* (Minneapolis: U Minnesota P, 1963) 51.

[30] "L'Italy Day in America," *Il Carroccio* VIII.1 (July 1918): 19.

[31] Rivka Shpak Lissak, *Pluralism and Progressives: Hull House and the Immigrants, 1890-1919* (Chicago: U Chicago P, 1989) 25-34.

[32] Richard Alba and Victor Nee, *Remaking the American Mainstream: Assimilation and Contemporary Immigration* (Cambridge, MA: Harvard UP, 2003) 140.

Italys in its domain," proclaimed St. Louis' *Globe-Democrat*.[33] U.S. war propaganda, especially the messages that the Wilson administration channeled by means of the Committee on Public Information, stressed that the members of the diverse ethnic groups living in the United States were "Americans all." The latter was the caption of a well-known Victory Liberty Loan poster by celebrated illustrator Howard Chandler Christy, featuring a honor roll of foreign-sounding names that included Italian-echoing Andrassi and Villotto.[34] In this way it is clear that the US government urged immigrant minorities to Americanize and come together across the divide of their different national extractions in order to support the fight against the authoritarian government of the German Kaiser.[35]

Such stimuli toward Americanization, however, often fell on deaf ears in the Little Italies. Italian Americans were interested less in contributing to "making the world safe for democracy" and in joining "the war to end all wars" as the two leading US slogans went, than in the liberation of the north-eastern regions of the Italian peninsula from under Austrian control.[36] Therefore, to many Italian immigrants and their children, the real enemy was not the Kaiser, as the US propaganda suggested, but his ally in Vienna because the latter was keeping the cities of Trento and Trieste and their hinterlands under his iron heel. For example, as few as two days after Italy had entered the war, a group of roughly 300 Ital-

---

[33] As quoted in Gary R. Mormino, *Immigrants on the Hill: Italian Americans in St. Louis, 1882-1982* (Urbana: U Illinois P, 1986) 101.

[34] Werner Sollors, "'Of Plymouth Rock and Jamestown and Ellis Island;' or, Ethnic Literature and Some Redefinitions of 'America,'" in Donald L. Horowitz and Gérald Noriel, eds., *Immigrants in Two Democracies: French and American Experience* (New York: New York UP, 1992) 211-12.

[35] Nancy Gentile Ford, *Americans All! Foreign-Born Soldiers in World War I* (College Station, TX: U Yexas P, 2001); Jeffrey E. Mirel, *Patriotic Pluralism: Americanization Education and European Immigrants* (Cambridge, MA: Harvard UP, 2010) 21-28.

[36] Alan Axelrod, *Selling the Great War: The Making of American Propaganda* (New York: Palgrave, 2009) 55, 61.

ian-American longshoremen seized the opportunity of the arrival of an Italian ship flying the *Tricolore* in New York City's harbor to stage a demonstration at the docks in support of their mother-land's fight for Trento and Trieste.[37] Likewise, in late November 1917 a few Italian-language newspapers did not hesitate to pub-lish editorials with the purpose of pressuring the US government into extending the range of its military operations and declaring war on the Austrian-Hungarian Empire, too.[38] North Providence's Lodge 636 of the Order Sons of Italy in America passed a resolu-tion to the same end and forwarded it to US President Woodrow Wilson.[39] Such appeals echoed the stand of the Italian government which — following the unexpected rout of its army in the battle of Caporetto between October 24 and November 12, 1917, when the Italian troops suffered over 10,000 casualties and were pushed 50 mile southwards to the Piave river[40] — started to urge Washington to fight against Austria-Hungary as well.[41]

Notwithstanding opposition from a few radical groups and newspapers of Anarchist and Socialist orientation, the Italian-language and Italian-focused press encouraged more than 65,000 reservists — out of a total of roughly 400,000 residing in the United States — to go back to their motherland to enlist in the Italian army. Some would eventually regret the decision to leave for the battle-fields after experiencing life on the frontlines. This was the case of a repatriate from California who, in September 1916, advised his nephew not to follow in his footsteps because "I swear at the day I

---

[37] Emilio Franzina, "Emigranti ed emigrati in America davanti al primo conflitto mondiale (1914-1918)," in *Stati Uniti e Italia nel nuovo scenario internazionale (1898-1918)*. Daniele Fiorentino and Matteo Sanfilippo, eds. (Rome: Gangemi, 2012) 149

[38] "For a Declaration of War against Austria-Hungary," *Il Cittadino*, November 22, 1917, 1; "Declare War on Austria," *Il Carroccio* VI.5 (November 1917): 403-4.

[39] "North Providence Italians Want War with Austrians," *Providence Journal*, November 12, 1912, 5.

[40] Nicola Labanca, *Caporetto: Storia di una disfatta* (Florence: Giunti, 1997).

[41] Saiu, *Stati Uniti e Italia nella Grande guerra*, 128-33.

returned" to fight.[42] But, at the beginning, they buoyantly answered the call of duty. *Il Telegrafo* claimed that, as early as the day following Italy's declaration of war on Austria, about 25,000 Italian nationals in the New York City area were ready to depart without waiting to be called up for active duty.[43] In the years of US neutrality, some immigrants even joined the Italian army although they had already acquired American citizenship. One of them was Pasquale DeCicco, a resident of New Haven, Connecticut.[44]

Their fellow ethnics who remained in the United States raised money to support the war efforts of their ancestral country and the families of the Italian soldiers, especially after the 1917 defeat of the Italian troops at Caporetto. For example, the Italian Club in Dorchester, Massachusetts, raised 1,200 dollars in a single day "to the benefit of people damaged by the Teutonic invasion."[45] Fraternal and beneficial organizations with little assets usually levied extra duties from their members to meet their commitments for the purchase of Italy's war bonds.[46] Women, too, contributed to the war efforts, for instance, by knitting woolen socks and undershirts for soldiers or by sending commodities like cigars and ciga-

---

[42] As quoted in Emilio Franzina, "Corrispondenze popolari fra le Americhe e l'Italia durante la prima guerra mondiale," *Archivio Storico dell'Emigrazione Italiana* XI (2015): 127.

[43] "I riservisti italiani a New York," *Il Telegrafo*, May 26, 1915, 3.

[44] Anthony V. Riccio, *The Italian-American Experience in New Haven: Images and Oral Histories* (Albany, NY: SUNY P, 2006) 303.

[45] "Italian Women Present $1,200 for Italian War Relief Work," unidentified and undated newspaper clipping [but 1917]; "Grande bazar a beneficio del danneggiati dell'invasione teutonica," leaflet, 1917, both in Rosa Marie Finocchietti Levis Papers [hereafter RMFLP], box 5, folder 122, Arthur and Elizabeth Schlesinger Library, Radcliffe Institute for Advanced Study, Harvard University, Cambridge, MA.

[46] Giorgio Corrente, "Un'altra loggia dei Figli d'Italia nella sottoscrizione pro-Patria," *Il Telegrafo*, December 8, 1917, 4-5.

rettes to the troops.[47] It was claimed that, in cooperation with the Red Cross, they sent 100,000 of such comfort kits from the Boston area alone.[48] Female members of service organizations also raised money to help Italian women and children who had been left destitute by the enlistment of their wage-earning husbands and fathers. For instance, the wives and daughters of numerous middle-class immigrants were active in the Boston-based New England Italian War Relief Fund, which was founded in June 1915 and aimed at "relieving the distress which the European War brings to non-combatant Italians."[49] Significantly, fund raisings for the Italian Red Cross continued successfully into the last year of the war among both un-naturalized immigrants and US citizens of Italian ancestry, although financial contributions for the motherland faced considerable challenges with new appeals for donations to the American Red Cross and the purchase of US Liberty Bonds after Washington joined the military conflict in April 1917.[50] Fundraising continued even after the end of the fighting. For instance, on November 5, 1918, after the news of the armistice had already reached the United States, the Italian consul in Denver, Colorado, still managed to collect 65,000 liras, roughly 7,775 dollars, within the local community.[51] A few days later, 740 dollars were raised in Chicago.[52]

---

[47] "La prima riunione del comitato delle donne italiane," *Il Progresso Italo-Americano*, August 11, 1915, 1; "Lana! Lana!," *Il Cittadino*, October 7, 1915, 2; "A voi donne italiane," *La Notizia*, undated newspaper clipping, RMFLP, box 1, scrapbooks, volume 1.

[48] "Italian Women's Club Filling 100,000 Comfort Kits for Soldiers," unidentified and undated newspaper clipping, RMFLP, box 5, folder 122.

[49] William R. Thayer, circular letter, February 27, 1917, RMFLP, box 5, folder 120.

[50] "Pro Patria Nostra," *La Trinacria*, January 12, 1918, 1; Mark I. Choate, *Emigrant Nation: The Making of Italy Abroad* (Cambridge, MA: Hatvard UP, 2008) 203

[51] "Gl'italiani negli Stati Uniti," *Il Carroccio*, VIII.5 (November 1918): 480.

[52] "Una raccolta di offerte a pro dei bisogni della Patria," *L'Italia*, November 17, 1918, 1.

A few male immigrants served in the U.S. army. The Italian-language press itself published information about how to enlist.[53] Some recruits were still Italian nationals and earned American citizenship as a reward for their military service. According to some estimates, servicemen of Italian birth and parentage made roughly 12 percent of the US troops, while Italian Americans were as little as 4 percent of the country's total population.[54] The 310th Infantry of the 78th Division, for instance, was "a heavily Italian regiment."[55] Similarly, a machine gun company of Connecticut's National Guard was made up almost exclusively by Italian-born soldiers.[56] The US Department of War set up a special division—the Foreign-speaking Soldier Subsection—not only to manage the foreign-born military personnel but also to Americanize such recruits.[57] As a result, Italian-born servicemen were given English lessons and introduced to American culture, including celebrations such as Thanksgiving.[58] Yet, in the view of *Il Momento*, an Italian-language weekly published in Philadelphia, even naturalized Italian-born soldiers serving in the U.S. armed forces should not forget their patriotic duties toward Italy.[59]

THE RESPONSE TO ITALY'S VICTORY

The surrender of the Austrian-Hungarian Empire on November 4, 1918 gave way to unapologetic pride and enthusiasm with cheers and parades to the sound of martial music in the Little

---

[53] "Per gli italiani registrati sotto la leva americana," *Il Telegrafo*, December 10, 1917, 3.

[54] Jerre Mangione and Ben Morreale, *La Storia: Five Centuries of the Italian American Experience* (New York: Harper Collins, 1992) 340.

[55] Laskin, *The Long Way Home*, 302.

[56] Sterba, *Good Americans*, 34-35, 44.

[57] Gentile Ford, *Americans All!*, 67-87, 114-116.

[58] Jennifer D. Keene, *World War I* (Westport: Greenwood, 2006) 111.

[59] "Il nostro dovere," *Il Momento*, August 4, 1917, 1.

Italies throughout the United States.[60] Besides rejoicing over their motherland's military triumph, Italian Americans rallied to curb the claims of the rising Yugoslavia over regions that were expected to be placed under Italy's sovereignty.[61] They also took specific pride in the proclamations of mayors from such cities as Philadelphia calling on residents to display the Italian flag along with the Stars and Stripes. Actually, both banners were hoisted one next to the other at the industrial plants where Italian-American laborers worked.[62] In terms of ethnic redress, it seemed that the shared war efforts of the United States and Italy had vindicated the immigrants' previous marginalization in their host society and eased both the newcomers' accommodation within the adoptive country and their identification with their ancestral roots without any fear of becoming future targets of xenophobia and condemnation. A biographer of La Guardia's wrote that "if, before the war, he was sensitive about his Italian ancestry [...], he returned self-assured, fully accepted."[63] The same happened to numerous Italian Americans, both servicemen and civilians, who profited by the wartime cooperation between their native and adoptive nations to delude themselves into concluding that they were eventually welcome in the United States. *Il Cittadino* was glad that, by celebrating Italy's military victory, the US press did justice to Italian Americans, too, after decades of discriminatory representations.[64] Chicago's *L'Italia* even hoped that the decline of German culture in the United States in the aftermath of Berlin's defeat would result in a redis-

---

[60] "Italians Celebrate Austria's Defeat," *Providence Journal*, November 5, 1918, 8; "Il giubilo in colonia," *Il Cittadino*, November 7, 1918, 1.

[61] "Grandiosa celebrazione per la vittoria italiana," *L'Italia*, November 17, 1918, 1.

[62] "Italians Exultant at Austria's Fall Hold Celebration," *Philadelphia Inquirer*, November 5, 1918, 1, 3; "Grande ed entusiastica celebrazione per la presa di Trento e Trieste," *Il Telegrafo*, November 6, 1918, 3.

[63] Thomas Kessner, *Fiorello La Guardia and the Making of Modern New York* (New York: McGraw-Hill, 1989) 56.

[64] "La verità in cammino," *Il Cittadino*, November 14, 1918, 1.

covery of Italian culture, which would make it easier to acclimate Italian immigrants and their progeny within American society without forcing the newcomers and their offspring to disavow their ancestral roots.[65]

These expectations let the residents of the Little Italies develop and cherish a sense of ethnic pride and nationalistic feelings that did not fade or need to be hidden away after the end of the conflict. The case of Providence offers an illuminating example. In this city regional antagonism and rivalries had interfered with Italy-related patriotic events. For example, these animosities had disrupted and caused the failure of public meetings like a 1912 gathering to celebrate the seizure of Libya from Turkish hands.[66] Conversely, in September 1920 the representatives of almost all the city's various local and regional societies attended a nationalistic rally on the occasion of the fiftieth anniversary of the annexation of Rome to the Kingdom of Italy.[67] Likewise, when General Armando Diaz, the victorious commander in chief of the Italian army in World War I, made a tour of the United States in the Fall of 1921, he received a triumphal welcome in every Italian-American community he visited.[68] On December 9, in Providence, work virtually stopped in the local "Little Italy" on Federal Hill and thousands of residents went out on the streets to acclaim Diaz as his motorcade passed through the district.[69]

In addition, in the first half of the 1920s, several social clubs were renamed for Piave, the so-called "sacred river of the homeland" because of the clashes that took place along its banks, or for other war-related symbols echoing Italy's victory, such as Vittorio

---

[65] "Scambio intellettuale tra Italia e America," *L'Italia*, December 30, 1917, 5.

[66] "La celebrazione per la Libia," *L'Eco del Rhode Island*, March 1, 1913, 1.

[67] "Italian Associations," *Providence Journal*, September 21, 1920, 5.

[68] V. Scarpaci, *The Journey of Italians in America* (Gretna, LA: Pelican, 2008) 291.

[69] "La giornata trionfale di Diaz in Providence," *L'Eco del Rhode Island*, December 15, 1921, 1; "General Armando Diaz, Commander of Italian Army, Visits Providence," *Providence Magazine* XXXIV.1 (January 1922): 21-27.

Veneto, the town next to the site of the victorious final battle fought by the Italian army.[70] These new denominations replaced the previous ones that had referred to the hometown or the native province of its affiliates. At the same time many associations changed their membership rules and opened their doors to all immigrants from Italy regardless of the newcomers' birthplaces in the native country.[71]

THE AFTERMATH OF WORLD WAR I

Historian Rudolph J. Vecoli has contended that "the First World War [...] was a transitory phenomenon which did not basically alter the apolitical character of the [Italian] immigrants."[72] Yet the rise of Italian Americans' wartime nationalism revealed a long-term echo particularly in the field of politics. The newcomers who had acquired US citizenship and their American-born offspring mobilized en masse in the fruitless effort to secure Washington's support for Italy's expansionistic demands at the peace conference in Paris. Specifically, they lobbied the American government to let Italy extend her sovereignty to the Croatian seaport of Fiume.[73] An association claiming the representation of about 50,000 immigrants from Trentino, Istria, and Dalmatia—including "many thousands naturalized American citizens"—urged Congress to back such re-

---

[70] Fortunato Minniti, *Il Piave* (Bologna: il Mulino, 2000) 123-131; Alessandro Marzo Magno, *Piave: Cronache di un fiume sacro* (Milan: il Saggiatore, 2010) 15-18; Alessandro Miniero, *Da Versailles al Milite Ignoto: Rituali e retoriche della vittoria in Europa (1919-1921)* (Rome: Gangemi, 2008) 76-78, 86-88.

[71] Loggia Piave, "Programma ricordo," Luigi Cipolla Papers, folder 1, Immigration History Research Center, University of Minnesota, Minneapolis; "Lodge #17 Vittorio Veneto," Records of the Italian Sons and Daughters of America, box 38, folder 7, Archives of Industrial Society, University of Pittsburgh, Pittsburgh.

[72] Rudolph J. Vecoli, "The Search for an Italian-American Identity: Continuity and Change," in *Italian Americans: New Perspectives in Italian Immigration and Ethnicity.* Silvano M. Tomasi, ed. (New York: Center for Migration Studies, 1985) 93.

[73] John B. Duff, "The Italians," in Joseph P. O'Grady, ed., *The Immigrants' Influence on Wilson's Peace Policies* (Lexington: U Kentucky P, 1967) 111-39.

quests.[74] Likewise the Italian Chamber of Commerce in Chicago showed its support in an open letter to Senator Lawrence Yates Sherman (R-IL).[75] Back from the battlefield, Congressman La Guardia became "one of the chief spokesmen for the Italian position" on Fiume, adding his authoritative voice to the campaign from his legislative seat in Washington.[76] Some Italian-American mouthpieces, such as *L'Eco del Rhode Island*, even endorsed the exploit of renowned and flamboyant poet Gabriele D'Annunzio, who led insurgent Italian troops to occupy Fiume under a self-proclaimed regency from early September 1919 to late December 1920, and raised money to finance his scheme.[77] But after President Woodrow Wilson, a Democrat, turned a deaf ear to this and other claims, Italian-language newspapers in Boston, Chicago, and Providence urged their readers to retaliate politically by casting their ballots for the Republican Party in the subsequent 1920 race for the White House.[78] An Italian-American Republican League was established to cash in on the disenchantment with Wilson among voters of Italian ancestry.[79] Indeed, a significant number of Italian Americans went over to the GOP and, between 1916 and 1920, their vote for the Democratic Party fell from 63 percent to 43 percent in Boston, from 68 percent to 31 percent in Chicago, from 63 percent to 47

---

[74] "L'Associazione politica tra gl'italiani redenti ai Senatori e Rappresentanti al Congresso," *Il Cittadino*, June 12, 1919, 1.

[75] Frank Bragno, "Per Fiume italiana," *Bollettino della Camera Italiana di Commercio* XI.8 (August 1919): 7.

[76] Howard Zinn, *La Guardia in Congress* (New York: Norton, 1958) 40.

[77] "Columbus Day pro Fiume italiana," *L'Eco del Rhode Island*, October 2, 1919, 1.

[78] "I connazionali d'America ripagheranno Woodrow Wilson degli oltraggi commessi contro l'Italia e le sue aspirazioni," *Gazzetta del Massachusetts*, 20 October 1920, 1; Humbert S. Nelli, "Chicago's Italian-Language Press and World War I," in Cordasco, ed., *Studies in Italian American Social History*, 72; "Perché gl'italiani debbono votare per il partito repubblicano," *L'Eco del Rhode Island*, October 28, 1920, 1-2.

[79] Arthur Mann, *La Guardia: A Fighter against His Times, 1882-1933* (Philadelphia: J. B. Lippincott, 1959) 125.

percent in New York City, and from 50.1 percent to 37.6 percent in Providence.[80] Even the Democratic presidential candidate, James M. Cox, would later acknowledge that he lost Italian Americans' support as they were "enraged because Fiume had been taken away from Italy."[81] Moreover, in 1919 La Guardia won election for president of New York City's Board of Aldermen on the Republican ticket with significant support from his Italian brethren in part because he had based his campaign on the slogan: "any Italo-American who votes the Democratic ticket this year is an Austrian bastard."[82]

CONCLUSION

World War I helped turn the many heterogeneous Little Italies into more cohesive communities whose members came to base their sense of belonging and attachment on their common Italian background. Such feelings overcame the previous fragmentation of the Italian-American colonies along sub-national lines. Furthermore, although historian David Laskin has maintained that immigrants who fought in the army of their adoptive country "became Americans,"[83] the new Italy-centered ethnic consciousness overshadowed any emerging U.S. identity, especially in the wake of Wilson's disregard for Rome's claims on Fiume. It even contributed to making some Italian Americans receptive of Fascist propaganda in the interwar years once the United States return to

---

[80] Joseph Huthmacher, *Massachusetts People and Politics, 1919-1933* (Cambridge, MA: Harvard UP, 1959) 20-22; David Burner, *The Politics of Provincialism: The Democratic Party in Transition, 1918-1932* (New York: Knopf, 1968) 236, 243; George J. Martin, *The American Catholic Voter: 200 Years of Political Impact* (South Bend, IN: Notre Dame UP, 2004) 188; Stefano Luconi, *The Italian-American Vote in Providence, Rhode Island, 1916-1948* (Madison, NJ: Fairleigh Dickinson UP, 2004) 135.

[81] James M. Cox, *Journey through My Years* (New York: Simon & Schuster, 1946) 273.

[82] As quoted in Mann, *La Guardia: A Fighter against His Times*, 114.

[83] Matteo Pretelli, *La via fascista alla democrazia americana: Cultura e propaganda nelle comunità italo-americane* (Viterbo: Sette Città, 2012).

"normalcy" in the 1920s included a resurgence of xenophobia and nativism that, as shown by the Quota Acts of 1921 and 1924, again marginalized Italian immigrants, stamping them as undesirable and inassimilable aliens.[84]

---

[84] Laskin, *The Long Way Home* xvii.

I Am(s):
Dantesque Strategies of Acceptance and Denial
And a Proposal

Martino Marazzi

UNIVERSITY OF MILAN "LA STATALE"

When in Rome, do as the Romans do. One usually tends to overlook the contribution that the Eternal City has played in the Great Migration, but still it wasn't by chance that Cesare Pascarella wrote *La scoperta de l'America* (1894) in *romanesco*, providing a model of sorts for future narratives of migration in the Roman dialect. Italians scattered *almost* everywhere from every part of the peninsula. So it is not only as an homage that I start with the Roman-American poetical voice of Alfredo Borgianini (Rome, 1882-Trenton, N.J., 1955), but rather as a nod to this long tradition.

I

Roma mia bella che me stai lontano
tremila mija e più tra terra e mare,
tu m'aricordi tante cose care
da scrivece un romanzo sano sano.

Benché sto qui ner suolo Americano,
pure in certi momenti, embe', me pare
d'esse tornato tra le cose rare
che me fanno avanta' d'esse Romano.

Me pare da rivive in que l'ambiente
in do' so nato, in dove c'ho vissuto
venticinque anni spenzieratamente.

Me pare da rivive in allegria
tra li compagni che ce so cresciuto,
me pare da riavecce Mamma mia…

[…]

IV

E adesso ar dunque: Pe' 'na fantasia
partii de botto senza amici intorno,
e l'anni da quer giorno me passorno
come passa quaggiù la ferrovia.

Più er tempo corre e più la nostargia
m'avvince, e penzo che si quarche giorno
eguale ar Figliol Prodico ritorno,
Roma mia bella nun me caccia' via.

Perdoname si credi c'ho mancato
co' l'imbarcamme e anna' tanto lontano,
perdoname, nun dimme rinnegato.

Nun me schifa', nun me guarda' in cagnesco.
Vabbe' so' cittadino Americano,
ma er core, er core è sempre Romanesco…[1]

I know it all too well, because I've heard this kind of criticism over and over: it sounds and it is amateurish and predictable. But it is not my intention to hail Borgianini as if he could soar to the unreachable heights of the giant Belli. What this self-taught poet deserves, though, is first of all that we evaluate his Muse by examining the cultural and historical context in which he lived and

---

[1] Alfredo Borgianini, *A te, Roma mia 1921*, in *Sonetti e Poesie Romanesche* (Trenton, New Jersey, 1948): 86, 89.

worked. And again, such a task is beyond the scope of the present contribution[2]; I will just point out that, despite the mawkishness of these lines, in his volume *Sonetti e Poesie Romanesche* (1948) Borgianini shows a rather considerable variety of tones and flaunts a certain metrical and linguistic awareness. To pull back the curtain on this vernacular intro, we should also bear in mind that the Roman question takes on very different colors in the memoirs of two other immigrants, the NYPD lieutenant Mike Fiaschetti (*You Gotta Be Rough*, 1930), and the leftist activist Carl Marzani (*The Education of a Reluctant Radical*, 5 vols., 1992-2002)[3]. Both Fiaschetti and Marzani wrote in English (although Fiaschetti's crime book also came out in a shorter Italian version, serialized in the popular daily *Corriere d'America*)—a fact that addresses the more substantial aspect of a general, and, I believe, more relevant, point: immigrant narratives comply with the dominant paradigms of their current country, which are reflected in their choice of language; immigrant literature reflects the country's cultural—and more specifically literary—history. And this is still mirrored in the way institutions of higher learning think and operate.

Not that I deny the role played by nations in shaping the curricula in the humanities. But the fact is that the culture lived by immigrants, the culture that the immigrant subjects produce and use in their interactions and in their more or less ethnic environments, and thus transmit to the following generations, this culture is, almost by nature, multifaceted, dialectic, and by necessity oriented toward a constant, grinding, negotiation between its various

---

[2] A first monographic attempt is John Vincent Aquilecchia's B.A. thesis *Alfredo Borgianini. Un poeta romanesco nel Nuovo Mondo*, relatore Martino Marazzi, Università degli Studi di Milano (2013-2014).

[3] Michael Fiaschetti, *You Gotta Be Rough: The Adventures of Detective Fiaschetti of the Italian Squad as told to Prosper Buranelli by Michael Fiaschetti* (Garden City, N.Y.: Doubleday, Doran & Company, 1930); Michael Fiaschetti, *Gioco duro*. Martino Marazzi, ed. (Cava de' Tirreni: Avagliano, 2003); Carl Marzani, *The Education of a Reluctant Radical*. Books 1-5 (New York: Topical Books, 1992-2002).

components. This, in a nutshell, is why it is so very difficult for immigrants to fit in, and why it is problematic — to say the least, — for scholars of immigrant cultures and history, to find a home in university departments (and modes of thought) that remain defined, and confined, by strict national parameters.

As a scholar interested in Italian culture and with a specific competence in its literary — and more broadly, written — dimension, I have long focused on its exogenous aspects for the simple reason that I have always found them to be more indicative of intellectual creativity, and more morally engaging, than what I consider the hackneyed rites of classical and neo-classical self-referentiality. This is not to say that immigrant cultures are *per se* innovative and not repetitious; but if as an Italian citizen I find it is my civic duty to make sense of the gigantic demographic fluxes affecting the peninsula, as an *italianista* by profession I do believe that first and foremost I have to open up the canon (as an old mentor of mine with a long Roman love story, Leslie Fiedler, taught me when I first set foot in the USA), if for no other reason than to reap new riches, and explore new dimensions of a country notoriously keen on the dialogue between power and the arts.

The fact that Ariosto locates on the island of Lampedusa ("Lipadusa. / Una isoletta è questa, che dal mare / medesmo che li cinge, è circonfusa", *OF* 40, 55) one of the crucial duels of his poem — that of Orlando and two other Christian paladins against three Saracen Kings — is obviously a *topos* that today resonates well beyond the merely rhetorical level. Even if we limit ourselves to the pillars of the Western canon, it is always a question of approaching it without denying our current point of view.

On the other hand, even a cursory exploration of the intellectual and literary debate of the teeming Italian American "colony" of the early decades almost invariably produces discoveries that shed new light on the Italian cultural landscape. Take for instance a rare publication like *Ultra*, a 1934 collection of miscellaneous writings celebrating the 15ᵗʰ anniversary of Local 89 of the International Ladies' Garment Workers' Union (ILGWU). Alongside poems by Arturo Giovannitti, we read excerpts from Walt Whitman and Ignazio Silone, Petr Kropotkin and Arturo Labriola, but also contributions that for a number of ideological, cultural and, yes, aesthetic reasons, one would be hard pressed to come across in the Italian publications of the same time: a short but eloquent letter of congratulations, in parallel German and Italian, from Alfred Einstein; a special insert of exquisite full-page wood-cuts showing New York (*La Città Incredibile*, by A. Scarpellini); and an article by Franz Boas debunking the *Mito ariano*[4].

Or take into consideration the elaborate and creative ways in which, from Da Ponte to the Dante Club and *La Follia di New York*, and later to Gerard Malanga, Lawrence Ferlinghetti, Joseph Tusiani, John Ciardi, Nick Tosches, and Robert Viscusi, Italians and Italian Americans have contributed to the canonization of Dante in the U.S.[5] Not only—and predictably—there is a discernible "Dantesque" element in Italian immigrant culture, but—on a narrower scale, which nonetheless reflects a heavy-handed symbolic predicament—Dante, and the inescapable classics, remain compulsory entries in the bibliography of any Italian literary scholar aspiring to a minimal degree of scientific and economic recognition.

This issue brings us to another aspect of the larger question, namely, the role of power structures in shaping cultural blueprints, and the hypostasis of the criterion of aesthetic excellence, whatever we mean by that. To put it bluntly—as an Italian Ameri-

---

[4] *Ultra*. Strenna commemorativa del XV anniversario della fondazione della Italian Dressmakers Union, Locale 89, I.L.G.W.U. (New York: Italian Labor Education Bureau—Liberal Press, Inc., no date [but 1934]).

[5] See my *"Our brother Dante." Dantesque Reappropriations in Italian America*, in *Dante politico. Ideological Reception across Boundaries*. Dennis Looney and Donatella Stocchi-Perucchio, eds. "Mediaevalia" (forthcoming). More in general, Martino Marazzi, *Danteum. Studi sul Dante imperiale del Novecento* (Firenze: Franco Cesati, 2015).

can colleague once told me off the record: "early Italian American literature sucks". But at least he said it jokingly (although, from a certain point of view, I certainly see his point); Italian colleagues are so prejudiced that they dismiss such material out of hand. Even the groundbreaking and innovative three-volume *Atlante della letteratura italiana* edited by Sergio Luzzatto and Gabriele Pedullà totally omits the culture of Italian emigration, with the customary exception of certain well-known political (usually anti-Fascist) exiles.[6] On this topic, it would be too easy and self-indulgent to open up a can of anecdotes. We rightly bemoan the sorry state of Italian American studies in Italy, and at the same time the reluctance to deal with figures and cultural products of the "new" Italy shaped by recent waves of immigration to the peninsula. But—despite groundbreaking works such as the anthology edited by Luigi Bonaffini and Joseph Perricone[7]—the silence surrounding other destinations of the Italian diaspora is still puzzling, to say the least. In the case, for instance, of the contagiously funny, multilingual, and thought-provoking *Les Ritals*, by François Cavanna (arguably *the* masterpiece of the Italo-French experience),[8] we should say that the refusal of *italianisti* and even more *francesisti* to accept it into their canon is actually *pénible*. Note that Cavanna, a second-generation Parisian artist of Italian descent and a legendary satirical illustrator and author, had been one of the founders of *Charlie Hebdo*: but academic disparagement is stronger than even curiosity. We have had mouthfuls of *Je suis Charlie* in the recent past: they don't seem to have reached certain ivory towers.

---

[6] *Atlante della letteratura italiana,* a cura di Sergio Luzzatto e Gabriele Pedullà. Volumi 1-3 (Torino: Einaudi, 2010-2012).

[7] Luigi Bonaffini—Joseph Perricone, eds., *Poets of the Italian Diaspora. A Bilingual Anthology* (New York: Fordham UP, 2014).

[8] François Cavanna, *Les Ritals* (Paris: Belfond, 1978).

In fact, such analyses must neither be exclusively limited to the American (as in Italian American) field, nor, indeed, only to forms of written culture. If what I stated above wishes to be seriously taken into consideration, we ought to value the Italian immigrant and multigenerational epic as a worldwide phenomenon. Yet, while this is obvious historically, it is not recognized as an area worthy of study either by Italian Departments of History or even in the far larger field of the humanities.

One needs only to peek out of the academic world to see that the topic of migration is being passionately addressed in other sectors, starting with the publishing arena. The scholarly output is growing by the year, and it is particularly impressive outside of Italy.[9] And yet, despite the rising curve of essays and conferences, the institutional offering—especially in Italy—of courses dealing with the cultural aspects of migration remains notably scant.

Such timidity—to be nice—is clearly at odds with the overall media discourse and indeed with individual everyday life, where, at every turn, the tragedies, trials, and questions posed by migration have become the staple of public debate and concern. It is the organic dichotomy of a deeply traditional culture that oxymoronically both talks and keeps silent, depending on the venue. We do not need to resort to Bourdieu to propose that, in such lofty realms, considerations of prestige act as vicarious forms of class

---

[9] For an updated overview, Franca Sinopoli, "Prospettiva transnazionale e ricerca di nuove politiche culturali nello studio della letteratura italiana contemporanea" in Luigi Bonaffini and Joseph Perricone, eds., *La Letteratura italiana nel mondo. Nuove prospettive* (Isernia: Iannone, 2015) 29-39. An excellent critical introduction to the North American dimension is Edvige Giunta and Kathleen Zamboni McCormick, eds., *Teaching Italian American Literature, Film, and Popular Culture* (New York: The Modern Language Association of America, 2010). An example of rigorous and in-depth analysis of the "new" Italian immigrant literature is Daniele Comberiati's *Scrivere nella lingua dell'altro. La letteratura degli immigrati in Italia (1989-2007)* (Bruxelles: Peter Lang, 2010).

distinctions. It is the pervasive Italian *perbenismo*, applied in the field of academic hierarchies. Or, as another American mentor of mine once memorably asked me, "Do you *really* think this is interesting?" The end result is that today, in Italian Universities, an *italianista* can well teach, from time to time, the literature of the Italian Great Migration, although nominally there is not any recognition of the dignity of the field *per se*.

This is why I am convinced that it is crucial, at this point, to try to win basic institutional recognition. By that I mean official teaching positions, linked to adequate hierarchical roles within the professorial roster. A direct consequence of the current situation is the impossibility of attracting students to this line of research. The functioning of academic life, in an Old World setting like the Italian, works along the lines of an elaborate metaphoric system which alludes to the reproductive mores of early modern family life. In effect, with both their field of research and their academic rigor disparaged, scholars of immigrant culture are treated as being under-age and academically impotent. Ironically, this impotence is the equivalent, within our rather abstract profession, of the dire challenges faced at every step along the way by immigrants. And again, as an *italianista* I see myself as having the privilege and the responsibility of activating a critical reflection on a huge phenomenon that has affected, as we know, well over 20 million Italians in the aftermath of the so-called Unification, and that, conversely, after the Fall of the Berlin Wall and the arrival in Bari of the Albanian cargo ship Vlora (August 1991) — to name just a couple of major instances — has changed the peninsula into a destination for migrants. If we are unable to perceive the *nemesis* in such a history, and are not troubled by the difficulty of coming to terms with it, then I am afraid that all our venerable classical education has proved quite futile.

Not that this comes as a surprise. The prerequisite of philology is the attribution of value to a certain text. This often fixates scholarly research at the "genetic" phase. A respectable Italian philologist spends years trying to determine the date of composition of Dante's *Monarchia*, relying on the erudite reconstructions of the German polymath Karl Witte; the fact that Hitler, seeking to inject cultural excellence into the Rome-Berlin Axis, brought as a gift to *il Duce*, during his visit to Rome in 1938, Karl Witte's translation of the *Divine Comedy* is usually treated as a footnote. While Luconi, Pretelli, myself and a few others have spent years going over the very rich columns of the Italian American press, a systematic exploration of the similar world of the ethnic, multilingual press in Italy today, is still to come. We sorely need to work as a collective, making room for the collaboration of colleagues well-versed in the languages and cultures of the current migrations. And in Italy we need to push the agenda for the opening of our Universities to the second generations and to the refugees. Look around in Italian college classrooms after high school and even after junior high, and you see an overwhelming majority of Italian kids, which is dramatically out of sync with the demographics of Italy today.

My invitation is thus to start considering the importance of an institutionally sanctioned field of migration studies (and to be more precise, of *Studi sull'emigrazione*), articulated if you will, at least provisionally, in two inter-related classes that I would tentatively name *Società e storia dell'emigrazione*, and *Cultura e lingua dell'emigrazione*. I would also invite our institutions to consider the epistemological opportunity offered by the study of what I propose to call a *changing culture* predicament, which should be read at the same time both as a transitive action (changing one's culture), and as a dynamic metamorphosis (a culture in the process of changing). A study of migrations must stress the socio-historical and material component, as well as the fact that we are dealing with a broader human condition of change and adaptability, and the resulting necessity of pluralizing one's life in many different ways. If Donna Gabaccia has rightly bemoaned the "tyranny of the national", Peter Carravetta is now articulating these questions with what he calls a "post-identitarian" approach.[10] This is part of the intellectual framework I find currently relevant to this topic.

We cannot hide the fact that being accepted goes beyond the personal matter of having one's individual career recognized as valid. Administering the traditional cultural landscape (*l'amministrazione dell'esistente*) is only a step away—if I can indulge in the creative malapropism dear to Roman popular poetry—from *la ministrazione dell'ex-sistente*, a warming up of old soups, and at the same time a governmental imposition (a typically Italian "ministerial" *ukase*) of models long gone.

On the contrary, admitting migration and migrants in contemporary culture contradicts the *favola bella* of Italy's cultural-centrism. Culture, in Italian society, deftly functions as an equalizer, or as an enzyme, that makes the social imbalances acceptable. Culture (in the more common Italian meaning of "high", humanistic, "classical" code) provides an alibi for accepting the class divisions in our midst; it works as an element of self-assurance, a mirror that reflects the fairest of them all, *Italia felix*. It must be noted that most Italian American intellectuals of the early days concurred. In other words, migrations carry with them, and activate, a far-flung critique of received wisdom. The time has come to finally act on Abdelmalek Sayad's call to "institutionalize an autonomous discourse on emigration".[11]

I would be tempted to paraphrase another great Roman writer, Ennio Flaiano, and say that *la situazione è grave ma non è seria*.

---

[10] Donna Gabaccia, "Is Everywhere Nowhere? Nomads, Nations, and the Immigrant Paradigm of United States History," *The Journal of American History* 86, 3 (December 1999): 1116; Peter Carravetta, *After Identity. Migration, Critique, Italian American Culture* (New York: Bordighera Press, 2017) 222.

[11] I quote from the Italian edition of Abdelmalek Sayad's *The Suffering of the Immigrant: La doppia assenza. Dalla illusione dell'emigrato alla sofferenza dell'immigrato*, a cura di Salvatore Palidda (Milano: Cortina, 2002) 169 [the original French edition came out in 1999]).

Unfortunately, I am not sure that this could apply to our current predicament. I want to stress, though, that narratives of migration are not limited to mere tragedy. Since we are dealing with a life-changing experience, expressions take the most varied forms. Think only of the amazing richness of such diverse works as Robert Orsi's *The Madonna of 115th Street*, the collected essays on "Italian Folk", on Sam Rodia's Watts Towers and on the needlework of Italian American women (edited respectively by Joseph Sciorra, Luisa Del Giudice, and again Sciorra and Edvige Giunta), and finally Sciorra's *Built with Faith*.[12]

But I'd like to end going back to where I started, closing with a short Italian American story which originates, again, with the Roman immigrant poet Alfredo Borgianini. This comes from a private letter sent jointly to me and Francesco Durante by one of his grandsons, Stephen Borgianini:

> I do want to pass on one funny story my Aunt Mable passed on to me. My grandfather was teaching a citizenship class in Trenton to recent Italian immigrants. He was teaching his students about the United States presidential line of succession and asked "If the president dies, who gets the job?" [...] after some discussion the answer given was "Gruerio's" the local funeral home in Trenton that did all the Italian funerals.[13]

---

[12] Robert A. Orsi, *The Madonna of 115th Street. Faith and Community in Italian Harlem, 1880-1950* (New Haven and London: Yale UP, 1985). Joseph Sciorra, ed., *Italian Folk. Vernacular Culture in Italian-American Lives* (New York: Fordham UP, 2010). Luisa Del Giudice, ed., *Sabato Rodia's Towers in Watts. Art, Migrations, Development* (New York: Fordham UP, 2014). Edvige Giunta and Joseph Sciorra, eds., *Embroidered Stories. Interpreting Women's Domestic Needlework from the Italian Diaspora* (Jackson, Miss.: UP of Mississippi, 2014). Joseph Sciorra, *Built with Faith. Italian American Imagination and Catholic Material Culture in New York City* (Knoxville, Tenn.: U Tennessee P, 2015).

[13] Email of Stephen A. Borgianini to Francesco Durante and myself, ca. January 2012.

It might be an easy way to start exploring the trope of Italian American funerals, something that has already produced its share of bibliographies and filmographies. What I particularly treasure here, and find a source of provisional respite, is the black humor — an element that institutions are never properly equipped with. But irony is easier to accept if you are an insider. The problem is that we, our subjects, our objects, are all still treated as outsiders, and frankly, *that* has never been very funny.

INDEX OF NAMES

SAGGISTICA

Taking its name from Italian–which means essays, essay writing, or non-fiction–*Saggistica* is a referred book series dedicated to the study of all topics and cultural productions that fall under what we might consider that larger umbrella of all things Italian and Italian American.

Vito Zagarrio
  The "Un-Happy Ending": Re-viewing The Cinema of Frank Capra. 2011. ISBN 978-1-59954-005-4. Volume 1.
Paolo A. Giordano, Editor
  The Hyphenate Writer and The Legacy of Exile. 2010. ISBN 978-1-59954-007-8. Volume 2.
Dennis Barone
  America/Trattabili. 2011. ISBN 978-1-59954-018-4. Volume 3.
Fred L. Gardaphè
  The Art of Reading Italian Americana. 2011. ISBN 978-1-59954-019-1. Volume 4.
Anthony Julian Tamburri
  Re-viewing Italian Americana: Generalities and Specificities on Cinema. 2011. ISBN 978-1-59954-020-7. Volume5.
Sheryl Lynn Postman
  An Italian Writer's Journey through American Realities: Giose Rimanelli's English Novels. "The most tormented decade of America: the 60s" ISBN 978-1-59954-034-4. Volume 6.
Luigi Fontanella
  Migrating Words: Italian Writers in the United States. 2012. ISBN 978-1-59954-041-2. Volume 7.
Peter Covino & Dennis Barone, Editors
  Essays on Italian American Literature and Culture. 2012. ISBN 978-1-59954-035-1. Volume 8.

Gianfranco Viesti
  Italy at the Crossroads. 2012. ISBN 978-1-59954-071-9.
  Volume 9.

Peter Carravetta, Editor
  *Discourse Boundary Creation (LOGOS TOPOS POIESIS): A
  Festschrift in Honor of Paolo Valesio.* ISBN 978-1-59954-
  036-8. Volume 10.

Antonio Vitti and Anthony Julian Tamburri, Editors
  Europe, Italy, and the Mediterranean. 2012. ISBN 978-1-
  59954-073-3. Volume 11.

Vincenzo Scotti
  *Pax Mafiosa or War: Twenty Years after the Palermo
  Massacres.* 2012. ISBN 978-1-59954-074-0. Volume 12.

Anthony Julian Tamburri, Editor
  Meditations on Identity. Meditazioni su identità. ISBN 978-1-
  59954-082-5. Volume 13.

Peter Carravetta, Editor
  *Theater of the Mind, Stage of History. A Festschrift in Honor
  of Mario Mignone.* ISBN 978-1-59954-083-2. Volume 14.

Lorenzo Del Boca
  *Italy's Lies. Debunk History's Lies So That Italy Might Become
  A "Normal Country".* ISBN 978-1-59954-084-9. Volume 15.

George Guida
  *Spectacles of Themselves. Essays in Italian American Popular
  Culture and Literature.* ISBN 978-1-59954-090-0. Volume
  16.

Antonio Vitti and Anthony Julian Tamburri, Editors
  *Mare Nostrum: prospettive di un dialogo tra alterità e
  mediterraneità.* ISBN 978-1-59954-100-6. Volume 17.

Patrizia Salvetti
  Rope and Soap. Lynchings of Italians in the United States.
  ISBN 978-1-59954-101-3. Volume 18.

Sheryl Lynn Postman and Anthony Julian Tamburri, Editors
  *Re-Reading Rimanelli in America: Six Decades in the Untied
  States.* 2016. ISBN 978-1-59954-102-0. Volume 19.

Pasquale Verdicchio
  Bound by Distance: Rethinking Nationalism through the Italian Diaspora. ISBN 978-1-59954-103-7. Volume 20.
Peter Carravetta
  After Identity: Migration, Critique, Italian American Culture. ISBN 978-1-59954-072-6. Volume 21.
Antonio Vitti and Anthony Julian Tamburri, Editors
  The Mediterranean As Seen by Insiders and Outsiders. ISBN 978-1-59954-107-5. Volume 22.
Eugenio Ragni
  Giose 1959: Un "Suicidio" Annunciato. ISBN 978-1-59954-109-9. Volume 23.
Quinto Antonelli
  Intimate History of the Great War. ISBN 978-1-59954-111-2. Volume 24.
Antonio Vitti and Anthony Julian Tamburri, Editors
  The Mediterranean Dreamed and Lived by Insiders and Outsiders. ISBN 978-1-59954-115-0. Volume 25.